GARDENING IN INDIA

Percy Lancaster's

Gardening in India

(An Amateur in an Indian Garden)

Second Edition

Revised by

TK Bose

Professor and Head

Department of Horticulture

Bidhan Chandra Krishi Viswa Vidyalaya

D Mukherjee

Secretary

The Agri-Horticultural Society of India

Kolkata

Oxford & IBH Publishing Co. Pvt. Ltd.

New Delhi

(*A Unit of* CBS Publishers & Distributors Pvt Ltd)

CBS Publishers & Distributors Pvt Ltd

New Delhi • Bengaluru • Chennai • Kochi • Kolkata • Mumbai

Hyderabad • Jharkhand • Nagpur • Patna • Pune • Uttarakhand

Percy Lancaster's

Gardening in India

Second Edition

ISBN-13: 978-81-204-0229-4

ISBN-10: 81-204-0229-4

Last Printing 2012, 2018 2024

OXFORD & IBH

New Delhi

(A Unit of CBS Publishers & Distributors Pvt Ltd)

CBS Publishers & Distributors Pvt Ltd

204 FIE, Patparganj Industrial Area, Delhi 110 092

E-mail: delhi@cbspd.com, cbspubs@airtelmail.in

Ph: 4934 4934 Fax: 4934 4935 Website: www.cbspd.com

e-mail: publishing@cbspd.com; publicity@cbspd.com

Branches

- **Bengaluru:** Seema House 2975, 17th Cross, K.R. Road, Banasankari 2nd Stage, Bengaluru 560 070, Karnataka
  Ph: +91-80-26771678/79 Fax: +91-80-26771680 e-mail: bangalore@cbspd.com
- **Chennai:** 7, Subbaraya Street, Shenoy Nagar, Chennai 600 030, Tamil Nadu
  Ph: +91-44-26680620, 26681266 Fax: +91-44-42032115 e-mail: chennai@cbspd.com
- **Kochi:** Ashana House, 39/1904, AM Thomas Road, Valanjambalam, Ernakulam 682 016, Kochi, Kerala
  Ph: +91-484-4059061-65,67 Fax: +91-484-4059065 e-mail: kochi@cbspd.com
- **Kolkata:** 6/B, Ground Floor, Rameswar Shaw Road, Kolkata-700014 (West Bengal), India
  Ph: +91-33-2289-1126, 2289-1127, 2289-1128 e-mail: kolkata@cbspd.com
- **Mumbai:** 83-C, Dr E Moses Road, Worli, Mumbai-400018, Maharashtra
  Ph: +91-22-24902340/41 Fax: +91-22-24902342 e-mail: mumbai@cbspd.com

Representatives

• **Hyderabad**	0-9885175004	• **Jharkhand**	0-9811541605	• **Nagpur**	0-9021734563
• **Patna**	0-9334159340	• **Pune**	0-9623451994	• **Uttarakhand**	0-9716462459

Printed at Chaman Enterprises, Daryaganj, New Delhi, India

PREFACE

In the First Edition of Gardening in India more than 20 chapters of the original book written by Late S. Percy Lancaster were revised. But later on the need for a chapter on Nursery Management was felt and accordingly the same was included in this Second Edition. A number of chapters viz. Annuals, Bulbous plants, Dahlia and Chrysanthemums, Orchids and Garden Design were thoroughly revised and enlarged for incorporating more essential informations including modern trends of cultural practices.

We feel that the professional and amateur gardeners will find this edition very useful for garden layout and cultivation of different types of garden plants.

CONTENTS

CHAPTER I

Some Principles of Gardening

It is not possible to know garden plants and learn gardening thoroughly by reading books and journals only. Practical experience and careful observations on the response to plant growth will give you the pleasure in growing plants successfully and the confidence in suggesting others to develop a good garden.

Some general principles might prove very useful to tackle problems in garden and avoid casualities and failures.

Knowledge of plants

If you want to develop, maintain and enjoy your garden according your ideas, you should have interest and knowledge about plant and plant growth. Otherwise it becomes a mali's garden. You cannot grow and appreciate many beautiful plants possible in your garden with less effort and expenditure. With little interest and time spent in the garden, one can very easily gain a fairly good knowledge about plants and their relation to soil and environment. You may then advise your Mali what and where to grow.

Knowledge of soils

Physical condition and chemical composition of the soil affect the fertility and plant growth. Porous soil, rich in organic matter and containing sufficient nutrients is ideal for most garden plants. Then the correct preparation, depth of it and after-care play a great part. Careless planting, keeping the soil wet or dry, exposure to extremes of heat or cold will also affect the plant growth.

While surface soil conditions cannot always be changed, a study of the sub-soil often helps a great deal. Test-holes dug in different parts of the garden may disclose a pocket of sand required for digging into stiff clay. The strata of 30 or 40 cm deep is sometimes far superior to the worn out surface earth and deep digging will improve the tilth of the soil. No soil should dryout too quickly ; but if this condition exists, it must be rectified if plants are to thrive. There must be at least 40 cm of soil for annuals, less than this would result in slow starvation and quick scouring of the soil. Change the top layer of soil from time to time by digging deep and thus permit the nutrients which are lodged in the bottom to come to the top. In digging, remember that sandy soil can be attended to almost immediately after rain but clay must be allowed to dry to some extent. Never let a crust form. When turning over soil always remove old roots and stones.

Cultivation of soil

This is the digging of land with the kodali or hoe or ploughing it, and many amateurs consider that the operation is sufficient to ensure a good tilth and all other desirable qualities. But this is an error. The worst soil can be made to grow plants if a little care is taken on digging and manuring. To get a slope on a plot of ground, dig towards the end which is desired to be lower. If it is done twice or thrice a natural fall will result. But the mere digging or ploughing of ground is not enough, subsequent disturbing of the surface soil must be carried out. If soil is allowed to crack after watering, a large proportion of the moisture escapes ; when the surface is forked lightly and the soil broken fine the disturbed area may dry but other capillary tubes having been broken, prevent the moisture from the lower layer being dispersed quickly. The rake can also be used and the surface of the soil scarified.

Drainage, surface

Dig a pit and half fill with stones but provide an outlet for water. On the hills, if a plot of ground has to be prepared for planting, build up the side toward the slope with a stone wall and after laying a base of stones of varying sizes, fill in the compost. The natural grading of land should also be noticed and care taken not to allow scour which will relieve the soil of a good percentage of the fertiliser worked into it.

On the plains, drainage is often difficult and raising the level of the land is the only solution, though expensive and impossible where the house is only on short lease. There should be a fall of a few cm to be at all effective.

Drainage, sub-soil

Drainage pipes are often laid with good effect to relieve land of the excess subsoil moisture. In the case of sandy soil these pipes of 10-15 cm in diameter should be laid at 16 m intervals, and about half this distance in clay soils. The water should be diverted to a sump or connected to a large drain or tank (the gradient is 1 : : 100 or 1 : : 300). When bedding down the pipes use cinders, broken brick or some such material to avoid the pipes being clogged quickly by earth. The roots of trees will rush to these areas because of the moisture and in time fill the pipes with rootlets. If pipes are not available a satisfactory drainage channel can be arranged by setting a triangular drain of tiles or stone slabs and filling in the space with clinkers or broken bricks.

Agricultural pipes of porous material with four rows of holes each and few cm apart running the length of the pipes can be purchased.

LIGHT AND SHADE IN THE GARDEN

Intensity and duration of sun light greatly influence growth and flowering of plants. Gardens in cities are often shaded partially, in some crowded locality almost fully, in such places common sun loving flowering plants including shrubs, annuals, roses, etc. will prove to be failure and so design for shade plants without affecting unity in the garden.

WATERING

Water is the medium which conveys the soluble nutrients in manure and fertilizer to the roots of the plant, at the same time providing the moisture. One good soaking is far preferable to repeated sprinklings ; over-watering damages the delicate root system, and weakens the vitality of the plant. The soil should be allowed to dry before next watering.

Daily sprinkling encourages surface roots which are liable to be affected through extremes of heat and cold and are damaged when the soil is loosened. Moreover, less labour is required to give a thorough soaking every few days.

No hard and fast rule can be laid down for watering as it depends entirely on the season of the year, the type of soil and the plant. During the winter months, certain bulbs and succulents are dormant, these naturally want little moisture. When spring comes, water has to be applied generously and during the hot summer you can hardly overdo watering. In the rains, except when there is a break, give the watering-can a rest. The average mali's favourite outdoor sport is wetting the ground daily, no matter what you may say, he is confident about his knowledge on gardening. Absorption of water does not take place as quickly in cold as in warm weather, therefore, watering should be withheld to a certain extent in winter and supplied also as a spray during hot dry periods. To test when a pot plant requires water, sound it with a wooden mallet, if it gives out a hollow sound it is dry, a dull sound ensures moist soil.

Water is essential in a garden and where this is not under pressure but has to be delivered by drain or channel maintain levels for the passage of water to ensure the minimum of labour necessary of its distribution.

A saucer of water kept continually under a pot is apt to damage the roots, moist sand is better, when the sand dries moisten it again.

Never water a plant near the crown ; the roots that make use of the moisture are along the sides of the pot. With shrubs in the ground, water should be applied 30 to 40 cm from the stem. The feeding roots of a tree are roughly at the same distance as the spread of the head from the trunk and water should, therefore, be accordingly given.

How to water

First see that the soil is lightly forked to allow water to penetrate ; even seed pans with a hardened surface should be scratched with a wooden splinter or else a few small holes made along the outer edge to allow the water to penetrate. A good way is to gradually lower the pan or pot into a tub of water till the soil is thoroughly soaked. Pot plants should be periodically soaked ; a sharp instrument run down the sides of the pot before watering is an easy method. With ordinary soil if the ground is thoroughly soaked it will be impossible to fork up the surface within 24 hours in the summer and twice or thrice as long in the winter months.

When to water

In the cold months, avoid giving water late in the evening when the nights are cold ; afternoon or early morning is better.

During the warm months late afternoon is better than early morning.

Never syringe foliage when the sun is up as there is the fear of the drops of water acting as burning glasses and damaging the leaf surface. Always use clean water as mud in suspension deposited on the leaf is troublesome to remove and spoil the foliage.

What to water

Do not give more water when the soil is already wet, nor it should be allowed to get bone dry. Pot plants require more water than those in the ground and by sounding the pot you can soon judge when water should be supplied. Keep the surface of the soil loose so that water may sink to the lower strata where the feeding roots lie. A plant that has faded through neglect, should in addition to a good watering, have the foliage syringed twice a day and transfer it in shade.

WHEN TO PLANT

What is the correct planting season ? (a) When plants are dormant, they can then be lifted carefully and can tolerate pruning of roots, with the coming of spring the plant will break into leaf. Dormant season planting takes place on the hills and in climate where there is a real winter.

(b) Spring starts growth but when this season merges into a severe summer one has to be careful ; if you look after the plants yourself, transplanting is best done in February. When very hot winds blow, newly planted stock will suffer and it is advisable to avoid planting till the first rains.

(c) Rainy season planting is perfectly safe, provided the soil does not get waterlogged. Drainage, therefore, is the main problem at this time, as the newly formed roots are prone to excessive moisture. Let a few showers fall to cool the atmosphere, then fork deeply and plant. The pits for planting can be excavated prior to the planting season.

Planting should be done when plants have the greatest chance of survival. Never take unnecessary risks by leaving the minimum of roots when lifting a plant ; avoid cutting any of the large ones. Always shade plants in hot dry weather and syringe the foliage in the late evening to further assist them to recover. When the normal flow of sap is held up for a day or two the plant hardly looses a leaf or on the other hand, when every leaf turns yellow and drops, this plant will live. Those plants with leaves that hang on the twigs and do not fall, with shoot-tips that droop, usually die. To save such seemingly hopeless cases, clip the tips, strip off the dead foliage, syringe frequently and keep the soil moist.

TRANSPLANTING

Transplanting is a simple operation and yet a number of plants collapses apparently for no rhyme or reason. Have the pit ready, moisten it with water and lower the lifted plant into place. Raise a ridge of earth around the plant to contain water, flood, then to make certain that the bottom soil is also wet run a bamboo splint down in several places to allow the water to penetrate. Shelter the plant and syringe the foliage at dusk for several days. Arrange for a supporting stake according to the height of the plant ; a tree guard will often save it from being damaged in an open public place.

In the hot months, do not risk transplanting during a spell of moist weather as the plant cannot stand it.

Before transplanting soak the pot or ground so that the ball of earth can be lifted easily. After repotting leave about 2-3 cm space between the rim of the pot and the ball of earth for watering purposes. Before transplanting seedlings of flowers and vegetables, withhold water for a day before the operation and flood immediately after planting.

Unless you have an exceptionally careful Mali, supervise transplanting personally. This will minimise the casualities.

Large plants should have moss or straw wrapped around their stems and periodically syringed and all soft sappy shoots should be pruned back to hard wood.

No matter how urgent the occasion, never plant in sodden soil ; if it is imperative to transplant during wet weather excavate the soil and replace with dry earth. No manure and very little leafmould should be used, the addition of sand to heavy clay is recommended and a basket of screened leafmould to a pit 1 m deep.

Newly planted trees should be cut back to the point where the stems are green. Do not allow plants to carry dead wood longer than is necessary. All deciduous fruit trees should be cut back and the new growth thus forced. Guard against deep planting which is responsible for a lot of collar rot. Plants of slow growth and hard wood must be planted firmly ; those of quick maturity and coarser root systems moderately ; give plenty of room to such as they are impatient of root disturbance.

When to transplant

The wet weather is safest though during the winter months dormant plants can safely be shifted. It depends on the care with which the operation is performed as to when you transplant. For transplanting seedlings use a bottomless milk tin, press down into the soil around the seedling to be lifted, cut through soil below the tin with a khurpi, transfer and press out ball of earth.

How to transfer

In order to transfer a pot plant to the ground, remove and loosen the ring of roots and place in the prepared hole. Any tree with a tap root should not be kept too long in a pot otherwise the most important anchor will become useless.

The transfer of a pot plant to pot, has been dealt with in the repotting section.

Transplanting of ground plants to pots. Here we are on different ground for if the soil is clay, the lifting operation is simple. Dig a trench of a larger diameter than you actually require severing the roots as you go round. Gradually reduce the ball of earth after under cutting to a size slightly smaller than the pot. Have the pot crocked and slightly covered with soil, place the plant in position and drift in fresh compost. Lightly ram the soil down and soak thoroughly.

The last type of transplanting refers to the removal of large bushes or trees from the ground to other situations. Some plants roughly taken out of the earth and thrown into a roughly dug pit will survive, others lifted with all the care and attention that it is possible to give them—die. The chief trouble lies in the delicate root system, the severance of the tap or main root without the supplementary roots coming into action. Open up the trench as suggested above but after severing the roots on one-third of the circle close it down again for a week. Should the plant show no signs of wilting carry on with the next, completing the circle within the month when the plant will be ready to lift. When lifting any large ball of earth it should be well tied with straw, grass or even gunny bags to prevent the earth from falling away. If by chance the earth should break, immediately prepare a thin paste of fresh cow manure and clay, one-third manure to two-third clay and dip the roots into this before planting. Shading, and frequent syringing in addition to watering are necessary. Prune the tips if they wilt or bend ; if the bush or tree has a heavy head of foliage reduce the branches before lifting as the leaves play an important part in transpiration and will get the sap moving and the roots to work but do not be too drastic in pruning. Transplanting, if carefully done, stimulates the formation of the fibrous roots, for the main roots are severed and the smaller ones develop to take their place.

How to toss out a plant

First, water the pot plant an hour before attention, then placing the pot upside down in the left hand with the stem of the plant between the extended fingers, hold the bottom of the pot with the right hand and tap the pot gently on the edge of a platform or log of wood raised from the ground to avoid damaging the plant which might otherwise come in contact with the ground. If roots show through the drainage hole push these back and sever any large tap root which looks as if it will prevent the release of the plant.

Potting

It is a common practice in garden plant to transfer it from a smaller pot to a larger one by gradual stages. In the majority of cases when a root comes to the limit of extension it curves and follows a course around the sides of the pot. The main roots travel as far as they can go before dividing into the fine roots with their root hairs which feed the plant. In a small pot it is not very far and naturally the plant benefits quickly by receiving a good food supply. Before the plant gets root bound, make the shift to a larger size ; the plant thus obtains the maximum nourishment that roots can provide with each successive shift. It becomes a far stronger plant when it reaches the last stage than if the transfer had been made to the large pot at the very commencement.

How to repot

When potting, place the crocks concave-side down, one over the drainage hole and build up around this and over, finishing off with smaller pieces then a layer of coarse screenings or half decayed leaves, or fibre. Fill in compost, leaving at least 2 cm of space for retaining water. Moss is ideal but often difficult to obtain. Small pieces of cinders, brick or gravel on the surface of the pot prevent the soil being washed away and also help to retain moisture and check evaporation. Never use too large a pot for a small size plant, as this does harm. A small sized pot can always give place to a larger size when necessary. Bury the old ball of soil 3 cm below the compost and ram the compost with a blunt stick to settle the plant. Gently jar the pot as this will help the soil to settle. Keep the pot in a shady spot at least two days before placing it in the sun and syringe regularly. The potting compost should never be used bone dry and always moisten it thoroughly before potting. If this is not done, very often moisture will not penetrate below the top 2 cm soil after the plant has been watered.

In very dry climate, where the heat affects the earthernware pot it is a good idea to place the pot in a larger pot with a layer of coarse sand and crocks between the two receptacles or partially bury the pot in the ground.

Plants in pots are usually placed anywhere and anyhow. Ants, earth worms, termite etc. often enter and cause trouble.

Always keep pot plants on a couple of bricks laid parallel so that the drainage hole has a clear passage, or else on a bed of clinkers, broken bricks or such materials.

When you receive a consignment of plants from Bangalore or Madras, remove the ball of red sticky soil and then plant in pot or ground.

When to repot

The best time of the year is during wet weather for any damage to the roots will not cause the death of the plant ; if the replanted specimens are kept in the shade, syringed and watered ; this work can be done any time of the year. Avoid transplanting the plant when new growth just commenced ; dormant bulbs or plants should be attended to just before the growth starts and not immediately after they have lost their leaves.

What to repot

Repotting of a plant will depend upon the rate of growth of both shoot and root. Chrysanthemums need repotting at intervals of 30-40 days, while a palm may remain in a pot for 4-5 years. Again when a plant grows rapidly it may need repotting every year but after few years change of pot is done less frequently. Specimen plants of fern and foliage plants are not repotted every year but some rich soil is incorporated to maintain the growth.

Shading

The shading of plants is sadly neglected and no thought is ever given to the direct rays striking one side of the plant. It is only when the plants are scorched and sunburnt that we realise what the sun can do. A rough mat screen, a few branches, or a green screen composed of *Tephrosia*, *arhar*, *jaint* or other quick growing plants will be helpful. A plant gets a set back when thus sunburnt ; a palm or anthurium, for instance takes a full season or more to make up the damaged foliage. Not only are the leaves destroyed but the entire system of the plant is adversely affected.

Staking

This may be called an art. It is necessary almost with all types of ornamental plants.

The mali often ties a branch to a stake so close that the bark is damaged badly and the growth of the plant affected. The tying material should be first fastened to the stake by a simple knot, then the tie passed over the twig or branch in a loop allowing for growth and yet not sufficiently loose to permit wind play. When large branches are to be staked a block of wood or bamboo or a pad of coir or gunny fixed to the branch over which the tying rope or wire is drawn, will prevent damage to the bark.

With bushy growth three or more stakes linked together with string forming large mesh interlacing is better. Carnations have special wire stakes which are efficient and inexpensive and stakes are removed at the end of the season. Trees or shrubs, that are loosely tied or with straggling growth are apt to be injured by high winds ; either reduce the growth or else tie them to substantial stakes.

Syringing

The syringe is not considered important by most amateurs, yet it makes a difference to a plant if the foliage is sprayed regularly. Insects and dust are removed and the cleansed leaf surfaces are useful for efficient functioning of the leaf. The air is also cooled and moistened even for a short while. First of all, use a fine jet to wet the surface of the leaf and loosen the dust and dirt. Follow this up with a second spraying slightly stronger to remove unwanted matter. If the syringing is done before the dew dries it will be more beneficial to the plant. If water alone fails to make much impression on the dirt use a soap solution.

New arrivals

When deciduous plants arrive after a long journey, especially from abroad, they should be potted off in a light compost without the admixture of any manure and placed in a cool dark room for a couple of days. Thoroughly wet the foliage and syringe the plants every day ; on the third day admit a little light so that the etiolated stems may become green. Gradually increase light and water till the plants can be taken into the open. Do not place in full sunlight for at least ten days.

On receiving plants from a nursery, examine the ball of earth around the roots as often this is a stiff clay, which has hardened on route to brick like consistency. During wet weather the removal of this ball by soaking and washing, and replanting in a more congenial compost is suggested. At other times, gently crack the ball by pressure and plant in light soil, filling the fissures with sandy soil to induce the roots to leave the hard shell.

Forcing

This is only possible where there is a dormant period and the sap is held up. Arrest growth by artificial wintering, i.e., withholding water ; at the desired season heavy flooding and warmth will rush along growth and consequently the flower bud. This principle is not always practicable on the plains and can only be tried within small limits with a few bulbs such as hyacinths, etc. Hot beds are not often required on the plains but if desired, can be made of rotting material, stable manure or mown grass, with top layer of 6 cm of soil. A glass frame placed on top will conserve heat. The bed should be renewed as the heat is reduced.

Off Season Attention

When one is acquainted with the period of dormancy, water should be withheld and every opportunity given for the rest that nature desires. Other plants that have a growing time varying with the seasons, but never dormant, should be attended to with common sense. Before flowering do not force leaf growth and therefore, be careful what fertilizers you use.

Follow the instructions and you will find a difference in the condition of your garden.

(1) Get advice from reliable source.

(2) Always buy the best seeds, it pays in the long run.

(3) Dig the ground deeply before planting.

(4) Manure carefully with recognised fertilizers.

(5) Aerate the soil while the plant is growing.

(6) Weed continually, not by fits and starts.

(7) Never over-water or over-manure a plant.

(8) Plant for succession in your garden but allow for a period of rest.

(9) Avoid a seasonal repetition in the annual and the vegetable garden.

(10) Remove flowers as they fade.

(11) Gather vegetables as they reach a fair size.

(12) Destroy weeds when first noticed.

CHAPTER II

Garden Design

The subject of garden planning is so diverse and complicated that it is very difficult to represent all ideas of completeness in one chapter. To plan and survey the land and to construct a house, expert advice of an architect or a civil engineer is essential to make the place habitable. In modern living consciousness of interior decoration, including furniture, wood work, wall furnishings, carpets, painting also need careful setting and the services of specialists are considered necessary for this purpose. In order to achieve a rewarding result, a garden should be designed carefully as it is a semi-permanent feature and frequent change in design is not possible. Garden design combines the aesthetic beauty, artistry, knowledge on growth and development of plants and at least the principles of garden maintenance at different seasons.

Before entering the subject of Garden Design one should know the definition of some terms which are commonly used and a short history of landscape gardening. A garden may be defined as a place for growing plants, exhibits various forms of plant life, which are consciously directed for ornamental or practical use or both. Now a days, we often use the term like landscape gardening, landscape architecture, landscape design etc. Arrangement of trees, shrubs, climbers and various other plants together with the building, walks, drives, artificial and natural features for the use of humanity is termed as 'landscape gardening'. 'Landscape architecture' is the art of arranging land and landscape for human use, convenience and enjoyment. 'Design' is the determination of the character of an object to serve a certain purpose known in advance. Design may be of two types—aesthetic and economic. Aesthetic design is purely attractive and pleasing in appearance, while economic design is meant to serve some practical and utilitarian purposes.

Landscape architecture should, in most cases satisfy in its design for both the purposes.

Although garden of different types differ in their arrangement and plant material used, some features such as water, fountains, walls and walks are commonly used in such a way as to take advantage of climatic conditions and to suit the principle of design. Garden may be of two types—formal and informal. In the formal garden we find symmetrical balance, with sharply defined edges, straight lines of planting, clipped hedges, man made levels and retaining walls. Informal gardens are asymmetrical with intelligent melting and merging points where planting is done in free flowing contours on curved lines and clipping is almost avoided. Le Notre, a French landscape designer who is best known for his Grandiose Palace garden at Versailles was the founder of what became known as the Grand Style in landscape architecture. In about 1750 informality in garden design came into practice due to the ingenuity of Mr. Kent. His idea was to create naturalistic effect. This was followed by Mr. Lancelot Brown, commonly known as Capability Brown who proceeded to tear out all features that could be possibly of old garden types. All traces of formality like terraces, yew hedges and geometrically shaped beds were abolished and the ground laid out in entirely new lines with miniature mountains, streams, crossed by bridges, paths, walks etc. in serpentine curves. Sir Humphery Repton appeared in England as landscape gardener in the year 1803, who believed in an organised plan and used plant material in the best possible way to create the desired effect so as to enhance the plan. Towards the end of the nineteenth century Mrs. Gertrude Jekyll introduced an act of adapting arrangement of living material to the site which has exerted a great influence on garden in England and America.

In order to layout a good garden some fundamental principles are to be followed.

(i) Garden should be reasonably laid out for the owners' comfort and convenience.

(ii) Simplicity in design should be the key note and undue complexity be avoided.

(iii) Variety in a garden gives the greatest pleasure. But attempting too much in a small space is not desirable.

(iv) The natural grade of the ground should be taken as a guide.

(v) The ground should be so designed that the entire garden is not visible at a glance. Even in a small plot it should not be possible to view the whole garden at a glance. It should be full of surprises, with each turn of the path revealing fresh vistas, or disclosing new interest.

(vi) Long and straight garden paths should be avoided.

(vii) Judicious employment of more number of plants of different varieties should be one of the most important fundamental approaches.

(viii) Colour and contrast in the garden are very much desirable which are lasting enjoyment and most satisfying means of creating interest in the garden.

Garden design involves attention to many considerations connected with the character and position of the site and its surroundings. Each particular site presents a problem to itself in relation to soil, position, aspect and evironment and the designer must carefully consider these factors. Artistic consideration and practical need of horticulture must synchronise. In garden planning proper growth and flowering of plants and the comfort and convenience of those who use the garden must always receive attention. Everything in the garden should be interdependent, the general picture distinguished by balance, unity of effect and a studied harmony of line and mass. There should be no exaggeration of special features, no discordant note to worry the eye, no forcing of effects. Gardens which are made haphazard are rarely successful, while over elaborating any feature destroys simplicity and breadth of effect. Hastening in planning a garden should always be avoided. Trained and skilled personnel should be engaged in designing and laying out gardens.

Before preparing a plan of the site any attempt for construction work and planting should be avoided. This is most important because certain mistakes cannot be rectified. As a rule, however, building, building entrances, windows, all walks, roads, paths, all physical features such as existing vegetation, water sources, rock, all views to be emphasised or screened, all terraces or other decided irregularities in the ground level, features of importance, should be located, named and shown on the map. With survey map completed, work on the preliminary plan can proceed. A preliminary plan should offer a practical workable scheme. It should be attractively drawn and present enough information to explain the ideas. A final plan represents a finished scheme on accepted programme of work. It should be completed in every detail and presented in a form suitable for its use. In the final plan according to the nature of development one may show the adopted scheme, general plan, planting arrangement, planting plan, the dimension and construction details, working plan, grading and drainage plan.

While laying out garden, intelligent and artistic allocations of major ground areas for different purposes are necessary to achieve the success. For the development of a home garden suitable arrangement of three essential portions (a) an approach (b) the service and (c) the outdoor living part or garden area are important. The approach is of two types—a walk to the front door for the general public use and the other a drive or walk to rear door and garage for general service purposes. The approaches should be direct, shortest possible and must occupy little space. Service area is meant for supply and disposal of waste such as garbage. Behind the service yard vegetable garden, nursery for propagation of plants, compost heap etc. can be located. All those activities, however, must be crowded into a minimum of space and screened from living area by a fence or planting. Atleast half of the area should be devoted to outdoor living or garden area which is to be beautified with living plants and other outdoor features.

On the front and side of the building there should be a lawn with low planting on the boundary line. In the rear portion of the building there should be again a lawn area bordered by terrace and planting beds. After coming to the final decision concerning the location of major areas one is ready to think in terms of actual landscape objects, paths, terraces, fences, trees, shrubs, climbers and annual beds etc.

The home ground should be planned between the property lines around the house, so that there is more outdoor living space. Grading of ground to get drainage away from building is necessary and if possible, the slope should be 20-30 cm in 20 metres. An area of paving between the house and the garden may take many forms and is increasingly becoming an essential feature of modern living ; water, pools, rocks, benches and seats are also playing important parts in modern design.

A continuously satisfying garden can be built with plants themselves, if one knows how to use them. Considerable thought should be given to the selection of plants in modern landscape. Before going for plantation we must know the main purposes of residential planting and these are to provide shade, make boundaries and give seclusion, soften architectural harshness, create a transition between the vertical lines of the house and the horizontal lines of the ground and to create beauty.

Plants should be chosen on the basis of size, form, structure, texture, colour and fragrance. It is advisable to use large material where size of the area permits. They should be moderately spaced for proper growth. Planting lines or curves in the garden add beauty and the curve should be very bold and supported by a bank of trees and shrubs which will create the structure of the garden. The height of planting is to be related with the width of bed and the bold outcurves automatically become the high point in planting. These high points or outcurves should be adjusted in such a way so that it will occur in just the right position to screen out all undesirable objects. In any circumstance, the high points or outcurves should not invade the corner of the plot. The piece of lawn, cutting in deeply towards the corner greatly increases the illusion of depth. The bold outcurves by itself do not give depth in garden unless it is strongly supported by heavy planting. The shrubs at the outcurves should be dwarf in height which will give more pleasing effect with the leaves and branches touching the ground. Amount of distribution of natural light should be assessed very well.

Neatness and simplicity in front of the house are very much desirable. Front garden should not be over crowded with planting neither should it remain without trees and shrubs etc. Planting must echo the formal or informal quality of the house, walk and drive to establish the pleasing character and neat and attractive perennials are selected. Fine foliaged plants are excellent as doorway accents for clapboard house, while broader foliage is pleasing with a house of stone or brick. Seasonal flowers can also be added for seasonal colour. It is better to decorate the entrance garden with seasonal flowers cultivated in pots, rather than in beds.

Back garden in combination with terrace, lawn, children corner, rockery, lily pool, and various kinds of plants and other features gives comfort and pleasure to the owner. Successful planning of this lot results in matching the unique characteristics of the property with personal requirement. Some degree of privacy is also desired. Generous boundary planting with shrubs, screening trees or climbers are helpful in this regard. This adds interest and depth to the views and creates a good setting for the house and outdoor living areas. Plants of distinctive qualities and suited to the particular need for planting in outdoor living areas are to be selected.

Some of the important feautures of gardens are described :

LAWN :

Lawn is one of the most important elements in the garden design, attractive at all times and providing a pleasant surrounding for house, trees, shrubs and flowers. One of the greatest charms of a garden is a beautifully kept, clean shaven, verdant lawn. To the designer grass is considered as the background on which the garden picture is built. It is the centre of social life which is always restful to the eyes. A patch of good velvety green lawn is desirable close to the house to secure a greater breadth and dignity to a place. Planting of any kind should not be encouraged which may encroach the broad expanse of lawn area before the house. The lawn or a portion of it, should always be seen from the best parts of the house, the choicest shrubs or the richest terrace gardens will satisfy in the same manner. The size of the lawn will depend very much on the availability of space, whereas the shape should be such that it creates an attractive appearance. The quantity of grass and the various levels of the lawns would all be settled with exactness in an architecturally treated garden but in a more natural and landscape portions of the ground there are a few conditions, the observance of which will make lawns pleasing or otherwise. Once the lawn is established it takes little effort to keep it growing beautifully.

ROCK GARDEN :

Rock garden is an interesting feature in the garden. In most of the gardens they are laid out in such a non-artistic way and badly contrived that it looks out of place and has no utility of any symmetrical balance with the garden. The common plan of heaping together a mass of stone and mineral curiosities into a grotto-like structure and sprinkling the whole with soil is the outcome of misunderstanding of the first principles. In laying out a garden to bring nature in home and like other features introduce rocks in the garden and feel happy to see plants growing well on rocks. In nature rocks serve as flower pots. So any attempt to imitate this natural condition should have naturalistic approach and good technical thinking.

It is better to select rocks from material which is porous and the soil in rock garden must be well drained. The rock garden should be as far removed from a formal environment as possible. The aim should be to imitate a piece of nature. If associated with walls, green houses or other artificial surroundings the illusion falls to pieces. It is also better to keep it away from the neighbourhood of trees, one great charm of the rock garden is its variety and that can be maintained by providing all the conditions of aspect and exposure demanded by various plants.

The rock garden may take the shape of a mountain or the stony slope of a hill, a rock crest or a peak. But whatever may be the plan in mind, it must have definiteness of scheme. All rock gardens should have planting pockets and compartments filled with rich soils on the slopes and should have adequate drainage. All rocks in the ground level should be burried two third leaving one third exposed to look like a natural out crop. Rocks of different shapes and sizes are combined and rooted in the ground to get the desired landscape effect. The actual outline and dimensions of the rockery depend entirely on the chosen site. A fairly steep slope of different characters facing south-east is a good spot for laying out a rock garden and it should not end abruptly. It is better to let it gradually merge into the general surface of the ground, some detached pieces of rock being placed on the level beyond the raised part of the rock garden, just as we find in nature.

Careful selection of plants and bulbs suitable for growing in rocks which give long flowering season and beautiful colour effect are desirable.

ROSARY :

Roses are grown in the garden with great love and sincerity in isolated beds or where the space permits they may be grown together in a special garden, termed the rosary or rosarium. Roses can be grown in a place by itself without a monotonous effect. The most common method is to cut the rose beds in grass and there is much to be said in favour of grass as a setting for roses. The beds should not be elaborate in outline nor too small. The groups should show a geometrical relation between their component beds. It is not unusual to carry a path through the rose garden, or to set it where two paths intersect at right angles. The point of intersection is sometimes marked by a sundial or vase. When a path or paths leads into the rose garden, the beds may be separated by gravel, thereby excluding grass altogether.

Establishing a rose garden involves three things, and these are (a) design, (b) choice of varieties and (c) preparation of soil and planting. Design will depend very much on available space in sunny location and personal taste. This may consist of a number of beds grouped together leaving paths and space of green velvety grass in between. This pleasant setting brightens the display of rose flowers of different types and varieties. Considering the growth habit of different types of roses Hybrid Tea roses may be grown in simple beds and Floribunda and Standard roses in border or along side the long paths, whereas Climber and Rambler roses on walls, rustic arches or fences. With various types and enormous varieties a complete garden may be laid out by using roses as planting material.

WATER GARDEN :

In landscape gardening use of water in their setting plays a prominent role for many obvious reasons. Garden designers have always produced the most satisfactory results, when they have been able to bring water in some way into their compositions. It is beautiful and attractive at all times and providing a pleasant everchanging surface varying with the change of season and weather. The murmuring stream or dripping waterfall attract the ears and eyes. The beauty of water-side planting is enhanced by charming reflections. Lovely hybrids of water-lilies and water loving plants are gaining much importance in modern gardening. If in any site of a garden, natural stream, pond or lake exists, water garden is at once assured by planting suitable plants. If no such natural facilities exist, an artificial pool must be formed in a sunny spot. It should fit in with the overall garden design. Available space and individual choice will determine the size and shape of the pool.

The music of flowing water, the beautiful forms which can be made to rise and fall and the association of architectural designs account for the deserved popularity of the fountain. The success of fountain, however, depends upon obtaining the water at sufficient pressure and skilful plumbing. If surrounded by a large basin or pond, upright jets may be adopted ; for smaller fountains, some simple form of bubbles or jets thrown out from the side of a central arrangement would generally be found most satisfactory.

A sheet of water is not only a welcome feature in the landscape, but also proves useful for boating and fishing in almost all seasons. The beauty of a lake also depends upon reflection of the objects upon the bank. Smoothness and softness of effect have been recommended as the best treatment of the surroundings of lake. The artificial treatment of water, especially when it is required to form a part of a formal scheme, is one of the most costly affairs in the whole practice of garden-craft.

When a rock garden combines with water garden it gives more attractive appearance. A formal garden of this type should have a conventional shape of pool with bold stone slab on the sides surrounded by straight paths and geometric beds. The informal type which is most desirable and should be the key note in the rock and water gardening. Here, the pool or a series of small pools should combine in artistic manner surrounded by rock garden.

BOG GARDEN :

Though not an important feature in garden design, bog garden is interesting if facilities to form such type of ground naturally exist at the site. It is not always advisable to level the low lying areas as it creates opportunity for growing some special kind of plants without taking help of any artificial means. Bog garden can be laid out in a marshy spot, partly in sun and in shade and plants can be selected depending upon the moisture on the ground. Deposition of organic matter markedly improves the growth of the plants. It should be specially designed in order to fit the overall plan of the garden.

WILD GARDEN :

With the increasing popularity for informal design in gardening, laying out wild garden is also getting importance in garden planning. It is the desire of man for direct communication with nature and naturalizing home-living with no touch of artificiality. Combinations of some plants are very attractive in wild garden e.g., fine leaved plants, ferns, climbers, grass, trailing shrubs and flowers if grown together in informal beds of rough undulated places. A wild garden will show its best when the plants have grown well and this type of garden should be attempted in large garden area. Designing a wild garden requires imagination and careful selection of plants depending on the growth habit of the plants.

TERRACE GARDEN :

Terrace garden is increasingly becoming an essential feature of modern garden. This is an area of paving between the garden and the house and it may be of various sizes and attractive shapes. In order to improve the look of the garden the terraces are constructed for several reasons e.g., (a) for cultivation of plants in pots or raised beds, (b) an outdoor area for sitting and dining (c) dirt-free children's play area etc.

Paving of terraces may be made by flag stone, native stone, brick concrete, wood or gravel. It is important to select the right colour and texture of paving material when planning a terrace. This creates interest in small area which brings beauty of growing things close to paving room and dining room windows at rear living area. Plant material for this area should be chosen with great care.

CHILDREN GARDEN :

Modern gardens are specially designed and adapted to provide maximum safety, fun and enjoyment for children of all ages. The elements of contended play are sand pits, sand, water, grass, rounded pebbles, a small flowering tree, miniature gardens and other game equipment. A planned yard in any semi-shady corner of the garden containing the above includes children's need in gardens.

KITCHEN GARDEN :

Most owners of garden, like to devote at least a small part of their garden area to some good varieties of fruit and vegetables which is a rewarding and fascinating garden project. Nothing tastes better than home grown fresh fruit and vegetables. In selecting a site for a kitchen garden, it is usually best to locate it in close proximity to the home and on no account should it be so arranged that a portion of the pleasure ground must be traversed to reach it. There are other points to be considered before laying out a kitchen garden. The garden should be laid out in a sunny place and enclosed by walls and good high hedge. A convenient water supply is a very important item and good walks in the kitchen garden as elsewhere are necessary. The size of kitchen garden is also a matter which needs careful consideration and for convenience of working it should be divided into quarters.

Kitchen garden as a whole seldom presents an attractive appearance, it should be located in such a place so that it does not spoil the garden picture. A delightful and attractive approach may, however, be made by way of arched opening in the wall. Cut flowers for the house may also be grown in this site. Formal design is the best for kitchen garden.

CONTAINER GARDENING :

It is one of the most interesting and popular methods of gardening. It widens the scope of making gardens indoor as well as outdoor and adds year round colour in the garden with minimum effort. Here lies the scope of using attractive containers of various types, of different shape and sizes ; simple shape and subdued colour are, however, desirable. Miniature gardens can even be laid out in one big container or by using series of small containers. For outdoor display large containers are better, small containers can be grouped for bold effect.

In order to soften bare steps, to separate terrace from lawn, to make partition, use of foliage and flowering plants tubbed or boxed is very effective.

STEPS FOR GROUND AND GARDENS : Steps are means of changing levels in the garden. They may be of brick, stone, concrete, wood, grass, or a combination of two or three of these. They should be of comfortable height and construction should be safe, durable and easy to maintain. Design of steps must fit in the overall landscape planning.

WALKS AND PATHS : Garden paths are used for recreative purposes and social intercourse, and should, therefore, offer an inducement for frequent use by well conceived and harmonious lines, easy gradients and perfect metalling or paving. Walks are the skeleton framework of a garden and a means of circulating around the place. To make the walks still more useful, seats and shelters may be provided in convenient positions. They should also be arranged in such a way that the beauty of the place may be exhibited. Walks and garden paths are also necessary for proper working and should be approximately levelled, if not cross-wise certainly length-wise and wherever a fall occurs it should be connected by steps ; sloping paths on a terrace are seldom a success.

Walks may be made of bricks, gravel, stone, concrete, wood, or grass depending on the availability of material and design. Much care is needed while planning and designing walks and paths. Paths of gravel or stepping stones through flower beds give an informal look. Stepping blocks, round paving blocks and angled squares also make the garden walk interesting. Stone, brick and concrete are suitable for the important and much-used paths in the garden. Delightful edging to garden paths may be made by planting lawn grass but it requires careful maintenance, otherwise it will spoil the look of the garden.

FENCES FOR UTILITY AND BEAUTY : Fence provides clearly defined boundary line, screening, security and allows the gardener to make the best use of the land. The materials may vary from split rails to the most sophisticated modern plastic or plywood sheet. The immediate surrounding and architecture of the house is important in deciding on the design of the fence. Sometimes fences support climbers and shrubs which assure considerable privacy.

Combination of stone walls and the common sheep wires look extremely interesting. When the ground is undulated and the line of fence arranged to fit the contour, some strong but simple form of continuous railing would make a good and cheap fence. Stone walls may be built in so many ways to correspond with the surroundings. As a cheap fence round a cottage garden, there are few forms which look so well in carpenter made lattice from bamboo slits. Whatever may be the material this should be made with good taste, ability and expert craftsmanship. Simplicity in design, charming and attractive appearance of fences are desirable. Hedges of different kinds and forms are also used for this purpose, this gives lasting pleasure, variety of hue and harmony with the surroundings.

GARDEN GATES : A gate with its attractive and simple design in garden welcomes the visitor and is a point of interest. It should be ornamental as well as functional. Its design must blend well with the architecture of the house, the fence or area surrounding them and should be at least one metre wide.

ARCHES AND PERGOLAS : Arches are generally used in garden to form a sort of screen or connecting link between one part of garden to another. They may be of different shapes and sizes with variety of design. Its proper place is astride a path and its avowed purpose is to support climbing plants.

Pergolas are a very pretty feature in a garden. A series of rustic arches embowered with climbers are termed as pergola. A path shaded with pergola is as much a necessity against the heat of the sun as a welcome visual feature. This may be used to cover a path leading from one part of the garden to another. The materials for making a pergola are brick, stone, timber or bamboo poles.

Arches and pergolas are to be erected in such a place of the garden that their design and existence harmonise with the entire planning of the garden. Climbers on the pergola should create interest at all seasons of the year.

GARDEN WALLS : Walls around a garden have almost infinite possibilities and variation in design, material and usefulness, and are usually constructed by using bricks, stones, flints and concrete blocks. They add beauty to the garden if designed properly. The architecture of the house and immediate surrounding of the place is also important in deciding on the architecture of the wall. It is usually desirable to have some planting on or near the wall which otherwise looks bare.

GREEN HOUSE AND GLASS HOUSE : Green house is essential to give shelter to all tender and special kind of plants which cannot grow in the open for months together. It also adds to the beauty of the garden, if properly designed and placed in a suitable place. Design of the green house should have close relation with the character and design of other features in the garden including the building.

In a tropical country glass house is not suitable to maintain plants in good condition but glass on the top protects the plants and seedlings from rains. Green house plants may also be grown in glass top green house in shade.

SUMMER HOUSE : The summer house is a useful adjunct as a shelter from wind and the scorching rays of the sun particularly during the hot months. It is also a pleasant feature in the garden, redeeming the general flatness of the site and offering an inducement to enjoy the garden even during the summer months. It is frequently used to hide some unsightly object on neighbouring premises. In locating the summer house two things are taken into consideration—its relation to the garden scheme as a factor in the general picturesque effect, and to the flowers in the garden. A summer house should not stand detached and isolated like a sentry box. If it is not convenient to place it against a boundary, it should remain associated with a tree or a group of trees or shrubs. It may stand among the flowers, where one may enjoy their fragrance and colour and hear the drone of bees. In any case the summer house should not be used as a store for flower pots, garden stakes, and tools.

GARDEN FURNITURES : Good design in garden furniture is as necessary as the selection of furuiture of the house itself. A wide range of attractive garden furnitures are used in modern garden design. They make outdoor living attractive and comfortable. To add fun and pleasure in the garden simple material and attractive designs are preferred.

SEATS : Comfortable seats are usually made of wood and fabric. Iron and stone seats are too hard and absorb temperature. Nylon, PVC and aluminium are largely used for making light and attractive furniture. Cast iron work for benches, tables and chairs look very charming in white colour.

BRIDGES : When water is introduced into the garden, particularly in the form of lake or canal it may be necessary to bridge the bank at some point, either as a matter of convenience or for the sake of an attractive feature. A well designed bridge has not only an aesthetic value but it is very useful in viewing the water vista. The design of a bridge should fit in with the character of the garden and unnecessary decoration should be avoided.

CHAPTER III

Trees

From time immemorial plants are associated with our life. We have appreciated the exquisite beauty of the world of plants through generations and trees are undoubtedly the most prominent group. Tree is a woody plant with a spreading crown, whose single trunk exceeds diameter of 15 cm and attains a certain height. To exclude shrubs, minimum height of a tree is fixed at 4 metres and any woody perennial attaining a height of more than 4 metres and up to 7 metres may be called a small tree. All trees are capable of producing seeds under favourable environmental condition and grow vigorously for many years.

A tree may show the height and shape of a shrub in a climatic condition different from the natural habitat and temperature, light, humidity and moisture and nutritional status of the soil are found to play important role on growth and flowering of plants. By manipulating the environment, delicate plants can be successfully grown if one knows the requirments of those plants. *Amherstia nobilis* can thrive in a place receiving morning sun for 2-3 hours and semishade for the rest of the day. The soil should be moist but porous.

Trees are very fascinating because of their graceful appearance and the abundance of bloom. They are grown for their economic importance or aesthetic value or both. Fruit trees are planted for fruits and forest plantation for other economic products like timber, fuel, tannins, oils, gums, resins, waxes, spices, beverages, narcotics and drugs.

The cultivation of trees for their aesthetic or recreational value is known as arboriculture. Here the individual tree is important in contrast to the wood as a crop as in forestry. They also exercise beneficial influences on climate and rainfall, ıeguate the water flow and prevent soil erosion. The purpose

Cassia nodosa

Bauhinia variegata

Pithecolobium saman

View of a large private garden

of this chapter is to focus the exquisite beauty and graceful charm of the flowering trees. The conspicuous or pretty flowers framed against the panorama of sailing clouds attune us with nature's rhythms and boundless joy at flowering time. A large number of trees in our country are resplendent in riotous colours at the flowering time and are capable of transforming the landscape.

The trees are the most permanent elements in landscape and a thorough knowledge of their ornamental properties, rate and mode of growth, their behaviour in different soil, situation and climate are essential. They should be planted carefully and thoughtfully for the benefit of height, shade, colour and vertical emphasis.

Avenues planted with trees are safer because their restful and scenic views, reduce the monotony of driving and provide shade to the exhausted pedestrians. Avenue trees are beautiful and safety enchanting feature of modern roads, reduce head-light glare from the oncoming traffic and provide a more pleasant drive with less distractions from the surroundings. Such medians are numerous in New Delhi and Chandigarh. Mostly indigenous shade and flowering trees are widely selected for landscaping these medians, where the traffic lanes are widely separated, rest parks with groves of trees have been provided. Such landscaped medians prevent the erosion of roadbarns and backslopes. We should aim at three objectives in planning and constructing of today's heavily travelled transportation arteries, —greater safety, reduced maintenance cost and general attractiveness. Systematic tree planting and landscaping contribute strongly to these objectives.

We have got large number of indigenous and exotic flowering trees which can be successfully utilized to beautify our cities, towns and villages. Along with the road plan, a plantation plan should be made and strictly adhered to. For the existing roads the dead and decaying trees should be re-placed systematically according to a plan. Beautifully planted avenues with flowering trees are pretty with the colour and beauty. The trees should not be patchy due to lack of aesthetic sense of those maintaining the roads. *Delonix regia, Anthocephalus indicus, Cassia nodosa, Bauhinia purpurea* will add colour and charm to an avenue. But shade and economic utility should be the main criterion for highways and *Lagerstroemia speciosa, Tamarindus indicus, Mangifera indica, Swietenia mahagoni* should be selected. One type of tree should be planted for a considerable length to provide a beautiful skyline and uniform crown but not in mixed patches.

Colour of the flowers is an important factor to consider in the selection of trees. Primary colours like red, yellow, blue and secondary colours like orange and purple show a very effective display. Green is also a secondary colour and the subtle tertiary colours derived from mixtures of these colour are also very attractive. Scarlet flowers of *Spathodea campanulata* or *Delonix regia* or mauve and purple or blue flowers of *Lagerstroemia* and *Jacaranda* look brightest in the grey asphalt roads. The power and effect of contrast colours should be kept in mind while planning tree planting. Many trees in our country burst into gorgeous blooms at a particular season, the colour of their flowers harmonize and appear more effective when planted in groups. *Cassia fistula, Delonix regia, Peltophorum ferrugineum, Lagerstroemia speciosa, Cassia nodosa* all bloom in May. The rich yellow contrasting with scarlet and deep mauve or pink form a striking colour scheme.

The value of trees as both labour-saving and attractive to the residents of any private garden has become increasingly evident. Many trees burst into bloom beautifully, while others afford a pleasing contrast with their decorative foliage. Although we have an abundance of flowering trees, selection of trees for private gardens which should create rhythm, accent, as well as balance in the garden and the dwelling place is rather difficult. One or two small flowering trees are often adequate selections and planting of trees should deserve just as much attention as is commonly given to the colour of the building, pool and paved path. Beauty and utility should be combined deftly. In small or medium gardens ornamental trees should be planted only in the boundaries as foundation planting and one small tree like *Callistemon, Bauhinia variegata, Amherstia nobilis* as an accent near the building. The knotted Neem or crowded growth of mango, guava or jackfruits produce ugly effect and make the most modern looking building look gloomy and depressing. The fruit trees should be planted to the back portion of the house where they are not visible from the entrance. A row of *Polyalthia pendula* often makes the approach road to the house very attractive. A group of *Plumeria* or *Cassia* at the boundaries add charm and grace to the house.

Many trees in India are actually natives of other countries. *Cryptomeria japonica*, the common conifer of Darjeeling has been introduced from Japan in the eighteenth century. Many beautiful trees from other tropical countries have been introduced by the British explorers and Missionaries. *Delonix regia, Colvillea racemosa* and *Kigelia pinnata* were brought from Madagascar ; *Jacaranda mimosaefolia* and *Tabebuia rosea* from Brazil ; *Brownea, Guaiacum* from West Indes ; *Enterolobium saman, Erythrina cristagalli, Coroupita guianensis* were introduced from tropical America. Australia with its diversified plant life, is the native home of many ornamental trees like *Acacia auriculiformis, Eucalyptus citriodora, Callistemon lanceolatus, Melaleuca leucadendron* and *Grevillea robusta*. *Spathodea campanulata, Kleinhovia hospita* are native of tropical Africa. Most of the pink *Cassia* and *Pterocarpus indicus, Saraca declinata* have been introduced from Malay and Java, *Amherstia nobilis* is a native of lower Burma.

List of our indigenous ornamental trees will be very long and it includes many colourful flowering trees like *Butea monosperma, Bauhinia purpurea, Cassia fistula, Lagerstroemia speciosa, Cochlospermum gossypium, Bombax malabaricum, Millingtonia hortensis, Dillenia indica* and *Saraca indica*. Trees with ornamental foliage indigenous to India include *Polyalthia longifolia, Putranjiva roxburghii, Melia azadirach, Mimusops elengi* and *Azadirachta indica*.

The best time for planting trees is during the rainy season (June-September). In northern India planting can be done in January-February before the new growth starts and 1-2 year old saplings have better chance of survival and early flowering. Large pits (1 metre in depth and diameter) should be prepared 2-3 months before planting. The soil is mixed with adequate amount of organic manure and bone meal and allowed to settle by exposing to rains or watering the pits. The tree saplings should have straight stem and undisturbed main shoot.

Before planting the ball of earth round the roots is cracked without damaging the roots and planted with root collar just below the ground level.

One sapling should be planted in each pit and casualties replaced without delay. Large saplings are expansive to handle and the mortality is likely to be greater. Very small seedlings on the other hand, do not grow well. During planting all dead and broken branches and roots are to be cut and removed. The soil around the plant should be firmly consolidated after planting, watered thoroughly and also staked. In the open and in public places tree seedlings are to be protected in gabions till they grow fairly large. Distance of planting trees usually varies from 5-14 metres depending on the size of the plant.

For better growth of the plant, the pits should be weeded and hoed to keep the soil loose and free from weeds. Most of the tropical trees have short dormancy period and monsoon is the season for maximum growth. Tree saplings may need watering in the summer months during the first two years after planting. The stem of the tree should be kept clean by removing the branches arising on it without allowing them to grow large and woody. Flowering trees seldom need any cutting back except *Gliricidia maculata.* In order to maintain the shape of the tree it is often necessary to remove the old branches. Crossed branches in the centre of the crown should also be cut off. On the stem or large branches holes are made by insect, rats, squirrel and birds or cracking of wood. The exposed surface of the hole is thoroughly cleaned by removing dead, and rotten wood, coated with coaltar or fungicides and filled with stonechips and cement.

BEAUTIFUL TREES

ACACIA AURICULIFORMIS (*Golden shower*)

Fam : Leguminosae

Beng.—*Swarna Jhuri*

This is an evergreen tree of graceful appearance which is said to have been introduced from Australia. The tree reaches to a height of about 20 m with waxy green, rather thin rounded crown ; bark light grey, somewhat fissured ; twigs green, without spines. Flowering is observed more or less all the year round, more abundantly in the summer and rains. Fruits flat curling up into a close coil when ripe, green then brown. The tree grows quickly in tropical and sub-tropical regions in all types of soil. It is planted on road side, parks and large private gardens.

ADANSONIA DIGITATA (*Baobab tree, Sourgourd*)

Fam : Bombacaceae

It is a native of tropical Africa, one of the largest trees of the world and lives for a thousand years. Though the tree attains a height of about 16-20 m but the trunk may attain an enormous girth. Flowers 15 cm wide, creamy white with a very strong smell, hang singly from flower-stalks 45-50 cm long ; appear in April-May.

The tree can be planted on sides of wide roads, avenues and in large parks and gardens. As the tree has comparatively shallow root it can be successfully transplanted.

ADENANTHERA PAVONINA (*Red Sandalwood, Coral pea*)

Fam : Leguminosae

Hindi—*Barigumehi* ; Beng.—*Ranjana* ; Tam.—*Animadumani* ; Tel.—*Bandigururenda*

A beautiful deciduous tree up to 20 metres tall, with uneven round crown ; bark pale pinkish grey. Small creamy yellow flower are borne in 8-15 cm long spikes at the axils of the leaves, in March-April. It is a fairly quick growing, recommended for planting on road side, parks and gardens.

ALBIZZIA LEBBEK (*East Indian Walnut*)

Fam : Leguminosae

Hindi—*Siris* ; Beng.—*Sirish* ; Tam.—*Vagei*

It is an ornamental tree chiefly grown for its attractive foliage and beautiful flowers. It has been extensively planted in gardens, along roadsides and in other places. The flowers are greenish white, becoming pale yellow of a somewhat heavy fragrance, appear chiefly in April and May ; sometimes earlier or later and the masses of yellowish white blossoms are conspicuous against the new foliage. The ripe pods are straw coloured, 16-25 cm long, 3 to 5 cm broad.

ALSTONIA MACROPHYLLA

Fam : Apocynaceae

A tall evergreen tree with a graceful outline ; leaves mostly in whorls of 3, elliptic-lanceolate 20-30 cm long. Flowers white, appear in loose axillary and terminal clusters at the end of the branches from July to September.

ALSTONIA SCHOLARIS (*Devil's tree*)

Hindi—*Chatian* ; Beng.—*Chatim* ; Tam.—*Palagaruda*

Usually the tree reaches a height of 15-20 m with greyish yellow to greyish brown bark and the crown is rather conical.

Flowers greenish white, scented, in many flowered cymes ; corolla tube finely hairy on the outside, about 0·8 cm long. Flowering is observed more or less all the year round but the peak period of flowering is from October to December.

AMHERSTIA NOBILIS

Fam : Leguminosae

This is one of the most beautiful flowering trees of the world, an evergreen tree indigenous in Tenasserium and cultivated in the warm humid regions of Burma and India.

Flowers are vermillion edged with yellow, appearing from March to May. They are arranged on large candelabra like racemes which arise from the axil of the leaves and frequently attain a length of 50-70 cm.

The plant is unusually slow growing, should be grown in semi-humid place protected from Western sun. It also requires well drained rich soil.

ANTHOCEPHALUS INDICUS

Fam : Rubiaceae

Hindi—*Kadam, Cadamb* ; Beng.—*Kadam* ; Tel.—*Kadambamu* ; Tam.—*Vellai-cadamba*

It is a tall deciduous tree having a height of 15-20 m with clean straight cylindrical stem and horizontal branches. Numerous small greenish yellow flowers are arranged or spherical heads 5 to 8 cm in diameter which are produced in June-August.

AZADIRACHTA INDICA (*Indian liac, Margosa tree*)

Fam : Meliaceae

Hindi and Beng.—*Neem*

A medium sized almost evergreen tree usually maintaining a height between 10-15 m.

The tree is very popular in India because of its high medicinal properties. The dark evergreen foliage gives a very showy appearance and it is also grown as an ornamental tree.

BAIKIAEA INSIGNIS

Fam : Leguminosae

It is an evergreen tree reaching a height of about 10-15 metres.

The plant bears many clusters of white flower, probably the largest among the tropical flowering trees, from April-June.

BARRINGTONIA ACUTANGULA (*Small Indian Oak*)

Fam : Lecythidaceae

Hindi—*Ingar*, *Neora* ; Beng.—*Hijal* ; Tel.—*Kadapa*

The tree is very common in Sub-Himalayan tracts, east of the Jamuna, in Bihar, Orissa, Bengal, Assam, Madhya Pradesh and South India ; also in Ceylon and Burma. It is found along the banks of streams, round the edges of swamps and in similar moist places. In April-May numerous long drooping spikes appear from the branches bearing many small pink flowers. The flowers are smaller than those produced on *B. racemosa*.

BARRINGTONIA RACEMOSA (*Indian oak*, *Bottlebrush oak*)

Hindi—*Ijjul* ; Beng.—*Samudraphul*

It is an evergreen tree, 10-16 m high usually found on sandy beaches and distributed from Ceylon and the Andamans to the Malay peninsula and Australia. Flowers large, 6 cm across ; petals white and the stamens tinted purple, the style long and prominent borne in long pendulous spike.

It grows into a handsome tree, sometime planted along road sides and also suitable for planting in swampy ground.

BAUHINIA PURPUREA (*Mountain ebony*, *Geranium tree*)

Fam : Leguminosae

Hindi—*Khairwall*, Beng.—*Rakta Kanchan*, *Deva Kanchan*, Tel.—*Kanchanam*, Tam.—*Mandari*

A nearly evergreen tree attaining a height 10-12 m growing sparingly throughout India. Flowers large about 6 cm across, in various tones of rose, purple, in few flowered clusters at the ends of the branches.

It is a very hardy tree, flowers profusely from October to March, when leaves fall off but not completely.

BAUHINIA VARIEGATA

Hindi—*Kachnar, Kiliar* ; Beng.—*Rakta Kambar* ; Tam.—*Segapu manchori*

It is a small sized tree with dark brown and more or less smooth bark, reaching to a height of about 6-8 m. Flowers in cluster of 5-7 in a short raceme or corymb, 5 cm across, large, fragrant, beautifully coloured with various shades of pink and purple appearing when the tree is leafless in February-March.

A variety with pure white flower (*B. variegata* var : Candida) is also a beautiful flowering plant and seen in gardens.

BIGNONIA MEGAPOTAMICA

Fam : Bignoniaceae

An evergreen tree of medium size growing up to a height of 10 m and produces clusters of light mauve flowers.

It is a quick growing tree in warm humid climate. The plant remains in bloom almost throughout the year but larger number of flowers develop from March to May.

BIXA ORELLANA (*Annatto tree*)

Fam : Bixaceae

Hindi & Beng.—*Latkan* ; Tam. & Tel.—*Japhra*

It is to some extent cultivated in Mysore and less extensively in Bombay, Assam and West Bengal.

Flowers cm across on upright terminal panicles 7-12 cm long, few flowers open at a time, in September ; petals white or pale pink, faintly dotted pink on the outside.

It is cultivated for the annatto dye prepared from the orange red pulp that covers the seeds.

BROWNEA COCCINEA (*West Indian Mountain Rose*)

Fam : Leguminosae

A medium sized evergreen tree with spreading and drooping branches.

Many large scarlet flowers are nicely arranged to form compact boquet which hang from the end of the branches from early March till the end of rainy season. Maximum flowering during March and April.

The plants should be grown in partial sun, as they cannot thrive in dry heat.

BROWNEA ARIZA

An evergreen tree indigenous to Tropical America. The usual height to which it can raise itself is 5 to 7 m.

Flowers orange scarlet, on globular drooping heads 10-12 cm across. The usual time of flowering is from February to June.

It is one of the best ornamental trees and looks extremely beautiful when it bears drooping new leaves, arising in the summer and rains.

BROWNEA GRANDICEPS

It is a rare tree, attains the height 4-5 m in 20 years. Many large, widely open, orange flowers in a well arranged compact cluster appear on older branches and some on the trunk near the ground. All the flowers open in a day or two facing the morning sun and start wilting in the same day.

BUTEA MONOSPERMA (*Flame of the Forest*)

Fam : Leguminosae

Beng.—*Palash*, Hindi—*Dhak*, *Palash*

It is a common but beautiful flowering tree in all the hotter parts of India except in very wet areas. Numerous clusters of large orange red flowers appear in February-March even on older branches ; petals 5-7 cm long covered with grey pubescents.

CAESALPINIA CORIARIA (*American sumach or Divi-divi*)

Fam : Leguminosae

Hindi.—*Dividivi*, Tam.—*Tividivi*, Tel.—*Dividivi*

The small spreading tree is indigenous to South America and West Indies and is now cultivated in the different parts of the country especially in Southern India.

Flowers greenish or yellowish, scented, arise in dense clusters at the end of the branch during April to July. Plants look very attractive when new light green leaves appear on new growth in March-April.

The tree is slow growing, begins to bear in 12-15 years and attains full bearing capacity in the twentieth year.

CAESALPINIA CACALACO

A rare but beautiful flowering evergreen tree, few specimens are found in the gardens of India.

Large number of long spikes appear at the end of the branch and bear numerous small yellow flowers from December to February. The petals are 0·5 cm long, yellow or orange marked with reddish spots.

CALLISTEMON LANCEOLATUS (*Bottle Brush*)

Fam : Myrtaceae

The plant is also known as "Bottle Brush" because the flower-bearing portions of the branches resemble bottle brushes in shape. Flowers in densely crowded cylindrical spikes 5 to 10 cm long, with long scarlet stamens projecting stiffy outwards. The flowering may be observed more or less throughout the year, especially from February to November.

The tree has pendulous branches, often grown on road side and in gardens.

CALOPHYLLUM INOPHYLLUM (*Alexandrian laurel, Dilo oil tree*)

Fam : Guttiferae

Beng. & Hindi—*Sultana champa, Punnag* ; Tel.—*Poona*, Tam.—*Punnai*

This is a medium sized evergreen tree with smooth grey bark and cylindrical branches reaching a height of about 15 m.

Flowers white, sweet scented 2 cm diameter, in loose axillary racemes at the end of the branches from June to October.

CASSIA FISTULA (*Indian laburnum*)

Fam : Leguminosae

Beng.—*Sondal*, *Amaltas* Tam.—*Konnai*, Tel.—*Rela* Hindi.—*Amaltas*, *Cirimalah*

It is a medium sized deciduous trees reaching a height of about 8-10 m, indigenous to India and cultivated in Tropical Africa, South America and West Indies.

Flowers 4 cm across, fragrant, golden yellow in hanging racemes up to 50 cm long from the old branches behind the leaves.

Cassia fistula is considered as one of the finest yellow flowering trees of the world. It is very popular in tropical India as road side tree and also commonly grown in gardens and parks.

CASSIA JAVANICA (*Java Cassia*)

It has widely spreading almost horizontal branches, brownish. Bright pink flowers arise in loose clusters on short leafless branches during April-May.

CASSIA MARGINATA (*Red Cassia*)

Tel.—*Urimidi*

Small tree, with short trunk and drooping branches. The flowers are smaller, terracotta appear in small axillary branches in June-July,

CASSIA NODOSA (*Pink Cassia*)

It is a deciduous tree attaining a height of 12 to 16 m distributed in India and many other countries such as Burma, China, Malayasia and Indonesia.

Flowers 2·5 cm wide, bright-pink fading to white, softly hairy, sweetly scented and appear in loose cluster along the branches during April-July.

CASSIA RENIGERA (*Burmese pink Cassia*)

The tree is indigenous to the dry zones of Burma and is now extensively grown in India and Malaya.

It is a medium sized deciduous tree reaching up to 10-12 m in height with a short trunk and a few upright branches bearing numerous slender drooping branchlets. Flowers are arranged in bunches along the branches, bright pink in colour and appear in April-May.

CASSIA SIAMEA

Tam.—*Beati*

In India it is frequently grown as a road side and avenue tree and also in parks.

The tree has a rounded crown becoming straggling with upright and drooping branches. Flowers 3 cm wide, bright yellow, on 30-40 cm long terminal panicle arising from June-January and flowering is at its best in October.

CASTANOSPERMUM AUSTRALE (*Moreton Bay Chestnut*, *Black bean*)

Fam : Leguminosae

The tree reaches a height of 16-20 m with dense foliage.

Flowers yellow-orange in many axillary loose raceme, are borne even on older branches in March to May, they remain almost hidden in dense dark green foliage.

CASUARINA EQUISETIFOLIA (*Australian oak*, *Beefwood*)

Fam : Casurinaceae

Hindi—*Janglijhau* ; Beng.—*Belatijhau*

It is a large evergreen tree chiefly Australian but can be found in E. Africa, and S. Pacific Islands, reaching a height of about 25 to 30 m ; main branches spreading or erect, smaller ones pendulous. The branches are much alike to that of a pine.

It is extensively cultivated as an avenue or ornamental tree, and used for checking erosion and afforesting sandy beaches. *C. equisetifolia* is a hardy, quick growing tree of unusual and elegent appearnce, extensively cultivated in sea shore and arid region.

CHORISIA SPECIOSA. (*Floss silk tree*)

Fam : Bombacaceae

A deciduous tree attaining a height of 10-15 m. Stem and branches, green with irregular cracks and large spines. Flowers appear on current year's growth in axillary clusters from mid September. Sepals thick, cup shaped with 5 lobes. Petals 5, free, up to 7 cm long, fleshy, pinkish outer surface, lower half of inner surface pinkish white, gradually fading to yellow and spotted brown.

COCHLOSPERMUM GOSSYPIUM.

Fam : Cochlospermaceae

Hindi—*Kumbi, Galgal* ; Beng.—*Gabdi* ; Tam.—*Tanakku* ; Tel.—*Kongu*

It is small or medium sized, deciduous, soft-wooded tree reaching a height of about 6-8 m. Flowers large, 6-8 cm across, bright yellow in colour arranged in terminal panicles which appear after leaf fall from December to April. It is a quick growing plant and starts flowering in 2 years.

COLVILLEA RACEMOSA (*Colville's Glory*)

Fam : Leguminosae

The tree is 15-20 m high with long spreading branches. When not in bloom it has the appearance of *Poinciana regia* but with thicker trunk and smaller foliage. Flowers orange scarlet in large racemes at the ends of the branches, about 45 cm long, drooping with up to 200 crowded flowers, opening from base. The usual time of flowering is July-September.

CORDIA SEBESTENA (*The scarlet Cordia or Aloe wood*)

Fam : Boraginaceae

Hindi—*Bhokar, Bohari*

It is a dwarf evergreen tree reaching a height of 6-8 m and distributed throughout India, Burma and Ceylon. Flowers orange scarlet in colour, arranged in terminal or axillary bunches, funnel shaped having tubular base and spreading lobes. Usual flowering time is from January to March but generally flowering is observed all the year round.

COROUPITA GUIANENSIS (*Cannon ball tree*)

Fam : Lecythidaceae

Hindi—*Sivalingam* ; Beng.—*Naglingam*

It is a tall soft-wooded deciduous tree, about 15-20 m high, with a large spreading crown. Flowers about 8·0 cm across, fragrant with concave petals, yellow and red tinged on the exterior and crimson lilac within, very showy, in racemes 75 cm to 1 metre long.

CRATAEVA ROXBURGHI (*Caper tree. Bengal quince*)

Fam : Capparidacae

Hindi—*Barna, Bilasi* ; Beng.—*Barun* ; Tam.--*Maralingam*

It is a small deciduous tree of graceful appearance reaching a height up to 10 m, distributed throughout the greater part of India and Burma, wild or cultivated.

Flowers, creamy turning yellow, 5 cm across appear in large cluster at the end of the branches. Flowering season is March-May.

CRESCENTIA CUJETE (*Calabash tree*)

Fam : Bignoniaceae

Hindi—*Bialyati bel* ; Tam.—*Tiruvothukkay*

It is a handsome tree with wide-spreading, well-foliated branches, reaching a height of about 10-15 m. Flowers develop from the old branches near the trunk and have a pale greenish yellow funnel shaped corolla finely veined with brown ; solitary, pendulous. Flowering is generally observed from April to June.

DALBERGIA LANCEOLARIA

Fam : Leguminosae

Hindi—*Takoli, Bithua* ; Beng.—*Chakemdia*

Tall deciduous tree with a straight somewhat but tressed stem. It is found scattered throughout India and in the tropical regions all over the world.

Numerous papilionaceous small, lilac flowers are arranged in panicles, mainly axillary. Flowering time is generally during the hot months.

DELONIX REGIA (*Gulmohar, Flame tree, Peacock flower*)

Fam : Leguminosae

Hindi and Beng.—*Gulmohar*

It is a large deciduous tree, native of Madagascar and reaching a height of 12-20 m with spreading branches, umbrella shaped crown and greyish bark. Flowers 5 cm wide, scarlet in colour with a mild scent, borne on long stalks in short axillary racemes forming panicles on the new shoots ; other portion of branches are bare of leaves.

It is one of the most beautiful and common flowering trees grown in India and very suitable for parks, roadside and also large private gardens.

DOLICHANDRONE SPATHACEA

Fam : Bignoniaceae

Beng.—*Goshingiah*

A tall deciduous tree with a rather slender crown. Flowers large white solitary or few flowered corymb. Corolla tubular, funnel shaped near the mouth, 10-15 cm long.

It is planted in the garden of Eastern India for its graceful habit and large beautiful flowers.

ENTEROLOBIUM SAMAN (*Rain tree*)

Fam : Leguminosae

Beng.—*Belatisiris*

It is one of the largest flowering trees, grown in India, spreading up to 20 m and also reaching the same or more height. Flowers in axillary solitary globose head up to 5 cm diameter on long peduncle. The numerous rosy stamens which project far beyond the rest of the flower are the showy part of the blooms.

Flowers appear from March to October, but the two main seasons are early hot weather and end of rains.

ERYTHRINA CRISTAGALLI (*Cockspur coral tree*)

Fam : Leguminosae

It is a small sized tree, native of Brazil and is now introduced in various gardens of India.

Flowers large 5 cm long pea shaped, crimson on a large terminal raceme, the keel nearly as long, as the down-folding standard, the wings rudimentary.

ERYTHRINA INDICA (*Coral tree*)

Hindi—*Pangra, Panjria* ; Beng.—*Palita mandar, Rakta mandar* ; Tam.—*Muraka* ; Tel.—*Barigamu*

It is a tall deciduous tree reaching a height up to 18 m; bark is smooth, yellowish or greenish grey. Flowers large, red 5 cm long, pea shaped in dense racemes 16-20 cm long which appear in February-May.

The tree is commonly planted in villages and along roadsides as shade trees and is used to make close hedges because it grows readily from massive cuttings and the prickles ward off intruders.

ERYTHRINA PARCALLI

It is medium sized evergreen tree. Stem yellowish with brown spines. Leaves trifoliate, mid rib and veins yellow, 8-12 cm long. Flowers yellow, 4 cm long on terminal raceme, are produced in March-May.

EUCALYPTUS CITRIODORA (*Lemon scented Eucalyptus*)

Fam : Myrtaceae

It is a tall handsome tree with slender tapering trunk usually attaining a height of about 40-50 m.

Flowers small white in terminal corymb of 3-5 flowered umbels, arising abundantly in March-April.

It is a beautiful tree of elegant appearance.

EUCALYPTUS GLOBULUS (*Blue gum*)

Tall, erect tree with greyish or bluish white bark. Leaves lanceolate, 15-20 cm long pendulous. Flowers solitary or 2-3 flowers bluish white.

The tree is a native of Australia and often grown in India for its graceful appearance and ornamental leaves.

EUCALYPTUS ROBUSTA (*Swamp Mahagony*)

A beautiful symmetrically branched tree. Bark persistent dark brown. Flowers small white, borne in clusters of 6-12 from near the base of the leaf. This species is hardy and suits well to wider range of soil and climatic condition. It is commonly grown in the gardens of tropical India.

FICUS BENGALENSIS (*Banyan*)

Fam : Moraceae

Hindi—Bar, Ber, Bor, Barged ; Beng.—Bot

A large evergreen tree, may attain a height of 30 m, branches spreading, almost horizontal.

The tree is indigenous near the foot of the Himalayas and Western India and is commonly planted all over the country.

FICUS COMOSA (*Java fig, Java Willow fig*)

Beng.—*Pakur*.

A handsome evergreen tree with spreading limbs and drooping branches. Leaves broadly elliptic, 5-8 cm long, assuminate glabrous and leathery. The receptacles sessile in axillary pairs, 1·2 cm in diameter, reddish orange when ripe.

The tree is a valuable avenue tree because of its graceful foliage and dense shade.

FICUS ELASTICA (*Rubber tree*)

Beng.—*Attah bar*

This is a large tree with fairly smooth reddish brown bark. Leaves alternate, elliptic, coriaceous shining 12-20 cm long.

The dark green glossy foliage is very handsome. Vegetatively propagated plants of smaller size are grown as house plants for indoor decoration.

FICUS INFECTORIA

Hindi—*Pilkhan, Kahimal, Pakri* ; Beng.—*Pakur, Pakar*.

This is a handsome quick growing tree with spreading branches, attaining a height of 15-18 m. This species is indigenous in most parts of India, Ceylon, Malaya and China. It is commonly planted on road sides in both wet and dry regions of India.

FICUS RELIGIOSA (*Peepul*)

Hindi—*Pipal, Pipli* ; Beng.—*Asvattha, Asud*.

A huge tree with greyish bark. Leaves smooth shining, broadly ovate, apex long and narrow, 10-18 cm long.

The tree is indigenous in Bengal and Burma and is cultivated all over India. Handsome dense foliage on the spreading branches gives a cool and pleasant shade under the tree.

FILICIUM DECIPIENS (*Fern tree*)

Fam : Sapindaceae

Hindi—*Katu*

A medium sized evergreen tree cultivated extensively in tropical regions of the world for its attractive foliage and graceful form. It grows better in humid atmosphere and in semi-shade.

GARDENIA LATIFOLIA

Fam : Rubiaceae

Small tree, indigenous in Bihar and West of India. Flower large solitary, axillary, white fading yellow, fragrant ; corolla tubular about 7 cm long, lobes expanded, 8 cm across.

This hardy plant should be grown more widely in parks and gardens.

GLIRICIDIA MACULATA (*Madurai shade tree*)

Fam : Liguminosae

Long straight and slender branches arise from a pruned tree and grow up to 6-8 m. In February, small white flowers appear in clusters which cover the greater part of the branches. The flowers are pea shaped with a pale yellow marks near the base of the upper petals.

This quickgrowing, beautiful flowering tree is planted on road side, gardens and also grown as shade tree for plantation crops.

GREVILLEA ROBUSTA (*Australian Silk Oak, Silver Oak*)

Fam : Proteaceae

This evergreen tree, a native of East Australia reaches a height of 25 m or more. Young shoots are covered with rusty hairs. Leaves compound pinnate type, 20 to 30 cm long, spirally arranged, divided into 5-11 pairs of segments, dull green above and silky white beneath. Flowers small, reddish orange in colour, 1·5 cm long, stalked, set along spike like inflorescence, appear in abundance during March-April.

GUSTAVIA AUGUSTA. (*Stinkwood*)

Fam : Lecythidaceae

The tree is 7-10 m high ; leaves large, ovate-lanceolate, dark green, grossy, 30-50 cm long, clustered at the end of the branches. Flowers large, about 10 cm across white or tinged pink, grouped at the ends of the leafy twigs, with 8 large petals.

HAEMATOXYLON CAMPECHIANUM. (*Log Wood, Campeachy wood*)

Fam : Leguminosae

Hindi—*Patang* ; Beng.—*Bokkan*

It is a medium-sized tree, reaching 8-10 m in height with a short crooked trunk. Flowers small, delicately scented and yellow in colour, appear in abundance in axillary raceme from January to March.

The tree is grown in small gardens for its ornamental foliage and scented flowers.

HIBISCUS POPULNEUS. (*Portia tree, Bhendi tree*)

Fam : Malvaceae

Hindi—*Parsipu, Paraspipal* ; Beng.—*Paras, Paraspipal*

This is a medium sized evergreen tree reaching a height of 7 to 10 m with smooth grey trunk and spreading uniformly. Flowers large, about 7 cm across axillary, at first yellow with purple centre, becoming entirely purple by evening. Flowering takes place throughout the year, but principally during the Summer.

HOLARRHENA ANTIDYSENTERICA (*Easter tree, Ivory tree*)

Fam : Apocynaceae

Hindi—*Karra, Dudhi* ; Beng.—*Kurchi*

A deciduous tree of medium height 7-10 m, indigenous throughout the plains of India. White scented flowers about 2-3 cm across appear in terminal cymes in March, and continues to bloom up to the middle of June. A second flush of flowers is often produced in September.

JACARANDA FILICIFOLIA (*Fern - leaved jacaranda*)

Fam : Bignoniaceae

A small tree with few slender branches. The leaves are divided into a large number of small pointed leaflets, 1·2 cm long. Numerous panicles of bright purplish blue flowers appear at the end of the branches. Corolla 3·5 cm long with 5 lobes (2+3).

This species can be distinguished from *J. ovalifolia* by its larger leaflets and smaller flowers. *J. filicifolia* flowers more freely in humid regions.

JACARANDA OVALIFOLIA (*Mimosa-leaved jacaranda*)

It is a medium sized, deciduous tree reaching a height of about 10 to 12 m.

The plant bears loose pyramidal panicles, 20-25 cm long and many brilliant purplish blue drooping flowers, each 3 cm long and 2·5 cm wide. Usual time of flowering is during March to June.

It is one of the finest flowering trees of the world, the blue flowers are very handsome, while the finely divided foliage makes it an ornamental tree.

KIGELIA PINNATIA *(Sausage tree, Cucumber tree)*

Fam : Bignoniaceae

It is a very useful road side tree, native of Mosambique and tropical Africa, commonly planted in hotter parts of India. The tree has a large spreading crown. Flower hang on a rope like stalk arising from the branch which may attain a length of 1·5 to 2 m. The petals are joined to form a broad marroon wide-mouth funnel with 5 spreading lobes, wrinkled and striped on the outside with lighter colour.

The tree is fairly fast growing, thrives well in all types of soil and environment in the tropics. It forms a well shaped tree for avenues and large gardens.

KLEINHOVIA HOSPITA *(Guest tree)*

Fam : Sterculiaceae

Beng.– Bota

It is an evergreen tree attaining a height of 18-20 m with a dense rounded crown. Flowers, in long terminal panicles, about 0·6 cm wide, soft pink appear almost all the year round but principally in August-September.

LARGERSTROEMIA SPECIOSA *(The Pride of India, Crepe flower)*

Fam : Lythraceae

Hindi—*Jarul* ; Beng.—*Jarul*.

It is a deciduous tree of 16-20 m in height, a native of S. E. Asia.

Large, beautiful flowers are borne on long erect and stout spike 25-35 cm in length, arising from the end of the branches during April to June. Petal 6-7, about 5 cm across opening from the base of the inflorescence. Freshly opened flowers are deep mauve, almost purple, fully open before sun is up and fade with a dull colour.

Another type *L. speciosa* 'Rosea' is a small tree about 6-8 m high with uniformly spreading crown. Rose coloured flowers appear on terminal panicle during February-April.

LAGERSTROEMIA THORELII

It is a medium sized plant with uniformly spreading crown and short trunk. The flowers develop on large axillary panicle, lilac or purple when first open, soon turn pink and finally white. Petals 6, wrinkled, about 3 cm across. The flowers appear from July to September.

MAGNOLIA GRANDIFLORA (*Lily tree, Laurel magnolia*)

Fam : Magnoliaceae

Hindi : *Anda Champa, Him Champa*

The plant may reach a height of 20 metres or more in cool and humid climate.

Flowers creamy white, sweetly scented, more or less cup shaped, 16-20 cm across. Flowering takes places during the hot weather, and each flower lasts for 2-4 days. It is a very slow growing plant but the large fragrant white flowers make it most attractive.

MAGNOLIA PTEROCARPA

Beng.—*Dulichampa*

It is a large evergeen tree with a rounded crown and large glossy and leathery leaves, 25-32 cm in length. The large white scented flowers 6-9 cm across have six fleshy petals which arise on a short stout stalk near the end of the branches in April-May. The plant should be grown in semi-shade and moist situation.

MELALEUCA LEUCADENDRON (*Cajeput oil tree, white bottle brush*)

Fam : Myrtaceae

Hindi—*Kaya puti* ; Beng.—*Cajuputi*

It is a medium sized evergreen tree reaching a height of about 18-20 metres with the dense greyish green crown and shout twisted trunk ; bark whitish or light grey, branches dropping down. Flowering may be observed more or less all the year round but more profusely in the summer and rains. Small whitish flowers with protruding stamens appear in narrow cylindrical spikes, 6-12 cm long and look like a bottle brush.

MELIA AZEDARACH (*Persin Lilac, China tree, India Lilac*)
Fam : Meliaceae
Hindi—*Bakain, Betain* ; Beng.—*Mahanim, Goranim*

It is a medium sized evergreen concial tree reaching a height of about 12 metres and more. Flowers 1·2—1·6 cm wide, fragrant, lilac in colour, arise on large axillary panicle. Deep purple stamens are surrounded by petals. Flowering is generally observed during the Summer. The tree grows rapidly and is widely planted on road sides and gardens particularly in the Northern India.

MESUA FERREA (*Iron wood tree*)
Fam : Guttiferae
Hindi—*Nag champa* ; Beng —*Nageswar.*

The evergreen tree, native of tropical Asia and reaching a height up to 6-8 meters. Flowers white, very fragrant, about 6 cm wide, look like magnolia when open. Flowering takes place during March-April. The plant should be grown in semi-shade and porous soil.

MICHELIA CHAMPACA (*Golden champa*)
Fam : Magnoliaceae
Hindi and Beng.— *Swaranchampa, Champa*

It is a medium sized tree, reaching a height up to 20 metres, the rather cylindrical or conical crown is supported by a few bold upright limbs. Flowers yellow, scented, 5 cm long, grow singly, each from the base of the leaves. Flowers appear in April and at intervals throughout the summer and rains. A variety of this species (*M. champaca* var. Alba) is a small tree producing creamy white flowers, less scented than the yellow one, blooming almost throughout the year.

MILLETIA OVALIFOLIA (*Jewels on a string*)
Fam : Leguminosae

The height attained by this tree varies from 10-12 meters, having a rounded crown and half-drooping branches. Flowers are very beautiful, pea shaped, mauve, arise in clusters at the axils of leafless shoots during March-April. Light green, glossy new leaves appear after flowering. The tree is commonly grown in garden and on roadside because of its dense foliage, beautiful flowers and attractive shape.

MILLINGTONIA HORTENSIS *(Indian Oak tree)*

Fam : Bignoniaceae

Hindi—*Akash nim*, *Belati nim* and Beng.—*Akash nim*

This tall evergreen tree grows to a height of 15-20 meters with drooping branchlets and open uneven crown. Bark is irregularly ridged and fissured ; very rough and corky. White and fragrant flowers are borne on 18-20 cm long, terminal, erect, panicles in November-December. The flowers are nocturnal, opening in the evening with delicate fragrance and falling off next morning. The tree is planted along the road-sides and in the gardens for its beautiful scented flowers and ornamental foliage. The tree breaks off with strong wind.

MIMUSOPS ELENGI (Indian Medlar)

Fam : Sapotaceae

Hindi—*Mulsari* and Beng.—*Bakul*

It is a large evergreen tree reaching a height of about 20 metres with dense, dark green round and spreading crown. Flowers white, fragrant, drooping, star-shaped nearly 1·5 cm across 1 to 6 together in the same leaf axil. Flowering takes place almost throughout the year but more profusely during April to June. A variety of this species with leaves variegated in different shades of yellow and green is a fine foliage tree.

MONODORA GRANDIFLORA

Fam : Annonaceae

A beautiful flowering tree, rare in Indian gardens, indigenous to tropical Africa. It grows up to 10 metres high. Solitary, axillary flowers in large number arise on new and older branches from November to February and hang on long stalk. Sepals 3, about 2·5 cm long, green with brown margin curved and curled inward. Petal 6, outer 3 ovate-lanceolate,

6 cm long first green then yellow with large brown spots on the margin curled and twisted, reddish brown inside ; inner 3 petals shortly clawed almost cordate, light yellow, small reddish brown spots more prominent inside.

Though the plant flowers profusely in warm humid regions of India but seldom produces seeds. It is also difficult to propagate vegetatively.

MUNTINGIA CALABURA *(Chinese Cherry)*

Fam : Tiliaceae

It is an evergreen tree up to about 7 metres high, with dense spreading crown and drooping branches. Flowers 2 cm wide, with white petals, arising in pairs in the leaf axil. Flowering is seen more or less all the year round. It is a common tree in gardens in the eastern part of India and is recommended for its quick-growing habit and ornamental quality.

PACHIRA INSIGNIS

Fam : Bombacaceae

A medium sized tree, native of South America, New leaves are very colourful, remain dark brown for a month or so, ultimately become green. Flower solitary or in axillary cluster of 2-3 appearing in March on a bare tree. Petals large fleshy brownish outside and purple inside 8-10 cm long. Numerous long purple silky stamens give a very attractive appearance.

PERMENTIERA CERIFERA *(Candle tree)*

Fam : Bignoniaceae

It is a small tree, native of Panama and Central America. Flowers funnel shapped white or slightly rosy ; solitary on trunk or larger branches ; 4-5 cm across, corolla lobes notched. Flowering is noticed from May to August. The tree can be propagated from seed or cuttings. It is planted as an ornamental plant because of its fine foliage and candle like fruits.

PELTOPHORUM INERME

(Braziletto wood, Rusty shield bearer)

Fam : Leguminosae

The tree is a native of Ceylon, the Andamans, Malayasia

and North Australia It may attain a height of 30 metres with a smooth grey bark and a spreading crown. Yellow flowers appear on large axillary or terminal panicle from middle of March to May and few minor flushes develop before and during the rainy season. The petals are curved along the margin. The plant is liked for its beautiful flowers and ornamental foliage and is a popular road side tree in the tropical parts of the country.

PLUMERIA (*Frangipani, Pagoda tree*)

Fam : Apocynaceae

Hindi—*Gobur Champa, Golainchi* ; Beng.—*Dalanaphul, Gorur Champa*

Large or medium sized deciduous trees with fleshy stem. Leaves large lanceolate or with rounded apex according to species and varieties, 25-40 cm long. Flowers large, 5-8 cm diameter, white or various shades of pink, yellow, red, on terminal cymes and scented. This is a popular and free flowering tree in tropical India. Many large clusters of flowers appear in summer months on a leafless tree except in *P. alba* which bears white flowes almost throughout the year. It grows in all types of soil and flowers better in poor porous soil. Cuttings root well in spring.

P. acuminata syn. *P. acutifolia* was described to possess oblong leaves, acute at both ends, and the only species cultivated and naturalised in many parts of India. Prain recorded only *P. acutifolia*, but colour of flower was not mentioned. Benthal distinguished *P. rubra*, *P. alba*, *P. tuberculata* and *P. bicolor* in Indian garden.

P. acuminata or *P. acutifolia* had also acuminate or acute leaves and did not show any distinct morphological character as *P. rubra* and *P. lutea*. In some specimens of *P. lutea*, rose or pink colour was completely absent and should be considered as a species and not a form of *P. rubra* as suggested by Woodson.

Thirtyone specimens showing variation in size and shape of leaves and colour of flowers were collected from gardens in

Calcutta and neighbourhood and the following classification is suggested :

P. obtusa : leaves oblanceolate or obovate with rounded apex, dark green, glossy, coriaceous ; flowers relaxed white with yellow throat ; petals spatulate.

P. alba : leaves oblanceolate, narrow, obtuse coriaceous ; flowers relaxed, white with yellow throat ; petal elliptic with rounded apex.

P. lutea : colour predominantly yellow, white also occurs, no pink or rose on the upper surface.

P. rubra : purple, red, rose or crimson in various shades with or without white and different shades of orange or yellow at the throat are also common.

P. rubra forma typica : colour predominantly shades of purple, red or crimson with or without orange or reddish orange throat, white being completely absent.

P. rubra forma tricolor : colour predominantly rose, pink, red, crimson or purple, orange or yellow conspicuous, with or without white on the upper surface.

P. rubra forma bicolour : white, yellow or orange predominant, pink, rose or red in the form of band, stripes or splashes both on the upper and lower surface of the petals.

POLYALTHIA LONGIFOLIA (*Debdar*, *Mast tree*, *Indian fir*)

Fam : Annonaceae

Hindi—*Asok*, *Devadaru* ; Beng.—*Devdaru*, *Devdar*.

It is a handsome evergreen tree indigenous to Ceylon and much cultivated in the garden and avenue in India and Burma. The height may reach up to 20 to 25 metres, the crown is conical in shape. The trees are cultivated in the garden and avenues for their graceful appearance. A beautiful weeping variety of this tree named P. *longifolia* var. *pendula* is very popular in India. The branches and leaves droops steeply downward.

PONGAMIA GLABRA (*Indian Beech, Poonga oil Plant*)

Fam : Leguminosae

Hindi—*Karanja, Kanja* ; Beng.—*Karanja, Dahur*

Tam.—*Ponga*

It is a moderate sized deciduous tree attaining a height of 10-15 metres with fairly dense, shining dark green leaves. In May and June, the lilac coloured or pale pink flowers in short axillary raceme are borne in great profusion. Each flower is shaped like that of a pea. The tree is suitable as an ornamental specimen mainly for its bright and handsome foliage.

PTEROCARPUS INDICUS (*Burmese Red wood, Padauk*)

Fam : Leguminosae

It has a spreading growth with drooping branches and reaches a height of 18-22m. In hot months, the plant is covered with clusters of golden yellow sweet scented flowers at the ends of the branches. Flowers appear in two or three flushes before the rains but they drop off quickly. Grown mostly as an ornamental and shade plant.

PTEROSPERMUM ACERIFOLIUM (*Kanak champa*)

Fam : Sterculiaceae

Hindi—*Kaniar* ; Beng.—*Kanak champa*

It is a large handsome evergreen tree native of the Himalayas, Assam and Burma. Flowers large, solitary or in pairs in the axils of the leaves, strongly fragrant, appearing during March-June. Sepals 5 fleshy about 10-12 cm long, brownish tomentose outside ; petals 5 white, membranous. The tree bears sweetly scented flowers are grown on road side and gardens. It grows well in both humid and dry areas.

PTERYGOTA ALATA (*Buddhas coconut*)

Fam : Sterculiaceae

Beng.—*Buddha narikella*

A tall deciduous tree, native of South Western India, Sikkim, Burma and the Andamans. The flowers which arise in dense axillary clusters are rusty brown outside and marked with red veins within. Flowering season is February-March, when old leaves begin to fall. It is a very quick growing tree and widely planted on road sides. A variety of this species (*P. alata* var : *Diversifolia*) has leaves of unequal shape and size and is called 'Pagla gach' (mad tree).

PUTRANJIVA ROXBURGHII (*Child Life Tree*)

Fam : Euphorbiaceae

Hindi and Beng.—*Putranjiva, Jiaputa*

It is an evergreen ornamental tree, native of tropical Asia and is distributed throughout the greater part of India. The tree usually attains a height of 12-16 metres and is nearly glabrous. Flowers small, axillary, single or in small clusters, yellow in colour, arising in the summer months. The tree is mainly used as an avenue tree because of the dense evergreen foliage on nearly pendulous branches.

SARACA INDICA (*Asoka tree*)

Fam : Leguminosae

Hindi—*Asok* ; Beng.—*Asoka*

It is a medium sized evergreen tree, reaching to a height of 8-10 metres, having an erect trunk covered with smooth dark brown bark ; branches are spreading. Flowers yellow or orange when first open in February, gradually turn vermillion. They arise in numerous clusters of various sizes, mainly from older branches and some from the trunk. The tree grows well in partial shade and porous soil. In India, it is considered as a sacred tree and said that Lord Buddha was born under its shade.

SARACA THAPINGENSIS

Normally the tree does not grow more than 8 metres high. Yellow flowers arise in large clusters, axillary and terminal, during December to March on order shoots and trunks. It is a rare tree but unusually attractive when the tree bears large clusters of bright yellow flower during Winter and Spring.

SCHLEICHERA OLEOSA (*Lac Tree*)

Fam : Sapindaceae

Hindi—*Kusum, Gausam* ; Beng.—*Kusam*

Large deciduous tree up to 20 metres high with dense and shady crown. Small yellowish-green flowers appear in short dense axillary clusters in February-March. Flowers are either male or hermaphrodiate. This hard tree, resistant to extreme dry climate should be widely used for planting on road sides particularly in areas where the plants are not attended carefully.

SPATHODEA CAMPANULATA (*Tulip tree, Scarlet bell tree*)

Fam : Bignoniaceae

It is a tall and erect handsome evergreen tree reaching a height up to 20 metres. Large colourful flowers appear in terminal clusters in early Febuary at the end of the branches. The petals are joined to form a wide bell 8-10 cm long, orange and crimson outside, red with yellow streaks inside, margins wavy and yellow. Spathodea an important addition among the introduced flowering trees in this country and is found to flower more abundantly in drier soil and climate.

STERCULIA VILLOSA

Fam : Sterculiaceae

Hindi—*Udal, Udar*

A moderate sized deciduous tree, 12-15 metres high. Flower small, membranous, male and hermaphrodite on pendulous panicles on leafless trees ; calyx yellow with purple centre, 1 cm diameter. The tree bears numerous clusters of flowers at the end of the shoots in Febuary-March. This quick growing plant should be used in green belts and parks.

SWIETENIA MAHOGANI (*Spanish mahogany*)

Fam : Meliaceae

Beng.—*Mahagani*

The crown is heavy dark green and dense ; bark dark grey and ridged. Flowers small, greenish yellow, 0·6 cm across in axillary or sub-terminal panicles. The tree yields the

Mahogony of Commerce. It is planted as road side tree in some parts of India.

TABEBUIA CHRYSANTHA

Fam : Bignoniaceae

A medium sized tree, South American in origin. In march, bright yellow funnel shaped flowers arise in large axillary clusters at the upper portion of the branches. Flowers about 4 cm long, petals expanded 5 lobed. It is a quick growing plant, very suitable for planting in gardens as one of the finest yellow flowering tree.

TABEBUIA ROSEA

Large tree of graceful appearance, reaches a height of about 20-25 metres. In late-February numerous funnel shaped rosy purple flowers arise in axillary clusters on leafless branches. Flower yellowish inside, 5 lobed, curved about 4 cm across. It grows quickly from seeds and the seedlings start flowering in 4-5 years. The wood is not hard and strong wind often breaks the branches.

TERMINALIA ARJUNA (*White murdah*)

Fam : Combretaceae

Hindi—*Arjun, Kawa* ; Beng.—*Arjun*

A large deciduous tree with horizontally spreading branches. Flowers on erect terminal panicles are borne in profusion in April-May. The tree is commonly planted on road side in the northern part of the country.

THEVETIA PERUVIANA (*Yellow oleander*)

Fam : Apocynaceae

Hindi—*Pilakanir, Zardkunel* ; Beng.—*Kolkaphul, Haldikarabi*

A small tree, native of West Indies, is widely grown in India. Flowers large, bright yellow, white or pinkish funnel shaped about 5 cm long borne in small clusters during the summer and rains. This free flowering small tree with numerous spreading branches grows well in both sun and semishade on any type of soil.

WRIGHTIA COCCINEA

Fam : Apocynaceae

Beng.—*Pallam*

It is a medium sized deciduous tree. Flowers deep red in small clusters at the end of the branches. Petals 5, thick about 4 cm across, joined at the base to form a short tube. It is occasionally grown for the handsome red velvety flowers which appear in March-April just after new leaves are formed.

CHAPTER IV

Shrubs

Shrubs are defined as woody, semiwoody or herbaceous perennial plants, branches arise from the base of the plants and grow up to a height of about 0·5 to 4 metres. The plants are usually erect and bushy but some are decumbent or prostrate. These are the most important garden plants not only because of the large number of cultivated species and varieties but also due to their wide range of variation in shape and size of the plants, leaves, growth habit, size, shape and colour of flowers. Most of the shrubs are very hardy, require little attention and grow in all types of soil. Although some plants flower almost throughout the year, in most cases it is seasonal and selection can be made in such a way that some plants in the shrubbery will be in bloom in different seasons of the year. Shrubs flower regularly every year and produce flower of almost all the important colours-white, light yellow, golden-yellow, pink, scarlet, salmon, crimson, rose, violet, light blue, deep blue and some are sweet scented. Most of these plants are fairly quick growing and when vegetatively propagated start flowering in the first year. Plants like *Bauhinia acuminata*, *Cassia alata*, *Galphimia* which are usually grown from seeds produce flowers in the first year.

According to the requirement of sunlight for growth and flowering, shrubs can be classified into three groups—(*i*) show normal growth and flowering in full sun (*ii*) grow only in partial shade (*iii*) can grow well both in sun and semishade.

Most of the tropical flowering plants are sun loving and growth and flowering are greatly affected by shade and it is also observed that lack of morning sun shows much more adverse effect than the afternoon sun. Plants like *Magnolia mutabilis*, *M. pumila*, *M. fuscata*, species of *Pentas*, *Olea fragrans*, *Nandina domestica*, *Wormia burbidgii*, *Beloperone amherstiae*, *Calliandra brevipes*, *Mussaenda erythrophylla*. *Calliandra houstonii* grow only in partial shade. In full sun these plants show signs of scorching during the hot weather and do not thrive. *Jatropha panduraefolia, J. rosea, Lemonia spectabilis, Hamelia patens, Brunfelsia grandiflora, B. americana, Cerbera fruticosa, Eranthemum laxiflorum, Crossandra, Daedalacanthus, Turnera elegans, Cestrum, Mussaenda frondosa, Thunbergia erecta,* grow well in full sun and also in semishade. Shrubs e.g. Crotons, *Polyscias, Eranthemum* have colourful foliage and grow well in shade where other plants fail to grow properly.

Shrubs show great variation in height, tall shrubs usually reach a height of 3 to 4 meters and dwarf shrubs grow only up to 0·4 to 1 meter and thus plants can be chosen from a large selection for growing in various places according to their suitability and utility.

In addition to their utility as flowering plants, shrubs are also used for hedges and screening. Acalyphas form the most colourful hedge, *Dodonia viscosa, Duranta plumerii, Clerodendron inerme* are usually grown as hedge plants. They are quick growing plants and stand severe and frequent pruning. *Hibiscus rosa-sinensis, Ixora chinensis, Bougainvillea, Barleria, Jasminum pubescens* and *Murraya exotica* are also used as hedge plants and produce showy flowers. *Cestrum, Bougainvillea, Jasminum pubescens, Murraya exotica, Jacquinia ruscifolia* can be grown for screening.

Hardy dwarf shrubs like *Lantana depressa, L. sellowiana, Russelia, Euphorbia splendens, Gardenia fortunei, Vinca rosea, Turnera* etc. are usually grown in rockery to add colour and also *Adenium, Jatropha podagrica* to break the monotony of succulents.

Ornamental plants are usually grown for their showy flowers or beautiful foliage but *Ochna wightiana* and *O. squarrosa* bear black fruits on red thalamus, and many yellow berries are found on *Duranta macrophylla* at the end of rainy season. Dark fruits of *Carissa carandas*, blue fruits of *Cestrum diurnum* and numerous red fruits on *Rauwolfia canescens* give a showy effect in the shrubbery.

Acalypha, *Phyllanthus*, *Excoecaria*, *Strobilanthes*, varieties of Croton, species of *Eranthemum*, *Polyscias*, *Manihot utilissima*, have leaves with two or more colours which are more attractive than their flowers. *Bougainvillea*, *Hibiscus*, *Malvaviscus*, *Citrus limonia*, *Duranta*, *Cordia*, *Tabernaemontana* with variegated leaves are also important garden plants.

SELECTION, PLANTING AND CULTIVATION OF SHRUBS

Like any other ornamental plant, selection of shrubs depends on availability and duration of sunlight at the site of planting, maximum height and spread of the plant, utility of plants i.e. foliage or flower, deciduous or evergreen and colour of flowers and season of flowering. It is always safe to plant shrubs during early monsoon. In the next two to three months of rains it will not only establish in the soil but will also start new growth and such plants thrive much better in the hot months of the year. Except hydrophytes garden plants are very susceptible to water logging and well drained site should always be selected. Waterlogging for few days or very wet soil adversely affect growth of most of the garden plants and a well grown plant cannot be obtained in such a place. *Hibiscus*, *Plumbago*, etc., do not even survive in a poor drained soil, *Bougainvillea* produces only vegetative growth in such condition.

Like fruit plants, growth and flowering of garden plants depend on initial preparation of soil before planting. For plants which will grow above 1·5 metres it is recommended to dig pit 70 cm in depth and diameter and mix 5 to 7 kg of well rotted cow manure and raise the soil of the pit to about 20 cm from the ground level. It should be done before or at the beginning of the monsoon so that with few showers the manure further decomposes and mixes with the soil and the loose soil settles. When cow manure is not available, leaf mould and a handful of bone meal may be mixed in the soil.

In gardens, shrubs are usually planted in three ways—(i) in the form of shrubbery, on a long strip of land where taller shrubs are grown at the back, those with medium height in the middle and dwarf ones at the front. In this design upper portions of all the plants in the shrubbery bearing flowers become clearly visible. Colour of flowers and time of flowering are also considered so that the shrubbery remains colourful throughout the year with bloom and foliage. (ii) In small garden or to break monotony of open space shrubs are often grown in groups and in this case few plants of the same variety or of different species are selected, (iii) Shrub is also grown as a specimen plant or in only one row along the border of the garden or a wall.

In order to give a brighter appearance in the rockery dwarf and hardy shrubs are also planted. *Russellia juncea*, *R. sarmentosa*, *Lantana depressa*, *L. sellowiana*, *Jatropha podagrica*, *Adenium obesum*, *Vinca rosea*, *Thespesia lampens*, *Turnera elegans*, *Malphigia coccigera* are useful shrubs for rock garden.

Distance of planting in a shrubbery depends on the size of the plants. Tall and bushy shrubs are generally planted at a distance of 1·5 to 2·5 ms. Shorter plants with less spreading habit can be grown at a distance of 0·5 to 1·5 metre.

Shrubs are watered in winter and more frequently in summer, slight wilting due to dry soil may cause defoliation and affect the growth of the plant. It is always advised to give thorough soaking to all plants than to sprinkle every day. Soaking of only surface soil encourages production of shallow root system which not only prevents utilisation of nutrient from lower level of the soil but also makes the plant more susceptible to drought.

Shrubs should be manured during the rainy season. Well decomposed farm yard manure can be dug in around the root region ; use of bone meal or hoof and horn meal once or twice a year also shows excellent result.

DESCRIPTION AND CULTIVATION

ACALYPHA : (*Euphorbiaceae*) Eng.—*Copperleaf*.

Acalyphas are colourful foliage shrubs used for many purposes. Most of the species and varieties have colourful leaves suitable as hedge plant and also add colour in the shrubbery. Acalyphas grow very quickly in a well-shaped bush on any type of soil and can also be used for screening an undesirable spot in the garden. These do best in full sun. While in partial shade, growth is affected and colour becomes less attractive. Pruning should be done in early Monsoon. Hedges are trimmed regularly.

A. godseffiana. The plants are dwarf and bushy, leaves are bright green edged creamy white.

A. hispida (Catstail). It is also a bushy shrub with green leaves hairy on the top and slightly pale beneath. Flowers bright red in drooping spike.

var. *Alba*—spikes creamy white.

A. hamiltoniana. The leaves are more or less like *A. godseffiana* but the plants are taller in height.

A. :vilkesiana. These are also coloured leaved shrubs from 1·8 to 3·0 m high. The leaves are blotched, mottled with different shades of red, crimson, brown.

var. Marginata—bronzy green, edged crimson.

var. Mosaica—bronzy green with orange and red markings.

var. Aliporensis—a spot from mosaica with creamy margins.

var. Macrophylla—large leaves, russet-brown blotched with pale spots.

var. Obovata—leaves obovate, bronzy green with rose pink margin.

var. Macafeana—leaves red blotched bronzy crimson.

var. Morifortanensys—leaves are bigger than marginata.

A. torta. Leaves cut into blunt segments, twisted, dark olive green.

A. illustris. Leaves ovate, margin cream and yellowish green.

ADENIUM OBESUM : (*Apocynaceae*)

Tall erect shrub up to 2·5 meters. Stem swollen at base, stem and branches succulent. Flowers many on terminal corymbs, funnel shaped, pinkish crimson lobes five, margin fringed darker in colour about 6·4 cm across, yellow inside with reddish longitudinal stripes.

It produces large showy flowers from June to September, succulent stem and branches give a peculiar appearance to the plant. It is an ideal rock garden plant and thrives in porous soil. Propagated from seeds and airlayers.

ALLAMANDA NERIFOLIA (*Apocynaceae*)

An evergreen shrub or half climber. Flowers large, showy, rich yellow on terminal panicle. A hardy, bushy shrub bearing large number of flowers in the summer and rains but smaller than *A. cathartica*. Propagation by cutting or layer.

A. VIOLACEA

An erect shrub 2·0 metres high, branches green and hirsute when young. Flowers on few flowered terminal cyme, large, showy, light violet.

It is a poor grower on its own roots and is grafted on *A. cathartica* var. Schottii. It requires a well-drained soil and a sunny spot and produces flowers in the hot and rainy season.

ANGELONIA GRANDIFLORA (*Scorphulariaceae*). Eng.—*Gorgon flower*.

Small bushy, perennial herb 0·4-0·5 metres high. Flowers, solitary arising from axil of almost each leaf on long pedicel, white with violet spots, upper lip 2 lobed, larger lower lip 3 lobed about 1·3 cm across. Var. *Alba*—flowers white.

ANGELONIA ANGUSTIFOLIA

Flowers deep violet on erect terminal racemes. Angelonias are usually grown as under shrub and thrive in partial shade and well drained soil. The plants bear flowers all the year round and maximum during cold months. Regular cleaning and pruning twice or thrice a year are necessary especially in the rains. Cuttings root profusely.

APHELANDRA CRISTATA : (*Acanthaceae*)

An erect shrub with spreading branches 0·9 to 1·2 m. high.

It is an evergreen shrub producing many spikes of scarlet flower in winter months. It grows well in partial shade where most of the flowering shrubs fail to grow. Propagation by cuttings.

ARGYREIA SPECIOSA : (*Convolvulaceae*)

Eng.—*Elephant Creeper*, Bengali—*Guguli*, Tel.—*Samudra-Pala.*

A very quick growing hard plant usually cultivated as hedge. It produces large showy flowers all the year round and more in the rainy season. The plants are pruned frequently, otherwise it spreads on all sides. Cuttings root very easily.

ARDISIA UMMELLATA : (*Myrisinaceae*) Eng.—*Spear flower*,

Large bushy shrub about 2·4 to 3·0 m high.

As there are many other ornamental shrubs more beautiful than *A. umbellata*, it is seldom grown in private gardens. In the summer and rainy season the plant bears numerous purplish flowers and red fruits. Propagation by seed or sucker.

ASYSTASIA COROMANDELIANA : (*Acanthaceae*)

Dwarf perennial herbaceous plant 0·3 to 0·5 m high grown in the shrubbery. Very hardy plant and can cover very quickly as an undershrub. Flowers few at one time in the summer and rains. Propagation by cutting.

ATALANTIA MONOPHYLLA (*Rutaceae*)

This is a tall shrub aboat 4·0 m high with stout axillary spines. The plant looks like a small tree because of its stout wocdy stem. It is a very slow growing plant and difficult to propagate where seeds are not produced. Small white scented flowers appear in the summer and rainy season in small clusters. Application of root promoting substances encourage root formation in gootie.

BARLERIA CRISTATA (*Acanthaceae*) Beng.—*Janti*

A dwarf bushy much branched shrub reaching a height of 0·75 to 1·5 m. Flowers purplish blue.

var. Dichotoma—flowers white.

B. STIGOSA

Bushy shrub like *B. cristata*. Flowers blue.

B. GIBSONII

Much branched bushy glabrous shrub. Flowers pale bluish purple in short axillary or terminal spike. Barlerias are commonly grown as hedge plants. It produces compact bushy growth and tolerate regular pruning. Numerous showy flowers appear in the early winter and it grows well in sun and partial shade. Tip cuttings root readily in the Monsoon.

BAUHINIA ACUMINATA (*Leguminoseae*)

Beng.—*Kanchan*. Hindi— *Kachnar*.

An erect bushy shrub with brownish hairy branches 3·0 m high, flowers snow white. It is a hardy plant and widely grown in private garden, parks and public places. It grows very quickly and flowers in the first year. Flowering continues for 7 months from March to September. In *B. acuminata*, seeds are produced abundantly and used for multiplication of plants.

B. GALPINI

A bushy rambling prostrate shrub, 1·8 to 2·4 m in height. Unlike *B. acuminata*, *B. galpinii* is fairly slow growing and does not flower before 3 years when grown from seeds. It produces large number of brick red flowers in the rains. Propagated from seeds and layers.

B. TOMENTOSA

An erect bushy, handsome, deciduous shrub which grows up to 2·5 m. The plant bears numerous sulphur yellow dropping flowers in the summer and rains, and grows in all types of soil. Seed pods are produced abundantly and the seedlings start flowering in the second year.

BELOPERONE AMERSTAE (*Acanthaceae*)

About 0·5 to 0·8 metre high, decumbent stem. Flowers long white, tutular with violet spots inside lower lips. Very quick growing bushy under-shrub suitable in semishade and flowers throughout the year. Propagation by cutting.

B. GUTTATA Eng.—*Shrimp plant*.

Dwarf shrub about 0·6 m high. Flowers rose purple in axillary spike. A free flowering undershrub which grows in partial shade and produces showy flowers throughout the year and more during the rainy season. Propagation by cutting.

A yellow flowering variety has been introduced.

BRUGMANSIA SUAVEOLENS (*Solanaceae*) Eng.—*Angel's Trumpet*

This shrub grows up to a height of 2·5 to 3·0 m. Flowers greenish white. A large hardy shrub flowering in the hot months. It thrives well in wet shady place and easily propagated from cuttings.

BRUNFELSIA AMERICANA (*Solanaceae*)

Shrub 1·5 to 2·0 m in height. Flowers white fading to yellow. It is a handsome perpetual flowering shrub of medium height and grows well in sun and semishade. Propagated by air layering.

B. GRANDIFLORA

It looks more or less like *B. americana* but has more bushy habit, larger and paler leaves and bigger flowers. *B. grandiflora* is one of the most useful shrub and bears large number of white and light yellow flowers throughout the year. Propagation by air layering.

BUDDLEIA ASIATICA (*Loganiaceae*)

Evergreen tall shrub about 3·0 m high. Flowers sweet scented. It grows well in semi shade and porous soil and flowers in February. Propagation by cutting.

B. LINDLEYANA

Bushy shrub about 2·0 m high. Flowers purplish violet. *B. lindleyana* likes partial shade and flowers for many months in the summer and rains. Propagation by cutting.

B. MADAGASCARIENSIS

An evergreen tall shrub with irregular bushy growth, shoots weak densely tomentose. Flowers orange yellow in terminal panicles. It grows up to a height of 2·5 m in full sun and semishade, and flowers in the early summer. Pruning is to be done almost every year to keep the plant in shape. Propagation by cutting.

BRYA EBENUS (*Leguminoseae*) Eng.—*Jamaica or Green ebony*

One of the most beautiful shrubs about 3·0 to 4·5 metres high, branches pendulous with small dark green leaves. Almost all the branches become covered with golden yellow pea-shaped flowers. The plant can be grown at the back of shrubbery or as a specimen plant in the garden. Seedlings are fairly quick growing, produce flowers in the third year and many times during the summer and rains. There are not many plants which are so showy with drooping branches covered with golden yellow flowers. The plant can be made dwarf and bushy by cutting the top of the main shoot. Airlayers root profusely.

CAESALPINIA GILLESI (*Leguminoseae)*

An erect shrub, height 1·5 to 2·0 m, flowers yellow. A bushy shrub with feathery foliage, flowering in the hot and rainy season. Propagation by seeds.

C. PULCHERRIMA *(Leguminoseae)*

Eng.—*Barbados Pride*, Beng.—*Krishnachura*

Beautiful bushy shrub with few prickles, about 2·5 to 3·0 metres high if pruned. Flowers orange-scarlet.

C. PULCHERRIMA var. Flaba (*Radhachura*) a variety with bright yellow flowers. If pruned properly every year, this plant forms an almost round shape and each new shoot bears a long panicle of flower on the top during the summer and rains. The plants should be pruned up to a height of 0·45 to 0·60 m in March. Propagation by seed.

CALLIANDRA BREVIPES *(Leguminoseae)*

This is a bushy shrub and under warm condition it grows about 0·7 to 1·2 m. Flowers in clusters almost globular in shape with numerous fine pink stamens. A dwarf shrub with fine feathery foliage, thrives in semishade and well drained soil. It flowers almost throughout the year, number increases in the winter. Plants are multiplied from seeds or layer.

C. HAEMATOCEPHALA

Tall bushy shrub about 2·5 m high, spreading habit. A well-shaped bushy, evergreen shrub with dark green foliage. The plant bears numerous crimson flowers in the autumn and winter. Seedlings do not grow quickly, so usually propagated from airlayers.

C. HOUSTONII

A perpetual flowering tall shrub about 2·5 m high. Growth irregular, branches terete, some erect others grow slightly above the ground. Flowers in clusters on terminal panicle.

C. HOUSTONII grows better in shady place than in full sun, flowers all the year round. Propagation by layering.

C. SPECIOSA

One of the best flowering shrubs under cultivation. Erect up to 2·0 m high. There should be at least one *C. speciosa* in every garden. Upper portion of the plant becomes covered with scarlet flowers at an interval of few days and continues all the year round. It should be grown in rich soil and full sun. The planities difficult to propagate vegetatively and usually grown from seeds.

C. TWEEDII

Calliandra tweedii flowers very freely all the year round. It is a hardy shrub suitable for growing in the shrubbery or as single plant. Like *Chaematocephala*, seedlings are also growing and can be propagated vegetatively by air or ground layering.

CALLICARPA CANA *(Verbenaceae)*

Beng.—*Arusha*

Bushy shrub about 2·5 m high. Flowers small lilac. A hardy and quick growing bushy shrub producing cluster of small lilac flowers at the axil of leaves during spring, hot and rainy season. Pruning is done after flowering to maintain the shape. Propagation by cutting.

CANANGA KIRKII *(Annonaceae)*

Tall shrub 2·5 to 3·0 m in height. Flowers solitary, greenish yellow on long stalk, fragrant. Flowers and foliage cannot be easily distinguished from a distance unless carefully observed. Flowers appear in March and continues up to September. Propagation by layering.

CANTHIUM GLABRUM : *(Rubiaceae)*

Tall evergreen shrub up to 3 m in height. Flowers in many flowered clusters or corymbs, white, sweet scented. Corolla tube about 2·0 cm long, lobes five, star shaped 1·3 cm across.

It flowers in the summer and large clusters of white flower give a very showy appearance. It can be propagated from cuttings or airlayer.

CAPPARIS ZEYLANICA (*Capperidaceae*)

Eng.—*Caper Bush*

A much branched shrub about 2 m high. Flowers showy. *Capparis* grows well in partial shade and well drained rich porous soil. It flowers in the early summer and continues till rainy season. Propagation by layering.

CARISSA CARANDAS (*Rubiacenae*)

Beng.—*Karamcha* ; Hindi—*Karanda* ; Tam—*Kalaka* ; Tel.—*Kalivikya*

Tall, evergreen shrub 2·5 to 3·5 m high, grown mainly for showy fruits. It flowers in early summer and fruit matures in June. The fruits are used for making pickles. Propagation by seed or cutting.

CARYOPTERIS MASTACANTHUS (*Verbenaceae*)

Eng.—*Blue Spirea*

Deciduous 1·8 to 2·4 m high. Flowers small violet blue. This species of *Caryopteris* has another variety producing pink flower but violet blue is more common.

It is a very hardy shrub and flowers in the winter and spring. Pruning should be done in the rainy season upto 0·5 to 0·75 m to allow new shoots to grow and flower. Propagation by cutting.

CASSIA ALATA (*Leguminoseae*)

Hindi—*Dadmurdan* ; Tam.—*Shinai agati* ; Tel.—*Sima avisl.*

Tall erect shrub not much branched as other *Cassia*, up to 2·5 m. It is a very quick growing shrub and starts flowering in the first year, erect terminal inflorescence bears yellow flowers in winter. Propagated by seed.

CASSIA GLAUCA

Tall bushy shrub 3·0 m high. It is a beautiful shrub with dark green foliage and large clusters of yellow flowers appear almost throughout the year. Propagation by seed.

CASSIA LAEVIGATA

Bushy shrub about 3·0 m high. *C. laevigata* is also a very hardy shrub suitable in both full sun and partial shade. The plant produces mass of yellow flowers for 8 to 10 months a year. Propagation by seeds.

CATESBAEA SPINOSA (*Rubiaceae*)

A spiny shrub about 1·5 to 2·0 m high with spreading branches. This slow growing hardy shrub has an unusual shape. The terminal branches droop down, creamy white funnel shaped flowers hang in summer and early rains in large number. Older plants produce fruits and seeds but the seedlings are slow growing.

CERBERA FRUTICOSA (*Apocynaceae*)

Bushy shrub about 2·5 m in height. Flower reddish white, tip and centre red. It is one of the best shrubs producting large number of showy flowers throughout the year. The plant has compact and bushy growth and grows well in sun and semi-shade. Propagation by airlayering.

CESTRUM AURANTIACUM (*Solanaceae*)

An erect or scrambling shrub, glabrous and pubescent when young. Flowers orange yellow. This species of *Cestrum* forms a bushy plant, and branches drooping on all sides. Flowering is profuse during the cold months and can grow in partial shade. Propagation by cutting.

CESTRUM DIURNUM (*Solanaceae*)

Eng.—*The Day Jasmine*

A quick growing evergreen bushy shrub with dark green foliage and white flowers, scented during the day. It flowers in the summer and continues till the end of rainy season. Pruning should be done after flowering. Propagation by seed or cutting.

CESTRUM PURPURESCENS

Tall rambling evergreen shrub produces spikes of reddish purple flowers in cold months and grows well in full sun and partial shade. Cuttings root easily.

CESTRUM NOCTURNUM

Eng.—*Lady of the Night*

A popular shrub extensively grown in the gardens. Numerous creamy white flowers open at night and are very sweet scented. It is very hardy and suitable for screening and can be trained on trellis. Propagation by cutting.

CITRUS LIMONIA var.—Variegata (*Rutaceae*)

This is a variety of lemon with variegated leaf. Plants grow up to 1·5 m. It is a good foliage shrub suitable for sunny spot, very hardy, quick growing and bushy. Pruning is necessary to keep the plant in shape. Propagation by air layering.

CLERODENDRON FRAGRANS (*Verbenaceae*)

About 1·5 m high. Flowers double white tinged with pink, very fragrant. A hardy and very useful shrub prducing large cluster of flowers during the hot and rainy season. It grows better in moist, semi-shady places. Propagation by separation of root sucker and cutting.

CLERODENDRON INERME

Eng.—*Forest Jasmine*

A straggling shrub, flowers white. *C. inerme* forms a compact, clean hedge and remains dark green throughout the year. It can be kept very low and does not produce leafless woody stem. Flowers appear in rains and easily propagated from cutting.

CLERODENDRON MACROSIPHON

It is a very free flowering dwarf shrub 1.0 high and produces mass of white flowers in several flushes during summer and rains. *C. macrosiphon* should be grown in the front row of a shrubbery. Propagated by cutting or layering.

CLERODENDRON SHIPHONANTHUS

Eng.—*Tubeflower*

A tall shrub about 2·5 m high. Common in Bengal and is also cultivated in partial shade in the gardens. Flowering commences in early monsoon followed by conspicuous dark blue fruits. Propagated by seeds.

Pritchardia grandis

Calliandr tweedii

Brunfelsia americana

Clerodendron macrosiphon

COFFEA BENGALENSIS (*Rubiaceae*)

A deciduous shrub about 1·8 m high. Flowers are produced on leafless plants during winter and the snow white flowers are very conspicuous. It is a hardy plant, grows in full sun and semishade. Black fruits remain attached on brown branches for few days. Propagation by seed or air layering.

CORDIA SEBESTENA (*Boraginaceae*)

It is a quick growing tall shrub producing clusters of orange flowers in the summer and rains. The seedlings bear flower in the second year.

CROSSANDRA NILOTICA (*Acanthaceae*)

This species of *Crossandra* is free flowering, dwarf shrub and grows well both in sun and partial shade. Propagation by cuttings.

CROSSANDRA UNDULAEFOLIA (*Acanthaceae*)

It is a free flowering under-shrub suitable for sun or semi-shade, quick growing and forms a small bushy plant. Orange flowers are produced profusely in the summer and rains. Propagation by cutting or layering.

DAEDALACANTHUS NERVOSUS (*Acanthaceae*)

About 1·5 high. It is one of the best winter flowering shrub producing indigo blue flowers which are not very common in perennial ornamental plants. *Daedalacanthus* grows well in partial shade and size and shape of the plant can be kept under control by pruning in the monsoon. Cuttings root easily.

DOMBEYA ROTUNDATA (*Sterculiaceae*)

Large bush shrub reaching a height of 3·5 m. This species of *Dombeya* produces numerous tufts of white flowers during the winter. The flowers do not fall off after they have faded but hang in ugly bunches till blown off by the wind. Propagation by air layering.

DURANTA MACROPHYLLA (*Verbenaceae*)

Eng.—*Golden dew drop*

It is a tall evergreen spineless shrub about 3 m high producing long panicles of blue flowers in the summer months. Yellow fruits remain on the plant for a number of days. It flowers well in full sun but also grows in partial shade. Propagation by seed or cutting.

DURANTA PLUMERI (*Verbenaceae*)

Tall much branches shrub with axillary spines, about 2·5 to 3·0 m high.

Var : *Alba*—flowers white.

Var : *Variegata*—flowers blue, foliage variegated.

It is usually grown as hedge and forms an inpenetrable barrier.

ERANTHEMUM (*Acanthaceae*)

Eranthemums are useful shrubs for shady and semishady places. These plants have colourful foliage and also showy flowers. Though most of the species except *E. laxiflorun* are grown mainly for foliage, one can see flowers in shade in summer where other flowering shrubs even fail to grow.

In full sun the leaves become less colourful, smaller in size and in the hot months *E. nigrum* shows signs of wilting. *E. laxiflorum* which is grown for flowers does best in partial shade, while in complete shade it may even die during the Monsoon. Well drained rich soil produces bushy plant of luxuriant growth. Plants can be made bushy and size can be controlled by pruning during the early monsoon. All species root from cuttings in about 3 weeks but tip cutting with terminal leaves produces better plant than the semi woody stem cuttings.

ERANTHEMUM ALBOMARGINATUM

Bushy, 1·5 m high. Leaves large, upper surface green with irregularly suffused grey, margin very irregular or coarsely toothed, green undersurface. Flowers on terminal panicle.

ERANTHEMUM BICOLOR

About 1·5 to 1·75 m high. Leaves with greenish yellow margin and also a part of lamina ; centre green or interrupted by greenish yellow patches. Flowers dark red.

ERANTHEMUM LAXIFLORUM

A handsome dwarf shrub flowering throughout the year and more abundantly in the rainy season. It grows better in partial shade and well drained soil. Propagation by cutting.

ERANTHEMUM NIGRUM

About 1·5 to 1·8 m high ; leaves with upper surface dark almost blackish, lower surface purplish with dark veins. Flower on terminal panicle, white with rose centre, upper one bi-lobbed.

ERANTHEMUM RETICULATUM

1·2 to 1·5 m high shrub. Younger leaves with yellow netted veins, older leaves green throughout. Flowers many on terminal panicle, white, reddish violet spot at the centre.

ERANTHEMUM TRICOLOR

About 1·5 m high. Upper surface of leaves greyish purple on dark green base, lower surface reddish with violet spots. Flowers red with white spots on terminal panicle.

EXCOECARIA BICOLOR (*Euphorbiaceae*)

Handsome bushy shrub up to 1·5 m high ; upper surface of leaves olive green glabrous, lower surface red. Flowers small yellow in axillary spike.

This is grown for the colorful leaves and suited well both in full sun and partial shade. Very small flowers are inconspicuous. Propagation by cutting or air layering.

FORTUNELLA JAPONICA (*Rutaceae*) *Kumquat.*

Tall handsome ornamental plant when in fruit, reaches a height of 2·4 m. Flowers small, scented. Flowers usually appear in the early rains and the fruits turn yellow in winter. It is very easy to grow and likes full sun. Propagation by airlayering.

FRANCISCEA HOPEANA (*Solanaceae*)

Eng.—*Yesterday-today-tomorrow*

Bushy shrub about 2·0 m. high. Flowers solitary, at first violet with yellow centre changing to purple and fading to almost white, sweet scented.

One of the most popular shrubs in cultivation because of the changing flowers colour, bushy growth and profuse flowering in the summer and rains. It grows well in full sun and partial shade. Propagation by layering.

GARDENIA JASMINOIDES (*Rubiaceae*)

Beng.—*Gandhraj*

A shrub reaching a height of 3·0 m. Gardenias are very popular shrubs grown in almost every garden, and produce many sweet scented white flowers in the summer months. These are very hardy and can be grown in any type of soil. Propagation by air layering.

GARDENIA JASMINOIDES var : *Fortunii*

Much branched shrub reaching a height of 1·5 to 2·0 m. Branches arise from the base of the stem thus forming a bush with dark green glossy foliage. Sweet scented white, flowers appear in early summer. Propagation by air layering.

GARDENIA JASMINOIDES var : *Veitchii*

Dwarf shrub 0·9 to 1·2 m high. It also produces many double white scented flowers in summer and is propagated by air layering.

LINDENIA RIVALIS (*Rubiaceae*)

Tall shrub, 2·4 to 3·0 m. Flower solitary terminal on short branches, white, scented. It is not commonly cultivated as small number of flowers appear in the summer and last for a short time. Propagated from air layers.

GMELINA ASIATICA (*Verbenaceae*)

Tall erect spiny shrub. Flowers yellow, irregularly bell shaped. This species of *Gmelina* forms erect growth and the flowers are smaller than *G. hystrix*. Propagation by air layering.

GMELINA HYSTRIX (*Verbenaceae*) Beng—*Bhadara*

Climbing spiny shrub. Flowers yellow, irregularly bell shaped, bracts large reddish purple, showy. It is a very quick growing evergreen shrub, and produces pendulous yellow flowers in the summer and rains. Severe pruning is to be done in August and odd shoot removed frequently to keep the growth under control. Propagation by air layering or cutting.

GRAPTOPHYLLUM HORTENSIS (*Acanthaceae*)

Foliage shrub, 1·2 to 1·5 m high, bushy and grows best in semi-shade and porous soil. It produces tuft of flowers in the hot months and is easily propagated from cutting. There are two varieties which vary in the foliage. The common variety has yellow and green patches, while in the other variety, the leaves have pink and bronze patches.

GUSTAVIA INSIGNIS (*Myrtaceae*)

A shrub 1·2 to 2·0 m high. Flowers showy, rose coloured, lower part cream white. A rare shrub, very slow growing but produces large showy flowers all the year round. Propagation very difficult even by ground layering.

HAMELIA PATENS (*Rubiaceae*)

Handsome perpetual flowering shrub, up to 2·5 m high. Flowers orange scarlet. It is one of the most common and useful shrubs and grows very well in semi-shade and full sun. It produces numerous small tubular flowers all the year round. Every year small branches in the centre should be removed. Propagation by air layering.

HAMILTONIA SUAVEOLENS (*Rubiaceae*) Beng.—*Bain Champa.*

Flowers small in terminal panicles, pale heliotrope, scented. It is a winter flowering shrub about 3 meters high and prefers semi-shade. The plants should be pruned after flowering and the cut branches used as cuttings for propagation.

HIBISCUS (*Malvaceae*)

These are the most useful flowering shrubs in Indian gardens. Four species, *H. syriacus*, *H. mutabilis*, *H. schizopetalous*, *H.*

collinus and the varieties of *H. rosa-sinensis* are commonly grown in tropical gardens.

Hibiscus rosa-sinensis (Jaba) has large number of hybrids and there is hardly any garden without it. 'Alipore beauty', 'Rubroplenus', 'Careno plenus' have large double flowers and plants may reach a height of 2-2·5 m, while 'Juno', 'Daffodil'. 'Pride of Ceylon' seldom grow above 1·2-1·7 meters. Varieties with single flowers have wider range of colour-white, yellow, orange, salmon, pink, mauve, in one or in combination with other colours, size of flowers also vary from 5–12 cm. Most varieties flower throughout the year in moderate climate and more abundantly in the late rains. 'Viceroy' produces small deep red flowers all the year round and beauty of 'Hawaii White' is never lost. 'Australian Rose', 'Deep Rose Saundorya', 'Sweet Heart', 'Netaji White', 'Daffodil', 'Agens', 'Pride of Ceylon' are popular and prolific bearers.

Hibiscus rosa-sinensis grows best under moderate temperature and relatively high humidity. Porous loamy soil suits best and water logging causes serious damage to the plants. Humus in the soil is not so essential while undecomposed organic matter causes root injury and greatly affect growth and flowering. In regions where soil is clayey, it is observed that careful preparation of pits and raising of planting bed definitely keep even the best and less hardy varieties in good condition for 5 to 6 years. In such cases the pit must be dug at least 75 cm in depth and diameter, well rotted dry screened leaf mould, sand and bone meal mixed with soil to form a loamy mixture. Raise the pit about 30 cm high from the ground level, flood the pit and allow the soil to settle down and planting should be done when the soil is slightly moist. In heavy rainfall areas with sticky soil best time for planting *Hibiscus* is early winter, If planting is done during the rainy season the roots do not find a favourable environment for growth as the soil remains soggy for 3 to 4 months. No more bulky organic matter will be required after initial preparation of pits, use handful of bone meal or hoof and horn or sterameal at least twice during the rainy season and mix it with the soil. A small quantity of blood meal will improve the colour of the flowers.

All the species of *Hibiscus* grow in full sun but few varieties of *H. rosa-sinensis,* however, thrive and flower well in partial shade e.g. Netaji White.

H. syriacus and *H. schizopetalous* and *H. rosa-sinensis* do not respond to pruning. Only *H. mutabilis* is drastically pruned after it has finished flowering. Pruning encourages a second-flush on the new shoots. In other species only dry or diseased shoots should be removed from the base.

H. rosa-sinensis becomes seriously infested by insects. Mites and red spiders cause curling of leaves which become unusually small in size and the plants stop further growth and flowering. Jassids are very dangerous insects and often kill the plants if they are not controlled at the early stage of attack. Weevils damage the plants in July-August, they bore the tip of the shoots and suck the sap. Propagated by cuttings, layering or budding.

It can be grown well in pot. Prepare rich but porous compost consisting of 2 parts laomy soil, I part screened leaf mould, 2 table spoonful bone meal for each 25 cm pot. Varieties which do not grow very large are suitable for pot cultivation e.g. 'Juno', 'Daffodil', 'Sweet Heart' and Hawaii White ! Keep the pot with the plant in full sun throughout the day except in the summer months when it may require shade in the afternoon. Do not water on moist soil. Use bone meal twice or thrice during the monsoon and liquid manure during the winter. Keep watch on the insects and protect the plants by spraying insecticides at regular intervals.

Many varieties of *H. rosa-sinensis* from Hawaii are now grown in India. They have unusually large flowers with attractive bright colours. The plants are propagated by cutting, layering, budding or grafting. In Calcutta budded plants do not grow so well as they do in Bangalore. Plants propagated by air or ground layering show better growth and flowering.

H. schizopetalous (Jhumka Jaba)—Tall glabrous much

branched shrub. Leaves ovate-elliptic, toothed glossy. Flowers pendulous on long peduncles, orange red, petals re-curved and beautifully cut at various length. Long staminal tube hang down with red anther.

This species is very hardy and grows in almost every type of soil and bears numerous pendulous flowers almost throughout the year.

H. syriacus. Erect much branched shrub, leaves short petioled, strongly 3 ribbed, lower ones mostly 3 lobed and with many rounded teeth or notches. Flowers are single or double, blue, purple, flesh colour and white differing according to variety.

Though *H. syriacus* can thrive under wide range of climate from tropical to temperate, flowering is at its best in dry and cooler climate. This species is not so popular as *H. rosasinensis*, in tropical gardens.

H. mutabilis (Sthalpadma) Tall shrub with few erect branches. Leaves cordate, 5 angled and toothed, hairy. Flowers large white, double changing gradually to deep pink.

This is frequently grown in the gardens of West Bengal and becomes very attractive when the plant bears large number of white or pink flowers in the autumn months. If grown from seeds, high percentage of seedlings produce single flowers. It prefers high humidity but porous soi' *H. mutabilis* is pruned after flowering which encourages second flush of flower and keeps the plant in shape.

It is also a favourite plant for a number of insects e.g. scale insects, wooly aphis, red spider ; caterpillar also greatly damages the plants. Propagated from cutting layers and seeds.

HIBISCUS COLLINUS

Tall and bushy shrub 2·5 to 3·0 m. Flowers white with purplish brown centre. A large evergreen shrub and produces showy flowers in the rainy season. The petals appear to be impreganted in vas. Propagation by seed or airlayering.

IOCHROMA TUBULOSA (*Solanaceae*)

Bushy shrub 1·5 to 1·8 m high. It flowers almost throughout the year and more during the summer and rains *Iochroma* survives in well drained soil in full sun. Drooping violet flowers in bunches are very showy and should be grown in a shrubbery. Propagation by cutting or air layering.

IXORA (*Rubiaceae*) Beng—*Rangan*

Ixoras are very popular and effective flowering shrubs in the tropical gardens. Almost all the species and varieties flower very freely in the summer and rains. They can grow on any soil but will respond to treatment with manure when the plant is bursting into bloom. Pruning after flowering is beneficial.

These plants are grown in shrubbery or as specimen plant. *Ixora singaporensis, I. macrothyrsa, I. rosea, I. barbata* and few varieties of *Ixora coccinea* produce well shaped plants and bear many large bunches of showy flowers. *I. chinensis* is often grown as hedge.

As a result of hybridisation and natural crossing many varieties have developed which are of horticultural importance. The species and varieties have been arranged according to the colour of flower.

Many types of *Ixora* produce seeds but cutting and layering are the common methods of propagation.

YELLOW AND ORANGE FLOWERS

Ixora lutea—An erect compact bushy shrub about 1·3 m high. Flowers yellow.

Ixora armenaica—Dwarf plant of weak habit with flowers salmon orange. It is of garden origin.

Ixora alipurensis—It is hybrid of *I. coccinea* and *I. venusta.* 1·5 m high, leaves like *I. coccinea.* Flowers deep orange with deeper tube.

Ixora coccinea var : Lancasteri, Hybrid of *I. coccinea*, var : Magnifica and *I. crocata.* Dwarf habit with large bunches of deep orange flowers, 20 to 30 in a bunch.

Ixora venusta—A plant of straggling habit, flowers buff yellow.

PINK FLOWERS

Ixora chinensis var : Rosea. A plant about 1·4 m high. Flowers pale pink becoming reddish in age.

Ixora westii—More or less like var : Rosea, flowers pale rose becoming bright rose.

Ixora rugosula—Compact growing habit with small crowded bunches of flowers, deep pink in colour.

SCARLET FLOWERS

Ixora coccinea—A compact shrub about 1·5 m tall. Flowers deep scarlet.

Ixora coccinea var : Bandhuca. It is more compact than above, flowers slightly larger.

Ixora coccinea var : Magnifica. The flowers in this type are very large, bright deep scarlet in colour, foliage broader.

Ixora splendida—Dwarf plants, about 1·3 meters. Flowers brilliant crimson.

Ixora chinensis—A small shrub about 1·5 m high.

Ixora sanguinea—A tall growing shrub of rather untidy appearance reaching a height of 2·5 m. Flowers pale scarlet in loose bunches.

Ixora macrothyrsa—This species grows tall upto 2·5 m. Flowers scarlet, appear in large clusters.

WHITE FLOWERS

Ixora barbata—A large shrub about 3 m or more. Flowers white.

Ixora parviflora—It becomes a tree, much branched. Flowers white sweet scented, dirty white and only last for few days.

Ixora undulata—A large evergreen shrub. Flowers white, sweet scented.

ORANGE SCARLET SHADES

Ixora chinensis var : Prince of orange. One of the finest varieties of *I. chinensis.* Compact shrub of neat growth, flowers deep buff changing to orange scarlet.

Ixora coccinea var : Dixiana. Very compact growth about 1·4 m high. Leaves small. Flowers orange scarlet deepening to scarlet.

Ixora coccinea var : Pilgrimii. Plants like Prince of Orange. Flowers bright orange-scarlet shaded crimson.

Ixora fulgens—Neat shrub about 1 to 1·4 m high. Flowers orange-scarlet in large bunches.

Ixora spectabilis—About 1 to 1·4 m high. Flowers appear like var : Dixiana except that of a deeper shade of red and bunches larger.

Ixora singaporensis—One of the finest Ixoras in cultivation. Tall bushy plants 2 to 2·5 m high. Leaves large 12 to 18 cm long, shining green. Flower cluster about 15 to 18 cm in diameter, brilliant orange scarlet.

JACQUINIA RUSCIFOLIA (*Theophastaceae*)

Handsome evergreen shrub about 2·4 to 3·0 m high. This slow growing shrub produces small orange flowers during the summer which remain hidden in the dense dark green foliage. Propagated by cutting or seed.

JASMINUM GRANDIFLORUM (*Oleaceae*) Beng. and Hindi—*Chemeli*.

A hardy scandent shrub of vigorous growth producing snow white fragrant flowers in the summer and rains. The plant is severely pruned after flowering to cheek the spreading habit. Propagated by layering.

JASMINUM PUBESCENS Beng.—*Kund*.

A scandent shrub, evergreen. Flowers white, single or double fragrant. *Jasminum pubescens* is a bushy shrub and can be trained on low trellis. Flowers appear in the form of sprays on pendulous branches in the early monsoon. The plants are pruned by removing interlaced growth to maintain size and shape and also to encourage flowering. If left untouched for one or two years the plant will throw out shoots in all directions and twine round other plants. Propagated by layering.

JASMINUM PUBESCENS var : Rubescens

A scandent shrub often grown as a bush. Flowers are produced in clusters on the tips of short axillary branch, inner surface white outer surface pink. This variety is one of the best winter flowering shrubs. Its growth is less than *J. pubescens.* Pruning should be done every year after flowering to remove unwanted branches.

JASMINUM SAMBAC Eng.—Arabian Jasmine, Beng.—*Belphul.*

A bushy weak stemmed shrub up to 1.0 m high with pubescent branches.

Var : Rai-flowers double.

Var : Motia-flowers double larger in size.

Var : Rai (Japanese)—flowers large double, profuse bloomer.

This species of *Jasminum* produces sweet and strongly scented flowers which are widely used in garland and other decorative purposes. The flowers have a good market in cities and towns. These are very hardy shrubs and flowers are produced in abundance for 4 to 5 months in the summer and rains. Large scale propagation is done by cuttings.

JATROPHA PANDURAEFOLIA (*Euphorbiaceae*)

A perpetual red flowering shrub, 3 m high. This quick growing plant does very well also in semi-shade. Light pruning becomes necessary to keep the branches in form otherwise it tends to grow irregularly. Propagation by cutting or air layering.

JATROPHA PODAGRICA (*Euphorbiaceae*)

A succulent shrub about 1·5 m high. The base of the stem and branches are swollen and light grey. Because of the peculiar gouty stem and hardy habit this plant is used in rockery. The orange red flower and branches of the inflorescence add colour to the feature. Usually propagated by division.

JUSTICIA MAGNIFICA 'Carnea' (*Acanthaceae*)

Erect shrub about 1·5 m. It produces large clusters of showy pink flowers almost all the year round and suits better in well drained soil and partial shade. Propagation by cutting.

LAGERSTROEMIA INDICA (*Lythraceae*) Eng.—Crape Myrtle, Beng—*Phurush*

Grows up to a height of 3 m. Flowers on long panicles 15·2 to 23·0 cm long, mauve.

Var : The Bride—delicate rose
Var : Rosea—deep pink
Var : Candida—white

Very hardy plant and flowers profusely from May to July. The plant does not grow very tall if pruning is done in January or early February up to a height of 0·5 m. The cut branches may be used as cutting for propagation.

LAGERSTROEMIA LANCASTERI

Tall shrub about 3·0 m. Flowers on terminal panicle 18·0 to 25·0 cm long. This hybrid *Lagerstroemia* grows into a tall shrub, if left unpruned for few years. Pruning should be done every year in February at a height of 0·45 to 0·60 m and new shoots bear long panicle of large mauve flowers in May. The leaves and flowers are bigger than the varieties of *Lagerstroemia indica*. Propagated by cutting or layering.

LANTANA CAMARA (*Verbenaceae*)

Prickly stemmed bushy shrub of 0·5 to 2·0 m. Flowers on compact heads. Fruits black round.

Var : Mixta—outer flowers opening yellow becoming saffron then brick red.

Var : Sanguinea—opening saffron yellow becoming bright red.

Var : Nivea—Tall growing, flowers white.

Var : Depressa—Plants semitrailing dwarf. Leaves smaller, flowers yellow.

LANTANA LILACINA

Leaves ovate-lanceolate, flowers bright rosy lilac on larger heads.

LANTANA SELLOWIANA

Trailing shrub. Flowers pale mauve on flat heads.

Though common, Lantanas are useful flowering shrubs. These are hardy, quick growing and flower throughout the year. *L. camara* var : Depressa has dwarf bushy growth seldom exceeding a height of 50 cm and produces numerous clusters golden yellow flowers. *L. sellowiana* is low growing and an ideal rock garden plant. Flowers appear in cold months and continues till the rains. All species and varieties of *Lantana* should be pruned severely in the rainy season. Propagation by cutting or layering.

LAWSONIA INERME (*Lythraceae*) Eng.—Tree Mignonette Beng.—*Mendhi*.

Tall, often growing up to 3·6 to 4·6 m.

Var : Alba-petals light yellow.

Var : Rubra—petals rose on light green sepal.

Both the varieties grow tall and appear to be small trees with stout woody stem. Crown is much branched and spreading and bears large panicle of numerous small flowers in the summer and rains. Propagation by seed and cutting. *Lawsonia* is usually grown as hedge.

LEMONIA SPECTABILIS : (*Rutaceae*)

Tall shrub 2·1 to 2·4 m high. Flowers crimson pink, two large green bracts with each flower. Like *Jatropha panduraefolia* it also flowers throughout the year and grows both in sun and semishade. Propagation by air layering.

MAGNOLIA FUSCATA : (*Magnoliaceae*)

Bushy shrub hardly exceeds 1·5 to 1·8 m in tropical conditions. Flowers yellowish green stained brown purple. Most delicate among the Magnolias described below. It should be grown in partial shade and porous soil. Flowers appear in summer and rains. Propagation by layering.

MAGNOLIA GRANDIFLORA

It is usually grown as a tall shrub reaching a height of 3·6 to 4·5 m. Flowers large, creamy white, fragrant. It is very slow growing and suitable as a specimen plant. Shining dark green leaves with rusty under surface are very conspicuous. Propagation by air layering.

MAGNOLIA MUTABILIS

Bushy shrub about 2·0 m high with straight long branches. arising from the base of the stem, dark green when not too old. Flowers yellow, scented. It grows only in shade and the soil should be well drained. Strong fragrance of the flowers indicates the presence of flowers. The flowers are about 3·8 cm long appear in the summer and rains but not always visible in the large dark green leaves. Propagation by air or ground layering.

MAGNOLIA PUMILA

Beng. & Hindi—*Jahuri Champa.*

Evergreen shrub about 1·5 m. Flowers cream, drooping, very fragrant at night. *Magnolia pumila* is suitable for semi-shade and well drained soil. Direct sunlight burns the leaves, flowering continues all the year round. Among the Magnolias this species produces more number of flowers in the summer and rains. Propagation by air layering.

MALVAVISCUS CONZATTII : (*Malavaceae*)

Eng.—*Scarlet cotton* Beng.—*Lanka Jaba.*

Var. Alba—flowers light pink.

Var. Variegata. Variegated leaf in yellow and green. It also produces red flowers.

Malvaviscus are common plants in gardens of Eastern India. It grows well in partial shade and can be kept low and bushy by pruning in early rains. The plant bears large number of tubular red flowers all the year round and the number increases in the early winter. Cuttings root easily.

MALPIGHIA COCCIGERA : (*Malpighiaceae*)

Dwarf bushy shrub 0·6 to 0·9 m high. Numerous pinkish white flowers on straight shoots and shining green leaves give a showy appearance during the summer and rainy season. It should be grown in full sun, thrive in any type of soil. Propagation by seed or layering.

MALPIGHIA GLABRA : (*Malpighiaceae*)
Eng.—*Barbados Cherry*

Much branched evergreen shrub about 2·5 m high. Dark green glabrous shrub producing numerous rose red flowers in the rainy season. Fruits are ornamental. Propagation by air layering.

MEMECYLON EDULE (*Melastomaceae*) Eng.—*Red iron wood*, Beng.—*Anjan*.

Handsome, bushy well shaped shrub about 2.4 m high. Flowers small blue in cluster in the axils of leaves and also from the stem. Fruit first red and turns black.

It is very slow growing and difficult to propagate vegetatively. The plant looks beautiful when the branches become covered with numerous clusters of blue flowers in April-May. *Memecylon* grows better in partial shade at the early stage. Propagated by seed.

MEMECYLON UMBELLATUM

Bushy well shaped shrub about 2·0 m high. A very interesting plant bearing numerous clusters of pinkish blue flowers at the axils of leaves and also on dark woody stem in few flushes during the hot months. It is a slow growing shrub and a seedling grows about 5·0 to 7·6 cm in one year in pot. Vegetative propagation has been found to be difficult.

MUEHLENBECKIA PLATYCLADOS (*Polygonaceae*)

Bushy evergreen glabrous shrub. 1·2 to 1·5 m high. It is a flat stemmed peculiar plant and grows better in partial shade. Numerous clusters of white flowers on dark green stem are very showy. Flowers are produced during the rains when plants also show vegetative growth. Propagation by cutting.

MURRAYA EXOTICA (*Rutaceae*) Eng.—*Chinese box* ; Beng. and Hindi—*Kamini.*

Tall shrub with greyish bark. Flowers white, strongly scented. From the strong scent of the flowers presence of *Murraya exotica* can be recognised from a distance.

It forms a well shaped large shrub with dark green leaves and can be grown as specimen plant. Flowers appear in several flushes in the summer and rains. Propagation by seeds or air layering.

MURRAYA ELONGATA—Plants bigger, leaves and flowers larger than *M. exotica.*

MUSSAENDA CORYMBOSA (*Rubiaceae*)

The plant is erect with slender branches and grows better in partial shade than in full sun. The expanded yellowish sepal are more abundant in the rainy season. Propagation by cutting or air layering.

MUSSAENDA ERYTHROPHYLLA

A semierect shrub about 1·0 to 1·5 m high. It produces scarlet velvety and leafy sepal except in the winter. The plants thrive in partial shade and the soil should be porous. Propagation by layering.

MUSSAENDA FRONDOSA

Eng.—*Dhoby bush* ; Beng.—*Sada pata.*

An ornamental shrub with spreading habit. *Mussaenda frondosa* is much more showy than the *M. corymbosa* because of its larger petaloid sepal and flower. Pruning is necessary to keep growth restricted and it is done after flowering. Flowers are produced in the summer and rains. Propagated by layering.

NANDINA DOMESTICA (*Berberidaceae*)

Handsome evergreen shrub 1·5 to 2·0 m high. Flowers white in large panicle. This is grown mainly for the handsome foliage and thrive well in shade. Propagation by seed or by division of clump.

NERIUM OLEANDER (*Apocynaceae*) Beng.—*Karabi.*

Erect shrub up to 2·5 m high. Flowers fragrant showy.

Var : Alboplenum—white single.

Var : Black Prince—dark crimson, double.

Var : Carneum—flesh pink, single.

Var : Flore-pleno—pink double.

Var : Rosea—deep rosy red.

Nerium is a very common and beautiful tall shrub with dark green foliage. Flowers are borne profusely in the summer on the top of the branches and are visible from a distance. It is very quick growing and easily propagated from air layer or cutting.

NYCTANTHES ARBORTRISTIS (*Oleaceae*)

Eng.—*Night Jasmine*, Beng.—*Shefalika*, Hindi—*Harsinghar.*

Tall bushy shrub with drooping branches, reaching a height up to 4 m. Flowers open at night and start falling in the morning. It is a free flowering popular tall shrub producing numerous sweet-scented flowers in the autumn and winter. It grows better in semi-shade. Propagation by seed.

OCHNA SQUARROSA (*Ochnaceae*)

Beng.—*Ramdhan champa.*

Tall shrub 2·4 to 3·0 m woody. It can be grown at the back of shrubbery, flowering profusely in hot months. The red sepals and the black fruits on the red thalamus are also very attractive. Usually propagated by seeds and the seedlings are slow growing at the beginning but grow much faster after 1-2 years.

OCHNA WIGHTIANA

Plants about 2·4 m high. It is also a slow growing plant and flowers after 3 years. *O. wightiana* is more free flowering than *O. squarrosa* and yellow flowers appear all the year round but maximum in the summer. Persistent sepals and fruits appear to be more showy than the flowers. Usually grown from seeds.

OLEA FRAGRANS (*Oleaceae*)

Shrub 1·5 to 1·8 m high. Flowers yellowish sweet scented. It is a delicate plant and requires well drained rich soil in a semishady place. Flowers appear many times a year. Propagation by layering.

PENTAS (*Rubiaceae*)

Dwarf perpetual flowering shrub erect or decumbent about 40-60 cm high.

Var : Alba—Flower white.

Var : Carnea—Flower pale lavender pink.

Var : Lilacina—Flower mauve.

Var : Kermesina—Woody erect shrub 1·2 to 1·5 m. Le pubescent on both sides, dull green, flower red.

Pentas grows well in semi-shade, in few months it forms a bushy plant and bears clusters of flowers throughout the year. *P. kermesina* can tolerate more sun. Old branches and the plant should be pruned in the early monsoon in order to maintain the shape. *Pentas* propagates readily from cuttings and can also be grown as a pot plant.

PETREA ARBOREA (*Verbenaceae*)

A tall woody shrub about 2·5 m high. It is a slow-growing shrub thriving well in rich soil and full sun. It produces purplish blue flowers in several flushes in the summer. The plant is not easily obtained because of the difficulty in propagation, best method being grafting on to *P. volubilis*.

PHYLLANTHUS NIVOSUS (*Euphorbiaceae*)

Bushy shrub about 1·8 m high. Flowers small greenish.

Var : Roseopictus—leaves mottled with pink, purple as well as green and white.

These plants are grown in the gardens for attractive foliage and bushy habit. In variety 'Roseopictus' pink colour in leaf becomes more prominent in winter. Propagation by seeds or cuttings.

PLUMBAGO CAPENSIS (*Plumbaginaceae*)

Dwarf, bushy subscandent shrub 0·8 to 1·0 m. Flowers azure blue with a slender stalk.

Var : Alba—white flowers.

There are few shrubs so beautiful like a blue plumbago in flower. The plants remain in flower for about 8-9 months of the year. Plumbagos are very susceptible to waterlogging and should be planted on raised beds in full sun. It has been observed that application of bone meal greatly improves growth and flowering. Seeds are rarely formed and layering is the common method of propagation.

PLUMBAGO ROSEA

Dwarf shrub up to about 1 metre high with scandent branches. Flowers brick red. In *P. rosea* flowers are not produced so abundantly as in *P. capensis* and growth is also much slower. It grows well in partial shade, flowering starts in the winter and continues for 2–3 months. Propagation by cutting or division of clump.

POINSETTIA PULCHERRIMA (*Euphorbia pulcherrima*) (*Euphorbiaceae*)

A shrub reaching a height of 3 m, bracts crimson.

Var : Albida—bract creamy yellow.

Var : Rose Queen—lovely shade of pink.

The large coloured bracts are very showy and during the winter poinsettias give a bright appearance in the shrubbery. Yellow variety produces smaller plants compared to the varieties with crimson bracts.

Poinsettias are very fast growing and grow best in full sun. In shade or semishade the plants become shorter in size with few thin branches. These are propagated from cuttings. Varieties with single row of bracts are more vigorous in growth than those with double rows.

Medium-sized plants with large number of bracts in several rows appearing on a length of stem have been introduced.

POLYSCIAS BALFOURIANA (*Araliaceae*)

Compact and bushy shrub about 2 m high. Stem bronze green speckled with grey. Leaves with long slender petiole, leaflets usually 3, round or reniform, heart shaped at base, very obtuse or broad at apex, blunt, coarsely toothed and sometimes with small spine tipped secondary teeth ; margined or spotted with white.

Var : Viride—leaves entirely with green variegation.

Var : Albicans—leaves perfectly creamy white in colour.

Var : Lancasteri—leaves perfectly oblong in shape, pale creamy white with border and edges dark green.

POLYSCIAS FILICIFOLIA

Erect glabrous shrub about 2 metres or more. Stem and leaf stalks purplish, thickly marked with white lenticels. Leaves variable, bright green, midrib purplish.

Var : Marginata—leaflets margined pale cream.

Var : Maculata—leaflets broad and pale green colour.

Var : Leptophylla—leaflets long, narrow, very dark shiny green.

POLYSCIAS GUILFOYLEI

Erect bushy glabrous shrub upto 2 m, much branched. Leaves large often 40 cm or more long, with more or less spotted or lined petiole, clasping at base ; usually margined white and often splashed grey, terminal leaflet large.

Var : Viride—leaves perfectly green.

Var : Monostrosa—foliage dark green margined cream with serration of leaf exaggerated into spinose teeth.

Var : Fissum—leaves dark green, deeply and unevenly cleft.

Var : Variegata—pale apple green or ivory white ground, margined and splashed darker green.

Var : Alipurensis—leaflets small irregularly lobed, deeply serrated, dark green with a splash of golden yellow at centre of each leaflet.

Var : Victoriae—leaves small, much divided into small segments of various shapes and sizes, green, margin creamy white.

POOTIA GRANDIFLORA (*Apocynaceae*)

Tall spreading shrub about 3 m high with long branches. Flowers white or creamy, scented. Few flowers are produced at one time and can be recommended in large shrubbery. Flowers appear in the summer and rains. Propagation by air layering.

PORTLANDIA GRANDIFLORA (*Rubiaceae*)

Tall glabrous shrub growing about 2·5 m high, flowers funnel shaped 7·6 to 10·2 cm long 3·8 to 5·0 cm across.

It is a beautiful shrub and flowers all the year round. Much better growth has been observed in rich well-drained soil and when protected from western sun or in partial shade. Flowers large white with pinkish inside. Plants are usually raised from seeds or propagated by air layering.

PROSOQUERIA LATIFOLIA (*Rubiaceae*) Eng.—*Needle flower*.

A large evergreen shrub reaching a height of 4 m. This tall shrub bears numerous clusters of pendulous flowers in March-April and flowers well in full sun. It can be propagated from air layers.

PUNICA GRANATUM (*Lythraceae*) Beng.—*Dalim* ; Hindi—*Anar*.

Tall deciduous shrub, 2·4 to 3·0 m high.

Var : Florepleno—flowers double red.

Var : Albopleno—flowers double white.

Var : Nana—dwarf 30 cm, narrow leaves, bears scarlet double flower and small fruits.

Large scarlet flowers are produced in the hot months and also in rains. Interlaced growth and weak branches should be removed. The variety grown as ornamental plant does not produce fruits. Propagation by air layering. Seeds are produced in the variety Nana.

QUASSIA AMARA (*Simarubaceae*)

In bloom, it looks like scarlet Salvia. Tall shrub up to 2·5 m high, brown stem. Select a spot, cut oft from western sun and you will be able to save your plant in the hot summer. It produces long spike of red flowers in the summer months. Propagation by layering.

RANDIA MACRANTHA (*Rubiaceae*)

Bushy shrub about 1·8 to 2·4 m high. It produces long pendulous pale greenish yellow flowers in the late summer and early rains and grows well in partial shade. Propagation by layering.

RANDIA MACULATA (*Gardenia stanleyana*)

Tall evergreen shrub 2·4 to 3·0 m high, shows better growth in partial shade. Many long pendulous flowers appear in the hot months. Propagation by air layering.

RAUWOLFIA CANESCENS (*Apocynaceae*)

Bushy evergreen shrub about 1·5 to 1·8 m high. Flowers small, white. Fruits many, showy, green at first gradually turn red and then black.

The plant always bears numerous round berries of various colours because of difference in maturity. Very easy to grow from seeds.

RONDELETIA SPECIOSA (*Rubiaceae*)

Bushy shrub about 1·5 to 2·0 m high. Flowers many, vermillion with conspicuous yellow throat. *Rondeletia* is slow growing and thrives in sun and partial shade. Flowers last for a much longer time than most of the shrubs and flowering continues for about 7–8 months in a year. Propagation by air or ground layering.

RUELLIA ROSEA (*Acanthaceae*)

A red flowering undershrub suitable for shady place. It flowers well in the summer and rainy season and can be propagated from cuttings.

RUSSELIA JUNCEA (*Scrophulariaceae*)

A much branched peculiar shrub almost prostrate with few erect branches about 0·8 m high. Branches whorled, smooth, angular and grooved. The flowers are produced at the tips of whorled branches. It is a useful dwarf shrub for rockery and shrubbery. It grows quickly, covers the ground and produces scarlet flowers in the summer and rains. Propagation by cuttings.

RUSSELIA SARMENTOSA

It is also a twiggy straggling shrub reaching about 1·2 m. Bears numerous red flowers in the summer and rains.

SANCHEZIA NOBILIS (*Acanthaceae*)

Quick-growing plant with showy foliage and long spike of flowers, suitable for shade or semishade. Stem square, pinkish yellow, grows in zigzag way and the plant attains a height of 0·9 to 1·5 m. Leaves large, veins light yellow, surface green. Flowers yellow, very shortly stalked.

Sanchezia nobilis is a useful bushy shrub both in ground and pot. Cuttings root easily.

SOLANUM MACRANTHUM (*Solanaceae*)

About 3·0 to 3·6 m high, much branched with yellowish prickles on stem and petiole. Flowers large, bluish violet. *Solanum macranthum* is a large shrub with spreading branches, grows quickly and flowering starts in the second year. Branches are brittle and break off easily and the plant has to be replaced after 4 to 5 years. Plants are raised from seeds.

SOLANUM RANTONNETII

An erect shrub reaching 0·9–1·2 m in height. Flowers violet with yellow centre. It thrives and flowers in the plains but does not grow into a well-shaped plant. Flowering starts in April–May and continues up to August. Propagation by cutting.

SERISSA FOETIDA (*Rubiaceae*)

Much branched dwarf bushy shrub about a metre high. Flowers white light pink beneath, densely packed in rounded clusters. The plants become very showy when many white flowers appear in the summer and rains. Propagation by layering.

SOPHORA TOMENTOSA (*Leguminosae*)

A large very free flowering shrub 2·4 to 3·0 m high. Flowers yellow pea-shaped. Pods remain attached to the plants. Almost every branch produces flowers on terminal end during the summer and rains. Seedlings flower in the third year.

STACHYTARPHETA MUTABILIS (*Verbenaceae*)

A semiwoody perennial bushy plant, 1·5 m high. Flowers crimson fading to rose, open from below upwards. *Stachytarpheta Indica* is another useful shrub with blue flowers.

Both the species are very hardy and fairly quick-growing medium shrub, flowering in the rains. It can be multiplied from seed or cuttings.

STEMMADENIA BELLA (*Apocynaceae*)

It is a large much branched shrub, almost appears to be a small tree. *Stemmadenia bella* can be grown in large garden. It produces many scented white flowers like that of double *Tabernaemontana* in the summer. Usually propagated by air layering.

STROBILANTHES DYERIANUS (*Acanthaceae*)

A subscandent shrub growing up to 0·6 to 0·9 m. Flowers long, pale violet. One of the most colourful foliage shrub in cultivation. It should be grown in well-drained soil and semishade and easily propagated from cuttings.

STROBILANTHES GLOMERATUS

Dwarf shrub about 1·5 m high. Flowers bluish purple, funnel-shaped, bracts showy pinkish purple, persistent, which appear in the hot months. Pruning in rains keeps the plants in shape. Like the other species of *Strobilanthes*, it also roots easily from cuttings.

STROBILANTHES ISOPHYLLUS (*Goldfussia isophylla*)

A dwarf much branched shrub about 0·6 to 0·9 m high with swollen joints. Flowers long funnel-shaped, blue and white.

An evergreen dwarf shrub suitable in partial shade.

STROPHANTHUS DICHOTOMOUS (*Apocynaceae*)

Erect shrub with stout branches about 2·6 m. Flowers light brownish yellow with long twisted limbs. It is a very well-shaped shrub with round spreading top. Flowers appear aimost throughout the year but mostly remain concealed in the foliage. It is not a common shrub. Propagation by air or ground layering.

TABERNAEMONTANA CORONARIA (*Apocynaceae*)

Eng.—*Cape Jasmine*, Beng. and Hindi—*Tagar*.

Very popular shrub, greyish green stem, about 2·5 meters high.

Var : flowers single white. Tall.
Var : flowers single white. Dwarf.
Var : flore pleno—flowers double white. Tall.
Var : variegata—flowers white double, foliage variegated.

A beautiful and popular evergreen shrub grown in almost every garden. Flowers are produced throughout the year but more during the summer and rainy season. The conspicuous white flowers against a dark green background are very attractive. Propagated easily by cuttings and air layering.

TECOMA GAUDICHAUDI (*Bignoniaceae*)

A large erect shrub up to 4 m high. This tall shrub is very quick-growing and likes sun. Large number of golden yollow

fragrant flowers appear in the hot months, but the plant is always with some flowers on it. It is selected for the back row of the shrubbery. Propagation by air layering or seed.

TECOMA STANS

Erect shrub up to about 3 m, more bushy than *T. gaudichaudi*. The tall yellow flowering shrub grows very quickly and seedling flowers in the second year and continues all the year round. It can be grown in sun and semishade.

THESPESIA LAMPANS (*Malvaceae*)

Dwarf bushy shrub 50 to 80 cm high. Flowers yellow with glossy brown centre. An undershrub producing large showy flowers in all seasons of the year and grows fairly fast. Plants are raised from seeds which bear flowers in the same year.

THUNBERGIA ERECTA (*Acanthaceae*)

Hardy bushy shrub almost erect, deciduous in winter. Flowers dark violet.

THUNBERGIA NATALENSIS

Plants almost erect, bushy and compact. It is very hardy, branching starts from the bottom and forms a bushy plant. Blue flowers appear in the summer and rains and easily propagated from cuttings. It can also grow and flower in partial shade.

TURNERA ZEYLANICA (*Turneraceae*)

Straggling under shrub about 50–70 cm high. Flower solitary arising from petiole, sessile pale yellow with purplish brown centre. *Turnera* produces numerous flowers all the year round and grows in both sun and semishade. It thrives well even in poor soil or rock garden and is propagated by layers.

URARIA CRINITA (*Leguminosae*)

Erect shrub with few branches about 1·2 to 2·4 m high. Flowers lavender, pea-shaped. Inflorescence remains on the plant for few months after petals drop.

URARIA PICTA

Hardy shrub with few branches 1·2 to 1·5 m high. Flowers pea-shaped, purplish. Urarias are very hardy shrubs, more suitable for rock garden than in shrubbery. Usually grown from seeds and flowers appear in the winter months.

VINCA ROSEA (*Apocynaceae*) Beng.—*Nayantara.*

Much branched dwarf and bushy shrub about 50–80 cm high.

Var : Alba – flowers white with rose centre.

Var : Rosae— flowers rose.

These are very hardy dwarf shrubs, produce numerous showy white or rose coloured flowers all the year round. The plants are grown mostly in rock gardens in full sun and also in the shrubbery. Propagation by seeds and cutting.

VITEX AGNUSCASTUS (*Verbenaceae*)

A blue flowering tall deciduous shrub 3 m high, aromatic. In summer and rains large number of compact spikes of fragrant blue flowers appear very frequently. In winter the leaves shed off and the plants look dry. Propagation by air layering.

VITEX TRIFOLIA

A deciduous much branched tall shrub about 3 m high. Flowers lavender. A hardy shrub commonly grown in the garden but *V. agnuscastus* is more showy and free flowering. It also flowers in hot months and is propagated by air layering.

WORMIA BURBIDGII (*Dilleniaceae*)

Bushy shrub. Large shining leaves of *Wormia* are not very common in shrubs. It should be planted in partial shade otherwise the leaves show signs of scorching in hot summer. Large yellow flowers are produced in the summer and rains. Plants are multiplied by layering or from seeds.

CHAPTER V

Climbers

Climbers are very important ornamental plants and the beauty of any garden can be greatly increased by carefully selecting and planting them in a suitable place. The growth habit and mass of colour give charming appearance. Climbers are very commonly used on arches and pergolas but in cities their utility enhanced for the purpose of screening the premises from adjacent houses and maintaining privacy. Bare walls can be most effectively decorated by growing colourful climbers on it. Fences and trellis also provide scope for the beautiful climbers to grow and display. It is often felt that among the various types of ornamental plants least interest is taken on climbers and only few species or varieties are found growing in a locality. Even a good amateur gardener seldom knows more than a dozen climbers and practical information regarding a large number of these plants are not readily available. Attempts have been made to include description of plants of horticultural interest and their utility and practical hints on cultivation of a large number of climbers suitable for tropical gardens.

Botanically, plants which have special structure to climb on supports are defined as climber. Another type of climbing plants grow spirally around another plant or support and do not possess tendrils, rootlets, shoots or thorn. These are known as twiners e.g., *Echites, Chonemorpha, Clerodendron*. Creepers cannot grow vertically on their own e.g., Morning Glory. All these types of plants are commonly known as climbers.

Most of the flowering climbers require full sun for growth and flowering ; few climbers, however, grow well in shade and flower e.g., *Thunbergia grandiflora, Clerodendron splendens. Jacquemontia violacea. Asparagus racemosus, Scindapsus, Philodendrons, Monstera deliciosa, Syngonium, Cissus discolor* are grown for beautiful foliage in shade or partial shade.

Scindapsus (Pothos) are the most popular climber in shade and when grown on tree trunk, the leaves grow large with very attractive shades of green and yellow. Philodendrons are also grown on tree trunks in shady places. *Ficus repens* (Indian ivy) is the most popular and widely grown plant for covering bare walls or pedestrals. No support is needed as the roots from the node grip the walls.

SCREENING

Climbers which grow quickly and cover the space thickly are mostly used for this purpose. Railway creeper (*Ipomoea palmata*), *Antigonon* and *Vernonia* are commonly selected. *Vernonia* has neat growth but the flowers are not showy. Some heavy climbers with colourful bloom can be recommended. These are *Clerodendron splendens, Derris scandens, Thunbergia, Adenocalymna calycina, Passiflora. Bignonia gracilis, Rhyncospermum, Bougainvillea. Ficus stipulata* is also an ideal climber for screening shady place. *Jacquemontia* is a light flowering climber used for this purpose.

IDEAL CLIMBERS FOR PERGOLA

Quisqualis, Poiveria densiflorum, Banisteria laurifolia, Derris scandens, Clerodendron splendens, Petrea volubilis, Pyrostegia venusta, P. purpurea, Adenocalymna calycina, Bougainvillea.

ANNUAL CLIMBER

Important annual climbers are sweet pea and heavenly blue morning glory (*Ipomea coerulea*), *Mina lobata* with yellow and orange red spikes and *Quamoclit vulgaris* with white, pink and red flowers are also popular annual climbers. *Thunbergia alata*, (Black Eyed Susan) in white, pale and deep yellow with and without the dark eye are perennial but often grown as annual. *Clitoria*, though a perennial, is often grown as annual and raised from seeds and flowers in two months. Blue flowers are very common but white and mauve colours are also seen ; the double blue flowering variety is the best.

CLIMBERS FOR POT CULTURE

For growing climbers in pots, light climbers or those with

bushy growth should be selected. Climbers should be planted in large pots (20–30 cm) and given suitable support to allow the plant to grow. Among the perennial climbers *Clematis flammula, Bignonia purpurea, Solanum seaforthianum, Tristellatia australis, Adenocalymna alicea, Clerodendron balfouriana, C. thomsoniae, Clitoria* should be selected for pot cultivation. Bougainvilleas in pots are usually treated as shrubs.

SOIL

Loamy soil with good drainage suits well to most of the climbers. Decayed cow or stable manure or leaf mould should be incorporated in the soil of the pit about 50 cm in depth and diameter in case of large and heavy climbers. For light climber, the pit may be 30 cm deep and 25 cm in diameter. Bone meal and leafmould show very good result if cow-manure is not available. Distance of planting depends on the species or variety and the purpose for which the climbers are used. Quick growing heavy climbers are planted at a distance of 3 m for screening, while light climbers for the same purpose may be grown at 1 m. To cover fences or walls closer planting is recommended. *Vernonia* and *Ficus repens* are planted at a distance of 15–30 cm.

As the climbers do not grow erect without support, main stem and the branches should be tied up with the support. This helps to grow and cover the space quickly. Like other perennial plants planting of climbers can be done any time of the year, early monsoon is the best.

Manuring encourages growth and flowering of climbers. Bone meal or hoof and horn once or twice in the monsoon will be beneficial to the plants.

PRUNING

Pruning of climbers has been discussed in a separate Chapter.

ADENOCALYMNA CALYCINA (*Bignoniaceae*)

Heavy climber. Leaflets 3 or 2, the terminal one is sometime modified into tendril, ovate-elliptic 7–10 cm long, 4–5 cm broad, shining green leathery. Flowers large, scented, yellow in terminal raceme about 5 cm long, funnel-shaped, lobes 5, almost equal roundish and spreading about 6 cm. Large yellow flowers are produced for several months from March to June.

Adenocalymna allicea—produces lavender flowers profusely in several flushes during Autumn and Spring.

ANTIGONON LEPTOPUS (*Polygonaceae*) *Coral vine, Love's chain.*

Tuberous rooted quick-growing climber. Stem slender green. Leaves alternate, cordate or hastate ovate 7·6 to 12.7 cm long, almost smooth, netted veins very prominent, undulate on the margins, petiole long, tendrils axillary. Flowers on axillary or terminal raceme, rosy red. Perianths five, outer 3 broad, ovate about 3·2 cm long, inner 2 narrower and smaller.

It is commonly grown in the garden for the purpose of screening and produces numerous flowers starting from the hot months till the beginning of winter. When grown on arches or pergolas it has to be cleaned and pruned after flowering.

Var : Alba—a variety with white flowers and less growth.

Var : Aliporensis—flowers deep red.

Antigonon guatemalense—This species has broader leaves with hairs. The flowers are almost double the size of *A. leptopus*.

ARISTOLOCHIA ORNITHOCEPHALA (*Aristolochiaceae*) *The bird's head, Birthwort.*

An extensive climber. Leaves reniform obtuse with deep sinus and large auricles at base. Flowers pale or dingy purple, solitary and are borne on peduncles 16 to 20 cm long, netted or spotted dark purple, tube purple and upper lip violet within lips 10 cm long, lower 12 to 17 cm wide. The pouch and tube are often dark shining purple in colour.

Var : *Macrophylla*—Leaves large, cordate kidney-shaped, flowers larger.

This climber is quick-growing and has extensive growth on walls and trellis. It has an offensive odour and flowering starts in October-November and can be propagated from cuttings or seeds.

Combretum comosum

Jacquemontia violacea

Thunbergia grandiflora

Passiflora coerulea

ARISTOLOCHIA ELEGANS, *Calico flower*, Beng.—*Pakhilata.*

Slender climber, glabrous. Leaves reniform-cordate 5·0 to 7·6 cm wide and as much long with wide sinus and rounded basal lobes, obtuse. Flowers solitary long stalked, the tube yellow green 3·5 cm long, the limb cordate circular 7·5 cm diameter, purple and white blotched, white on the exterior, with yellow eye.

It is a small flowering species, an ideal light climber and grows freely from seeds. Curious pouch-shaped flowers are abundantly produced during the hot months. Unpleasant odour is absent in this species.

ARISTOLOCHIA GRANDIFLORA (*A. gigas*) *Pelican flower*, *Swan flower.*

A shrubby climber, leaves alternate, heart shaped, downy, slender pointed. Flowers solitary, the flower bud resembles the head of a pelican. The posterior wall of the tube expands into a hood which is pressed back upon the bulb ; the great expanded cordate-ovate limb about 20·0 to 25·0 cm across, wavy margined, purple blotched and veined terminating in a long and slender ciliated tail.

var. *Sturtevantii* has larger flowers and commonly grown.

It is a heavy climber producing large peculiar flowers with offensive odour and should be grown away from the house. Usually propagated by layer though seeds give rise to new plants. The flowers appear on strong growth in October-November and weak shoots may be removed.

ARTABOTRYS ODORATISSIMUS (*Annonaceae*) Beng.—*Kantali Champa.*

A large woody climber or half-scandent shrub. Leaves alternate oblong, oblong-lanceolate leathery, glabrous, dark green upper surface, 12 to 16 cm long 3 to 5 cm wide. Flower solitary, axillary or 2–3 flowers, greenish to yellow very fragrant. Petals flat lanceolate, about 5 cm long. Peduncles often hard and hooked.

This huge climber finds very little space in private gardens in cities. Strongly scented flowers announce the presence of the plant.

BANISTERIA CHRYSOPHYLLA (*Heteropteris chrysophylla*) (*Malpighiaceae*)

Large, evergreen twining climber. Branches woody, brown clothed with dense rusty hairs. Leaves opposite obovate, leathery, dark green, glabrous upper surface, lower surface and veins pubescent about 8 to 12 cm long, 5–9 cm wide. Flowers orange turning reddish in axillary panicles.

BANISTERIA LAURIFOLIA

A heavy evergreen climbing shrub. Branches terete covered with whitish matted hairs when young. Leaves opposite, elliptic, elliptic-obovate coriaceous, dark olive green above, 7·6 to 12·7 cm long about 6·3 cm wide. Flowers on trichotomous umbellate panicle, yellow about 1·2 cm across. Petals 5 alternate with the sepals, orbicular with a short claw 8 mm long, margins toothed.

Strong support is necessary for this extensive climber, it produces showy yellow flowers in hot months.

BEAUMONTIA GRANDIFLORA (*Apocynaceae*) *Nepal Trumpet creeper.*

A heavy evergreen climber with latex. Young shoots tinted rose and rusty haired. Leaves opposite, broad, oblong-ovate-apiculate, smooth and shining above, downy beneath, rusty hairy at first, 16·2 to 25·4 cm long, coriaceous. Flowers large many in terminal or axillary cymes. Calyx of 5 oblanceolate segments dark red or reddish brown in colour, about 3·8 cm long. Corolla 7·6 to 12·7 cm long, white greenish outside near base, throat dark, tube short, limb bell shaped, lobes 5 rounded acute about 8 cm across.

A huge dark evergreen climber grows very quickly and can tolerate light shade. It produces large funnel-shaped white flowers in February. Pruning should be done every year in rainy season. Propagation by layering.

BOUGAINVILLEA (*Nyctiginaceae*) Beng.—*Bagan bilash.*

It is a popular ornamental plant in Indian garden and grown both as shrub and climber. The genus is known to owe its origin to tropical and central America. As early as 1789 Commerson, a French Botanist named this genus *Bougainvillea* in honour of L. A. de Bougainvillea, the famous french navigator, based upon the specimen collected during Bougainville's voyage around the world.

It is a much branched woody plant. Leaves simple, alternate, generally ovate, oblong or lanceolate in shape, membranous to somewhat leathery in texture. Stiff thorns arise from the axil of many leaves. Flowers in a group of three, occasionally four or five on brightly coloured bract which are characteristically conspicuous feature of this genus, ovate or cordate in shape. Perianth tubular up to 2·5 cm long, opening in five rayed stars.

The different varieties of *Bougainvillea* belong to three natural species viz., *B. glabra*, *B. peruviana* and *B. spectabilis*, and two hybrids *B. buttiana* (*B. peruviana* × *B. glabra*) and *B. spectoglabra* (*B. spectabilis* × *B. glabra*).

BOUGAINVILLEA GLABRA

Plants almost glabrous with usually small straight spines. Leaves glabrous or with very short hairs, evenly elliptic to oblong-lanceolate. Bract elliptic or elliptic-lanceolate, cordate at the base ; perianth tubular distinctly swollen at the middle and 5 angled above the constriction. Few popular varieties—

(1) Dream	Bracts phlox purple
(2) Dr. R. R. Pal	Bracts large, bright crimson
(3) Formosa	Bracts mauve, veins pinkish
(4) Gopal	Bracts dark crimson
(5) Partha	Bracts orange when young, turning spirea red, perianth whitish
(6) Refulgens	Bracts cyclamen purple ; perpetual flowering

(7)	Snow Queen	Bracts white
(8)	Trinidad	Bracts pinkish white, perianth greenish

BOUGAINVILLEA PERUVIANA

Spreading spiny plants ; spines straight when young, curved on maturity. Leaves broadly ovate, glabrous or minute hairs present, cuneate at the base. Bracts smaller than those of *B. glabra*. Varieties—

(1)	Lady Hudson	Bracts pale pink
(2)	Princes Margaret Rose	Bracts fuchsia purple, perianth tube greenish purple.

BOUGAINVILLEA SPECTABILIS

The branches and shoots hairy, spines woody up to 3·5 cm long. Leaves ovate, densely tomentose on both surfaces. Flowers arise laterally from the branches. Bracts ovate to elliptic in shape, cordate at about 3·5 cm long and 3 cm wide. Perianth tubular hairy about 2·5 cm long ending in 5 star-shaped lobes. Few popular varieties—

(1)	Mrs. Frazer	Bracts phlox purple, perianth tube pinkish green
(2)	Purple robe	Bracts purple
(3)	Red glory	Bracts ruby red, perianth scarlet
(4)	Tomato	Bracts spiral red, perianth tube reddish

BOUGAINVILLEA BUTTIANA

Branches usually hairy when young, become glabrous on maturity. Leaves broadly ovate or cordate. Spines of medium size, up to 1·5 cm long. Bracts comparatively smaller and falling off earlier than in other species, elliptical ; perianth tube constricted at the middle. Few popular varieties—

(1)	Mrs. Butt	Bracts cardinal red
(2)	Louis Wathen	Bract, brick-red, perianth tube without star, a sport from Scarlet Queen
(3)	Mrs. McLean	Young bracts orange, old ones pale mauve.
(4)	Scarlet Queen	Bracts cardinal red
(5)	Scarlet Queen Variegata	Leaves variegated with various shades of yellow and pink. Bracts like Scarlet Queen.

BOUGAINVILLEA SPECTOGLABRA

Dr. R. E. Holttum reported that first of these hybrids developed by natural crossing at Tenerife in about 1900. Hybrids of this group were raised in the West Indies, in Calcutta by S. Percey Lancaster, in Queensland by W. F. Turley. Good cultivars are Turleys' Special, Mrs. Lancaster, Aida, Jubilee, Maharaja of Mysore and Mrs. H C. Buck. Variety Mary Palmer originated in India as a bud sport from Mrs. H. C. Buck and Thima from Mary Palmer.

DOUBLE VARIETIES

Several varieties originated recently by bud mutation in the Philippines from *B. buttiana*. In these varieties, instead of one flower at the base of each primary bract there is a little shoot bearing a variable number of smaller bracts of the same colour with or without rudimentary flowers on some of them. Four such varieties have been introduced to this country.

var. Mahara — Bracts deep purple.

var. Roosevelt's delight—Salmon with orange shade.

var. Double White

var. Double Pink

bougainvillea grows in all types of soil, varying from sandy to clayey, but sandyloam is the best. It does not prefer fertile or moist soil, dry atmosphere favours flowering. Too much humidity and moisture in the soil during autumn and winter encourage growth of leaf. Once established in the ground, it seldom needs watering even during the hot months. Flowering is better in pot plants, if watering can be restricted.

Bougainvillea should not be manured heavily, bone meal helps in growth and flowering of pot plants. Superphosphate after the rains will encourage flowering in plants in ground and pot.

Flowers appear on current year's shoot and pruning is necessary to encourage flowering and to keep plants in shape. If left untouched, it produces numerous thin shoots which do not bear flowers and these branches should be removed leaving few mature shoots of medium thickness. Vegetative growth takes place almost throughout the year but more vigorously in the rainy season. Pruning should be done in May-June after the plants have finished flowering. In order to reduce the height of plants, rejuvenate old plants in ground, severe pruning is recommended at a height of 1 to 1·5 metres. Watershoots which often arise after pruning, more frequently in the rainy season, should be removed from the base.

For growing Bougainvilleas in pots the size of the pots should not be very large for the plants, pot-bound condition favours flowering. They are transferred in larger pots when the roots completely fill the pots. The plants are propagated by cuttings and layering.

CAMOENSIA MAXIMA (*Leguminosae*)

Vigorous evergreen shrubby climber ; stem woody, green glabrous ; leaf trifoliate, leaflets—obovate glabrous coriaceous abruptly slender pointed, 7·6 to 10·2 cm long margin undulate. Flowers large papilionaceous 4 to 8 flowers on axillary peduncles, white tinged gold and fringed at the edges of the petals about 7·6 cm wide. *Camoensia maxima* bears long sprays of flowers in the hot months.

CAMPSIS GRANDIFLORA (*Bignoniaceae*) *Large flowered Tecoma, Chinese Trumpet Creeper.*

Deciduous climber. Leaves opposite, compound; leaflets 7 to 9 ovate or ovate-oblong coarsely toothed glabrous 3·8 to 7·6 cm long. Flowers in 6 to 12 flowered terminal pendulous panicle. Corolla 5·0 cm long, shorter and broader than *C. radicans*, deep orange and red widening trumpet-like from a funnel-shaped tube, cut half way into 5 rounded lobes.

It is a very hardy climber and produces large number of orange scarlet flowers in the rainy season. It should be pruned in winter when deciduous. Very easily propagated by root suckers and cuttings.

CAMPSIS JASMINOIDES

A climbing shrub. Leaves opposite, compound; leaflets 5 to 9 elliptic to lanceolate entire, glabrous, dark green in colour 2·5 to 3·8 cm long. Flowers in many flowered axillary or terminal corymbose panicles. Corolla tubular, expanding into 5 almost round lobes 5·0 cm across white or rosy pink, colour deeper in throat.

It is an ideal climber for a small garden, evergreen and flowers many times in summer. This species grows well on small trellis.

CAMPSIS RADICANS, *Trumpet Vine*

A scandent deciduous climber clasping by means of adventitous roots. Leaves opposite, compound; leaflets 9 to 11 ovate to ovate-oblong 3·8 to 6·3 cm long, glossy green above downy on veins beneath, toothed. Flowers 4 to 12 in terminal clusters, trumpet shaped. Corolla 6·3 to 7·6 cm long, orange in colour with a scarlet limb about 3·8 cm wide at the mouth with 5 short, broad rounded lobes.

It is an ideal climber for covering bare walls as the aerial roots cling on the walls. It remains constantly in bloom in the rainy season and is easily propagated by cutting or root suckers.

var. *Gulfoylii*—A hybrid between *C. grandiflora* and *C. radicans* is intermediate in colour producing pretty apricot terracotta flowers.

CHONEMORPHA MACROPHYLLA (*Apocynaceae*)

An evergreen heavy climber. Stem pubescent with white latex. Leaves opposite, orbicular or obovate upto 25 cm long and 10 to 15 cm wide, wedge-shaped at base, pale and hairy beneath. Flowers white, fragrant, borne in terminal cymes. Corolla tube very short 6·3 cm across, white, yellowish in the throat.

It is suitable for pergola or other strong support. Fragrant white flowers appear in abundance, during the hot months. Propagation by layering.

CLEMATIS FLAMMULA (*Ranunculaceae*)

A slender low-growing climber. Leaves usually bipinnate dark green, often trifoliate ; leaflets narrowly lanceolate entire, glabrous 1·3 to 3·2 cm long. Flowers very fragrant, small 1·9 to 2·5 cm across pure white in loose panicle upto 20-30 cm long, Sepals 4-linear oblong.

Clematis flammula has less growth but flowers heavily on large panicles in the early rains. It is ideal for small gardens on low walls or wire nettings. It likes porous soil and partial shade. Propagation by layering.

CLEMATIS PANICULATA

A vigorous deciduous climber. Leaves opposite, compound; leaflets 3 to 5 ovate cordate 3·8 to 7·6 cm long entire, glabrous. Flowers white, fragrant in axillary or terminal panicles about 7·6 to 10·2 cm long. Sepals 4 oblong about 3·2 cm across.

Clematis Paniculata is a hardy climber and often grown on strong trellis. Numerous star-shaped flowers appear in summer and early rains.

CLERODENDRON SPLENDENS (*Verbenaceae*)

Vigorous evergreen climber. Stem slender woody glabrous slightly angled. Leaves simple opposite, oblong cordate or elliptic, dark green glossy 10 to 16 cm long. Flowers scarlet in terminal or axillary corymbose clusters about 12 to 18 cm wide. Corolla tube very slender 1·8 cm long, limb about 2·5 cm across.

It is a quick-growing climber producing many large clusters of scarlet flowers during winter and also useful for screening. Heavy pruning should be done in the rains. Propagation can be done by separation of root suckers and layering.

CLITORIA TERNATEA (*Leguminosae*) *Mussel Shell Climber*, Beng.—*Aparajita*.

A twining climber. Leaves pinnately compound, alternate; leaflets 5 sometime 7, oval or oblong, terminal one is the largest. Flowers solitary blue about 3 cm with beautiful marking on the standard and yellowish inside. Pods long with 5 to 6 seeds.

Double blue is better than the single, white and mauve are also grown. Though a perennial it is easily raised from seeds annually and flowering starts in 2 months.

COMBRETUM COMOSUM (*Poiveria comosum*) (*Combretaceae*)

Shrubby climber. Stem woody ; young shoot green covered with brown hairs. Leaves simple, opposite, elliptic 7 to 10 cm long, 3 to 5 cm broad. Flowers orange red in compact terminal spikes, usually remain horizontal with flowers only on the upper part of the spike. Corolla tube 1·3 cm long, 4 triangular lobes.

Combretum comosum has denser foliage than *C. densiflorum* and bears dull coloured spikes from February to June.

COMBRETUM DENSIFLORUM (*Poiveria densiflorum*)

Climbing shrub. Stem woody brownish, young shoots green, glabrous. Leaves simple, opposite oblong-lanceolate, 8 to 15 cm long, shining green on both surfaces. Flowers in loose flat, terminal panicle, closely arranged almost sessile, brilliant scarlet ; petals about 1 cm across, stamens 10.

Because of shrubby habit *C. densiflorum* is difficult to train on pergolas and arches. It bears flat spikes of scarlet flowers from November to May.

CONGEA TOMENTOSA (*Verbenaceae*)

Strong woody climber. Stem woody, brown, tomentose when young. Leaves opposite ovate or ovate-elliptic, leathery, tomentose on both surface more on the lower surface, 9 to 12 cm long 5 to 9 cm wide. Inflorescence, a large compound terminal panicle, main branches pubescens, opposite. Peduncles supported by bract at the top, 3 bracteoles velvety tomentose on the upper surface.

This heavy climber is fairly fast growing and requires strong support. Numerous pinkish mauve bracts appear during December to March.

DERRIS SCANDENS (*Leguminoseae*) Beng.—*Noalata.*

Vigorous, evergreen, woody climber. Leaves compound; leaflets 9 to 15, terminal one, ovate or elliptic, dark green glabrous, coriaceous, 2·5 to 6·3 cm long. Flowers numerous pinkish white, in long axillary raceme ; standard white tinged pink about 1·3 cm long, wings pink shorter. Pod numerous about 3·8 cm long.

It is a heavy climber and requires strong support. The plant bears large number of spikes of numerous pinkish white flowers from March to August. Grown from seeds or propagated by layering.

DILLENIA SARMENTOSA (*Tritiacera sarmentosa*) (*Dilleniaceae*)

A large evergreen climber. Stem stout, woody, brownish scaly bark. Leaves alternate. obvate leathery, both surfaces rough dentate, 12 to 18 cm long, 4 to 8 cm wide, dark green. Flower small scented, white, in terminal panicles.

It has a very attractive evergreen foliage. Sweet-scented flowers appear in the summer months.

FARADAYA SPLENDIDA (*Verbenaceae*)

Tall woody, heavy climber ; stem green. Leaves large ovate, 6-10 cm long leathery. Flowers white in terminal panicle, corolla tube about 3 cm long, lobes 4, one larger than the others. Stamens 4 long. Flowers appear in the summer months.

HIPTAGE MADHABLATA (*Malpighiaceae*) Beng.—*Madhabilata.*

A large evergreen climbing shrub. Stem woody dark brown. Leaves opposite, elliptic, 10·2 to 16·2 cm long about 7·6 cm wide coriaceous. Flowers white on terminal or axillary panicles, terminal ones are larger than axillary panicles. Petals 5 silky outside, 4 equal in size white in colour, fifth one smaller pale yellow.

Another heavy climber with sweet-scented yellow and white flowers. Flowers appear in February.

HOLMSKIOLDIA SANGUINEA (*Verbenaceae*) *Cup and Saucer Plant.*

A straggling shrub. Leaves opposite, ovate or elliptic-ovate, 5·0 to 10·0 cm long, dentate, dark green above pale beneath. Flowers in terminal or axillary raceme or panicle. Calyx gamosepalous bell shaped about 1·8 cm diameter, reddish or orange in colour. Corolla tubular 2·5 cm long, 2 lipped. Fruit a drupe, ovoid in shape.

It has an untidy growth. The flowers are produced in large numbers in winter and plant should be grown in full sun. Pruning should be done closely after flowering. Propagation by layering or cutting.

IPOMOEA LOBATA (*Convolvulaceae*)

An annual climber. Leaves cordate with a broad sinus, 3 lobed. Flowers orange or crimson many on spiral cyme, 1·3 to 1·9 cm wide when open ; corolla salver shaped, tubular below forming a bag-like limb with 5 lobes. Stamens protrude through the corolla.

IPOMOEA PALMATA, *Railway Creeper.*

A perennial vigorous climber. Leaves 5·0 to 7·6 cm in diameter, cut nearly to the base 5 to 7 lobes, entire, elliptic or lanceolate. Flowers purple, 5·0 to 6·3 cm across often 3 flowered cyme. Corolla campanulate, colour deeper in the throat.

IPOMOEA PURPUREA, *Common Morning Glory.*

It is also a quick-growing climber. Leaves entire, ovate-cordate, 7·6 to 12·7 cm long pubescent on both surfaces. Flowers large funnel shaped, few on axillary peduncles, about 6·3 to 7·6 cm across, white, pale blue or purple.

IPOMOEA RUBRO-COERULEA

Another annual climber of extensive growth. Leaves alternate cordate 6·3 to 10·2 cm long, wavy surface. Flowers 3 to 4 on axillary peduncles. Corolla funnel shaped about 7·6 to 10·2 cm across, azure blue with five angles.

Scarlet and white flowers, single and double, commonly grown in the winter months from seeds.

JACQUEMONTIA VIOLACEA (*Convolvulaceae*)

Handsome light climber. Stem slender green. Leaves alternate, cordate, 2·5 to 4·4 cm long, membranous slightly pubescent. Flowers violet blue, 5 to 12 on loose cymose cluster. Corolla short, funnel form about 3·2 cm across, 5 angled.

It is a light type of blue flowering climber, very suitable for neat screening in semishade. Flowers are produced almost throughout the year. The plant has to be replaced after 3 years.

JASMINUM HUMILE (*Oleaceae*)

A shrubby climber. Leaves alternate, compound imparipinnate ; leaflets 3-5 elliptic or ovate, terminal one larger than laterals. Flowers yellow on terminal corymbose panicle. Calyx tube very short 5 lobed. Corolla tube about 2 cm long 5 lobed ; lobes broadly ovate reflexed when fully open about 2 cm across.

Like few other species of *Jasminum*, *J. humile* is grown on trellis or suitable support. This evergreen plant does not flower very well in lower Bengal. Flowers usually appear in the summer and pruning is done after flowering.

LONICERA HILDEBRANDIATA (*Caprifoliaceae*) *Giant Honeysuckle.*

A huge evergreen climber. Leaves opposite, broadly ovate 7·6 to 12·7 cm long 5·0 to 8·9 cm wide. Flowers are borne in pairs on leaf axils forming a terminal raceme ; corolla 4 to 5 cm long, slender tube, about 5 cm across creamy white turning orange.

LONICERA JAPONICA *Japanese Honeysuckle.*

It is an evergreen quick-growing climber. Leaves opposite ovate or oblong ovate 3·8 to 7·6 cm long, entire downy on both sides. Flowers borne in axillary pairs, white changing to yellow with age, about 3·8 cm long.

MELODINOUS MONOGYNOUS (*Apocynaceae*)

This heavy climber is often grown as a straggling bush. Branches glabrous green but turning brown when old. Leaves, opposite, elliptic or oblong-lanceolate, glabrous 10 to 14 cm long. Flowers white, scented on trichotomously branched terminal panicles. Corolla tube 2 cm long ending in five ovate lobes, spreading about 2·5 cm across.

An evergreen heavy climber often grows as a bush. White vanilla scented flowers appear during March-May.

ODONTADENIA SPECIOSA (*Apocynaceae*)

Large shrubby climber. Leaves opposite, oblong-ovate, leathery, smooth, dark green 12 to 18 cm long. Flowers large yellow, scented in loose cyme. Corolla tube funnel shaped, lobes about 6 cm across.

Odontadenia speciosa bears large, yellow delicately scented flowers in loose cyme almost throughout the year.

PASSIFLORA COERULEA (*Passifloraceae*)

A vigorous climber. Stipule leafy, cordate, toothed. Leaves divided nearly to the petiole into 5 lanceolate or lance-elliptic segments 10·2 to 16·2 cm across. Flowers solitary, large 7·6 cm across, axillary. Bracts large ovate-cordate about 2·5 cm in length. Petals 5 oblong-obtuse, pale pink in colour. Corona 5·0 cm across, outer filaments blue at top, white in the middle and purple at base.

PASSIFLORA EDULIS

Woody, strong and spreading climber. Stem angular slightly downy or glabrous. Tendrils axillary, long simple. Leaves alternate large, 10·2 to 12·7 cm long and wide deeply 3 lobed ; lobes ovate, glandular, toothed. Flowers solitary terminal or axillary, 3 leafy bracts, 5 lobed greenish with short crown. Petals 5 about 2 cm long, oblong white often tinted with purple. Corona in several rows white in the upper half, violet or purple below. Fruit globular, oblong, thickly purple dotted.

PASSIFLORA KERMESIANA

Glabrous climber. Stem slender. Leaves alternate 5·0 to 9·8 cm long 5·0 to 10·2 cm wide ; 3 lobed, lobes oblong ovate sometimes faintly toothed purplish beneath. Flowers 6·3 cm across, stalk 7·6 to 10·2 cm long. Sepals and petals scarlet, narrow, oblong. Corona 2·5 cm wide, outer filaments violet, purple inner ones united into a short tube.

This red flowering species does not flower well in hot and humid regions. Leaves are yellowish green and growth is also slower than other species.

PASSIFLORA LAURI, *Jamaica Honeysuckle.*

Strong glabrous climber. Leaves oblong to broadly ovate-oblong, 7·6 to 12·7 cm long 3·8 to 7·6 cm wide leathery. Flowers fragrant 5·0 to 7·6 cm wide ; sepals narrow oblong, green outside, red within ; petals red. Corona with the outer filaments 1·8 cm long, purple but banded with red, blue and white.

PASSIFLORA QUADRANGULARIS, *Giant Granadilla.*

Strong glabrous climber. Stem stout, 4 angled, winged. Leaves alternate, broadly ovate, cordate 10·2 to 20·3 cm long, 7·6 to 10·2 cm wide, white glabrous. Flowers solitary, axillary 6·3 cm across. Sepals ovate 4·4 cm long greenish outside, pink inside. Petals 5 oblong, ovate pink or mauve outside, white or blue inside. Corona 5 ranked with reddish purple and white at the base, blue in the middle ; fruits oblong-ovoid, yellow, longitudinally 3 grooved up to 20·3 cm long, edible.

PERGULARIA ODORATISSIMA (*Asclepiadaceae*) *West Coast Creeper*, Beng.—*Kunja Labanga Lata.*

Evergreen light climber. Leaves alternate cordate, membraneous glabrous, 4 to 6 cm long. Flowers, greenish yellow, scented, on umbels. Corolla tube oblong about 1·5 cm, lobes 5 salver shaped about 1·4 cm across wooly within.

The species of *Pergularia* produces greenish yellow flowers in clusters almost throughout the year.

PETREA VOLUBILIS (*Verbenaceae*) *Purple Wreath.*

A woody climber with greyish bark. Leaves opposite ovate-elliptic or ovate, coriaceous dull green above, brighter green beneath, rough 7·6 to 17·8 cm long, 6·3 to 10·2 cm wide entire. Flowers many on long drooping receme about 22 to 30 cm long. Calyx tube very short, 5 lobes oblong lilac or bluish in colour about 1·9 cm long. Corolla tube 0·8 cm long, five-lobed deep blue in colour.

Petrea volubilis is a shrubby climber and bears long spikes of star-shaped purple blue flowers in the hot months. It grows and flowers best in full sun. Propagation by layering or cutting.

PORANA PANICULATA (*Convolvulaceae*)

Strong shrubby climber. Leaves alternate, cordate 7·6 to 12·7 cm long, glabrous above, pubescent beneath, undulate margin. Flowers numerous on panicles terminating each branchlet. Corolla glabrous, campanulate white, small.

Flowers appear in great profusion in December. The heart-shaped foliage is grey green in colour and tiny funnel-shaped scented flowers are massed in sprays.

PORANA RACEMOSA (*Snow Wreath*)

Evergreen perennial climber. Branches almost woody, green when young with raised white warts forming a rough surface. Leaves simple alternate, cordate, dark green glossy 3·5 cm long. Flowers white, star-shaped in small raceme. Corolla tubular, lobes 5 lanceolate.

Porana racemosa bears masses of small white flowers during the summer and rains.

PYROSTEGIA MAGNIFICA (*Bignoniaceae*)

A shrubby climber. Leaves compound opposite consisting of 2 leaflets ; leaflets obovate-oblong 5·0 to 8·9 cm and 5·0 cm wide, dull green on both surfaces. Flowers large borne on axillary or terminal cyme, purplish violet in colour. Corolla tubular funnel shaped 5·0 cm long ending in 5 orbicular lobes about 5·0 cm across.

It is not a popular climber in Indian garden. Flowers are few to give any showy appearance. Propagation by cuttings or layering.

PYROSTEGIA PURPUREA

An evergreen climber. Leaves compound, leaflets 3 ovate to ovate-oblong about 5·0 to 7·6 cm long mostly toothed bright green above paler beneath. Flowers 4 to 10 rosy purple in axillary cyme. Corolla funnel shaped about 5·0 cm long, lobes 5 spreading about 6 cm across.

This ideal climber produces flowers in large bunches 6 to 8 times a year in the summer and rains and should be grown on trellis or low walls. Propagated from layers.

PYROSTEGIA TWEEDIANA, *Cat's claw.*

Slender evergreen climber. Leaves opposite compound. Leaflets 2 lanceolate and pointed cordate, 7·6 cm or less in length with terminal 3-partite clawlike tendril. Flowers trumpet shaped beautifully borne in pairs, bright yellow with deeper yellow lines in the throat. Corolla with a short tube about 5·0 cm long, the limb of rounded spreading lobes 5·0 to 6·5 cm across.

The climber forms masses of dark green foliage and yellow flowers on the tall trees or strong support. Propagation by seed or layering.

PYROSTEGIA VENUSTA *Golden Shower.*

A deciduous climber climbing extensively by means of tendrils. Leaves compound, two leaflets with a terminal branched tendril or sometimes with three leaflets ; leaflets ovate or ovate oblong 5·0 to 7·5 cm long, glabrous on the upper surface. Flowers many, drooping on corymbose cyme. Corolla tubular about 6·3 cm long golden, gradually expanding in five linear lobes, lobes curve backwards and form two leaps when flowers open.

It is one of the best flowering climbers producing showers of golden flowers in January-February. It is slow growing and gives a showy appearance on an eastern wall. Propagation by layering.

QUISQUALIS INDICA (*Combretaceae*) *Rangoon Creeper.*

A large, vigorous climber. Stem green and become light brown with age. Leaves opposite, oblong or elliptic, entire membranous about 7·6 cm long, hairy on the veins. Flowers are borne on pendulous racemes axillary or terminal. The flowers are first white, turn pink and finally red. Corolla tube slender greenish 5·0 cm long, five petals expanded about 1·8 to 2·5 cm across.

Quisqualis indica is a common climber, very hardy and quick growing. Numerous bunches of drooping pink, white and red flowers appear during the hot months and early rains.

ROUPELLIA GRATA (*Solanaceae*)

A large evergreen shrubby climber. Stem woody, dark when old. Leaves opposite, elliptic, oblong, glabrous, coriaceous entire 5·0 to 8 cm long, 3·8 to 6·3 cm wide, dark green above. Flowers large in few flowered cyme, white, tints of purple, scented about 3·8 cm long and across ; petals 5 broad, obovate, margin fringed. Buds deep purple. This large growing heavy shrubby climber require strong support and much space. It is suitable for trellis and pergolas and flowers in the hot months. Propagation by cutting or layering.

SOLANUM JASMINOIDES (*Solanaceae*) *Potato Vine*

A slender shrub. Leaves alternate, lanceolate or ovate lanceolate, up to 4·4 cm long entire, glabrous on both surfaces.

Flowers bluish white star shaped arranged in terminal cymose panicle. Corolla 5 lobed about 2 cm across.

S. jasminoides grows well in porous soil, cooler climate and prefers partial shade. Flowers appear in the hot months.

SOLANUM SEAFORTHIANUM (*Blue Potato Creeper*)

Slender, slightly woody climber. Leaves alternate with 3 leaflets, 3·8 to 5·0 cm long or the upper ones simple lanceolate, ovate-lanceolate, entire or undulate margins. Flowers numerous in long drooping axillary panicles. Corolla 5, light purple or blue, star-shaped about 2·5 cm across.

This light evergreen climber produces clusters of flowers throughout the hot months and likes porous soil.

SOLANUM WENDLANDII

Tall climbing shrub with few scattered prickles on stem, branches and petiole. Leaves bright green, variable, upper most simple oblong, cordate or 3 lobed, sometimes with side lobes or otherwise cut ; lower on branches 16·2 to 25·4 cm long, pinnate below with 4 to 6 pairs of leaflets or lobes which are ovate or oblong. Flowers lilac blue, 3·8 cm across in large cymes.

It should be grown in porous soil. The flowers are borne, in large sprays from April to August. Propagation by layering.

STEPHANOTIS FLORIBUNDA (*Asclepiadaceae*) *Madagascar Chaplet flower*.

Slender climber. Leaves opposite, oval or ovate-elliptic, thick shining green 6·3 to 8·9 cm long. Flowers pure white, highly scented produced in large bunches. Corolla tube 2·5 cm long, segments ovate-oblong about 1·3 cm across.

It is one of the finest light climber bearing strongly scented waxy white flowers during the hot and wet season. Propagation by layering.

STIGMAPHYLLON CILIATUM (*Malpighiaceae*)

A slender climber, young stem covered with dense white hairs. Leaves opposite, ovate or nearly round deeply cordate at base, glaucous. Flowers yellow on umbel like corymbs, axillary, with 3-4 flowers. Petal 5 about 3 cm across, 4 equal in size, one smaller, all clawed, limbs round oblong fringed.

STIGMAPHYLLON PERIPLOCIFOLIUM

Stem cylindrical, brown. Young stem and leaves covered with hairs, glabrous with age. Leaves opposite elliptic-oblong, leathery 3·8 to 7·6 cm long, two glands at the base of the lamina. Flowers yellow arranged in raceme, about 2 cm in diameter. Petals 5, four subequal in size, the fifth smaller.

THUNBERGIA ALATA (*Acanthaceae*) *Black-eyed Susan.*

Annual climber. Stem square, hairy. Leaves opposite ovate cordate, petiole winged, up to 5·0 cm long and 3·8 cm wide, rough pubescent. Flowers solitary on axillary peduncles. Bracteoles 2 spathe like ovate, pubescent on both surface. Corolla tube infundibuliform ending in 5 large segments.

var. Alba—white with a blackish centre.

var. Aurantiaca—bright orange with dark centre.

var. Sulphurea—sulphur yellow.

Annual climber of various colours grown from seeds.

THUNBERGIA FRAGRANS

A slender climber. Leaves with wingless petioles, ovate-lanceolate or triangular ovate-cordate at base upto 6·3 cm long and 3·8 cm wide angularly toothed. Flowers axillary white without scent. Corolla tube narrow, limb spreading 2·5 cm in diameter.

THUNBERGIA GRANDIFLORA

Large, woody climber. Leaves opposite, broadly ovate, angularly cordate and toothed or lobed, rough on both surfaces about 10·2 cm long and 7·6 to 10·2 cm broad. Flowers solitary or in short stout racemes. Corolla tube short, conical at base ending in 5 lobes about 7·6 cm across, whitish, lower half shading into the blue lobes, yellow inside.

var. Alba—flowers white.

It is a heavy climber and should be grown on very strong

support. The hanging sprays of flowers, blue or white are generously produced from March throughout the rains.

THUNBERGIA LAURIFOLIA

A shrubby climber. Stem terete, smooth except when young. Leaves opposite, ovate, oblong—lanceolate rounded at the base, entire or slightly toothed, 15 cm long about 6·3 cm wide. Flowers borne in axillary or terminal raceme. Corolla tube cylindrical, swelling above, funnel-shaped with spreading large 5 lobed limb about 6·3 cm across pale blue, white or yellow in the throat.

THUNBERGIA MYSORENSIS

Climbing shrub with long slender branches. Leaves opposite, elliptic or oblong—lanceolate, entire or somewhat distantly toothed 10·3 to 16·2 cm long, 3·2 to 5·0 cm broad. Flowers on long pendulous raceme, yellow. Corolla 3·8 cm long purple enclosed by the spathe like bract ; limb 4 lobed, upper lip erect, concave with reflexed side lobes, lower lip of 3 subequal spreading lobes, 5·0 cm across.

TRACHELOSPERMUM JASMINOIDES (*Apocynaceae*) *Star Jasmine.*

A large evergreen climbing shrub with white latex. Leaves opposite, elliptic-lanceolate glabrous, entire glossy, 2·5 to 3·8 cm long. Flower small, white, fragrant, on few flowered cyme. Corolla tube short about 0·8 cm long inflated above, ending in five lobes, spreading with wavy and reflexed margins.

It grows well in partial shade and is suitable for screen. Scented flowers are produced in the hot months.

TRISTELLATIA AUSTRIALIS (*Malpighiaceae*)

Very beautiful climber with prominent lenticel. Leaves opposite ovate or ovate-oblong, 6·0 cm long, 1·9 to 3·8 cm wide, dull green, entire glabrous. Flowers in terminal raceme 7·6 to 16·2 cm long, opposite pairs, petal yellow ovate-oblong about 1·3 cm long, filament red.

It is an ideal light evergreen climber and produces numerous star-shaped yellow flowers throughout the year.

UVARIA ODORATA *(Annonaceae)*

It is a shrubby climber. Stem stout; leaves alternate, ovate-lanceolate, glabrous, upper surface shining, lower surface downy, margin undulate, 7 to 12 cm long, 2·5 to 4·0 cm wide. Flowers solitary, yellowish green, scented, petals 6 in 2 rows.

Uvaria can also be grown as a bush. It produces scented pale yellow flowers in the rainy season. The fragrance is milder than the flowers of Artabotrys. Propagation by layering.

VALLARIS HEYNEI *(Apocynaceae)*

A climber with dark grey bark. Leaves opposite, elliptic or oblong 5·0 to 10·0 cm long upto 3·8 cm wide, slender pointed. Flowers white, fragrant in axillary cyme, 3-6 flowered. Corolla tube short narrow cylindrical ending in five orbicular petals 1·3 cm across.

An evergreen strong growing climber, bearing greenish white sweet-scented flowers from February to April. Propagation by layering.

VERNONIA ELAEGNIFOLIA *(Compositae)*

Very quick growing evergreen climber. Stem pendulous usually not much branched, whitish when young. Leaves simple alternate, lanceolate, broader at the upper portion, irregularly toothed margin. Flowers white in small axillary head.

It is an useful and popular climber for screening. The pendulous branches hang close to the support and form a neat screen. It is very quick growing and the cuttings root easily in the monsoon.

WISTERIA SINENSIS *(Leguminosae)*

Large woody climber. Leaves odd pinnately compound alternate, pale green ; leaflets 5 pairs, ovate-elliptic. Flowers purplish blue or pink about 1·4 cm long, very showy on long raceme ; standard large, reflexed.

One of the best climbers in cool, dry place, seldom produces flowers in the plains of West Bengal. Purplish blue flowers are borne on long pendulous panicle in April-May.

CHAPTER VI

Green House Plants

In tropical climate, Green House is an important place where green house or shade-loving foliage plants are kept. Green House reduces temperature, provides shade and more humidity than in the open. If properly constructed, keeping in view the availability of light and circulation of air, Green House may also be used for growing orchids both epiphytic and terrestrial.

SITUATION

We have to depend a good deal on the ground available. East and south sun is excellent for the green house which can remain open on both these sides, but it should be shaded on the north and the west. Where one cannot obtain the right site, more shade should be given on the north and the west. Never build the fern house in the shade of heavy foliaged trees as the drip from the leaves is certain to damage plants.

CONSTRUCTION

A plan should be prepared before constructing the green house together with plan of beds and paths on the ground. Haphazard construction will result wastage of money and the purpose will not be served.

A green house on the Hills is seldom seen. Natural conditions do not call for such a structure, but a glass house in which the more tropical varieties can be kept and saved from sharp frosts is imperative. Out in the open, under the shade of trees, a rustic arrangement of raised beds and sunken plots with a stream running through it will contain all the ferns and other different types of plants that thrive at the various elevations. Here Primula of many kinds will grow.

THATCHING

This is an important matter. Too heavy shade draws up the foliage and makes it sappy and weak, too little on the other hand, allows the sun to burn and destroy the colour. To obtain the happy medium, allow 50% of sunlight to filter through during the hottest months, in the rains when the sun is not so strong and the sky overcast for long periods, the thatching should be thinned out. As the days shorten, the sun loses its intensity and the shading material can be reduced but do this gradually. Dry palm leaves shrivel in the heat and are eaten by caterpillars as well, while during the wet weather the leaves rot and the shade is thus naturally reduced. Grass usually collapses, but never thatch too thickly with this material.

Hessian is too heavy except for just a short period of the year and this material rots with wet weather unless preserved with crude oil paint. If not tied down carefully, heavy winds are apt to blow the covering to pieces. Coarse coir string last long and commonly used being woven in and out of the wire netting but it does not allow for any reduction of shade.

ARRANGEMENT OF POTS

If space is limited, pots are usually arranged on wooden benches but resting on cinders they do better. Trays of sheet iron or galvanised material should be used where brickwork cannot be arranged for and if these are filled with cinders, plants will grow strongly. Where woodwork is the only material available, have the wood creosoted, tarred or painted thoroughly ; keep it scrupulously clean and every now and then shift the pots so that any washings of earth do not collect on the wood. Avoid a draughty fern house and shelter it from the north or from whatever direction the wind blows.

DESIGN OF BED

Work from a plan allowing at least 1 m between beds, make the shapes as simple as possible but irregular in outline such as triangles with curved sides and rounded angles, etc.

Do not make the general design too regular. In a large green house, for instance, if a narrow bed is arranged up against the north-east side, do not carry the idea right round the house ; repeat it on the south-west.

In planting green house plants do not make the slope too regular, a dwarf plant taller than the undergrowth is an excellent way of breaking up the rockery. Follow nature, group in colonies or several plants together especially of the dwarf and medium sized varieties. Ornamental climbers up the posts or grown on rustic branches are also very artistic.

When building a rockery, do not make the slope of earth too steep, terracing is far preferable with brickwork as a backing. Arrange for good drainage, a core of large clinkers or cinders with a fall to some drain. The bank of earth can be held in position with clinkers, fused bricks or lumps of roof rubbish i.e., mortar and broken brick united in a conglomerate mass. These are piled so as to dovetail into each other will hold the earth in position.

Selaginella argentea, *Pillea*, *Zebrina*, *Nephrolepis*, *Adiantum ciliatum*, *Fittonia*, *Pellionia* and *Cyanotis*, etc help to cover the nakedness of the bare stone and in time germinating ferns add their foliage.

Prepare the top layer of earth say 15 cm deep with equal parts of fine cinder or gravel, leafmould and sand. When planting any deeper rooting plant, use some extra compost to fill the pit. Fork up the soil every few months but once ground is covered with small plants this must, of course, cease. Once a year, however, as the rains break, it is advisable to lift *Selaginella*, fork up the soil, add a top dressing of manure and then replant smaller plants.

WATERING

If the soil is porous there will be no difficulty about flooding or watering through a watering can without the rose during the hot months. A good syringing in the early hours will also help and to further create a moist atmosphere flood the paths every morning. During the rains look out for drip which is fatal to foliage and see that the exposed portions of earth, which are rather steeply banked do not get washed away.

CARE AND ATTENTION

Remove dead and dying foliage. Never make the mistake of having too many deciduous plants in one spot and this will show a gap in the cold weather. It is a good plan to sink 15 or 20 cm empty pots here and there in the rockery into which cineraria, geranium (Pelargonium) etc, can be placed and removed as they finish blooming. In this way a fern house can be made quite gay for many months of the year. During the off season foliage plants can fill the vacancies.

GREEN HOUSE PLANTS

Achimenes Herbaceous perennial plants with scaly underground stems, flowers funnel shaped, show various colours, solitary or in clusters. These form very good plants for hanging baskets. A mixture of 2 parts leafmould and 1 part soil is a good compost. Some popular varieties include—

var. Coccinea—flowers bright scarlet.

var. Dazzler—plants of compact growth, large red flowers.

var. Grandiflora—many large red-purple flowers.

var. Longiflora—flowers violet blue.

Aechmea. Colourful flowers appear in large inflorescence from the crown of the plants. The plants require moderate shade to full sun. Leaves are ligulate or sword like margins sometimes spiny. Propagation by suckers and offsets. Very light and porous compost consisting of leafmould, moss, soil and sand will be an ideal medium for the growth of the plant.

Aglaonema includes several popular and hardy green-house plants suitable for any shady place. They grow well in a rich sandy soil. Propagation by tip cutting or stem cutting.

A. commutatum. Leaves oblong-lanceolate, 20-30 cm long, rounded at base, green silvery marking.

A. costatum. Broadly ovate, dark green glossy leaves spotted white and with a white midrib.

A. modestum. Leaves green leathery, ovate-acuminate.

A. oblongifolium. Leaves linear oblong, dark green, stiff, about 30-45 cm long, base acute.

A. oblongifolium var. Curtisii. Elliptic, thick leaves, bluish green, feathery markings of silvery grey.

A. pseudobracteatum. Leaves ovate-lanceolate deep green, variegated with light green or creamy white and leaf base white mottled green.

A. roebelinii. Large ovate leaves, thick, leathery, greyish green, variegated silver.

Alocasia has many species with beautiful foliage. Some are hardy natives of India. The rhizomatous plants with attractive foliage prefer moist and shady situation and a porous soil, rich in organic matter.

A. (*Cyrtosperma*) *johnsonii*. Very showy plant. Leaves sagittate, about 30 cm long, widely spreading basal lobes olive green with crimson veins. Stalk light green with rosy spots and bands and upward pointing spines.

A. korthalsii (*Thibautiana*). Sagittate leaves, olive greyish green, veins silvery or greyish silver, purple beneath.

A. lowii. Leaves cordate-sagittate, 30-40 cm long, leathery olive green with thick greyish white ribs, deeply purple beneath.

var. Grandis. Leaves broad, slightly cordate at base, deep metallic brownish green, veins greyish green.

var. Veitchii. Base deeply lobed, main veins wide whitish margin, others greyish white.

A. macrorhiza var Variegata. Robust plant, large leaves, sagittate up to 60 cm long, light green blotched and mottled with white.

A. sanderiana. Well-shaped plants. Leaves sagittate, sinuate shining, metallic silver-green with greyish white veins, margins deeply lobed and white, purplish beneath.

Ananus (Pineapple). Herbaceous perennials producing leaves rigid, spiny and in a rosette form. Varieties with variegated leaves are grown as ornamental plants. Light soil, rich in organic matter favours the growth of this plant.

A. comosus var. Variegatus. Leaves green broadly margined, creamy yellow, tinged red towards the margin.

Anthurium—There are about 500 species of these tropical perennial plants and about 120 species and varieties are grown as ornamental plants. Anthuriums like a warm, moist climate and a shady situation. They have fleshy rhizomatous stems which can be cut into pieces with a node on each piece and gives rise to a new plant. The compost should be porous consisting of 1 part soil, 2 parts leafmould, 1 part each of well rotted cow manure and cinder or lime rubbish. Though all the species and varieties may flower but only some of them are grown for their showy spathes, white or coloured. The spathes are large, on erect peduncle, usually heart-shaped, rigid and have a waxy appearance. Some species have large beautiful leaves.

A. andraeanum. Stem short and erect, leaves oblong, cordate, 20-25 cm long. Stalk slender, longer than the blade ; spathe erect, scarlet cordate 10 cm long.

var. album. Leaves round cordate waxy, white spathe.

var. rhodochlorum. Deeply cordate leaves, spathe salmon-red.

var : rubrum. Large waxy quilted spathe of dark crimson.

A large number of varieties have been developed as a result of hybridisation between *A. andraeanum*, *A. ornatum*, *A. nymphaefolium*, *A. magnificum*, *A. lindenianum*, *A. splendidum*, *A. signatum* and *A. veitchii*.

A. crassinvervum—Plants with rosette of fleshy shining green elliptic leaves, 75-90 cm long.

A. crystallinum—Large cordate leaves velvety green, veins white.

A. digitatum—Plants of climbing habit, leaves palmately compound, dark green.

A. pittieri—Lanceolate, dark green, leathery leaves.

A. scolopendrium—Large plants, leaves long elliptic, dark green depressed veins in centre.

A. warocqueanum—Large ovate-lanceolate leaves, velvety, deep green with ivory veins, delicate and difficult to grow.

Aspidistra elatior—It has a rhizomatous stem, leaves oblong-lanceolate, leathery 40-50cm long, dark green.

A. elatior var Variegata—Decorative foliage striped and banded green and white in varied width. It is a hardy shade loving plant and thrives well in well-drained soil. Propagation by division of the rhizomatous stem with leaf.

Rex Begonias are grown for the beautiful foliage and prefer a moist atmosphere and a shady situation. Direct sun burns the leaves and wet soil cause rotting of the rhizome. The soil for such plants should be very porous and consists of 2 parts leafmould, 1 part each of soil and sand.

Large number of varieties are in cultivation, some popular varieties are described below.

var. Fairy. Very similar to above but has larger leaf. The whole undersurface of the leaf is maroon crimson.

Var. Her Majesty. Blackish satiny reddish purple with olive green zones, rosy silver blotches.

var. Hoar Frost. The predominant colour is silver, with irregular zones of dark metallic green along the principal veins and pink along the edge of the leaf.

var. Mikado. Centre of leaf purple, spilling into metallic silver, edge silvery purple.

Var. Peace. Similar to Silver Queen except that all silver is overlaid with rosy purple.

var. President. Quilted leaf, deep green, raised areas a clear silver.

var. Salamander. Leaves olive green blotched and pearled with silver.

var. Silver Queen. Soft silvery grey except along veins in centre and the margin metallic green.

Bertolonia Dwarf herbaceous plant with very beautiful leaves. Well-drained soil and semishade situations should be provided for better growth.

B. marmorata. Leaves ovate-oblong 5 veins, vivid bright.

B. mosaica. Streaks of pure white, rich purple beneath.

Billbergia. Plants look more or less like *Aechmea* and *Bromellia.* The leaves are sword-shaped with or without marginal spines. Flowers are produced as a terminal spike or in panicles. Propagation by suckers.

Caladiums are very popular, widely grown in tropical countries and have colourful foliage. There are numerous varieties showing variation in colour and in some cases, shape and size of leaves vary. The leaves usually peltate-sagittate but lance-shaped leaves are also common. The corms remain dormant in winter and sprouting starts in early summer. Soil should be porous and rich in organic matter and nutrient. In the summer months the plants require shade but in the monsoon they should be exposed to more sun in order to form a well-shaped plant and prominent colour.

var. E. O. Orpet. Lanceolate leaves, glossy red shading bright red margin.

var. Queen's Delight. Lanceolate leaves, greenish cream, white centre and pink blotches, margins green.

var. Red frill. Strap leaf, rosy red with main veins scarlet ending towards deep green, wavy margin.

var. Ripple. Bushy growth, lance leaves, white, transparent areas of lavender pink, green towards apex, veins greenish.

Miss Muffet, Ace of Hearts, Debutante, Fire Chief, Elizabeth Dixon, Kabootie, Mrs Sanders, are a few attractive broad-leaved varieties.

Calathea constitutes many species of green-house plants grown for ornamental foliage. It is a rhizomatous herbaceous plant and grows rapidly in warm humid condition. The plants are multiplied by division in the rainy season.

C. clossonii. Small plant of compact habit, thin leathery narrow lanceolate, yellow surface with blotches of green on both side of the midrib.

C. insignis. Long narrow linear leaves, wavy margins, yellow green with alternate large and small oval lateral blotches, dark olive green.

C. kegeliana. About 25 cm high. Stalk short, blade large, oblique ovate leathery surface, silvery grey patterned with lateral veins and lance shaped bands of yellowish to dark green.

C. magnifica. Dwarf plants, large oblique-elliptic leaves, olive green with large darker green feathery band, greyish outside and on both side of midrib.

C. medio-picta. Plants dwarf about 35 cm high, blade about 22 cm long, dull green with medium white feathery band, pale green beneath.

C. metallica. Leaf with short slender stalk, blade unequal, oblong about 20-22 cm long, dark green with white median zone and zigzag bands towards margin, purple beneath.

C. ornata var. Roseo lineata. Narrow ovate leaves, dark green regularly marked with uniform pairs of rosy red lateral stripes, purple beneath.

C. picturata. Plants very showy, about 35-45 cm high ; stalk 20-22 cm, blade elliptic unequal sided, thin leathery, green white line between midrib and margin above, purple beneath.

C. princeps. Plants reach a height of 75-90 cm, leaf stalk tall, blade oblong dark green with feathery centre band and yellow green base.

C. zebrina. About 45 to 60 cm high. Blade oblong lanceolate about 45 cm long, velvety deep green with alternate pale band above, purple beneath.

Chlorophytums are grown for their foliage. They can tolerate both shade and partial shade. Propagation by offsets or division.

Chlorophytum comosum var. Variegata. Rosette of large leaves 30-40 cm long, linear, green, margin white.

C. comosum var. Vittatum. Smaller plants, leaves in rosette, narrow linear, dark green, banded white in centre.

Cordyline terminalis has many varieties differing in shades and intensity of colour, shape and size of leaves. Some varieties have green leaves with streaks and feathery blotches of red or pink, while others show red, dark red to almost copper pink or purple. A particular variety may not display the same colour in young and mature leaves ; intensity of light, humidity, temperature and also manuring affect the colour of the leaves.

These plants remain colourful in semi-shade, dense shade brings dull colour and direct sun causes scorching of leaves.

The soil or pot compost should contain adequate organic matter, preferably well-rotted cow manure. These plants can be propagated from seeds and the seedlings show a wide variation of characters and new varieties are thus raised. Vegetative propagation is done by means of stem cutting or air layering of the top. From cuttings the plants grow slowly and do not attain a good size before 3 years. Air layering of the top gives a large plant with the foliage.

var. Baptisii. Broadly lanceolate, recurved, dark green to bronzy variegated with pink, cream and yellow.

var. Firebrand. Neat growth, well-arranged leaves lanceolate, stiff purplish red with glaucous sheen.

var. Margaret Storey. Elliptic lanceolate leaves with pink or red splashes on green foliage.

var. Tricolor. Rosette of broad leaves beautifully variegated red and creamy pink on a base of fresh green.

There are many other varieties in cultivation, raised in the garden of the Agri-Horticultural Society of India.

Costus speciosus. Erect perennial herb, leaves large, elliptic dark green, hairy, flowers terminal in a dense spike, bracts reddish. Flowers large white, margins frilled.

Cryptanthus (Tillandsia). Herbaceous plants with turred leaves. The shape of the plants and decorative foliage are very attractive. Propagation by suckers.

C. bivittatus var. Lueddemannii. Large leaves about 22 cm long, strap-shaped, undulate margin, sharply toothed, green with 2 broad buff coloured bands.

C. bivittatus var. Minor. Smaller plants with rosette of small compact leaves, light olive green with two pale bands overcast with salmon rose.

C. zonatus. Rosette of lanceolate leaves, brownish green with light brown irregular cross bands.

C. zonatus fuscus. Rosette of larger leaves, bronzy and green with silver cross bands.

C. zonatus viridis. Bronzy green with silvery cross band.

Ctenanthe. Herbaceous plants which grow in partial shade. Stalks of leaves are separated, lamina linear or ovate oblong. Some species form short stalked leaves on the erect stem. Propagation by division of clumps or separation of short stalked part.

C. compressa. About 60 cm high ; leaf stalk about 15 cm, blade elliptic-oblong green on both sides.

C. humilis. It has erect stalks bearing short stalked narrow leaves.

Curculigo recurvata. It looks like a young palm and grows into large clumps about 90 cm high. Leaves large, lanceolate, green stalks long, flowers yellow in dense heads. It grows in partial shade. Propagation by division.

Cyclanthus bipartitus. Erect rhizomatous perennial herb. Leaves large, clustered forked into two ; segments lanceolate, stalks long sheathing at base. These hardy plants grow better in semishade and can be easily multiplied by division of crown and rhizome.

Dieffenbachia consists of very popular and hardy, shade-loving plants commonly used in pots for indoor decoration. They grow quickly and form well-shaped plants and those with variegated leaves are very showy. These plants, grow in partial shade in any type of well-drained soil but adequate organic matter certainly helps to make the leaves more attractive.

The cut top with a portion of stem placed in sandy soil sends out strong roots. The stem may also be cut into pieces and each cutting will give rise to a new plant.

D. picta. This is the most common species. Leaves oblong slender, pointed, dark green, closely spotted or blotched with white or pale green.

var. *Bausei*. Leaves yellowish green, margined and irregularly spotted dark green and also spotted white, stalk white.

D. bowmannii. Leaves very large, broad 30 cm wide, deep

Asplenium nidus

Vanda hybrid

Philodendron imbe

Cattleya hybrid

rich green with irregular parallel markings of cream and light green.

D. costata. Leaves oval, broad dull green and occasional lighter blotches.

D. daguense. Robust appearance, stem short thick dark green. Leaves thick, heavy, leathery, rich shining green, thick-raised midrib and depressed veins.

var. *Magnifica.* Robust plant, broad ovate leaves, soft shining green, depressed veins, few white blotches.

D. seguine var. Decora. Very hardy, robust plant. Leaves deep green with light yellow green marking on both sides of the midrib ; petiole white.

D. seguine var. Irrorata. Leaves oblong, pointed, thin predominantly yellow green with dark green blotches and margin.

var. *Superba.* Compact growth, larger and thicker leaves, more creamy white colour on the glossy green leaf blade.

Dracaenas are commonly grown in shady places both in the open or green houses. Some species and varieties grow tall in the open and form definite stem with tuft of leaves on the top, while few species do well in pots and require more care. Even the hardy green leaved types when exposed to full sun in hot summer show scorching on leaves. Dracaena may remain unbranched but if the tip is removed or injured it starts branching. Species or varieties with showy and variegated foliage should be grown in light soil rich in organic matter.

D. deremensis var. Bausii. The white marginal bands are closed towards the centre separated by green stripe.

D. deremensis var. Longii. It is a delicate variety, pure white band at the centre.

D. deremensis var. Warneckeii. This variety requires shade and cannot tolerate direct sun. The stem is stout and erect and grows up to 3-4·5 m. Leaves lanceolate, 5 cm wide and 30-40 cm long sessile, leathery bright green, streaked milky green centre bordered by a white band on each side, bright green margin.

D. draco. This species forms the largest plant among the

genus, may grow up to 6 to 7·5 m. Large strong trunk branched. Leaves crowded on the top, lance shaped, thick green.

D. fragrans. It is the most common and hardy species, can grow up to 4-5 m, erect branches or unbranched. Leaves large 37-50 cm wide, oblanceolate, laxly recurved. Flowers yellow in cluster on long panicles.

D. fragrans var. Massangeana. Leaves large striped and banded light green and yellow at the centre.

D. fragrans var. Victoria. This variety is hardy, slow growing and require semishade. Leaves large pendant, yellowish or silvery green centre bordered by cream to golden yellow, broad margin.

D. godsseffiana. Small bushy plants with many thin branches ; leaves leathery, elliptic 5-6 cm long, glossy dark green with irregular yellow spots, turn white when mature.

D. goldieana. This fine foliage plant, requires warm-humid condition and very good compost. Leaves ovate, leathery glossy dark green marked with cross band of pale green maturing to white.

D. marginata, *D. hookeriana*, *D. americana* are green leaved species.

D. sanderiana. Erect habit and neat growth. Leaves lanceolate twisted, 15-20 cm long and 5-6 cm wide, green broadly margined in white.

Episcia. A few species of this genus are perennial herbs with beautiful foliage, require a moist climate and semishade but are very susceptible to excessive moisture in the soil which causes rotting. Stolons produce plants at the nodes which are separated for multiplication.

E. cupreata. This species has many varieties differing in colour of leaves. The plants are prostrate almost of creeping habit and ideal for hanging baskets. The leaves are oval or elliptic, almost a metallic copper faintly marked silver, thick, soft hairy.

var. Acajou. A hybrid with dark coppery leaves, veins and central area bright silver green.

var. Variegata. Leaves dark green to coppery, bluish silver in the centre, lateral veins silvery.

var. Silver Sheen. An attractive foliage variety. Most of the leaves and outer veins bright silver grey leaving only the marginal area coppery green.

E. reptans is another species with ornamental foliage.

Ficus elastica. The India rubber plant. Though it grows into a large tree, small plants in pots are favourite house plants. The leaves are oblong 12-15 cm long, 7-10 cm wide, thick leathery glossy deep green, young leaves enclosed in a rosy sheath.

Ficus elastica var. Decora has the midrib red on the under surface of the young leaves.

Ficus elastica var. Variegata. The leaves are longer and narrower than Decora and emerge light green tinged with pink, a wide creamy margin, when mature the central portion becomes patched with lighter or darker green and a narrow margin of cream.

Rooted cuttings or air layers are grown in pots, the compost consists of 2 parts loamy soil, 1 part each of leafmould and cow manure, ½ part sand and tablespoonful of bonemeal per 15 cm pot.

Fittonia has several species of low-growing ornamental foliage plants with overlapping foliage that completely cover the soil. These plants grow well in porous soil under warm damp conditions. One part each of sandy soil and leafmould will constitute a porous compost suitable for fittonia. Propagation by cuttings.

F. argyroneura. Leaves oval about 7-8 cm long, 5-6 cm wide, bright green heavily netted white.

F. pearcei has deep red netting.

F. verschaffeltii. The plant closely resembles F. argyroneura. The leaves are slightly larger but with red netting.

Gynura aurantiaca. Herbaceous erect plant. Stem and leaf covered with violet hairs. Leaves ovate toothed, flowers yellow. Propagation by cutting.

Heliconia. The plants look like a dwarf plantain. Some species are grown for flowers while others have handsome foliage. These plants grow in semishade and in almost all types of soil.

H. brasiliensis (Lobster's claw). Up to 2·4 m high, large linear long green leaves on long stalks. Inflorescence about 60 cm long 30 cm wide, bracts scarlet tipped yellow. Flowers greenish yellow or red.

H. humilis. About 2·4 m tall, leaves large on long stalks, oblong resembling a banana. The inflorescence is very showy, erect, bracts broad shaped on both sides, salmon red, green toward tip, ridge greenish yellow, flowers yellowish white.

H. metallica. Slender perennial herb about 1.2 to 1.5 m high. Oblong leaves on long red stalk, shimmering velvety emerald green, purplish red beneath.

H. psittacorum (Parrot flower). Plants slender, leaves lanceolate, narrow, leathery. Inflorescence erect, orange long pointed bracts tipped red. Flowers yellow.

Homalomena. Several species of this genus are grown as foliage plants in shade in the open and also in green houses. They grow well in rich and porous soil. Propagation by division.

H. rubescens. Stout stem, leaves heart-shaped reddish green on long brown red petiole, sunken veins.

H. wallisii. Low and compact growth. Leaves ovate oblong, slightly oblique, slender pointed 15-22 cm long, dark olive green beautifully blotched with yellowish silver, margin silvery.

Impatiens sultani (Zanzibar Balsam). A tender succulent but a hardy fernery plant. It is perennial and covered with brilliant orange scarlet to white flowers for many months of the year. Easily propagated by cutting or seeds. A wide range in colour now available.

Iresine grows equally well in sun or shade and is used as an edge plant. Easily propagated by cutting.

I. herbstii. Bushy sub-shrub 30-45 cm high, stem and

branches bright carmine, deep crimson beneath, leaves emerginate.

var. Aureo reticulata. Leaves fresh green with yellow veins, stem and petiole red.

I. lindenii. Stem red, leaves ovate-acuminate, rich deep blood red.

Marantas are beautiful foliage herbaceous plants of dwarf and compact growth, the leaves of some species fold upward in the evening. Suitable for cultivation in shade or partial shade. Soil should be well drained, excess moisture even for a few days may cause death of the plants. Propagation by division of crown.

M. bicolor. Low-growing plants with oval leaves about 15 cm long, dark green with grey feathered centre and greyish green margin.

M. leuconeura. Leaves oval, about 15 cm long rest on the ground ; the surface pale greyish green with a row of chocolate blotches on both sides of the midrib.

Pandanus. It is not strictly a green house plant as it can tolerate good amount of direct sun. In the summer, however, the leaves show scorching if exposed to full sun. They are very hardy, thrive as a house plant because of its adaptation to varied conditions and grow well also in poor soil but cannot stand waterlogging. Suckers arise from the stem which can be separated for multiplication.

P. baptistii. Leaves spirally arranged, stiff, channeled about 75 cm long, bluish green with several yellow stripes at the centre, without thorns at the margin.

P. sanderi. Stout compact growth. Leaves large, sword shaped, shining green with longitudinal stripes and band of light and golden yellow, margin spiny.

P. veitchii. Leaves grow in the form of rosette 75-90 cm long, narrow to long point, leathery, somewhat drooping, shining to light green, lined and broady margined with cream white, small spines along the edge and beneath.

Pellionia is a creeping herb with showy foliage. It grows in a shady moist situation. Sandy loam soil suits them and they are propagated by division or cuttings. Pellionias can also be grown in hanging baskets or trail on rocks in a shady rockery or the green house.

P. daveauana. Stem succulent, leaves obliquely elliptic 2-5 cm long, dark bronzy yellow, tinged violet on broad band of bright green centre.

P. pulchra. Succulent stem. Leaves soft thick obliquely oval, 13 cm long, light green to greyish.

Peperomia. This genus has many species and varieties in cultivation as ornamental foliage plants. These plants are succulent and herbaceous quick growing and ideal plants for the green house. They grow well on raised ground but the soil must be very porous. Direct sun should always be avoided and humidity maintained throughout the year. The soil should consist of 2 parts garden, soil, 1 part leafmould, 1 part well-rotted cow dung and 1 part sand or lime rubbish. Peperomias are easily propagated from stem or leaf cuttings in sand or sand and leafmould.

P. clusifolia. Erect habit, thick fleshy leaves obovate, waxy olive green, purplish margin.

P. obtusifolia var. Variegata. Small erect plants about 30 cm high. Leaves thick, obovate elliptic, bluntly pointed 3-6 cm wide, 6-10 cm long, waxy irregularly flecked with creamy-white and light yellow.

P. peltifolia. Low growing plant. Leaves peltate slight cupped, bluish green, faintly marked with silver between veins.

P. sandersii. Leaves arise in rosette, petiole red, lamina peltate bright green, glossy with silvery bands between the veins.

P. verschaffeltii, *P. bicolor*, *P. arifolia*, *P. glabella*, *P. Japonica* and many other species and varieties are grown in the green house.

Philodendron includes many useful climbers in shade or semishade grown for foliage when most of the flowering climbers fail to thrive. Some species, however, have short stem and grow as bush with rosette of leaves. Philodendrons can grow in all types of porous soil. The climber sends out roots from the nodes in contact with bark of trees of other support. Damp and shady place is ideal for the growth of these plants. It is propagated by cutting of stem pieces.

P. andreanum. Very beautiful climber with large, pendulous, velvety, oblong-sagittate leaves, dark olive green suffused with copper.

P. hastatum. Large arrow-shaped leaves pendulous, later hastate, fresh green, veins pale and ascending.

P. lacerum. Young leaves ovate entire, later deeply crenately incised, deeply sinuate at base 20-25 cm long.

P. mamei. It is a very slow-growing climber. Leaves large cordate, greyish green, marbled with silvery areas between the veins, petiole flattened green suffused pink, edges horny.

P. micans. Slender climber, leaves cordate, velvety bronze above and purplish beneath.

P. pertusum. Small leaves are roundish entire, later pinnatisect.

P. selloum. Large, often scandent on tree. Stem short producing aerial roots to strike the ground, leaves pendent, bipinnate about 60 cm long.

P. squamiferum. Twisted climber, leaves 15-25 cm long pinnatifid 5 lobed, centre lobe broad ovate, basal lobes short ; petiole, 10-20 cm, terete covered with green to red bristles.

Many other species of Philodendron are also grown as foliage plants.

Pilea muscosa is commonly known as the artillery plant because it discharges a cloud of pollen. The plant is very hardy and is a great favourite for green house and outdoor rockeries in shade and for hanging baskets. Propagated from cuttings. Low-growing plants about 15 cm high, herbaceous, succulent. Leaves obovate, minute, blunt, glossy green.

Pleomele. The species and varieties of this genus resemble *Dracaena.*

P. thalioides. A well-shaped plant about 45-60 cm high.

Leaves lance-shaped leathery 30-45 cm long, glossy dark green without midrib, clasping leaf base.

P. reflexa var. Variegata. The plant is much branched and of shrubby growth. Densely covered with lanceolate leaves, leathery, 10-15 cm long, two wide bands of golden yellow towards the margin.

Sansevieria. The genus constitutes many species and varieties of harbaceous perennials with short thick rhizome and are perhaps the most common foliage plant in gardens of tropical India. Leaves of various shapes and sizes arise in clusters or in regular order. Some are bordered with yellow. The plants grow in shade, partial shade and some species tolerate direct sun. Sansevieras can be grown on the poorest soils. Propagation is mainly done by the division of rhizome or clump.

S. cylindrica. Leaves round, slightly arching about 90-120 cm long, usually grooved, dark green with grey green cross band.

S. trifasciata. Leaves erect, stiff straight 30-90 cm long, linear-lanceolate, stout pointed tip, banded on both sides with transverse bands light, dull or whitish green and deep green to blackish green, glaucous above.

S. trifasciata var. Laurentii. This variety is the most popular among the Sansevieras. The leaves are like that of *S. trifasciata* having yellow border on both sides of the deep green light banded centre.

S. stuckyi. Leaves cylindrical, 75-90 cm long, dark green with light cross bands, slightly grooved longitudinally.

Spathiphyllum. These are evergreen perennial herbs, like the shade of a fernery and the leaves turn yellow if exposed to bright light. They grow rapidly and form clumps from an underground root stock.

S. cannaefolium. This is a commonly grown species of Spathiphyllum. Leaves large 15-20 cm long on a ribbed petiole, thick leathery tapering towards base, dull dark green. Spathe large greenish outside, white inside, spadix long cream.

S. commutatum. Leaves elliptic 20-25 cm long, fresh green.

Short thick spadix is white becoming green. Spathe broad, leathery cream white turning green beneath with age.

Setcrasea purpurea. Low-growing herbaceous stem, soft brittle purple oval-oblong leaves about 10 cm long, 3 cm broad, violet purple on both surfaces, flowers on erect stalk, 3 petaled colour purple. It is one of the best showy foliage plants and grow easily in porous soil with a little leafmould or cow manure. The colour of the foliage becomes deep when grown in partial to full sunlight. To get good colour, never plant Setcrasea in complete shade or under trees. Propagation by cuttings.

Syngonium. It is a foliage climber for green houses or shady places and is ideal on small posts or trellis. The plants are very hardy and grow in any types of soil. Propagation by cutting.

S. podophyllum is commonly grown in the green house. Leaves sagittate, thin green, in later stages becomes 5-7 lobed.

S. podophyllum var. Albolineatum. Leaves with silver-white centre and veins. Mature leaves green.

S. podophyllum var. Atrovirens. Leaves shaded ivory to greenish white, margin green.

S. wendlandi. Leaves trilobed ; adult 3 sects, 10-15 cm long, deep green velvety sharply contrasting white veins in the early stage, green when mature.

Tacca aspera var. Cristata. It is a perennial herb with curious flowers. Leaves oblong-lanceolate 30-45 cm long on long petiole, dark green glossy, veins pinnate, depressed. Flowers dark brown almost black, involucre of 4 bracts, upper 2 large erect, flat, the lower ones smaller.

Xanthosoma lindenii. Handsome perennial foliage plants. Large, arrow-shaped leaves with hastate veins 30 cm long, glabrous deep green midrib, and main veins ivory white.

var. Magnificum. Leaves larger than the species.

Zebrina pendula (Wandering Jew). It is a common foliage plant and grows well in partial shade. The plants spread quickly and creep on the surface of the soil. They are also very useful for hanging baskets. The leaves are oval in shape 5 cm long, main colour grey green, edges dark green and large purple stripe at the centre. The soil should be kept just moist, excess moisture in the soil causes rotting of stem. Roots come out from the nodes in contact with soil or moist surface.

Z. pendula var. Discolor. Leaves nile green, edged with metallic purple, two narrow silver bands in the middle of both the sides, purple beneath.

FERNS

The Hills are the natural home of most of our ferns and it is quite impossible to acclimatise some of the varieties found at high elevations. Ferns do best in a north or a north-east aspect where they get the morning sun and none in the afternoon but in the shelter of - fernery they will grow in any situation. *Nephrolepis exaltata* and such hardy varieties can stand the full sun during the Monsoon and winter months but need to be shaded for a couple of months during the hot weather. Fans and electric light have a bad effect on delicate ferns in pots, wherever possible these plants should be frequently changed and given a week or two out of doors to recuperate.

Use medium-sized pots, 16-20 cm are good enough except for specimens, while shallow seed pans of 25-35 cm diameter and 10 cm depth are better than 25 or 30 cm ordinary pots. When transplanting, do not commence with a bushy plant, for, as the fern grows and spreads, it will soon fill the pot with roots and lose strength.

Ferns are propagated by spores, bulbils that form on the leaf, stolons or runners that throw up a plant at the end, rhizome which is a continuation of the thickened stem and caude or a main stem that has to be divided.

Fern spores take 14-21 days to germinate and should be sown on a prepared bed or pan containing 1 part each of broken brick and coarse sand, loam and leafmould. Level the pan and sow, keep damp and if a sheet of glass is laid over the top results are better. Prick out when large enough to handle.

Don't bury the crown of the fern below the soil, a common mistake which accounts for many deaths. Syringe the foliage every few days in dry weather.

COMPOST FOR FERNS

The chief trouble with ferns usually lies in the wrong compost which *malis* use. Use one-third each leafmould, garden soil, not clay and coarse sand or clinkers. If at all possible, substitute old roof rubbish and pounded up lime mortar for the sand, charcoal and small pieces of broken brick should also be added to the compost. Ferns in pots should not be kept in a saucer of water but given a thorough soaking every day during the hot weather or a daily watering over head. If kept continually indoors, water once every couple of days during the cold and wet weather. A dusting of crushed limestone every few months will correct any tendency to sourness of the soil and do no harm to the plant, a pinch of bone meal or bone dust during the rains will ensure leafy plants in the cold weather.

Repot ferns every year, split up crowded pots removing all dead portions of stem and roots without the entire removal of soil.

Ferns enjoy a moist situation and if planted on a rockery with a block of fused bricks or conglomerable for them to nestle up to, they will repay you by depositing spores to increase their species. Hundreds of new plants will spring up once the stone has become covered with vegetable mould or a lichen like substance.

MANURE

While ferns seldom require manure, a little bone meal worked into the soil every year when the plants are repotted together with crushed limestone does benefit the plant. Liquid cow manure is also helpful.

WHAT TO GROW

The following list of hardy ferns might be of assistance to the amateur.

FOR HANGING BASKETS

Nephrolepis bostoniensis and other types, *Adiantum caudatum*, *Lygodium scandens* (Snake tongue), various kinds of *Polypodium* and *Davallia*, *Selaginella* of sorts.

FOR INDOOR DECORATION

Adiantum capillus-veneris, (Maiden Hair) *Cyrtomium falcatum*, *Pteris victoriae*, *P. mariesii*, *P. cretica albo-lineata*, *Nephrolepis piersonii*, *N. rufescens*, *N. furcans* and *N. cordifolia*, *Davallia fijiensis*, species of *Polypodium*, *Blechnum occidentale*, *Onychium japonicum*.

FOR OUTDOOR WORK IN POTS

Polypodium different types, *Nephrolepis furcans*, *N. exaltata*; *Nephrodium cuspidatum*, *Pteris longifolia*, *P. ensiformis*, *P. ludens*, *P. serrulata*, *Adiantum trapeziforme*, *A. peruvianum*, *A. hybridum*, *A. tenerum*, *A. fergusonii* and *A. victoriae*; *Aspidium* (Wood fern), *Asplenium* (Spleenwort), *Cheilanthes* (Silver fern), *Lastrea* (Beech fern).

HILLS

The selection is infinitely greater on the Hills and all the more delicate types of *Asplenium*, *Acrostichum*, *Gleichenia*, etc., thrive luxuriantly together with *Osmunda*, *Dicksonia*, *Angiopteris* and other tree ferns. Soil difficulties do not arise for the local material suits them and moist conditions are such that except when they have been lately planted little water is required. In winter a mulch of pine needles or straw will pull the more delicate kinds through severe frosts.

GENERAL PLANTING IN THE GROUND

In a fernery the selection can be varied according to the growers' own fancy and a collection of 20-30 varieties easily obtained.

Specimen forming varieties are *Adiantum peruvianum*, Glory of Moordrecht, a hardy type of Farleyense, *Asplenum nidus*, *Pteris quadriaurita*, *Nephrolepis cordifolia*, *N. gigantea*, *Gymnogramma sulphurea* (Gold fern) and *G. tatarica* (Silver fern), climbing types are *Lygodium*, *Diplazium*, *Acrostichum* and *Selaginella laevigata*.

Selaginella is useful for covering a rockery, *S. caulescens argentea* has a silvery appearance, *S. metallica*, blue and *rubella*, bronzy, *S. serpens* is very hardy but coarse, *S. erythropus*, *S. africana*, *S. braunei*, *S. gracilis* and *S. haematodes* are dwarf bushy growing. Taller kinds are *S. wallichii* and *S. lobbi*.

MARSH LOVING

While ferns can stand a lot of moisture they should not be subjected to overhead drip or the roots allowed to lie in water ; if the roots go towards water well and good, *Acrostichum* (Elephant's ear), *Angiopteris* (Turnip Fern), *Ceratopteris* (Pod Fern) and *Marsilea* (Water Fern) are known to thrive in swampy land and will grow in moist situations.

EPIPHYTIC

These are the *Drynaria*, *Platycerium* (Elkshorn or Staghorn), *Phegopteris* (Oak Ferns) and *Davallia* (Haresfoot) which are purely epiphytic, the first two living on tree trunks the others, though rooting in soil, are more at home on the bark of trees.

PESTS AND DISEASES

Most ferns are attacked by a caterpillar, green or grey black in colour, discovered only when the leaflets disappear. A careful search soon reveals the insects either at the roots or camouflaged as a portion of the stem.

A scale insect is common on indoor ferns, often the foliage is so affected as to require entire removal to eradicate the pest.

On occassion, white ants (termites) eat away the fronds from just below ground level, a grasshopper or cricket is another sinner in this way. If the old dead roots and steams are not regularly cleaned out, fungus and insects are invited to add to the troubles of the amateur.

Green fly and red spider as well as slugs and snails attack ferns. Use insecticide in low dose so that leaves are not damaged particularly of the specimen plants.

HOUSE PLANTS

House plants and shade-loving plants are widely grown in pots and used for indoor decoration. All shade plants, however, cannot be considered as ideal house plants as the condition of rooms and other shady places in the house with walls on the sides and the top covered permanently create less favourable atmosphere for the growth of shade or green house plants. Like arrangement of cut flowers, decoration of room with potted plants is becoming popular in modern living. Hardy types of green house plants which can tolerate more shade and adverse condition are usually recommended for indoor decoration. Plants producing showy flowers require full or partial sun for growth and flowering, while house plants have mostly beautifully variegated foliage or attractive green colour.

CARE OF HOUSE PLANTS

These plants should remain evergreen and grow into well-shaped plants of attractive appearance. Growth of all types of plants are adversely affected, if kept in airconditioned rooms or under fan. No plant can grow in darkness for indefinite period so the house plants should be exposed to morning sun after few days, direct midday sun will burn the leaves. Excess watering is to be avoided, keep the soil just moist and watering may be minimised in winter months but never allow the soil to become bone dry. Smoke and gas are also injurious to all types of plants. Handful of well-rotted cow manure or small amount of bone meal should be dug into the pots twice or thrice a year specially in the rainy season, fertilizers tend to make the plants more succulent and less hardy. Use pot according to the size and shape of the plants and better result will be obtained by repotting these plants into larger size pot when the roots become pot bound than to use a large pot for a small plant. The potted plants should be kept in a container so that water coming out the drainage holes of the pot does not spoil the table or room. The second container is in most cases decorative. A number of species and varieties showing variation in growth habit and colour of the foliage can also be grown in a pot. In the latter method of arrangement, usually tall and erect plant or a climber held on stake is planted in the middle and encircled by those of less height or of creeping habit to give showy appearance.

COMPOST

Compost for shade-loving foliage plants, in general should be light so that water drains out readily. Composition of compost, however, depends on the types of plants. Ferns will show healthy growth with 1 part each of leafmould, garden soil and sand or lime rubbish. For *Dieffenbachia*, *Aglaonema*, *Calathea*, *Anthurium*, *Philodendron*, etc., use leafmould, garden soil, cow manure and sand in the proportion of 1 : 2 : 1 : 1. Begonias require a lighter soil. One part each of leafmould and cow manure and 2 parts of loamy soil is a good compost for *Pandanus*, *Sanseviera* and crotons. In the compost, use 1 tablespoon of bone meal per 20 cm pot.

CHAPTER VII

Annuals

Importance, site, layout and cultivation

Annuals are an important group of flowering plants widely used for garden decoration, cut flowers and pot plants. Few types, however, are grown for attractive foliage. They have large number of species and many varieties which not only show variations in height and growth habit but also in the shape, size and colour of flowers. Annuals are very easy to grow, flower profusely in a short time in numerous shades of colour. Due to variation in the season of growth and flowering, several species grow well in summer and rains, while the majority of annuals are cultivated in the winter months in the plains.

SITE AND LAYOUT OF ANNUAL GARDEN

Most of the annuals require full sun, shade for few hours in the morning or midday adversely affects growth and flowering ; western sun, however, is less important. The annuals are grown in mixed border or only one variety in a small bed. A strip of green grass in front of mixed border or between two beds improve the display of colour. It should be sufficiently wide for the use of lawn mower. The space for a mixed border should be large and of informal design. Plants varying in height and colour are planted in groups, tall plants at the back and shorter one gradually towards the front. Tall plants of Hollyhock, seedling Dahlia, Lady's lace should go at the back ; plants of intermediate height, e.g., Antirrhinum, Cornflower, Salvia, Larkspur are grown in the next group ; the third clumps may consists of Dianthus, Aster, Wall flower, Anchusa, Calendula and Allysum, Phlox, Pansy, Brachycome, Candytuft should be selected for the front patches. In small bed, usually one

Aster

Pansy

Salvia

Petunia

type of annual of attractive colour is grown. Salvia, Antirrhinum, Dianthus, Aster, Phlox are selected depending on the size and position of the bed.

Loamy and porous soil rich in organic matter is good for the growth and flowering of annuals. If the soil is clayey, addition of lime in the rainy season will be useful to break the stiff soil and use of adequate organic manure will make the soil porous. Where the soil is sandy add clay if possible, for one cannot depend entirely on manure to improve the texture of the soil.

It is more artistic to allow the front annuals to fall over on the grass edge than to keep them in a straight line. To stiffen a wide herbaceous border, it is advisable to plant flowering and foliage shrubs which will act as a foil to the annuals and provide at the same time colour when the annuals are small or the beds empty. A sketch of a mixed annual border on a sheet of paper will be of assistance to amateurs who are diffident about risking their own ideas directly on the field.

SOWING OF SEEDS

Seeds of annuals are sown in bed or shallow seed pan. The seed compost should consist of 1 part each of garden soil and finely screened dry leafmould. The compost should be slightly moist before sowing, otherwise the water will not soak readily and the seeds will float on water. Sow the seeds thinly and cover with a fine layer of screened leafmould. It is always safe to use fresh soil for sowing and mix some sand if the soil is clayey. Protect the seed pan or the bed from rains after the seeds have been sown. When the seedlings start sprouting, exposure to sunlight should be gradually increased, so that before transplanting they become sufficiently strong to bear the full-day sun. The seedlings are severly damaged by fungul disease under conditions of high humidity and cloudy weather and it can be effectively controlled by the application of fungicide. Most of the seedlings become ready for transplanting at four-leaved stage. If it is desired to see the beds of annuals in bloom in late December or early January, sow the seeds in September and transplant the seedlings in October. For a display of colour in early February, sowing should be done in early October. Double and large flowering Petunia, Cineraria, Carnation and Stock, which require about 5 months to come to flower, should be sown earlier.

PREPARATION OF BEDS AND TRANSPLANTING OF SEEDLINGS

The beds should be throughly dug at least 30-40 cm deep as the rain ceases and the soil is dry. The clods should be broken, soil pulverised and dug again to make the soil of uniform tilth throughout the depth of the cultivated layer. Well-rotted cow manure should be mixed at the time of preparation of the soil. At the time of transplanting, a small hole is prepared and the seedlings are planted with the root just covered with soil. It is gently pressed to keep the seedling erect and watered through a rose can while taking out the seedlings from the seed bed or pan, care should be taken to minimise the damage of roots. Seedlings will establish in the ground in about a week, if light watering is done when necessary.

WATERING AND MANURING

The common mistake of daily watering whether the plant requires moisture or not causes more damage than anything else. After the seedlings have started new growth, they are watered profusely, weeds removed from these beds when it is just moist and the soil is allowed to dry before it is again flooded. This simple practice is the secret for successful cultivation of annuals.

Organic matter not only supplies nutrient to the soil but greatly improves its physical condition. Cow manure is the best and easily available organic manure. Fresh or half-rotted manure should never be used just before planting of seedlings. Chemical fertilizers should be used in very small dose. Mixture of chemical fertilizers and organic manure in the form of solution, if applied in low concentration during the vegetative phase of the plants will greatly improve the growth and also the quality and quantity of flowers. Fertilizers can also be used on the soil as dry powder followed by flooding.

EARLY BLOOMING ANNUALS :

There are occasions when display of colour in a garden becomes necessary before the time of normal flowering with most of the annuals. Ageratum, Alyssum, Balsam, Browalia, Candytuft, Celosia, Dianthus, Gomphrena, Marigold, Salvia, Sunflower and Zinnia are some of the early blooming annuals.

SHADE TOLERANT ANNUALS :

No annual can thrive in full shade, but where light is dappled and filters through a light tree the following will thrive. It must be remembered that the quality and quantity of bloom will necessarily be poorer.

Ageratum, Alyssum, Begonia, Calceolaria, Calendula, Candytuft, Cineraria, Clarkia, Dahlia, Delphinium, Godetia, Impatiens, Larkspur, Lobelia, Lupin, Myosotis, Nicotiana, Pansy, Phlox, Salvia, Verbena and Vinca.

ANNUALS FOR ROCKERY :

A rock garden in sun may not be entirely composed of cacti and succulents and patches of colour will brighten it. In a rock garden hardy types of dwarf annuals which thrive and flower in poor soil are usually selected. Ageratum, Alyssum, Arctotis, Brachycome, Nasturtium, Phlox, Portulaca, Verbena are some annuals suitable for this purpose.

DESCRIPTION, VARIETIES, GROWTH HABIT AND CULTIVATION

Ageratum conyzoides (*A. mexicanum*) (*Compositae*) *Ageratum.*

Popular annual flowering plant for beds and pots. The height varies from 15-40 cm depending on the variety. It develops into well-shaped plant with dark green foliage and the dwarf varieties are compact and widely grown for edging and in a mixed border. Blue or its shades like azure blue, dark blue are normally selected for gardens ; salmon, pink and white are not so popular. In the plains, seeds are sown from September to November and the plants flower in 2-3 months after sowing. Pinching of taller varieties is done to make the plants bushy. Removal of faded flowers promoted flowering for a longer period.

ALTHAEA ROSEA (*Malvaceae*) *Hollyhock*

It is a popular flowering plant throughout the world and commonly known as hollyhock. In tropical climate, hollyhock is treated as an annual, while in the hills it is grown as a perennial. The height of the plant varies from 1·0 to 2·5 m. Large flowers 8-12 cm across appear on long erect stem at the axils of the leaves. It is mainly used at the back of the mixed border or along a wall. Plants of shorter height also make good pot plants. The flowers open successively from below towards the tip of the spike and continues to bloom for a long time till the temperature rises high, when almost all other annuals dry up. A wide range of flower colour is recorded in hollyhock, eg. white, cream, yellow, rose, lilac, purple, scarlet and crimson. The flowers may be single, double and semi-double. The plants grow better when directly sown in site and extra seedlings are removed to maintain a distance of 50-60 cm. Seeds should be sown in September-October to get bloom during January to April.

ALYSSUM MARITIMUM (*Cruciferae*) *Sweet alyssum, madwort.*

It is a low-growing annual (12-20 cm) globular in shape with narrow leaves. It is frequently used in gardens for edging, borders, beds, hanging baskets, pots and in pavements, rock-eries, crevices of the wall. The small spikes of white, rose, deep rose and violet purple scented flower appear in 40-45 days after germination. It can tolerate semi shade.

AMARANTHUS CAUDATUS (*Amaranthaceae*) *Love-lies—bleeding.*

This species is commonly grown in pots or in beds as a

flowering annual during winter months and produces long pendulous plume like or headed spike, purplish crimson, light green and white in colour. The plants are quick growing and make a good display in groups in mixed border. The flower spike lasts for many days.

AMARANTHUS HYBRIDA (Princes Feather) is about 1 m in height and bears erect crimson red plume like spikes. Its cultivation is similar to that of *A. caudatus*. *A. tricolor splendens* is one of brightest foliage plant, about 50-90 cm in height. The leaves are deep scarlet marked with patches of yellow or bronze green. *A. tricolor rubra* has bright red leaves. The seeds are sown in February and March and seedlings grow into a well-shaped plant in about 2 months and continues to thrive during the summer and early rains. It grows well in pots and can be effectively displayed as foliage plants during the season.

ANCHUSA CAPENSIS (*Boraginaceae*) *Bugloss, Cape Forget-me-not.*

In the plains it is grown as an annual flowering plant in the winter months. The plant is 40-50 cm high, much branched and bears small azure blue flowers with white centre. Seeds are sown during September to November and the plant blooms after 4 months from sowing. They thrive well in porous soil and sunny location.

ANTIRRHINUM MAJUS (*Scrophulariaceae*) *Snapdragon.*

Antirrhinum is one of the most popular annual grown in garden. The plants have dark green narrow leaves, bear tubular flower with spreading irregular lobes on long erect spikes at the end of main stem and branches. According to the height of the plant, antirrhinum is divided into 4 groups-tall (80-120 cm), intermediate (55-75 cm), dwarf (25-50 cm) and miniature (15-20 cm). There are varieties with ruffled or double flowers.

Tall varieties with long erect spikes are very attractive at the background of a mixed border. The cut flowers are very showy and last long. Intermediate varieties in one or mixed colour are useful for planting in small beds or in patches in mixed border and as pot plants. Dwarf varieties have compact appearance and produces large number of smaller spikes at the tip of the branches. These varieties are commonly grown in beds, rock gardens, pots and window boxes. Seeds are sown during September to November. The soil should be porous but rich in organic matter and nutrients. In antirrhinum there is a wide range of colour except blue and with one or more colours of attractive shade.

Tetra or tetraploid varieties with larger flowers and double flowered varieties are spectacular improvement in the recent years. Those plants have large funnel-shaped flowers, lobes widely open, slightly ruffled at the edges. F_1 hybrids of antirrhinum are vigorous plants and show better flowering than the common varieties.

ARCTOTIS GRANDIS (*Compositae*) *African daisy.*

The species is commonly grown in the gardens of northern India. It grows best in porous soil, prolonged low temperature and less humidity. An appreciable improvement has been made in this species and the hybrids show wider range of colour and larger flowers. Normally *A. grandis* attains a height of 50-80 cms and bears white daisy like flowers with lilac centre. Large flowered hybrids, developed as a result of crosses between the species and hybrids, show various attractive colours like orange, pink, yellow, crimson, bronze and different shades of colour. Arctotis is very useful for bedding and rock gardens and also as pot plants. The seeds are sown in September-October in the plains and in March-April in the hills. Flowers appear in about 4 months from sowing.

BRACHYCOME IBERIDIFOLIA (*Compositae*) *Swan River Daisy.*

It is one of the most popular annuals for gardens and produces many flowers in one plant at a time. Height varies from 20-40 cms depending on the climate and soil. In eastern India it seldom reaches a height of more than 20 cm, whereas in northern India it often grows up to 30-40 cm. The plants have fine feathery foliage and small daisy like flowers (2·0 cm) in white, blue, purple and pink. Flowering starts after 3 to 3½ months of sowing and continue for 2-3 months. Pinching of shoots at the vegetative stage induces profuse flowering.

BROWALLIA ELATA (*Solanaceae*) *Amethyst flower.*

Browallia is a medium sized plant (30-40 cm height), produces small blue or violet flowers in the axis of the leaves. It grows well in warm humid condition and seeds are sown in May-June. Browallia develops into an attractive plants in pot and is also grown in beds.

CALCEOLARIA (*Scrophulariaceae*) *Slipperwort, Pouch flower.*

Calceolarias are normally grown in the hills in a cool humid condition. *C. pinnata* with pale yellow flowers, grows and flowers in the plains of northern India in semishady location.

Among the horticultural species which are hybrids, *C. herbeohybrida* also known as hybrid grandiflora, produces clusters of flowers in a wide range of colours including orange, yellow, red, rose, brown, purple, blotched and spotted in a very attractive manner. In the hills, seeds are sown in seed pan during July-August in glass house under protection from rains, frost etc. and flowers appear during April-July. In the plains of northern India seeds are sown in September-October, produce flowers in February.

CALENDULA OFFICINALIS (*Compositae*) *Pot marigold.*

Calendula is a popular annual in Indian gardens grown in beds and pots. The plant has a dwarf, rosette growth, bears flower heads 6-10 cm in diameter on stout stalk, 20-30 cm in length. Large double flowers are attractive, singles and semi-doubles bear large number of blooms, in various shades of yellow and orange. The plants grow well in rich porous but moist soil and flower in 2½-3 months.

CALLISTEPHUS CHINENSIS (*Compositae*) *China aster.*

Aster is one of the most popular flowering plants throughout the world. In the plains only annual types are grown, but many species of perennial asters are cultivated in temperate countries. They are grown extensively in beds for the attractive flowers of various shapes and colour. Cut asters last long and are used in vases and floral decoration. Height of the plants varies from 15 to 60 cm depending on the type and variety. There are various types e.g., Giant of California, Ostrichplume, Commet, varying in the shape of the head and size, shape and arrangements of the florets. Wide range of colours include white, pink, rose, blue, scarlet, crimson, mauve, purple etc. Aster grows well in porous soil rich in organic matter in full sun. In the plains the seeds are usually sown in September-October, sowing in July-August is also possible in low rainfall area and plants bloom after 3½ to 5 months depending on type, variety and climate.

CELOSIA PLUMOSA (*Amaranthacea*) *Cockscomb.*

Cockscomb is a hardy annual and can be grown in winter, summer and rainy season.

C. plumosa produces long silky feathery flower spike in various colours like red, orange, orange scarlet, yellow and white. The height varies considerably from 80 cm in the tall ones to 25 cm in the dwarf varieties and intermediate ones having medium height in between.

The feathery varieties with attractive shining spikes makes a good display in a mixed border. Dwarf types are good pot plants.

The variety Cristata (*C. plumosa* var. cristata) produces crested flower heads, resembling the comb of cock in various colours like red, rose, orange, scarlet, bright scarlet, white, yellow, golden yellow etc. The height varies from 15 cm to 90 cm depending on the varieties.

The seeds are sown in January-February, May-June and September-October for flowering in the summer, rains and winter respectively. Seedlings are transplanted at 4-6 leaves stage. Flowers appear in 2½ to 3 months after transplanting.

CENTAUREA AMERICANA (Compositae) *American Sweet Sultan, Basket flower.*

Plants are tall, approximately 1·0 to 1·5 m high, commonly grown at the back of mixed herbaceous border. American sweet sultan is a hardy plant and during the winter bear purple flowers. The plants usually take 2 to 2½ months to flower from the date of sowing. Flowers are large, 5-7 cm in diameter and are very commonly used as cut flowers.

CENTAUREA CYANUS, *Cornflower*.

The plants are tall. attaining a height up to 1 meter and are commonly grown at the back of mixed border. As the flowers last long, they are also used as cut flowers. Cornflower is a hardy winter annual in the plains and seeds are sown in September-October, flowers are produced in 3 to 3½ months. There are varieties with pink, rose, maroon, purple, blue and white, mostly single ; double flowered varieties are also grown.

CENTAUREA MOSCHATA, *Sweet Sultan.*

Sweet sultan is a tall growing hardy (1·0 to 1·2 m) annual, bearing attractive scented flowers in white, mauve, purple or yellow colours. Yellow Sweet sultan is less vigorous and more susceptible to excess moisture in the soil and shorter in height than other varieties. These free flowering garden annuals are commonly grown in mixed border and are excellent for cutting.

CHRYSANTHEMUM *(Compositae) Annual Chrysanthemum.*

Annual chrysanthemums comprise of three species, *Chrysanthemum segetum* (Corn Marigold), *C. coronarium* (Crown Daisy) and *C. carinatum.*

Corn marigold grows about 40 to 60 cm high and bears flowers 5·0 cm across in shades of white and yellow. Double flowered varieties are also available in this type.

The crown daisy is much branched plants with finely cut foliage reaching a height up to 1 meter, size of the flowers varies from 2·5 to 4 cm and colour is usually in shade of yellow and white. Both single and double flowered varieties are found, but single is common.

The tricoloured chrysanthemum (*C. carinatum*) are the best type in this group. The plants have finely cut leaves and bear large flowers variously coloured in white, yellow, scarlet, orange, purple, mahagony in the form of a ring. Disc appear at the centre and upper part of the petals.

Annual chrysanthemums are free flowering and grow in all types of soil in sunny situation in beds or pots and used as cut flowers.

CLARKIA ELEGANS (*Onagraceae*) *Mountain garland, Clarkia.*

Plants are of medium height (60-80 cm), bears attractive single or double flowers in white, pink, salmon, rose, carmine and scarlet at the axil of the leaves. Clarkia makes a good display of colour in groups and are commonly grown in beds or pots. If prefers a well-drained rich soil on the dry side and grows well in full sun and partial shade. Flowering starts in 2 to 2½ months from germination of seeds.

CLEOME SPINOSA (*Capparidaceae*) *Spider plant.*

The plants are tall (1·0 to 1·3 m) much branched and spiny-long protruding stamens and the four petals resemble spider, and the flowers are borne in large clusters at the end of the main stem and branches. In the plains it can be grown in winter and summer and flowers appear within 3 months after germination of seeds. Seeds are sown in September-October and January-February for winter and summer flowering respectively and seedlings are transplanted 40-60 cm apart. Colour of flowers are pink, rose and white.

CLIANTHUS DAMPIERI (*Leguminosae*) *Parrot's bill, Lobster's claw.*

An attractive winter annual producing clusters of large colourful curiously shaped flowers. The plants are very suitable for growing in pots and well drained soil in beds, in sunny situation. The soil should be kept on the dry side.

The flowers are 7-8 cm long orange scarlet in colour with a black raised centre.

Seeds are sown during September-October in a porous sandy compost and the seedlings are protected from excess moisture or rains.

COREOPSIS (*Compositae*) *Calliopsis, Tick-seed.*

Coreopsis tinctoria and *C. drummondii* are the two species of annuals commonly grown in gardens. *C. tinctoria* reaches a height of 40–80 cm, produces finely cut leaves and the flowers have one row of petals of yellow, brown or crimson brown. *C. drummondii* is medium in height (40-60 cm), bears larger bright yellow flowers with brown centre.

Coreopsis can be grown in summer, rains and winter in any type of porous soil. In the hills, the seeds are sown in March-April and August-September.

It is a very popular plant for mixed border and cut flower.

COSMOS BIPINNATUS (*Compositae*) *Cosmea, Cosmos.*

It is a free flowering popular annual, used for bedding, in mixed border and as cut flower and grows well in sun and semishade in all types of soil. Though cosmos is known as a winter annual, it flowers early in the season, beginning from September and continues till March. The plants are tall (80–120 cm), much branched with feathery foliage and bear large flowers in pink, rose, crimson, lavender or white in colour. There are varieties with double flowers. Cosmos is best sown *in situ* though transplanting is not uncommon. Early sowing can be done in June-July in low rainfall areas and flowering commences in 2½ months.

CYNOGLOSSUM AMABILE (*Boraginaceae*) *Chinese Forget-me-not.*

It is a blue flowering hardy annual attaining a height of about 30 cm and grows well in porous soil in full sun or semi shade. Small blue sweet scented flowers are borne in small clusters in the winter months. It has a white variety also. It is ideal for bedding, borders and rock garden and grows under trees and in shrubbery. In the plains, seeds are sown in September-October and the seedlings begin to flower in about 3 months.

DELPHINIUM (*Ranunculaceae*)

Perennial delphinium though widely grown in the hills, is found to grow well as annual in the plains of northern India. Most of the cultivated varieties are hybrid between *D. elatum* and other species like *D. formosum*, *D. cardinale*, *D. belladona* and *D. nudicaule*. Perennial delphinium is tall (1·5 m) much branched with lobes and cut leaves, flowers appear on erect stout spike and colours include white, pink, lavender, lilac, purple pale and deep blue. Delphinium is ideal for mixed border, background and cut flowers. It is propagated from seeds, division and cuttings, the last two methods are only possible in the hill where it is grown as perennial.

Larkspur, cultivated in gardens consists of two species *D. ajacis*, the hyacinth flowered and *D. consolida* the stock flowered larkspur.

The plants are tall (80-120 cm), erect, branched with fine feathery foliage. Spikes of blue, purple, lilac, salmon rose or white flowers, single or double arise in large number. Larkspur is excellent as cut flower and for growing in mixed border, along hedges and in semishade.

Seeds are sown in October-November, in the plains germination is better in lower temperature. In the hills it can be sown in March-April or during August to October. Larkspur shows satisfactory growth and flowers in well-drained light soil and takes about 3 months to bloom.

DIANTHUS BARBATUS (*Caryophyllaceae*) *Sweet willam.*

Sweet william has both annual and biennial strains. Annuals are grown in the plains, while biennials are grown in the hills. Annual varieties are 20-35 cm tall, have dark green foliage and flowers single or double in large rounded and showy clusters at the end of the branches. The flowers have a wide range of colours white, maroon, purple red, pink, purple, rose pink, etc., self-coloured or zoned and variously coloured.

Sweet william is widely grown in the plains and hills in beds, borders and are good for cut flowers.

The seeds are sown in September to October and the seedlings will flower during December to March. Biennial varieties take longer time to flower than the annual ones and are usually grown in hills.

DIANTHUS CARYOPHYLLUS *Carnation.*

Carnation is one of the most popular annual grown in Garden ; excellent for bedding, herbaceous borders, edging, pots and as cut flowers. In plains carnation is grown as a winter annual but cultivated as a perennial in hills. They grow and flower well in loamy soil and under full sun. Propagation by seeds and stem cuttings.

Plants are medium tall, about 40-90 cm high. Stems grey green, narrow with swollen nodes. Leaves narrow, thick and often curves at the tip. Flowers single or double with smooth or fringed edged petals, sweet fragrance like cloves. Terminal flowers are white, cream, yellow, pink, rose, red, scarlet, crimson, purple, maroon, orange etc. with selfs, striped, flaked and combination of different colours.

Seeds are sown during August-September in the plains to get flowers from February. Flowering starts in 5 months from germination.

DIANTHUS CHINENSIS, *Indian Pink.*

Dianthus is one of the most popular and beautiful garden annuals. The plants are 15 to 35 cm high and bear large rounded head of flowers, self-coloured in white, pink, rose, scarlet, crimson, violet, maroon, mauve, purple, etc., or zoned, spotted or blotched in various colours. There are two types of Dianthus—Heddewgii or Japanese pink and the fringed pink. The Heddewgii varieties are dwarf (15-25 cm) plants, free flowering, attractively coloured with single and double flowers having fringed and beautiful margin. The laciniatus varieties are taller (30-35 cm), flowers single or double beautifully coloured with finely fringed petals.

The pinks are excellent for beds, border, rock gardens and cut flowers. They grow and flower well in loamy soil and full sun. Seeds are sown during September-November and the seedlings bear flower in about 3 months.

DIMORPHOTHECA SINUATA (*D. aurantiaca*) (Compositae) *African Daisy, Star of the Veldt.*

Dimorphotheca makes attractive display of colour in porous soil and cooler climate. The growth and flowering are adversely affected in heavy and moist soil. The plants are ideal for planting in beds, border, pots and for cut flowers. They are 30-50 cm tall with narrow leaves and bear large shining daisy like flowers in white, bluish white, golden, rose, salmon, pink, reddish purple on long stalk and continue to flower for a long time.

The seeds are sown in September-October and flowering starts in about 7 to 9 weeks.

ECHIUM PLANTAGINEUM (*Boraginaceae*) *Tower of Jewels.*

Echium is not a very popular garden annual. The height varies from 40-90 cm depending on the type. The plants are bushy, erect and hairy, produces large number of small cup-shaped flowers of various colours like blue, purple blue, pink, mauve and white. It is suitable for border, pot and beds and thrive in all types of soil in summer and winter and also in full sun and semishade.

The seeds are sown in January-February or September-November for flowering in summer and winter respectively.

ESCHSCHOLZIA CALIFORNICA (*Papaveraceae*) *Californian poppy.*

It is a popular and free flowering annual, widely grown in beds, borders and in pots. The plants are dwarf with rosette growth and large number of extremely showy flowers are borne on stalk. The flower may be single, semidouble or double in several colour, e.g. golden yellow, lemon, orange, cream or creamy white, orange red, crimson, rose pink or bronze.

Californian poppy grows better, if sown *in situ* and the seedlings thinned out at 20-25 cm apart. Sowing of seeds in beds is done during September-October in plains and in March-April in the hills. The plants are susceptible to excess moisture and grows well in porous soil under full sun.

GAILLARDIA PULCHELLA (*Compositae*) *Blanket flower*.

It makes a fine display of colours, commonly grown in summer and rains and continues to flower for a long time. It is excellent for bedding, borders and also as a cut flower.

The cultivated types are *G. pulchella picta* produces large single flower and *G. pulchella lorenziana* bears double flowers in several attractive colours of yellow, bronze and smoky red. There are some perennial varieties with large single flowers.

For summer flowers, seeds are sown during December-January and in March-April for the seedlings to flower in the rainy season. The seedlings take about 3½ to 4 months to flower.

GAZANIA SPLENDENS (*Compositae*) *Gazania*.

A low growing (15-25) cm semi trailing plant with leaves silvery on the under surface and shining dark green above. Gazania is an ideal annual for rock garden and also makes a colour display in borders and pots.

The flowers are large attractive, variously coloured in orange, pink, brown red, yellow or white and flowering continues for a long time.

The seeds are sown in September-October in the plains and during March-April in the hills. They can be also vegetatively propagated from cuttings and layers. The seedlings flower in 3 to 3½ months and thrive best in well drained soil in a sunny situation.

GODETIA GRANDIFLORA (*Onagraceae*) *Satin flower*, *Godetia*.

Varieties of godetia cultivated in the gardens are hybrids of *G. grandiflora* and *G. amoena*. Godetia attains medium height (40-50 cm) bushy and bears bell-shaped single or double flowers in loose spikes. It is suitable for beds, borders, pot and as cut flowers and thrive well in porous soil, colour of the flowers may be pink, purple, crimson, carmine and orange red and various other shades of red and pink.

The seeds are sown in September-October to get flowers during December-January. In the hills the seeds are sown in March-April and in August-October.

GOMPHRENA GLOBOSA (*Amaranthaceae*) *Globe amaranth.*

It is grown in summer and rainy season, in bed and pots and flowers are used in decoration both fresh and dry. Globe amaranth is a hardy, free flowering plant, grows in all types of soil and reaches a height between 20 to 40 cm depending on the type and variety. The flowers are small, about 2 cm across, button like round spikes in white, pink, violet, rose or pale orange.

The seeds are sown in February-March and May-June for flowering in summer and rains respectively.

GYPSOPHILA (*Caryophyllaceae*)

Two species or gypsophila, *G. elegans* and *G. oldhamiana* are grown in gardens as annuals.

G elegans is medium in height (45-60 cm) much branched and bears numerous small pure white flowers. Although the flowering does not continue for a long time, it shows a very effective contrast in a mixed border. It is also widely used for floral arrangement. The plants grow better, if sown *in situ* and seedlings thinned out 20-25 cm apart. Sowing is done in September-November.

G. oldhamiana is 40-50 cm tall plant with broader leaves, greyish green in colour. Flowers in rose pink and its shades, appear in clusters at the end of the branches.

HELIANTHUS (*Compositae*) *Sunflower.*

The different varieties of sunflower grown for garden decoration can be grouped into two species—*Helianthus annus* and *H. dubilis*. Height of *H. annus* vary from 60 cm to 2·5 metres. Large single yellow flowered and large chrysanthemum flowered varieties are common. There are also large double flowered varieties plants of medium or dwarf height. Plants during the summer has chocholate, bronze or wine red flowers. A strain producing chocolate, bronze and wine red flowers are very attractive and popular in gardens.

Miniature or Japanese sunflower belongs to the species *H. dubilis*. The plants are much branched, bushy, 120 cm in height and bear small yellow flowers

Sunflowers can be grown as summer and rainy season annuals for beds and borders. The seeds are sown from January-June and the seedlings transplanted after about 3 weeks. The seeds may be sown *in situ.*

HELICHRYSUM BRACTEATUM (*Compositae*) *Everlasting flower.*

Helichrysum produces excellent cut flowers and the dry flowers last long. It is very free flowering, bears fairly large flowers of various colour, crimson, dark red, rose, salmon, yellow, pink and white on erect plants 80-120 cm in height.

For drying, the flowers are cut when half open and hung in a dry, cool place till they are thoroughly dried. Helichrysum is mainly grown in borders and the seedlings start flowering after 3 to 3½ months.

HELIOTROPIUM ARBORESCENS (*H. peruvianum*) (*Boraginaceae*) *Heliotrope.*

In the plains Heliotrops are grown as an annual during winter in bed, mixed border and pots. The plant is about 40-50 cm in height, produces scented flowers of pink, deep violet, purple and white. It grows well in rich loamy soil in full sun. Seeds are sown in September-November and to get bloom during January to March. In the hills seeds are sown during March-April.

HELIPTERUM ROSEUM (*Acroclinium roseum*) (*Compositae*) *Acroclinium.*

Acroclinium produces beautiful double daisy like flowers on 40-50 cm tall plants. Colour of the flower may be white, rose or reddish brown with centre of yellow or dark shade and the papery flowers last long when cut or dried. The plants thrive well in porous soil and sunny situation.

IBERIS UMBELLATUM and I. AMARA (*Cruciferae*) *Candytuft*.

Both the species are commonly known as candytuft and are widely grown in bed, border, for edging and in window boxes. *I. umbellatum* are much branched dwarf plants (15-30 cm) producing clusters of white, rose pink, carmine flowers at the end of the branches. Varieties bearing white flowers are popular edge plants.

I. amara is also known as hyacinth flowered candytuft. The plants are erect and produce large spike of white flower like that of a hyacinth. This type also form well-shaped pot plant. The seeds are sown *in situ* or the seedlings transplanted. Time of sowing in plains is September to November and in the hills during summer or autumn. Seedlings start flowering after 2 to 2½ months.

IMPATIENS BALSAMINA (*Balsaminaceae*) *Balsam*.

Balsam is a popular flowering plant in this country and widely grown in summer and rains. The plants are 20-60 cm tall usually branched and bushy and bear large number of single, semi-double or double flowers. The colours may be white, pink, rose purple, crimson, blue mauve and in various shades and also striped. Camellia flowered type is the best. Dwarf varieties (20-25 cm high) bear large number of flowers on the main stem and branches and make a beautiful display of colour.

The plants grow well in rich, porous but moist soil and in high humidity in sunny places. They can also be grown in semishade. The seeds are sown in January-February for summer flowering and in May-June to obtain blooms during the rains. In case of Balsam, the best method is to sow the seeds *in situ* and thin out the seedlings. Transplanting can also be done.

KOCHIA TRICHOPHYLLA (*Chenopodiaceae*) *Summer cypress, Burning Bush*.

Kochia grows into a well-shaped plant oval or rounded in form. The fine foliage is light green in colour and showy. At maturity the leaves turn coppery red and small flowers produced on the plant resemble a burning bush.

Kochia is grown in summer and rains and are commonly grown in pots for decoration. In bed, it is grown as back ground for annuals and usually attains a height of 50-80 cm. Seeds are sown during February to April. The plants grow well in rich and porous soil.

LATHYRUS ODORATUS (*Leguminosae*) *Sweet Pea.*

Sweet pea is usually grown as annual climber and trained on trailis, temporary support or on dry branches. There are numerous varieties of sweet pea and flower colours may be white, pink, rose, purple, maroon, red, scarlet brown, salmon, lavender and various other shades. Marked improvement in sweet pea has been done by hybridisation and mutation.

When grown as climber the seeds are sown *in situ* in a well-prepared and manured narrow strip of land at a distance of 8-10 cm. The seedlings are thinned out keeping plants at a distance of 15-20 cm. Two rows of plants at 30-35 cm apart will, however, cover the support and produce large number of flowers to make a more colourful display. Sweet pea grows extremely well if trenches are prepared by deep digging and throughly mixed with adequate amount of rotted cow manure. In the plains the seeds are sown in September-October and in the hills in March-April or during August-October. Dwarf varieties (25-30 cm high) are grown in beds or borders.

LIMONIUM SINUATUM (*Plumbaginaceae*) *Statice, Sea Lavender.*

Although statice is a biennial, it is grown as an annual. The plants are 40-60 cm tall and flowers are borne in loose and short one sided spike on the end of the branches. The flowers are white, lavender, mauve, blue, salmon pink, carmine and pink. Another popular species *L. suworowii* is 40-60 cm tall, grows in rosette and bears long branched spike of rose coloured flower.

Statice makes excellent pot plants and are also used in mixed borders. The flowers are ideal for cuttings. The plants grow better if seeds are sown *in situ* in a rich and porous soil and flower in 3 to 3½ months after sowing.

LINARIA MAROCCANA (*Scrophulariaceae*) *Linaria, Toadflax.*

Plants are bushy, dwarf, much branched, 20-30 cm in height. Small antirrhinum like flowers are borne in short spikes and the colours are white, yellow, pink, rose, purple, red, blue and bicoloured or blotched. The plants are grown in beds, borders, rock garden and in pots.

The seeds may be sown in permanent beds or the seedlings may be transplanted.

LINUM GRANDIFLORUM var : Rubrum (*Linaceae*) *Scarlet flax.*

The plants are 40-60 cm tall with narrow leaves. Flowers are about 2·5 cm across, scarlet with dark centres and borne in loose heads at the end of the stems. Linum can be grown in bed and border and makes a colourful display.

LOBELIA ERINUS (*Campanulaceae*) *Lobelia.*

The blue flowering variety of Lobelia is widely grown as edging in Western countries. Apart from various shades of blue, it has red and white flowering varieties also. The plants are compact, bushy, dwarf (10-20 cm) and bear numerous flowers (1·9 cm across). They are also ideal for pots, beds, borders and window boxes and grow well in cold climate in rich and moist soil.

The seeds are sown in September-October in the plains and in March-April in the hills and flowering starts in 3 to 3½ months from sowing.

LUPINUS HARTWEGII (*Luguminosae*) *Lupin.*

Among the annual flowering species *L. hartwegii* is commonly grown in the gardens. It has a very attractive appearance and large erect spikes of pea-shaped flowers are borne at the end of the branches. Colour of flowers in different varieties includes white, pink and blue. Lupin is ideal for growing in beds, border, pot and are used as cut flowers.

• Perennial species are suitable for the hills. *L. polyphyllus* has a wide range of flower colours like crimson, white, rose, orange, various shades of blue, pink, purple and lavender. Lupins do best when sown at the permanent site in September-October in the plains and in March-April in the hills. They grow well in light and porous soil in partial shade.

MYOSOTIS ALPESTRIS (*Boraginaceae*) *Forget-me-not.*

The plants are 30-40 cm tall, much branched, bushy and bear cluster of small flowers at the end of the branches. Colour of the flower is white, pink, sky blue or dark blue.

Myosotis flourishes well in pots and beds and can be grown in rock garden and mixed borders.

Seeds are sown in September-October in the plains and flowering starts after about 5 months.

NEMESIA STRUMOSA (*Scrophulariaceae*) *Nemesia.*

Nemesia grows well in cool climate. The plants are 15-30 cm high and have bushy habit. Small attractive flowers appear on spikes and colours are white, pink, red, rose, blue and yellow. It is ideal for cut flower, pots, beds and border. The varieties with shorter height are grown in rock gardens and edges.

NICOTIANA ALATA (*N. affinis*) (*Solanaceae*) *Flowering Tobacco.*

Nicotiana is a popular annual flowering plant grown in border and bed. The plants are 70-100 cm high, much branched, bear large funnel-shaped flowers on loose spike. The sweet scented flowers are pink, red, rose, pale green, maroon, white, smoky purple. Flowers of many varieties open in the evening, day blooming varieties are also available. The plants thrive well in rich but porous soil.

NIGELLA DAMASCENA (*Ranunculaceae*) *Love-in-a mist.*

It is not a popular annual in Indian garden but it is quite attractive when in flower. The plants are erect, 40-50 cm tall with finely cut dark green leaves. The flowers 3·0 to 4·0 cm across, white, rose or blue in colour, sky and dark blue are spectacular. Nigella is good for cut flower, pots and border.

PAPAVER RHOEAS (*Papaveraceae*) *Shirley poppy, Corn Poppy.*

It is a common and attractive annual, bearing large cup-shaped single or double flowers on long erect stalks about 50-80 cm in height. The colour of the flowers are white, pink, scarlet, rose, blue, maroon. In single, there are varieties with contrasting edges. Doubles are taller, more attractive and the flower retain longer than the singles.

Poppy is excellent for bed and herbaceous borders. It grows better if sown directly in the bed and the seedlings thinned out at a distance of 20-25 cm. Soil should be light and well drained.

PETUNIa HYBRIDA (*Solanaceae*) *Petunia*.

Petunia is a popular and colourful annual commonly grown in beds, herbaceous border and in pots and window boxes. The plants may be 20-35 cm in height with trailing branches and produce many funnel-shaped flowers. There are various types of petunia which show marked difference in growth, size, shape and colour of the flowers.

(i) *Bedding*—Hardy, free flowering type, bearing numerous small (4 cm across) funnel-shaped flowers. The colours are white, pink, blue, violet, rose and red.

(ii) *Grandifloras*—This type is a comparatively low-growing plant and produces large (10-12 cm) single flower of attractive colour. The edge of the flowers is smooth, frilled or ruffled.

(iii) *Doubles*—Double petunias are magnificient flowers. The plants are widely grown in beds, border and pots. In the plains seeds are sown during August to October. The plants flower well in rich, porous soil and require 3-4 months to initiate flower. Doubles are also propagated vegetatively in the hills. In Japan, USA and Europe all double petunias are being produced by hybridisation.

PHLOX DRUMMONDII (*Polemoniaceae*) *Pholox*.

Phlox is a popular annual throughout the world. It is widely grown in beds, border, pot, boxes and rock garden. The types include *Grandiflora* with large flowers, *Nana compacta* having dwarf growth habit and star type producing star-shaped flowers. Many colours exist in grandiflora—white, light yellow, pink, rose, scarlet, crimson, dark blue, violet blue, violet etc. Nana compacta and star type produce compact bunch of flowers.

Phlox is easy to cultivate and flowers well in rich soil. Seeds are sown in August-October and seedlings begin to flower with 3 to 3½ months.

PIMPINELLA MONOICA (*Umbelliferae*) *Lady's lace.*

It is a tall growing annual (130-180 cm) with finely cut foliage and bearing small white flowers on loose heads at the end of the branches. Lady's lace is grown in borders and in shrubbery. The flowers are commonly used for floral decoration.

Seeds are sown in September-October and the seedlings flower in about 3 months.

PORTULACA GRANDIFLORA (*Portulaceae*) *Portulaca.*

This is a low growing (8-12 cm high) plant with narrow and fleshy leaves. Single or double flowers, very attractive in pink, rose, orange, scarlet, white and lavender, appear at the end of small branches. Portulaca is grown in border, rock garden and pots and flowers open in sun. It thrives well in porous soil and flowers for long period during the winter, spring and early summer. The perennial type with double deep rose flower is effectively used in rock garden, window boxes.

Annual type is grown from seeds and the perennials from cutting.

SALPIGLOSSIS SINUATA (*Solanaceae*) *Velvet flower.*

It is a beautiful annual, grown in subtropical or temperate and in tropical region having prolonged winter. The plant grows up to a height 70 cm and bears funnel-shaped flowers of velvety appearance. The colour of flower may be white, deep yellow, orange, scarlet, deep violet, blue, beautifully netted or veined.

In the plains it is grown like other winter annuals and sown directly at permanent site or transplanted from seed bed.

SALVIA (*Labiatae*) *Sage.*

Three species of Salvia are often grown as annual in this country—*Salvia splendens*, *S. coccinea* and *S. farinacea.*

S. splendens, is commonly known as scarlet sage. Height of the plant may vary from 20-70 cm depending on the variety. Bright scarlet flowers appear on long spike at the end of the branches, other colours include salmon, pink and violet.

S. coccinea—Several varieties of this species bearing red, scarlet, pink or white flowers on terminal spikes are grown in Southern India.

S. farinacea—The plants are 50-70 cm high, produces spikes of small blue or white flower.

Salvia, particularly *S. splendens* is widely grown in garden for bedding, in border, pots and the dwarf variety in rock garden. It can be grown in semishade.

SAPONARIA CALABRICA (*Caryophyllaceae*) *Soapwort.*

This is a dwarf annual and excellent for cut flowers, borders and rock garden. It produces star-shaped pink flowers in loose clusters. Saponaria is grown during the winter in the plains, sown in September-October and the seedlings flower in 2-3 months.

SCABIOSA ATROPURPUREA (*Dipsacaceae*) *Pincushion flower, Mourning Bride.*

Scabious is a beautiful annual, flourishes well in long and cool winter in the plains. The height varies from 40-90 cm, bears flower in compact pin cushion like rounded head at the ends of long erect stem.

Colour of the flower may be white, yellow, pink, rose, scarlet crimson, purple, lavender, mauve and blue. It is ideal for border and pots.

The seedlings require about 4 to 4½ months to flower.

SENECIO CRUENTUS (Compositae) *Cineraria.*

Cineraria grows best in shade or semishade where most of the annuals will make very poor display. It is excellent as pot plant and in beds in suitable situation. The plants grow well in porous soil and comparatively long winter. In the plains, seeds are sown in September-October and the plants will be in flower during February-March. Seeds are sown in March-

April in the hills. The height of the plant varies from 30-60 cm. Large clusters of head appear at the terminal end of the branches and the colours are white, pink, blue, violet, red, scarlet or purple. Varieties showing different colours at the centre and in rings are also available. Singles are more popular than the doubles.

TAGETES (*Compositae*) *Marigold.*

Marigold is a popular name among the flowers. There are two common types of marigold, African (*Tagetes erecta*) and French (*Tagetes patula*). It is widely grown in beds, pots, rock gardens and as cut flower for making garlands, bouquets and also for worship.

AFRICAN MARIGOLD

Many varieties of African marigold have been evolved, which show variation in the height of plant, shape and size of flower. The height of plants ranges from 60-100 cm or more, colours are lemon yellow, golden yellow and orange and recently another colour nearest to white is also available. Size of the flower may vary from 5 to 15 cm, carnation flowered type normally produces large flowers. Dwarf chrysanthemum flowered varieties are very useful for bedding.

F_1 hybrids are superior to the common varieties.

FRENCH MARIGOLD

French marigold is a popular flower throughout the world, having a wider range of colour than the African type. It grows very easily, plant has dwarf, bushy growth (10-32 cm high) almost rounded in shape and bears large number of flowers of attractive colour. The flower colour may be yellow, golden, rusty red, mahagony, orange, deep-scarlet and often blotched, stripped or spotted in different colours. The heads may be single or double.

Although marigold can be grown throughout the year, mild winter is favourable for its growth and flowering. Hence, it is widely grown in the winter months in the plains and the seeds are sown in September-October. In the hills, sowing is done in

March-April. French marigold flowers profusely in porous soil, while growth and flowering in African type are better in rich and moist soil.

TROPAEOLUM MAJUS (*Tropaeolaceae*) (*Nasturtium*)

Nasturtium may be a climber or a dwarf compact bush, the latter type is popular in Indian garden and grown in beds, borders, hanging baskets and window boxes. It grows and flowers well in light and porous soil, rich soil tends to produce excessive vegetative growth, causes delay in flowering and reduces the number of flowers which remain inconspicious in the large green foliage. Removal of leaves before flowering makes a good display of colour. Nasturtium flowers may be single, semidouble and double and the colours are yellow, orange, scarlet or mahagony ; some varieties have various shades or stripes in contrasting colour.

The plants grow well, if the seeds are sown *in situ*, but transplanting is also done and require about 2 months to flower.

VERBENA (*Verbenaceae*)

In verbena, there are two types—annual flowering (*Verbena hybrida*) and perennial type (*V. erinoides*). Annual flowering type is commonly grown in the plains during the winter and the seeds are sown in September-October. This popular annual is grown in border, edges, rockeries and also in pots and boxes. Tuft of flowers in white, pink, rose, mauve, purple, violet or blue with contrasting centre, appear abundantly on low-growing spreading plants, 15-25 cm in height.

The perennial species are low growing with finely cut foliage, flowering in summer and colours are white, pink or mauve.

VIOLA TRICOLOR HORTENSIS (*Violaceae*) *Pansy*

Pansy is a beautiful flowering plant and popular throughout the world. It is grown as an annual in the plains and used in beds, border, edging, pots and window boxes. It can be also grown in semishade. The plants are low growing, compact, about 18-22 cm in height having dark green foliage. The flower arises on a stalk above the plant and may be white, pink rose, orange, yellow, blue, violet, red, purple, in clear colour or beautifully marked, blotched or stripped. Size of the flower may vary between 6-10 cm across.

F_1 hybrids are very popular because of vigorous growth and production of large number of flowers of better size.

Viola (*Viola cornuta*) produces smaller self-coloured flowers (2·0 to 4·0 cm) on vigorous and compact plants. The flowers are yellow, white, apricot, violet or violet blue.

ZINNIA ELEGANS (*Compositae*) (*Zinnia*)

It is a popular flowering annual for summer and rains. There are many types and numerous varieties in zinnia varying in the plant height and size, shape and colour of flowers. The height may vary from 25-100 cm or more. Some popular types are Dahlia flowered, Burpeeana, Giant of California, Haageana, Thumbelina, Cupid, Lilliput and Joni Thumb. Colour of flowers may be white, yellow, pink, rose, orange, scarlet, violet, red, lilac, etc. and size of flowers may vary from 3-12 cm.

F_1 hybrids have vigorous growth and are free flowering.

The seeds of zinnia are sown from January to June for flowering during summer and rains. First flower bud appearing on small seedling is removed to induce branching. Zinnia grows well in light soil, rich in organic matter. The seedlings may be transplanted or the seeds sown *in situ.* The plants are highly susceptible to leaf curl virus in the plains.

Zinnia linearis is a dwarf and bushy plant, reaching a height of 20-25 cm. It grows well in winter and summer and produces numerous small white or orange flowers. The plants are very suitable for growing in beds, border and pots and continue to flower for several months.

CHAPTER VIII

Bulbous plants

Importance, Cultivation, Propagation and Storage of Bulbs

In horticulture, the word bulb includes underground modified stems which are used for propagation e.g. bulb, corm, tuber and rhizome. Plants with tuberous roots are also grouped as bulbous plants. A large number of these plants producing attractive flowers are grown in the hills and are commercially important plants in floriculture. Many types, however, flower well. both in plains and hills but the season of growth and flowering may vary.

A bulbous plant has normally three phases during a year—growth, flowering and dormancy. Vegetative growth may precede flowering as in *Gladiolus* or flowering starts before the leaf emerges, e.g., *Amaryllis*, *Haemanthus*. After growth and flowering, the plants in most cases, enter into rest period and the duration of dormancy varies with the type of plants and environmental conditions like temperature and humidity.

Bulbs which grow and flower well in the hills include *Agapanthus*, *Anemone*, *Cylamen*, .*Eurycles*, *Fritillaria*, *Iris*, *Ixia*, *Hyacinth*, *Moraea*, *Montbretia*, *Nerine*, *Paeonia*, *Kniphofia*, *Ornithogalum*, *Ranunculus*, *Tulip*, *Watsonia*, *Sparaxis*, *Zantedeschia* Tuberous Begonia, etc. Although some hardy types of *Freesia*, *Daffodil*, *Narcissus*, *Gloxinia*, and *Lilium* may flower in plains but they do not show very attractive display of colour and often fail to flower in the second year.

PLANTING

Bulbous plants are grown in beds, shrubbery, herbaceous border, grassy land and in pots and bowl. Bulbs, corms, rhizome or tuber are usually planted when they have shown signs of sprouting after dormancy. In Canna, however, the rhizomes are taken out of bed in growing condition and replanted after a week or so.

The planting materials are normally placed deep in the soil and the soil around it is gently pressed. The depth of planting varies with the type of plants and size of bulbs. For most of the bulbous plants grown in tropical garden, the planting depth is between 3-10 cm.

Bulbs prefer loam or sandy loam soil. In stiff clay, rooting is delayed and too much moisture often causes rotting. If the soil is not perfectly well-drained, the bulbs may be planted on a bed of sand. Watering is not required after planting as the fleshy underground stems contain sufficient food materials to develop initial growth of root and shoot. Before root formation, watering proves injurious to the bulbs and helps in rotting.

Most of these plants prefer sunny situation, while *Eucharis*, *Zephyranthes* thrive better in semishade ; few types, e.g. *Pancratium*, *Haemanthus*, *Zephyranthes* grow and flower well in sun and semishade. Bulbs, corms and tubers should not come in direct contact with fresh organic manure, rhizomes are not usually affected. Time of planting depends on the season of flowering, environmental condition of the region and condition of the planting material. In the plains, *Gladiolus* is planted from September to November, whereas in the hills. the planting season is normally from April-June. *Amaryllis*, *Hippeastrum*, *Haemanthus* are planted in January-February to obtain flowers in March-April. *Caladium* and *Canna* are put in the ground in May.

LIFTING AND STORAGE

After the above ground portion dries out the bulbs are lifted out carefully. The root and shoot are cut and the bulbs are cleaned before storage. They should be stored in dark, dry and airy place until the time of next planting. Storage condition is very important for obtaining healthy bulbs. If the humidity is very high, fungus develops on the bulbs and causes rotting. In a very dry atmosphere the bulbs shrivel and may lose viability.

It is not necessary to lift all types of bulbous plants every year. *Amaryllis*, *tuberose*, *Caladium*, *Pancratium*, *Zephyranthes* may remain in the ground for three years before they are lifted. But water should be withheld when the bulbs are lying in dormant condition in ground or pot. *Gladiolus*, on the other hand, has to be lifted out every year after drying of leaves.

PROPAGATION

Bulbs, corms, tubers and rhizomes are used for vegetative propagation. Various methods and structures used for propagation are as follows :

(a) Division of clump—Rhizomatous plants like *Canna*, *Alpinia* can be divided into small clumps.

(b) Offsets produced laterally are separated for multiplication.

(c) Cormlets or bulblets produce new plants.

(d) Scales of Lilium are separated and used for propagation.

(e) Bulbil arising from the axils of leaves produce new plants.

(f) Pieces of bulb disc with leaves or rhizome also develop new plants.

Description and Method of Cultivation

AMARYLLIS (*Amaryllidaceae*)

Amaryllis belladona is the only species of the genus, a native of South Africa. It is a plant with strap-shaped, glossy, green leaves and producing few large funnel-shaped flowers on a stout stalk, from March-May. Leaves appear at the end of the flowering season and die out before the winter sets in. In warm humid region the plants retain leaves throught the year and bear flower during the season. Offsets, developed from the original bulb are separated for multiplication. Bulbs are planted 5-8 cm deep in December-January and the plants grow well in rich and porous soil. Amaryllis is not disturbed for several years at one place and the plants continue to produce new bulbs and flowers. It is very suitable for planting in border, shrubbery and in pot. Although rose or rosy pink colour is common, white to purplish colour are also found.

CALADIUM (*Araceae*)

The genus comprises of about 16 herbaceous perennial species with tuberous rhizome. They are a native of tropical America and are widely grown in warm humid climate for the beautiful and attractive foliage produced during the rainy season. Some of the important and interesting species are *Caladium bicolor, C. humboldtii, C. picturatum, C. schomburgkii*. Numerous varieties have been raised particularly from *C. bicolor.*

Leaves are usually peltate-segittate, stalks variegated, blades are with very many shades of colour, e.g. variegated green, blue green, dark green, light green, spotted with white, red, transparent white, etc. Leaf veins may be red, silvery or green. Leaf margins are coloured with purple, white, yellow or red. In some species, shape of the blade is lanceolate-sagittate. Flowers are unisexual.

The pot compost for planting *Caladium* should be prepared by mixing loamy soil with leafmould and well-decomposed cow dung manure. It prefers moist but porous soil. Application of liquid manure at frequent intervals enhances growth and improves colour of foliage.

Caladium is propagated through division of the tuberous rhizome and rarely by seeds. It is planted in summer and leaves show a fine display of colour in the rainy season.

The leaves start fading in autumn and water is gradually withheld until they have withered. In dormant condition, the rhizome may be allowed to remain in the soil or dug out and stored in a cool and dry place.

COOPERIA (*Amaryllidaceae*)

The genus is named after Joseph Cooper, an English gardener, comprises about 6 species native of North America, and differing from *Zephyranthes* by the long perianthtube and erect anthers. They are tender bulbous plants with the habit of *Zephyranthes* but blooms only at night. Important species are *C. drummondii* and *C. pedunculata.* Flowers are fragrant, white, sometimes tinged with red or pink.

Flowers are solitary, the perianth subtended by a bract like spathe. Leaves are long, narrow flat and twisted and appear along with the flower.

It is cultivated in a semishady location and in sandy loam soil. Addition of well-rotted compost, sand and charcoal dust in beds or pots is beneficial.

Cooperia is propagated by bulbs. It is planted during spring in rock garden, border or in pots and starts blooming during May-June.

COOPERANTHES (*Amaryllidaceae*)

This genus is a product of intergeneric hybrid between species of *Cooperia* and *Zephyranthes*, first raised in 1900 by Percy Lancaster at the Agri-Horticultural Society, Alipore, Calcutta. Hybrid between *Cooperia oberwettii* x *Zephyranthes robusta* is known as Alipore Beauty, is probably the best known *Cooperanthes*. Flowers are light lilac, rose or white.

It grows well in well-drained sandy loam soil, rich in organic matter and in semishade.

Cooperanthes are propagated by bulbs. They are planted in the spring and the plants start flowering by the end of summer. They are grown both in bed or in pot and are good as cut flowers.

CRINUM (*Amaryllidaceae*)

The genus *Crinum*, comprises more than 100 species of large and showy flowering bulbous plants. They are closely allied to *Amaryllis* and distinguished by the longer perianth tube. The species cross freely and many fine hybrids of *Crinum*, between *Crinum* and *Amaryllis* and *Crinum* and *Hymenocallis* are known. Some of the important cultivated species and hybrids are *C. longifolium*, *C. mooriei*, *C. powellii*, *C. variabile*, *C. asiaticum*, *C. augustum*, *C. careyanum*,

Pancratium

Water lilies

A herbaceous border of a garden

Haemanthus

C. yuccaeflorum, *C. giganteum*, *C. zeylanicum*. Flowers are usually white or in shades of red and purple.

The stems arise from the tunicated bulbs with a more or less elongated neck. Leaves are large, about 150 cm long and 12-15 cm wide, evergreen or deciduous, depending on the species. Flowers are regular, often highly scented, tube narrow, with six segments and usually funnel-shaped. In some species flowers are 30 cm long and 15 cm wide.

Most of the species prefer shade or semishady location for planting. Crinums usually have large bulbs, sometimes as much as 60 to 80 cm long with numerous fleshy roots. If planted in beds, the soil should be dug to a depth of two to three feet, mixed up well with sufficient quantity of rottep cow dung and compost. It can also be grown in large pots containing soil rich in organic matter.

Bulbs should be of good size and planting is done to a depth below the ground level, twice the size of the bulbs. The plant will grow and flower for years, if watered in the summer months and top dressed with fresh loamy soil around new vegetative growth. Bulbs are planted in April to get flower during the rainy season.

EUCHARIS GRANDIFLORA (*E. amazonica*) (Amaryllidaceae)

Eucharis is an important bulbous plant, popularly known as 'Amazon Lily'. It prefers semishade and flowers better in plains than on the hills.

The bulbs are globular in shape, leaves large lanceolate. The flowers are about 7 cm across, white, sweet-scented, 5-7 blooms appear on a stalk. *Eucharis* grows better in pots than in the ground and the compost should be rather rich and heavy instead of sandy, but must not be often disturbed. It flowers in the summer and rains and the leaves begin to wither before the winter.

GLADIOLUS *(Iridiaceae)*

Gladioli are among the most beautiful flowers, blossoming from October to March in plains and during June to September in the Hills. This genus comprises more than 150 species of perennial herbs with base of stem swollen into a corm. Most of them have their origin in South Africa, although a few originated from Europe. The species in cultivation and of considerable importance include :

G. cardinalis, *G. childsii*, *G. colvillei*, *G. gandavensis*, *G. lemoinei*, *G.nanceianus*, *G. nanus*, *G. primulinus*, *G. psittacinus*, *G. purpureoauratus*, *G. saundersii*. The numerous crosses have evolved large number of varieties of varying characters and it is almost impossible to keep up with and enumerate the different varieties of gladioli. Wide range of attractive colour shades may be grouped into white, yellow, cream shaded pink, orange, pale pink on white, pink on cream apricot, salmon, cherry red, orange-scarlet, crimson, purple, mauve and violet etc.

Gladioli prefer sunny situation with light sandy soil, with pH between 6 to 7. If the soil is heavy, addition of river sand and charcoal improves the soil condition. They grow well both in pot and in beds and the magnificent spikes brighten the garden and room as cut flower. Two parts sandy loam soil, mixed with one part of each well-rotted cow dung manure and leafmould and a handful of bone meal is recommended for pot culture. If planted in beds the ground should be dug deep and well-decayed compost at the rate of 4 kg per metre mixed thoroughly and left for sun drying at least for a fortnight. At planting time fresh manure should not be used, but a dressing of bonemeal, superphosphate and wood ash may be given with advantage. In the plains, planting is usually done during September-November and in the hills from April-June, but the flowering season may be extended by early and late planting.

Gladioli are propagated by seeds, corms and cormlets. New varieties are raised from seeds. Seeds germinate freely and the seedlings grown carefully, will flower in the second year. Large flower spikes, however, develop after 3-4 years when the corms attain a good size. Gladioli corms are planted 8 to 10 cm deep into the soil, at a distance of 20-30 cm between the rows and the plants. Application of liquid manure, once at the vegetative stage and again after the formation of flower buds has been found very effective.

The flowering spikes appear in 60-90 days after planting, the flowers continue to open in succession from below upwards and the open flowers remain fresh for a number of days. After flowering, the leaves begin to turn yellow and wither. The plants are then lifted with the corms and cormlets and kept in a dry shady place for a week for drying. The corms are thoroughly cleaned, the cormlets separated and stored on a layer of sand in a dry, cool, airy and shady place until the next planting season. The corms should be examined regularly and those showing sign of rotting or fungus growth should be removed. They are also stored in cold storage but in a dry atmosphere.

GLORIOSA *(Liliaceae)*

As the name implies, the genus *Gloriose* means 'full of glory', popularly known as climbing or creeping lily. They are tall creeping plants, support themselves by means of tendril which arises from leaves. This genus comprises about six species of rhizomatous plants native of Africa and tropical Asia. Important species, commonly grown in the gardens in India are *G. superba* and *G. rothschildiana*.

Leaves are oblong, lanceolate. Flowers are showy on long pedicels in leaf axils, perianth of 6 distinct long segments ; stamens six with versatile anthers.

Well-drained soil in a sunny location is ideal for planting Gloriosa and the attractive flowers make a fine display of colour when trained on bamboo frame work or low trellis.

Gloriosa is vegetatively propagated from rhizome which may be cut in pieces and planted to a depth of 3-4 cm in April-May.

The plant flowers in July-August. After flowering is over the plant begins to wither and rhizome becomes dormant. If left undisturbed, *Gloriosa* continues to produce flowers for several years in the same place. Application of liquid manure once at the active phase of vegetative growth and another just before flowering is recommended.

HAEMANTHUS (*Amaryllidaceae*)

Haemanthus is one of the popular and attractive bulbous lants, commonly known as Football Lily or Blood Lily. The genus comprises nearly 60 species, native of South and tropical Africa. The flowers are red, crimson, scarlet, pink and some species are white or pale green in colour. Some of the important species are *H. multiflorus*, *H. magnifica*, *H. lindenii*, *H. albo-maculaius*, *H. coccineus*, *H. tigrinus*, and *H. candidus*.

Bulbs are usually large with thick skin. Stems green, short, thick and fleshy. Leaves are usually large and luxuriant, turn yellow and dry in the winter months, the scape is sometimes curiously coloured. Inflorescence is a dense, many flowered umbel, perianth straight and erect with a short cylindrical tube. Flowers are showy and produced in ball-like heads. Fruits berry like, indehiscent. Flowers often appear before the leaves or sometimes simultaneously.

To plant in beds, the soil is deep dug and mixed with well-rotten compost and planted 40 cm apart. It grows well in pot and small pot is preferred. Application of organic manure in the rains and liquid manure before flowering is beneficial and the plants will continue to flower for several years in the same place.

They are propagated by offsets, which should be detached from the mother plant during spring. The bulbs are planted in pots or in beds during spring season to get bloom in summer and early part of rainy season.

HEDYCHIUM (*Zingiberaceae*)

Hedychium consists of 40 species of rhizomatous herbs native of Asia and several species are grown for their beautiful and fragrant flowers in both plains and hills. It prefers semi-shade and moist soil and produces many flowered large spikes during July-October. The leaves die before winter.

SPECIES GROWN IN GARDEN

H. coronarium is a hardy species, reaching a height of 1 to 1·5 metre and producing scented white flowers.

H. coccineum is a tall plant and bears scarlet flowers.

H. flavum produces long spikes of highly-scented yellow flowers in August-September.

HEMEROCALLIS (*Liliaceae*)

Hemerocallis is popularly known as Day Lily as the flowers last for a day and the blossoms fade at night. This genus consists of more than a dozen species and they are mostly native of China and Japan. The plants are very hardy, stout rooted, glabrous, perennial herbaceous plants, admired for their showy blooms.

Some of the common species are *H. flava*, *H. citrina*, *H. aurantiaca* and *H. multiflora*.

The leaves are almost grass like, 2 ranked at the base of the scape. Flowers are lily like, large funnel shaped, yellow or reddish orange or brown in colour. Though the individual flower last for a day, but many flowers open successively to keep the lasting beauty for a long period.

Hemerocallis grows in wide variety of soil. While planting, the ground should be dug to a depth of 50 to 60 cm and mixed up with well-rotten compost. They take a year or two to establish properly and should not be disturbed very frequently. Planting is done in February to March and flowering continues from May to August.

Propagation is by division of the clumps and also by seeds. Some of the species are self-sterile and seeds can be obtained easily by crossing two species. Many new-varieties with attractive large flowers of various colours have developed by hybridisation.

After 4-5 years, *Hemerocallis* clumps may be forked out during January-February, separated and can be replanted again in the planting season.

HIPPEASTRUM (*Amaryllidaceae*)

Hippeastrum, commonly known as Royal Dutch Amaryllis is one of the finest flowering bulbous plants. The flowers of Royal Dutch Amaryllis are larger, open widely, about 15-20 cm across, tube is shorter and the plant develops larger bulb than *Amaryllis belladona.* The spectacular flowers have various shade of bright colour and wide range of variation exists in varieties developed by hybridisation. *Hippeastrum* produced by Ludwig are famous throughout the world. A double flowered variety is also available.

The leaves are broader than Amaryllis and do not dry out in the plains. The bulbs are lifted in November-December, stored in dry cool place for a few weeks and replanted in January-February.

Hippeastrums develop flower during March-April and application of liquid organic manure before emergence of flower stalk improves the size and quality of flowers.

Improved varieties of *Hippeastrum* have developed as a result of hybridisation among the species and varieties and *H. equestre*, *H. aulicum*, *H. stylosum* and *H. reticulatum* has been widely used in crossing.

HYMENOCALLIS (*Amaryllidaceae*)

This genus comprises about 40 species of bulbous plants native of South America (one in Africa i.e., *H. speciosa*) cultivated for beautiful fragrant flowers, consisting of narrow green white petals with large coronas and protruding stamens. Some of the important species are *H. macrostephana*, *H. harrisiana*, *H. speciosa*, *H. caribaea*, *H. calathina*, *H. rotata*, *H. amancaes*, *H. tubiflora.* Flowers are white, except *H. amancaes* which is bright yellow.

Well-drained soil in sunny location is good for planting *Hymenocallis.* The bulbs are planted just below the surface of the soil during February to get the bloom in the month of May. The soil should be prepared by mixing 2 parts of loamy soil, one part of each well-rotten cow dung manure and leafmould. Watering should be given freely during the growing season. So long the plants remain healthy, transplanting or shifting from pot to pot is not recommended. Whenever necessary bulbs are dug out during September-October and stored in dry place for planting in February next year. *Hymenocallis* is propagated by bulbs.

NELUMBO (*Nymphaeaceae*)

Nelumbo or *Nelumbium*, popularly known as Lotus is a flower of national importance in India. The genus consists of two species—the one bearing yellow flower and the other produces white or pinkish flower.

The plant has rhizomatous stem, large peltate leaves standing well above the ground and it spreads rapidly in shallow water or wet soil. Like *Nymphaea*, Lotus prefers soil rich in organic matter and flowers profusely in summer and rains. Lotus do not grow well in lily pools and so tank is ideal for it. *N. lutea* bears scented yellow flowers 15-20 cm across. *N. nucifera* is common in India. The flowers are white or pink, 20-25 cm in diameter. Lotus is propagated by rhizome or seed.

NYMPHAEA (*Nymphaeaceae*)

The Water Lily is the most popular flowering plant in water garden. The genus comprises of 40 species of aquatic, rhizomatous plants widely grown in tank, lily pool, streams, lakes and in suitable earthenware containers.

The leaves are oval or round in shape, floating on the water or standing above the water surface. The flowers are very attractive, show various colours : white, yellow, pink, red, blue and shades of colour are found in the varieties developed by hybridisation.

Water Lily prefers clay soil rich in organic matter and sunny location. The rhizomes are planted in soil in the bed of the tank or lily pool or in baskets or pots filled with rich clay soil and then placed in the tank in March-April. In the gardens in cities and towns water lily is often planted in large earthenware container filled with water and a layer of soil. In several species and varieties leaves do not develop in the winter months and the rhizomes remain dormant. Vegetative growth starts in spring and flowers appear during the summer, rains and early winter.

In some species flowers open in day time while in other blooms open at night and close during the day. The species of Nymphaea commonly grown in water garden are as follows :

N. caerulea produces light blue flowers, 7-10 cm across, day blooming.

N. lotus, the night blooming water lily, bearing white flower 12-15 cm across.

N. odorata, a white flowering and fragrant water lily. The flowers are 8-15 cm across.

N. pubescens, has white flowers, 8-12 cm across.

N. stellata, a species commonly found in the warm humid region of India. It produces pale blue flowers about 10-16 cm in diameter.

Nymphaea is progagated from rhizomes, bulbils and seeds. Most of the species and varieties thrive and flower well at water depth between 50 to 150 cm.

POLYANTHES TUBEROSA (*Amaryllidaceae*) *Tuberose.*

Tuberose (*Polianthes tuberosa*), a native of maxico, is widely grown in the plains of India and blooms profusely during the summer and rains, flaunting its fragrance outdoors and indoors. Most artistic garland, floral ornaments, bouquets and button holes are made from these flowers. The long spike of flowers is excellent for table decoration. The flowers remain fresh for days together and bathe the atmosphere with their sweet pleasant fragrance.

The tuber is bulb-shaped and the plant is commonly classed among the 'Bulbs'. The leaves are 70-80 cm long, narrow, linear and radical, bright green in colour. The flowering stalk which emerges from the centre of the cluster of leaves is about 80-120 cm long bearing successively smaller long pointed clasping leaves, uppermost ones are much reduced and bract-like. The flower buds are tubular. Flowers are 5-6 cm long, borne in pairs in an open spike pure wavy white, highly fragrant, tube 2·5 to 3·0 cm long, slightly bent near the base, expanding widely where it meets the oblong obtuse segments.

There are three types of tuberose in cultivation—'single' with one row of corolla segments ; 'semi-double' bearing flowers with two to three rows of segments and 'double' having more than three rows of corolla segments. Though there is no popular named variety in tuberose. 'The Pearl' is known to be a variety in the double flowered type. A variety with variegated leaf bearing single flowers is also grown. Single flowered type is more widely cultivated than the other types.

The bulbs remain dormant during the winter months in places where the temperature is low and if early planting is desired, the dormancy can be successfully broken by dipping the bulbs in 4% thiourea solution for one hour. Normally tuberose begins to flower in 90-95 days after planting. It flowers during the summer and rains (April-September) in the plains of eastern part of the country and from May to July on the hills, while in milder climate tuberose flowers well throughout the year.

Bulbs having diameter 2·0 and 2·5 cm show satisfactory growth and flowering. The average life of a flower spike is about 10-15 days *in situ*, while that of an individual flower varies from 4-6 days. Vase life of a spike varies from 7-10 days, depending on the environment and change of water. The spikes remain fresh for a longer period, if kept in 4% sugar solution.

Tuberose can be successfully grown in pots, beds, borders shrubberies and rockeries. Propagation is by means of seeds and bulbs. Vegetative propagation is commonly practiced and desirable too, because such plants produce better flowers within a short period after planting.

The land should be throughly cultivated until the soil comes to good tilth. A good amount of rotted cow dung or farm yard manure should be incorporated with the soil at least 10-15 days before planting. The bulbs are planted 4-5 cm deep in beds in March-April in the plains and in May-June on the hills. The planting distance between the bulbs is 10-15 cm, while the rows are spaced 25 cm apart. For pot cultivation 1-2 bulbs are planted in a 20 cm pot.

A fertilizer mixture containing 6 gms of urea, 16 gms each of superphosphate (single) and muriate of potash per square meter has been found to show satisfactory growth and flowering. The above mixture should be applied in two equal doses—the first dose before planting and the second one, 4 weeks after sprouting of the bulb.

Commercial growers dig out bulbs 3 years after planting. They are stored in a cool, dry and shady place and planted again in the following spring.

ZEPHYRANTHES (*Amaryllidaceae*)

Zephyranthes has a fanciful meaning i.e., the 'West-wind Flower', commonly known as Zephyr Flower or Fairy Lily. The Genus has about 50 species of bulbous flowering plants, native of warmer region of America. It is related to *Habranthus*, *Pyrolirion* and *Hippeastrum*. Some of the popular species are *Z. candida*, *Z. citrina*, *Z. grandiflora*, *Z. rosea*, *Z. macrosiphon*, *Z. tubispatha*, and *Z. Verecunda*. The flowers are with many colour ranges i.e., white, yellow and various shades of pink.

Zephyranthes is a hardy bulbous herb. Leaves are filiform or linear or may be strap shaped. Flowers solitary, peduncle elongated, slender, hollow ; perianth funnel-shaped, erect or slightly inclined, stamens 6, stigma 3-fid.

Zephyranthes is planted in beds, pots and border. They grow well in sandy loam soil and addition of well-rotten compost or leafmould is beneficial.

It is commonly propagated by separating the bulbs, sometimes through seeds. Bulbs are planted in spring, 30 to 40 mm deep and 12 to 15 cm apart. They flower during summer and rains and make a very colourful display specially in rains. Top dressing of organic manure once a year in the rainy season will promote flowering and the bulbs may be left undisturbed for many years.

CHAPTER IX

Canna

Cannas are very important and popular perennial flowering plants and grow abundantly in the humid tropical regions throughout the world. They are very hardy and thus grown easily and successfully. The flowers have many shades of colour, appear throughout the year and make a wonderful display of colour which can hardly be surpassed by any other perennial plant. Cannas are frequently grown in private gardens but more extensively in the public gardens. As the flowers do not last long as cut flowers and are very common garden plants, visitors do not show much interest to pluck the flowers or pamage the plants. Cannas alone with their various shades of colour can make a garden quiet attractive.

The genus Canna has about 50 species, native of Tropical America and Asia and the following three species of Canna are considered to be the parents of the present cultivated varieties.

1. CANNA INDICA (*Indian shot*)

Rhizome stout, stem slender green 1 to 1·2 m high. Leaves oblong 45-60 cm long green, flower in simple raceme or in pairs ; sepals-short, waxy ; petals-pale pink, lanceolate ; staminodes 3 red or rose about 5 cm long.

2. CANNA FLACCIDA

Stem rather slender, 1·2 to 2 m high. Leaves ovate-lanceolate 20-30 cm long. Flowers few flowered raceme, pale yellow to sulphur ; sepals-small ; petals-linear-lanceolate, up to 7 cm long ; staminodes–3 about 7 cm long.

3. CANNA LUTEA

Stem green 1 to 1·2 meters high. Leaves oblong or broad-lanceolate, 25-40 cm long. Flowers on simple raceme pale yellow ; sepals-ob ong green white margined ; petals-lanceolate pale yellowish white ; staminodes pale yellow.

In India improvement of canna has chiefly been achieved through hybridisation and the pioneer work in this line was taken up at the Agri-Horticultural Society, Calcutta in 1890. A large number of varieties have been developed as a result of hybridisation and selection for a period of 45 years and these varieties are now commonly grown in the gardens. Depending on the size and shape of the flowers, cannas have been classified as follows :

Crozy and gladiolus flower :

These are improved hybrids raised by Anne in about 1850 and Vilmorin in 1880.

ALIPORE HYBRIDS :

The selections are the results of 45 years of hybridisation and are a great improvement on the crozy types from which they are derived. The size of the flowers markedly increased with a wide range of colour.

Giant or Orchid flower :

Originated in Italy and was very popular for many years. The large blooms of silky appearance resemble the Flag Iris, but not very hardy.

DREADNAUGHT :

A great advance on the ordinary crozy or gladiolous flowered canna both as regards the individual flowers and bunches.

DWARF :

This type include varieties which does not exceed the height of 70-80 cm at any time of the year and are very effective for breeding purpose.

BOUQUET :

In this class an ideal variety 'cupid' has flowers on closely branched spikes. The plants of this variety are also dwarf.

CANDLEABRA :

This is a distinct break. The main flower stalk branches and as many as 8-12 spikes are produced instead of two or three.

MINIATURE :

This is small flowering type derived by crossing a society's dwarf hybrid with Canna indica. The spikes are neat and compact.

Cannas can also be divided into several classes according to the colour of the flowers.

1. Selfs—without spots or margin, one colour only.
2. Spotted—usually a shade of red on cream or yellow ground or red spots on orange or red ground.
3. Striped red on a cream or a yellow ground.
4. Margin yellow.
5. Margined with a darker shade than the ground colour.
6. Flaked red or orange on a paler ground.
7. Splashed orange on a deeper ground.

The shades of colour cover a wide range from creamy white through yellow, orange and pink to an intense maroon red. There is no blue or purple colour in canna. There are also few varieties with dark leaves usually reddish purple, also producing dark red flowers. In one variety, however, the leaves are striped yellow.

CULTIVATION

Canna is commonly propagated by rhizome. Seeds are used for raising new varieties through hybridisation. The seeds have hard seed-coat and take a long time to germinate, if the seeds are not treated with hot water or rubbed on a sand paper. The rhizomes are collected in the month of May and then planted to get the full benefit of the Monsoon and a strong clump forms before the winter. The soil is prepared by digging at least 50 cm deep, breaking the clods and mixing in fresh stable manure at the rate of 100 kg to a bed of 10 sq. metre.

The rhizomes are buried 3 cm below the surface of the soil and thoroughly flooded. If the weather is hot and dry, shade is provided for a few days. Planting is done at a distance of 30-40 cm between the rows and the plant. Within six weeks after planting first flower spikes appear which should be removed to encourage better growth. The bed should be kept free from weeds by frequent weeding. After the rain ceases and the soil thoroughly dries, it is loosened and allowed to dry. Digging and watering of the bed are necessary at least once a month in the winter and more frequent flooding is recommended to keep the soil moist. A mulch of manure given in early November and another in January will keep the plants in flower throughout the year. Canna is replanted every year. The rhizome is lifted with a forked hoe, cleaned properly and the top growth cut leaving a stem of about 15 cm. The clump is then split taking only the strongest root and stored in a shady place for a week or so before replanting. The canna beds should be kept clean by collecting faded flowers and removing dry leaves.

Cannas can also be grown in 30-35 cm pot and the compost should consist of 2 parts stable manure and 1 part garden soil. The potted plants should be replanted every 6-9 months as the roots become pot bound.

PESTS AND DISEASES

Cannas are hardy plants and are particularly free of diseases. Caterpillars occasionally attack the leaves specially during the rainy seasons and bettles sometime destroy the flowers. Application of insecticides like Malathion, Basudin, etc. will keep away the insects.

NAMES OF SOME GOOD VARIETIES OF CANNAS AND THEIR FLOWER COLOUR

American Beauty	Handsome orange scarlet flowers.
Apricot	Buff-yellow base overspread with salmon pink.

Aurora Borealis	Canary-yellow with rose pink centre, beautifully rayed.
Carmine king	Bright carmine-red with yellow centre.
Cleopatra	Orange terracotta. Light purple leaves.
Dorris	Pale salmon-pink. Flowers very pretty.
Golden Wedding	Yellow. Dwarf plants with very lasting flowers.
Louis Cayeux	Large flowers with bright rosy scarlet colour.
Mrs Herbert Hoover	Beautiful flowers with deep water-melon pink colour.
Mrs Pierre S. du Pont	Very charming flowers with crinkled edges and light water-melon pink colouration.
Rosamond Coles	Dark reddish-orange with deep orange yellow border.
Rosea gigantea	Very large flowers with soft rose to carmine-pink colour.
Statue of Liberty	Plants with bronze coloured leaves and blazing flame-red flowers.
Susquehana	Dwarf plants with rose-pink flowers.
The President	Beautiful large flowers with rich growing scarlet colour.
Yellow King Humbert	Bi-coloured flowers. Bright yellow petals marked with crimson dots.

CHAPTER IX

Cacti and Succulents

In Plant Kingdom one finds all sorts of variation ranging from microscopic life to large Banyan tree. Cacti are a group of plants with peculiar shape and size and mostly adopted for desert life. The adverse environment has made these plants unusual in appearance and provided morphological, anatomical, and physiological safeguards to thrive and flourish under such condition.

The Cactaceae are perennial herbs or shrubs, annual species being non-existent, with more or less fleshy stems, usually jointed. The leaves are rarely perfect and permanent, but are generally absent or rudimentary or fugacious or reduced to mere minute scales. In *Pereskia* the leaves look like normal flattened leaves as in other dicots.

In the genera *Echinopsis*, *Rebutia*, *Lobivia*, *Echinocactus*, *Astrophytum* and *Lophophora*, the stem is globular or ovoid or cylindrical, very fleshy, usually with many ribs, acute or rounded, straight, wavy or spiral, more or less notched, with areoles and spines and the flowers are borne on the areoles at the top or at the sides.

The stem of *Opuntia* is always a typical joint whether it is globular, cylindrical or flattened. The joint is, therefore, a stem which when properly formed ceases to grow at the apex, but continues to grow in size and thickness until it reaches its full development and then the rudimentary fleshy cylindrical leaves drop off and the spines grow to their full size.

Spines are of two types. The real spines, vary in length according to species and in most cases very stiff, acute, needle-like, awlshaped, tortuous, arched or hooked and develop on the outer or lower areole or bud. On the upper or inner areole, just above the spines hairs develop which are flexible or

Aloe variegata

A rock garden

A collection of grafted cactus

Glass house with Cacti and succulents

more or less stiff bristles. The spines and bristles of cacti are often a terror particularly in the operations of planting and repotting.

The largest and finest flowers of the Cactaceae are mostly nocturnal. They open at sunset and display all their glory in the dark hours of the night and droop and fade away at dawn.

CLIMATE

Cacti can tolerate wide range of temperature. In fact, with the exception of the purely tropical species all cacti are able to tolerate without much inconvenience lower temperatures than those obtaining in their native habitat. Very high temperature or very low temperature adversely affect the growth of many species of cacti. At a temperature above 35°C under the blazing sun, plants may show sign of scorching or turn yellow. In such condition the plants should be shaded off. Most epiphytic species require half-shade and a moist atmosphere.

SOIL

The soil for cacti, in general should be porous and permeable. Almost all species thrive well in a porous calcareous soil and there is a number of species for which a calcareous soil is necessary. Lime mortar from old buildings, hard limestones, marble or even crushed valves of oysters or other shell fish, roughly powdered and passed through a sieve to remove the fine dust, provide an excellent material to add to the soil. Some old leafmould, thoroughly rotted should form a part of the compost. Very well-rotted cow manure is also an useful ingredient in the compost for the cacti. Undecomposed organic matter is sure to give trouble and causes rotting of roots. Chemical fertilizers force growth and due to excessive succulence the plant becomes susceptible to drought and infection. Small quantities of bone meal, superphosphate or basic slag may be added to the compost. The compost should be watered and allowed to remain for few months before using it. A small quantity of charcoal powder also helps to keep the soil porous and sweet and prevents infection of roots. On the other hand, a soil which keeps moist or forms a green coat or crust on the surface, is either badly drained or unsuitable and should be changed without delay.

Garden loam 2 parts, sand, old mortar or limestone gravel and leafmould 1 part of each and some crushed charcoal are suitable for *Cleistocactus, Espostoa, Oreocereus, Borzicactus* etc. For *Cereus, Cephalocereus, Pachycereus, Lemaireocereus, Harrisia* and other *Cereus,* use garden loam 2 parts, old mortar or limestone gravel, leafmould or manure 1 part of each ; some crushed charcoal may be added.

PLANTING AND POTTING

Many hardy cacti are also grown in ground particularly in the rockeries. The land should be sloping and the soil porous and calcareous.

The best time for planting and potting is just at the commencement of the growing season in spring. The soil should not be too wet and it is always safe to place some dry soil beneath and around the roots. If roots are damaged at the time of planting, watering should be stopped for few days to allow the wounded roots to dry and heal. In order to promote new roots little watering is done to keep the compost just moist. Water may be given more freely later on, when the temparature rises and new growth develops.

Well-baked earthen pots are suitable for cacti, glazed or painted pots hamper the aeration of the roots.

In potting or repotting cacti, it is safe to select the pots just large enough to contain the plant. Pots which are too large have two disadvantages. When watered they retain too much moisture, retain it too long and appear as constant danger to the plant. Moreover, the roots take too long to reach the sides of the pot and spread, thus causing a delay in growth and flowering.

The pots should be filled for about one-third with crocks or other drainage material, the large curved pieces to be placed on the holes and bottom and the hole topped over by a thin layer of thick gravel, shingle or crocks, broken into small pieces.

If it is found that the roots have become pot-bound it is advisable to break off the pot with a sharp blow, instead of risking damage to the plant in trying to take it out and save the pot. The plant to be repotted should be kept dry so that it easily comes out without injuring the roots and crocks are removed carefully. The plant should be replanted just as deep down as in the previous pot. However, experience has shown that small plants, seedings and also the cuttings are best planted close to the sides of the pot, as the young roots at once reach the side of the pot, spread out quickly, grow better and are less liable to rotting from occasional excess of moisture. This practice of planting cacti along the sides of the pot is now generally adopted by nurserymen and there is ample proof that the plants make quicker and healthier growth. Unless the soil is in a perfectly dry condition, newly potted plants should not be watered for two or three days, but just lightly sprayed once or twice a day and placed in shade for about one week, afterwards in half-shade for at least an equal period before removing them to full sun.

WATERING

It is a very important practice for cultivation of cacti. Under natural condition these plants are adapted to severe drought. Their external structures and also the physiological condition clearly indicate very little requirement of water.

In the summer months, when the cacti grow, watering is done frequently. If these plants are kept in open in small pots daily watering may be necessary. Every time the soil is to be drenched completely so that excess water comes out through the drainage hole. At the resting period, during the winter months roots remain inactive and watering should be minimised gradually from the autumn. While watering, one should be careful that water does not accumulate in the depression of the plant. In *Echinopsis*, *Echinocactus*, *Rebutia* the growing point on the top may rot. Fine spraying or syringing of water may be done in the morning.

PROPAGATION

SOWING OF SEED

Cacti can be grown from seeds but the seedlings grow slowly and take long time to form a specimen. It is commonly used by commercial growers and amateurs who specialise and aim at a large collection of these plants.

The seed compost consists of equal quantity of leafmould and sand and some amount of loam, powdered brick and charcoal. Seed pan or shallow pans are used for sowing and half the depth of the pot is crocked. The pans are filled with the compost leaving about 3 to 4 cms on the top. The soil is then gently pressed and levelled. Seeds are sown uniformly, pressed down in the soil and thin layer of sand spread on the top. The compost is watered by placing the pot in water and allowing it to enter through the bottom and side holes. The pot is covered with a paper or glass pane. Cacti can be sown successfully from March to September. Germination may take place from 7 days to one month. When the sedlings are 1·5 to 2 cm in diameter and in the case of tall-growing species unless about 4 to 5 cm high, they are taken out without injuring rootlets and planted in small pots containing the same compost as used for grown up plants. After potting it is transferred in shade and watering is best done by spraying after a day or so. A number of seedlings may also be transplanted into a bigger pot at a distance of 3-4 cm.

PROPAGATION BY CUTTING OR OFFSET

Propagation by cutting or offset is an easy method of getting larger plants and also the only way of perpetuating hybrids and valuable plants. Species with solitary globular stem cannot be propagated by this method. Tall-growing species with single stem sends out shoots if the top portion is cut which can be used as the cutting but the specimen plant is lost. The branches thus formed are also detached and multiplied.

The cuttings are cut clean with a sharp knife and kept in airy and shady place for drying. The period of drying may vary from seven days to one month. The cutting is then planted in sand and leafmould or in the usual compost and kept in semishade till rooting. During the time of root formation watering is done sparingly even in the summer months. Formation of roots in the cuttings is indicated by new growth on them.

Cutting of *Cerei* including *Harissia, Selenicereus* should be of convenient length, *Pachycereus, Lemaireocereus* are cut at a constriction. In braching species of *Mammillaria* and *Rebutia,* the clumps are divided into smaller clumps. Species of *Trichocereus, Cleistocactus, Echinocereus,* etc. are best propagated by separating the suckers which arise from the lower part of the stem. Cuttings of *Epiphyllum* are best taken across the broad part of the flat stem.

PROPAGATION BY GRAFTING

Propagation by grafting is a useful method of propagation. Generally a weak growing species is grafted on a strong growing stock, the weak scion improves the vigour and stock is weakened. Species of *Selenicereus, Trichocereus, Harrisia, Cereus, Opuntia, Cleistocactus,* etc. are commonly used as stock.

The grafting may take the form of an inverted wedge. The top of the stock is cut as a wedge which is inserted in wedge-shaped cavity at the lower end of the scion for proper union. It is very important that the sides of the wedge and cavity should come in close contact and the top of the stock fit in the bottom of the cleft.

For grafting *Cephalocereus, Oreocereus* and *Espostoa,* clean horizontal cut is made on both stock and scion. The scion is kept fixed on the stock by giving a moderate pressure by tying the scion with the potted stock. To avoid injury a piece of folded cloth is placed on the top of the scion and the string is tied on it. After a month the pressure is released. The cut end of the stock and scion instead of being horizontal may also be inclined at an angle of 45 degrees as in the case of tongue graft.

Cacti can also be grafted by making a clean cone or inverted pyramid at the base of the scion and inserted in a caving made into the upper end of the stock. The scion is then tied in the usual manner. Grafting is also done in the summer months when the humidity is very low. High humidity causes rotting.

SOME COMMON CACTI

Astrophytum is known as Starcactus because of the large well-formed ribs. Surface is covered with star like hair or scales. Stem globular, flowers borne on the aeroles near the top. *Astrophytum asterias*, *A. myriostigma* and *A. capricorne* and their varieties are very popular.

Borzicactus has slender, weak stem, many ribs, with numerous aeroles. *Cleistocactus* also appears like *Borzicactus*, stem slender, erect, often throwing off shoots or branched with numerous ribs.

Cereus forms a group of tall erect or prostrate, branched, ribbed or having angular stems. *Cephalocereus* has tall columner stem solitary or branched at the base. Aeorles woolly or hairy. *Lemairocereus* has tall erect stem branching from the base. Aeroles mostly with stout spines.

Oreocereus: Columnar in appearance, hairy, often known as the Old Man of the Andes. Spines are very strong. Red flower appear on matured plants. *O. celsianus* and *O. hendricksenianus* form good specimens.

Species of *Trichocereus* are hardy and can be easily grown, typically branched from the base and form large clumps. Ribs many, usually very spiny.

Corypantha: The plants look like mammillaria, but tubercles are grooved. Flowers mostly yellow, larger than those of *Mammillaria.*

Echinocactus has large barrel-shaped appearance with prominent ribs and numerous strong species. Large yellow flowers appear at the top. *E. grusonii* is a popular golden-yellowed spined cactus. The stem may be 70 cm across and about 80 cm high. *Echinocereus* is a group of hardy cacti, very easy to grow. Stems roundish, oval or elongated, branching at base, erect or prostrate, ribs many. Aeroles woolly with spines.

Echinopsis is another group of hardy and widely grown cactus. Stem cylindrical, globular, solitary or in cluster with many acute ribs continuous or notched. At least 36 species are in cultivation.

Epiphyllum is also an epiphytic plant with woody main stems and flat leaf like branches, toothed or notched on both sides. Aeroles small situated in the notches often associated with bristles. Flowers large, showy open at night time. *Epiphyllum hookeri*, *E. phyllanthus* and *E. strictum* are common. Large number of hybrids are cultivated in the western countries.

Espostoa: Woolly or hairy columnar plants, spines are less conspicuous than *Oreocereus*. Small flowers are almost hidden. *E. lanata* and *E. dautwitzii* are commonly grown by amatuers.

Ferocactus means ferocious cactus and the spines are long, thick and stiff. Stem is large round or cylindrical with permanent ribs.

Gymnocalycium has about 50 species with globular stem and many well-marked ribs straight or irregular. Spines prominent; flowers large.

Mammillaria is the largest genus in Cactaceae with 200 recognised species. Plants are globular, oval or cylindrical branched or in cluster. Ribs are absent, tubercles in spiral rows, woolly or hairy in the axils. Flowers small, borne in the axils of the tubercles around the upper part of the stem.

Nopalea has flat-jointed stem and looks like Opuntia.

Notocactus: Globular or columnar in shape easy-growing and free-flowering. The flowers are usually yellow with red stigma. *N. concinnus*, *N. haselbergii*, and *N. leninghausii* are few widely grown species.

Opuntia is a very commonly grown cactus, naturally occuring on road sides, rocky or sandy places. They are differentiated by their flat-jointed stem. Some are quite attractive, having red or yellow bristles. The genus includes over 300 species.

Parodia : Small plants, mostly globular, some are cylindrical, very spiny ; bears large attractive flowers. *P. aureispina*, *P. chrysacanthion*, *P. microsperma* form well-shaped plants and bear colourful flowers.

Pereskia—Large shruby plants much branched, spiny. Leaves large well-formed fleshy and permanent ; flower showy.

P. aculeata, *P. grandiflora* and *P. bleo* are commonly grown. *P. aculeata* var Rubescens has reddish leaves. It can be grown in a large rock garden.

Rebutia has many species of small globular plants producing offsets. The flowers appear on small plants and vary in colour. *R. deminuta*, *R. fiebrigii*, *R. marsoneri*, *R. senilis* are popular.

Cacti are often found growing on large trees and branches, hanging like snakes. These are epiphytic or semi-epiphytic. Plants belonging to genera *Aporocactus*, *Hylocereus*, *Selenicereus*, *Weberocereus*, *Werckleocereus* are epiphytic. *Hylocereus* and *Selenicereus* are commonly seen.

SUCCULENTS

The reason for the occurrence of succulence in plants is lack of adequate supply of moisture together with heat and sunshine. In the deserts and the semideserts the occurrence of succulents is readily understandable. In the alpine regions also where the atmosphere is physiologically dry for plant hardly differ from the dry desert region. It is necessary for the plants on high mountains to withstand drought and vegetation of succulent appearance are commonly seen. In the seacoast or salt deserts salinity results in the formation of succulent plants. Most of the succulents occur in the South African deserts and in the Cape Province. Succulents also occur in the deserts of the

Sahara. Curious forms of giant succulents plants are native to the Isle of Socotra. Many beautiful and interesting succulents come from Canary Isles. In the stony and the calcarious soil of the Southern and the Western sides, numerous succulents such as, *Agave*, *Echevaria*, *Sedum* and xerophyllum thorny bushes grow in abundance.

Succulents, that is, juicy plants are among the most specialized plant form and they are the expression of peculiar condition of soil and climate. As the plants grow in the severe shortage of water in the deserts and semideserts they are adopted to conserve water and to reduce transpiration. The water storage tissue occupies almost the whole leaf or the shoot and is surrounded by a thin layer of assimilating tissues. The leaves or the shoots may contain water as much as 95% of their volume. It is also of interest to note, that the water content in the leaves is very mucilagenous which is very important for its retention of water. During the dry period, the plants are usually completely at rest and look dead since they have shrunken and the surface of the leaf dried up. But they recover very quickly after the first rain, in a short time produce new leaves and show new growth by the swelling of the plant body. In ornamental horticulture, these succulent plants are used for their peculiar shape, decorative foliage or showy flowers and constitute the most important plants in the rock gardens.

CULTIVATION

Watering of succulent plant is one of the most important points that the grower has to acquire. Like cacti the resting period of most of the succulent comes in winter and the growing period during the spring and the summer months. This is, however, not true with all types of succulents as some species begin to grow in June, July and August and their resting period is in the spring and the early summer. *Hawarthia*, *Gasteria* should not be allowed to dry too much and the soil should be only moderately moist. During the winter month, the soil for *Huernia* and *Stapelia*, should be kept just moist so that the roots are not dried up. *Euphorbia* should be watered freely during the growing period but very little during the resting period in the winter months. In this case also when watering is done the soil should be soaked thoroughly and sprinkling of water on the surface soil be altogether avoided. Whenever possible rain water should be used in pots. Like other plants succulents should also be grown in clay pots which are porous, i.e., water and air pass through them. The pots must be provided with drainage holes so that superfluous water can pass out readily. The shape and size of the pots should be in proportion to the root system of the plant. *Aloe*, *Agave* etc. should be grown in large pots on account of their large roots. Many Euphorbias also need deep pots. For shallow-rooted plants like most of the *Gasteria*, *Haworthia*, *Stapelia* shallow pots should be used.

SOIL

Light porous soil is best for succulents. Undecomposed organic matter should never be used. Well-decomposed leafmould and cow manure, loamy soil, sharp sand, crushed, brick and charcoal constitute the ingredient of the compost for succulents. For many species, addition of lime is recommended, the best form being mortar rubble. For most of the Crassulas the following compost is recommended :

3 parts leafmould
1 part well-rotted cow manure
1 part loam
1 part crushed brick
6 parts sharp sand

For *Euphorbia*, *Aloe* and *Agave* use a compost consisting of 1 part each of cow manure, leafmould and loam and 2 parts sharp sand ; *Echeveria*, *Aeonium* and similar less sensitive plants generally require loamy soil which is not too porous. Repotting should be carried out at the beginning of the growing period. Quick-growing plants should be repotted once every year. Species which grow less freely need not be repotted every year. The plants should be taken out very carefully with minimum injury to the roots and then firmly replanted in a bigger sized pot in the compost of the same composition.

PROPAGATION

Since almost all succulents flower and produce seeds propagation by means of viable seeds is a practical method. Raising from seed becomes essential when large number of plants of one species are to be grown for commercial purpose. The best time for sowing seed is the spring. The most important factor for the germination of seed is the heat and atmospheric moisture. At a temperature between 30° to 35°C and the relative moisture content of the air of about 90% most seeds germinate quickly. After germination of seeds the seedlings should be removed in drier place. The seeds compost should also be very porous mainly containing well-rotted dry leafmould mixed with twice the quantity of washed coarse sand. Shallow pans are commonly used for sowing seeds filled with the compost and covered with a thin layer of sand. The seeds are then scattered thinly on the sand again covered with sand to a depth not greater than the size of the seed itself. After sowing, the pots should be kept in glass frame or covered with a glass pane. Watering is done either by spraying through a fine rose or keeping the pot on a vessel containing water. When the seedlings come up, the young plants are transplanted in a compost containing 3 parts leafmould, 1 part old cow manure mixed with soil, 1 part mortar rubble, 1 part loam, 6 parts clean sand. The young seedlings should be kept dry during the resting period. Like older plants the young seedlings, however, should not be exposed to extreme climatic conditions.

VEGETATIVE PROPAGATION

Almost all succulents can also be propagated vegetatively. As the succulents are fleshy, the parts removed must be carefully handled. The growth is cut off with a sharp knife and kept in an airy, dry place so that the cut surface becomes dry and covers itself with a shine. Cuttings should be taken from mature growth, little woody rather than too soft, for soft cuttings rot easily. It is not always necessary to use the terminal cuttings, lateral shoots may also be used. Aloe and Agave produce offsets and these are used for multiplication of plants. When large enough, these offsets are separated from the plants, a little below the surface of the soil and treated as cuttings. In many cases offsets are found to produce roots while attached to the plants and they can be potted after separation. Though it is not possible to multiply all types of succulents from leaf cuttings, species of Crassulaceae lend themselves successfully to this method of propagation.

The leaves are carefully detached from *Crassula*, *Cotyledon*, *Echeveria*, *Sedum* etc. and dried like the stem cuttings. *Haworthia* and *Gasteria* also produce shoots at the base of the cuttings. A few succulents such as *Kalanchoe* bears on the edges of the leaves small adventious buds which may be detached and used as cuttings. The rooting medium for all types of cuttings whether from shoot, leaf or buds should contain sand and dry leafmould in the proportion of 2 : 1. As a rule shoot cuttings root quicker than leaf cutting and the rooted cutting should be carefully removed and potted in the compost recommended for the plant.

SOME COMMON SUCCULENTS

Adenium obesum—Fleshy, thick-twisted stem grown in rock garden, about 2 m high ; flowers pink.

Aeonium—Succulent herbaceous plants with woody and branched stems, leaves in the form of rosette at the ends of the branches. Some species have no distinct stem and rosette arises close to the ground.

A. sedifolium, *A. tabuliforme* and *A. undulatum*, are common species.

A. haworthii has bluish green leaves, edges reddish brown and iook like flower of marble.

Agave—These are the common succulent plants with xerophytic appearance, leaves in the form of rosette, firm, hard and sword-shaped, usually spiny at the margin and tip, sometimes smooth at the margin but the apex is stout and pointed. The plants die after flowering. Adventitous buds often form at the axils of the panicle branches.

A. americana—Stemless rosette, margins spiny, curved. The variegated forms are commonly grown in rock gardens.

A. americana var. Marginata. Variegated form with margin pale yellow or cream.

A. americana var. Mediopicta—Leaves with yellowish stripe in the centre.

A. angustifola var. Variegata—Compact rosette, very firm leaves, margin whitish, middle green.

A. atrovirens, A. attenuata, A. philiphera, A. sisalana, are some of the common agaves.

Aloes are a group of succulent plants, hårdy and widely found in tropical countries, plants stemless or with short stem or sometimes tree-like. Leaves mostly in rosette, fleshy, margin entire or toothed surface may be spinous sometimes with markings or stripes.

Aloe variegata—Plants form densely rosette of leaves arranged in three ranks, upper surface concave, lower surface keeled. dark green with transverse white bands arranged irregularly.

A. zebrina—Leaves linear-lanceolate, in rosette, upper surface flat fleshy, green with numerous white spot.

Bowiea volubilis—Perennial herb with large light green spherical bulbs.

Caralluma—Succulent perennial herbs, 4 to 6 angled dentate sometimes creeping stem or semi erect grow in clump.

C. sprengeri—Stem much branched 8-10 cm high, 4-angled, angles toothed, light green with reddish spots.

C. turneri—Plant taller, stem 4 angled dentate, green with purple spots.

Ceropegia—Succulent perennial harb, stem leafless or twining with opposite leaves, lanceolate or cordate. Flowers showing various colours.

Cissus cactiformis—Climbing succulent plants 4-angled, winged, constricted at the internode. *Cissus quadrangularis* is also a climbing shrub, 4-angled constricted at the nodes, leaves cordate, falling off.

Cotyledon—Succulent herb or shrub, usually grows in clumps. Leaves spirally crowded, thick and fleshy. Flowers pendulous from terminal branches.

C. dobiculate—Erect shrub, leaves opposite crowded at the tips of the branches, obovate, narrowed into a short stalk.

Crassula—This genus has more than 300 species and forms the most important group of succulents. These are usually herbaceous plants or semishrub with succulent branches and twigs. Leaves opposite often crowded into a rosette usually sessile. Flowers small, mostly numerous in terminal or lateral cymes.

Echeveria—Perennial herbaceous much branched succulents. Leaves spirally arranged in rosette, fleshy and thick, various shapes and size. Flowers appear from the leaf axils, usually bell-shaped.

Echeveria agavoidis—Looks like a rosette of leaves, compact ovate with brown tips. Flowers pink.

E. glauca—This species has rosette of leaves, rarely any distinct stem with many offsets. Leaves broadly obovate, spatulate, wedge-shaped towards the base, margin reddish.

E. elegans—It also forms plants with rosette of leaves, obovate rounded above, pointed tip.

Euphorbia—Euphorbias are also common succulents in tropical country, They are usually thorny, fleshy. In many cases they resemble cacti in many ways. Few species have large prominent leaves.

E. antiquorum—Much branched thorny succulent, stem 4 to 5 angled, branches usually 3-angled constricted joint-like. Spines spreading on small roundish shields.

E. candelabrum—Tall tree-like branches 4-angled.

E. cooperi—Spiny much branched succulent, 5 to 6 angled, divided into many joints usually constricted, angles with grey throny edges and spines.

E. tirucalli—Much branched, woody succulent, branches jointed, dark green in colour.

Fourcroya—Plants are like agave with tufted leaves, margin spiny or dentate leathery.

F. gigantea—Large oblong oblanceolate leaves, flat undulate margin, fresh glossy green, margin entire.

F. gigantea var. Mediopicta—Leaves with creamy white or pale yellow longitudinal centre.

F. selloa var. Marginata—Leaves variegated, margins yellow.

Gasteria—It is a showy succulent, leaves long, thick firm mostly distichous.

G. marmorata—Leaves lanceolate long, densely distichous, rounded tapering apex, dark green, darker mottled.

G. parvifolia—Stemless, distichous leaves, reddish, glabrous, glossy spotted on both sides.

Gastrolea—It forms as a result of intergeneric hybrid between Gasteria and Aloe.

Graptopetalum—Perennial plants, look more or less like Echeveria. Leaves in rosette, thick and fleshy.

G. rusby—Plants small, rosette of compact leaves, thick ovate, whitish.

Haworthia—Low-growing perennial herbs, leaves in rosette or in compact rows, fleshy with smooth tubercles, tip usually stiff.

H. attenuata—This species has few sub-species.

H. attenuata var. Clariperla—Leaves in the form of rosette, wholly covered with small tubercles arranged in series or irregularly scattered.

H. greenii—It bears large number of leaves, reddish or light brownish green in the sun. Leaves compressed, loosely arranged incurved ; upper surface glabrous, back side with longitudinal lines.

H. reinwardtii—It is popular species of *Haworthia* with few sub-species. This species usually has large number of leaves loosely arranged, tubercles conspicuous arranged in various fashions.

Kalanchoe tubiflora—Erect plant, mostly unbranched, leaves almost cylindrical, somewhat broad in the upper surface.

Nolina—Small tree, succulent stout trunk swollen at the base and tapering towards apex. Leaves long, narrow, leathery.

N. recurvata—Base of the stem almost globose. Leaves thin, long recurved, in tuft.

S. pachyphytum—Perennial herbaceous plants. Leaves alternate, fleshy thick sometimes in rosette.

P. bracteosum—Leaves oblanceolate, blunt at the apex, curved.

P. compactum, *P. hookeri* *P. oviferum*, are also few showy species.

Pachyveria—Intergeneric hybrid between *Pachyphytum* and *Echeveria*. Plants look like *Echeveria* and *Pachyphytum*. Leaves succulent, fleshy in rosette on short stem.

Pedilanthus—These are succulent shrub or sub-shrub with latex.

P. carinatus—Much branched shrub, dark green erect stem. Leaves ovate-lanceolate, leathery, fleshy.

Pelargonium—Several species of Pelargonium commonly grown in milder climate have succulent stems. P. juttae has globular stem.

Portulacaria afra—Succulent shrub ; stem horizontal spreading. Leaves opposite, obovate, thick, glabrous, shining green.

Sedum—These are annual, biennial or perennial herbs or shrubs. Branches herbaceous or slightly woody, dichotomously branched, erect creeping. Leaves mostly alternate, flat or cylindrical and in most cases they are closely set on the stem.

S. compactum—Low growing herbaceous plant. Leaves obovate, obtuse on short rosette.

S. morganianum—Creeping sub-shrubs. Leaves numerous, thick fleshy, lanceolate.

S. neudum—Small sub shrubs. Leaves alternate, obovate-oblong, thick, blunt at the tip.

S. pachyphyllum, *S. moranense*, *S. stahlii* and numerous other species and varieties are grown for their curious and ornamental importance.

Sempervivum—These are a group of low-growing perennial herbaceous plant found in the rock gardens of temperate countries. The leaves are arranged in the form of rosette, thick fleshy, green, reddish or bluish in colour, giabrous or hairy.

Senecio—This genus comprises 1300 species and distributed all over the world.

Stapelia—Perennial succulent herb, stem fleshy erect, branched at base and forming clumps, 4-angled, the angles are toothed, green and also reddish. Flowers are of curious shape usually arise from the base of the stem.

CHAPTER XI

Palms and Conifers

PALMS

The large family of palms are prominent in the vegetable world for their grace and grandeur which are specially remarkable in regions where plams grow naturally. Linnaeus appropriately termed them 'princes of the vegetable kingdom'. There are some 1150 sp of palms known and they may be divided into two main classes, feather or pinnate leaved and fan or flabelliform leaved. Most palms have upright and straight stems. Some are bushy giving rise to many off shoots, a few are naturally branched while others are huge climbers. Palms are very little known to amateur but a number of species can be grown in pots or in ground and may show better effect than flowering trees depending on the situation. Palms form very beautiful pot plants and the following species are specially recommended for this purpose.

Chrysalidocarpus lutescens	*Phoenix roebelenii*
Elaeis guineensis	*P. rupicola*
Hyophorbe verschaffeltii	*Pritchardia grandis*
Kentia McArthuri	*P. pacifica*
Livistona chinensis	*Raphis humilis*
L rotundifolia	*Thrinax argentia*

One part each of leafmould and well-rotted cow manure and 2 parts garden soil is a safe mixture, an addition of a table spoonful of bone meal for every 25 cm pot will give good result. Application of small dose of ammonium sulphate brightens the colour of the leaves.

In the early part of this century, Royal Palm (*Oreodoxa*) had been frequently used in the garden mainly on the both sides of the road for a symmetrical appearance. The palms still stand gracefully in some well known gardens. Other species, however, are not frequently grown in the ground in the private gardens except clumps of *Caryota mitis* or *Kentia McArthuri*. The fan leaved types *Pritchardia*, *Washingtonia*, *Thrinax* and *Sabal* are very attractive till the long bare stem does not show prominence. In Botanic Gardens and also in large public gardens, palms in groups especially near the tanks and lakes greatly improve the vista.

FEATHER LEAVED PALMS

Acanthophoenix crinita—Height 15–20 m, densely armed with black needle-shaped spines. Leaves long 3 to 4 m, ovate, stalk densely hairy.

Areca triandra—6 to 8 m high. Stem cylindrical with basal off shoots. Leaf 1 to 1·15 m long, 6 to many pinnae ; petiole about 1 m long.

Arenga saccharifera—10–13 m high. Leaf 1 to 1·7 m long, white or silvery beneath ; leaf stalk smooth ; leaflets are like those of *Caryota*, irregularly toothed above.

Bentickea nicobarica—The genus has been named in honour of Lord William Bentick. Tall spineless graceful palm 20 to 30 m high. Stem thick 25–30 cm. leaf long 1·7 to 2·5 m ; leaflet 25–60 cm long lobed at the tip.

Caryota mitis—Spineless stout-ringed stem. Flowering is very commonly observed. Stem up to 7 m high. 8–12 cm thick. Leaves 15–20 cm long, obliquely wedge-shaped, irregularly toothed leaflets.

Caryota urens– Stem about 20–27 m high, to about 50 cm thick without suckers. Leaf 3·5 m long, 1·3 to 2 m wide ; leaflets obliquely wedge-shaped, leathery, toothed.

Chrysalidocarpus lutescens—Stem 10–13 m high, 8–14 cm thick, cylindrical smooth. Leaves long pinnate ; leaflets 30–50 pairs about 60 cm, lanceolate dark green in colour.

Dictyosperma album—This genus has only one species of slender trunk with a terminal crown of pinnate leaves. Height up to 10 m. Leaves 2 to 2·5 m long, pinnate ; leaflets 60 cm long bright green on both sides ; stalk whitish.

var. Aureum—Leaflets dark green, stalk yellow.

var. Rubrum—Main veins and leaf margins dark red.

Elaeis guineensis (Oil palm)—About 10 m high. Stems stout deeply ringed, not spiny. Leaves 3·5 to 5 m long, dark green ; stalk spiny toothed ; leaflets linear, lanceolate, acute.

Hyophorbe amaricaulis—It is a stout palm 20 m high, bottle-shaped near the base. Leaves pinnate 1·2 m long ; leaflets 40–60 pairs ; stalk dark maroon, glaucous with an orange line along the edges of midrib.

Hyophorbe verschaffeltii—7 to 10 m high, swollen about half the length of the trunk. Leaves 1·2–2m long arching on the top ; leaflets 30–50 pairs about 60 cm long, yellow band from the upper part of the leaf sheaths to the end of the blade.

Kentia McArthuri—This is a very common and hardy palm 3·5 to 5 m high. Leaves pinnate 12–23 cm long, obliquely cut at the apex. Suckers are freely formed at the base and produce bushy plant.

Oreodoxa regia—Stem about 13–20 m high, greyish, smooth with swollen base, very elegant. Leaves 2·5 to 3·5 m long, pinnate, leaflets 75 cm long, linear acuminate.

Phoenix reclinata—Stem 7–9 m. Leaves pinnate, bright green ; leaflets about 30 cm long, lanceolate.

Phoenix roebelenii—A very beautiful palm. Leaves 30–45 cm long ; leaflets 15–20 cm shinning dark green. It does not grow above 60–90 cm.

Phoenix rupicola—Stem about 5–7 m high, 15–20 cm thickness, solitary and slender. Leaves 2·5 to 3·5 m, dark green, petiole short ; leaflets two-ranked.

Ptychoraphis augusta—Slender smooth tall trunk. Leaves 1·8 to 2·4 m long, leaflets 30–60 cm linear, bright green.

FAN LEAVED PALM

Chamaerops humilis—It is the only palm native to Europe, grows up to a height of 1·8 to 3·5 m with a number of off shoots at the base and stiff dark fibres near the crown of leaves. Leaves fan-shaped about 45 cm long grey green, split nearly to base into narrow segments ; stalk about 1·2 m long, stiff sharp spines along the margin.

var. Arborescens—tree like with stem 1·8 to 4·2 m high.

var. Argentea—leaves silvery green.

var. Elegans—a slender form of elegant habit.

Corypha elata (Talipot)—About 20–24 m high, Leaves, 2–3 m across, 80-100 leaflets, stalk about 3 m long.

Hyphaene thebaica (Doum Palm)—About 13-15 m high. Stem is frequently branched, unarmed. Leaves large fan-shaped in crowns at the ends of the branches of the stem.

Latania commersonii—Stem about 1·8 to 2·0 m high, ringed, slender. Leaves fan-shaped in a terminal tuft, very deeply cut, segment margined with chocolate red bands and fine tooth-like spines ; stalk long, smooth, deep red.

Licuala grandis—1·8 to 2·5 m high. Leaves about 20 in crown, bright green ; stalk 60-90 cm long slender spiny ; blade about 90 cm across, orbicular somewhat wavy, margin cleft into 60 cm lobes.

Licuala pelteta—4·5 m high. Leaves fan-shaped peltet ; leaflets long wedge-shaped, many nerved ; stalk prickly on margin.

Licuala spinosa—Leaves fan-shaped, large ; stalk stout with large spines on the margin.

Livistona chinensis—Stem about 1·8 to 2·5 m high ; grey ringed. Leaves many, fan shaped about 1·2 m across, cut into linear lanceolate segments ; deeply forked between them, lower part of the stalk covered with crown of spines.

Livistona rotundifolia—Stem about 13-15 m high. Leaves almost round, 90 to 120 cm across deeply cut with slender points, tips two-fid, stalks 1·6 to 2 m long with sharp spiny margin. *Livistona chinensis*, *L. australis* and *L. mouritiana* are also grown in tropics.

Pritchardia pacifica—Leaves fan-shaped up to 1·2 m long, 90 cm wide, densely covered with whitish brown tomentum when young ; segment 80-90, petiole about 90 cm long.

Raphis humilis—It is a commonly grown palm producing bushy clumps from the suckers. Height varies from 1·2 to 2 m fan-shaped leaved with many segments.

Sabal adansonii—(Blue palm)—Stem short buried in the earth and the palm appears stemless. Leaves 60-90 cm long, glaucous circular in its outline ; segments cleft at the apex.

Sabal palmetto—Erect stem ; leaves about 1-2 m long, cordate, deeply cut.

Stevensonia grandiflora—Stem very spiny when young, about 13-15 m high. Petiole 25-45 cm long, blade cuneate, obovate 1·2 to 2 m long.

Thrinax argentea—Upto 5 m high. Blade shorter than petiole, fan shaped. Silvery grey beneath.

Thrinax excelsa—Leaves pale green above, glaucous beneath ; segments cut 2/3 of the leaf blade.

Washingtonia filifera—It is also a fan-leaved palm with stout erect stem. Dry leaves remain on the trunk for a long time. Margins of the petiole armed upto the middle, about 1 m long, blades circular, segments many, upto 1 m in diameter. Segments margined with numerous fibre about 15-30 cm long.

CONIFERS

In tropical gardens the scope for growing the conifers is limited to few species, while in sub-tropical and temperate region conifers constitute very important and showy group of plants. They are used as avenue plants, on roadside, in gardens and parks, on the bank of lakes, pools or flowing water. Many species and varieties show symmetrical growth and are frequently used in formal garden. Several species, unusually attractive in appearance are often grown in Japanese garden and rock garden. They are also grown as specimen trees, hedge and as pot plants.

SOME CONIFERS FOR TROPICAL GARDEN :

Araucaria—A group of showy everygreen trees with symmetrically spreading branches. Though a popular pot plant, it grows well in ground, if protected from the midday sun in the hot months. The potted plants should be kept in shade or green house during the summer. Rich loamy soil, application of manure and suitable growing condition retain the lower branches for many years. Plants of this genus are commonly used as 'Christmas tree'. Each year the plants produce a whorl of branch which are horizontal and spreading in different direction.

A. bidwilli—Branches in whorls, long, drooping. Leaves 4-5 cm long, 1 cm or more in width leathery narrowing to a stiff point.

A. cookii—Species commonly grown in pots. In the ground it forms tall erect tree. Leaves 1 cm long and awl-shaped, densely arranged and curving inward.

A. cunninghamii—This species has also horizontal branches with tuft of branchlets near the apex. Leaves are of 2 kinds.

A. excelsa—A beautiful plant with crowded branches, horizontal and branchlets drooping. Leaves rather soft, awl-shaped, curving inwards and densely arranged.

Cupressus sempervirens—This is the only species of the genus which can be successfully grown in the tropical region. Commonly known as Mediterranean Cypress. There are two distinct forms of this species, one stiff and erect, grows upto 15 m, the other with spreading branches.

Cycas is commonly seen in large gardens and looks like a palm. Tuft of large and spreading leaves on brownish trunk is very graceful and attractive. It grows well in partial shade.

It thrives well in poor but well-drained soil. In large pot *C. revoluta* will remain for a number of years. New leaves are susceptible to insect attack. Suckers form on *Cycas* which can be detached from the plants for multiplication in addition to seeds.

Cycas circinalis—Erect stem, may grow upto 10 m or more, branching is common. Leaves 2·4 to 5 m long covered with reddish brown hairs when young ; leaflets linear lanceolate, darkgreen glossy.

Cycas revoluta—1·8 to 2·5 m high. Leaves 1 to 1·5 m long, leaflets narrower than *C. circinalis*.

Juniperus—Hardy evergreen trees and shrubs of this genus are grown in tropical, sub-tropical and temperate climate as ornamental plants. Leaves needle-shaped, narrow scale-like. Junipers thrive best in sandy loam soil and prefer sunny open situation. The erect species are grown along the paths in parks and gardens, lawn and in shrubberies and dwarf species are suitable for rock garden. All the species can be propagated from seeds and cuttings.

Macrozamia is a group of conifer, few species, however, thrive well in hot and humid climate. They grow well in pots in shade in poor but porous soil.

Pinus—A genus of about 70 species of evergreen trees mainly distributed in the temperate zone. *Pinus roxburghii* can be grown in tropical part. It is a very slow-growing conifer and need partial shade and well-drained soil. Leaves long, needle shaped.

Podocarpus—Several species of this evergreen plants have been found to thrive well in warm humid climate.

P. macrophylla—It can be grown in semishade, well-drained and rich soil. Like other conifer, *Podocarpus* is fairly slow growing at the early stage. It reaches a height of 10 m, densely covered with large green leathery leaves.

P. neriifolia grows into a tall tree upto 13 m. Leaves narrow lance-shaped, 10-15 cm long, 5-7 mm wide.

Thuja (Arbor-Vitae) a group of popular evergreen plants is widely grown in tropical, sub-tropical and temperate gardens and also as decorative plants in pots. Most species and varieties are pyramidal or rounded in shape with much-branched shoots, clothed with small scale-like leaves. Because of the symmetrical habit they are favourites in formal garden. Besides their utility as pot plants, Thujas are also used at hedge plants. *Thuja occidentalis* and *T. orientalis* are commonly grown in tropical gardens. Many varieties or forms of these species are available in the Western countries. The plants in general, like rich, porous, slightly moist soil. Propagation is by seed or cutting.

Thuja occidentalis—This species of Thuja, though grows as tree, does not reach a height above 5 m in warm humid environment. The plant has compact growth with short horizonal branches, leaves acute, ovate.

Some of the best known varieties are Alba, Compacta, Cristata, Douglasii, Pyramidalis, Pumila and Woodwardii.

T. orientalis—Pyramidal in appearance with spreading and ascending branches, branchlets thin ; leaves rhombic ovate bright green. This species is widely grown in the tropical parts of India.

J. Communis (Common juniper), Hindi—*Arar*

Grows upto about 12 m depending on the environment. Leaves linear, spreading sharp-pointed, 1 to 1·5 cm long.

var. Fastigiata—compact and elegant growth

var. Pendula—shrub with spreading and pendulous branches.

J. Macracarpa—Shrub or small trees about 4 m high, pyramidal in shape, leaves linear lanceolate, spiny pointed, 1 to 1·5 cm long.

J. Macropoda (Dhupi)

It is commonly grown in the Himalayan region as forest tree.

J. Prostrata

Procumbent, usually with trailing branches, with numerous short branches ; leaves scale-like acute, bluish green or steel blue

J. Sabina, Hindi—*Bhil*

Dwarf, 1·5 to 3 m tall. Leaves needle-shaped acute.

var. Tamariscifolia—grows upto 1·5 m, leaves needle-shaped, bright green.

CHAPTER—XII

Hedge and Edge Plants

HEDGE

Hedge is an important adjunct to every garden but should not be multiplied out of all reasons. It is necessary to demarcate the garden from public road and from adjacent gardens particularly in flat gardens. Besides its utility as screens, hedge is necessary between flower and vegetable garden, to provide a background for annuals if shrubbery does not exist and also to enclose a rose garden or a children's corner in a park or public garden. A wind screen is also wanted when strong breezes, hot or cold, blow from one direction during certain seasons of the year or when we wish for protection from frosts. One should screen the manure pit, potting area, servants' quarters and other unsightly views.

How to Grow Hedges

The majority of hedges are propagated by cuttings out where seed can be obtained the cost of raising a large number of plants is considerably reduced.

Sowing of hedge seed should be done in a nursery whenever possible as the care of a long row of plants in their delicate stage is difficult. If this cannot be carried out sow at the following rates per 100 metres ; *Duranta* 1 kg, *Inga dulcis* 1 kg. Jaint (*Sesbania*) 150 gms, Mendi (*Lawsonia*) 250 gms, *Dodonea* (Sanatta) 250 gms.

Hard seed such as that of *Acacia modesta* should be soaked in warm water for 24 hours.

SELECTION OF PLANTS

Shrubs

All Acalyphas do not stand constant pruning especially, *A. bicolor*, but *A. mosaica*, *A. hamiltoniana* and the small leaved kinds can be clipped. A hedge of *Breynia rhamnioides* is often seen in gardens and is very ornamental when in berry.

Bauhinia acuminata in spite of its large leaves makes an effective display of white flowers even when brought to a shape.

Caesalpinia pulcherrima ages fast when severely pruned but if trimmed slightly it provides tall hedge.

Clerodendron inerme forms neat hedge or edge of varying height from 20 cm to 2 metres. It forms a compact hedge between 20-120 cm. *C. inerme* is not touched by cattle and white ants leave it alone.

Duranta in its many varieties holds first place in Bengal, *D. variegata* being very ornamental. Next comes *Lawsonia* (Mendhi) which is better in dry localities than in lower Bengal. *Dodonea viscosa* (Sanatta) is also an up country hedge but this latter should not be cut back as it is liable to die off in three or four years. *Nerium* and *Tecoma* are two others that might be used. *Dracaena fragrans* and *D. stricta* are good hedges for a shady spot. *Hibiscus* of several kinds form excellent hedges but *H. liliflorus* and *H. schizopetalus* are chiefly used.

Ehretia buxifolia as well as *Serissa foetida* and *Malpighia coccigera* are small leaved evergreens for shady situations. *Polyscias* (Aralia) of many kinds, *Codiaeum* (Croton), *Eranthemum* and *Graptophyllum* are ornamental shade loving hedge plants. Crotons of the narrow leaved and small foliage varieties are better hedges than those with large foliage. *Plumbago capensis* and *P. zeylanica*, *Meyenia* (*Thunbergia*) *erecta* and *M. affinis* are dwarf types of flowering shrubs that can be used for a hedge. In Bangalore we have seen *Plumbago capensis* cut down to 15 cm and in bloom. Other shrubs that can be used for hedges are *Caryopteris*, *Mussaenda*, *Rhapiolepis* and *Rondeletia*.

Euphorbia pulcherrima, if backed or having a supporting hedge in front can provide a fine mass of colour in the cold months. The last pruning should be done in August-September.

Jacquinia ruscifolia is an evergreen hedge with orange red flowers and needle-tipped leaves, an ideal hedge but difficult to propagate. *Justicia gendarussa* can be clipped to 15 cm or allowed to grow upto a metre.

Lagerstroemia indica in many colour variations, though bare in the cold weather, is a fine flowering hedge in April-June and if two colours are planted alternately provides a pretty effect when in bloom.

Ligustrum neilgherriensis, one of the privets, is not to be despised and the *Lantana*, though so frightful a weed, can be retained as a dwarf plant with frequent clipping though the non-seeding types are recommended. We must not forget the carounda, *Carissa carandas*, which is prickly, has white flowers and finally bears ornamental fruit ; *C. paucinervis* makes a better hedge as it is more compact growing.

Malvaviscus can be cut back to form a 1 metre hedge or allowed to grow 2-3 metres high. When in bloom, it is very effective.

Murraya (Kamini) and *Tropis aspera* (Sheora) are slow growing but clip well. *Jasminum pubescens*, *Coffea bengalensis*, *Barleria* (Jhati), *Ixora* especially *I. ragoosula*, *I. coccinea* and *I. strica*, *Daedalacanthus* and *Strobilanthes* are flowering hedges that are well known and easily grown.

Pandanus, the Screw Pine, is throny and apt to occupy much room in a small garden. It is not recommended as it harbours snakes and vermins ; the dwarf bamboo on the other hand, *Bambusa nana* is taboo for the same reason but actually a bamboo hedge can be kept clean and clipped. Both grow on the poorest of soils.

Roses form excellent hedges and many of the cacti such as *Cereus*, *Opuntia* as well as *Euphorbia antiquorum*, *E. trigona* and *E. tirucalli* are used in exposed positions for hedge work. *Pedilanthus tithymaloides* will be found as hedges surrounding village huts. Being poisonous to cattle it is left severely alone.

Sesbania aegyptiaca (Jaint) is a fast-growing hedge reaching a height of 2 metres in a couple of months ; it must be grown from seed and is a great favourite in the drier parts of India for a tall temporary boundary hedge. After two years it commences to become rugged and should be replaced. Another quick hedge is *Cajanus indicus* (Arhar) but this grows too rapidly in Bengal.

Thuja orientalis is an excellent evergreen hedge. 2-3 metres in height.

At an elevation of over 1000 metres a different type of plant is cultivated for hedges. Here are some varieties : *Spirea, Kerria japonica, Berberis* (Barberry), *Habrothamnus elegans, Fuchsia, Heliotrope, Euonymus, Ligustrum* (Privet), *Buxus* (Box) *Hydrangea, Philadelphus, Hibiscus syriacus, Cupressus* and *Ancuba.*

Trees

For very tall hedge several trees lend themselves to pruning : *Polyalthia longifolia* is one of the best, *Putrànjiva roxburghii, P. acuminata, Anogeissus, Diospyros embryopteris Grevillea robusta* and *Pithecolobium* are others that can be recommended. *Pongamia glabra* and *Inga dulics* are also used. *Thevetia nerifolia, Erythrina* of many kinds, *Haematoxylon campechianum, Schinus terebinthifolius, Cryptomeria, Cupressus* and other conifers are considered good when cut back to a height of 3-4 metres.

Acacia modesta is much grown in the Punjab and *Inga dulcis* for wealth of throns and neatness, though both these are great favourites of the white ant.

Casuarina equistifola if pruned before a large trunk forms, makes a very neat hedge. *Acacia farnesiana* and *Parkinsonia aculeata* are both useful but do better in dry situations.

Pisonia alba (Tree Lettuce) which forms hedges of pale coloured foliage, is grown in South India and Ceylon but not elsewhere to any extent.

Prosopis spicigera and *P. juliflora* can be clipped and kept low, soon becoming impenetrable, as those who have tried to force a way through soon discover. Commence cutting back when the seedlings are 20 cm high and repeat when the shoots are 40 cm a quick thick hedge from the very beginning is then ensured.

Thevetia nerifolia is poisonous to cattle and goats and make a neat-clipped hedge 3-4 metres high.

Climbers

On a wire fencing *Jacquemontia violacea* is ideal, *Ipomea palmata* (Railway Creeper) and *I. sincrata* and *Antigonon* (Sandwich Island Creeper), *Clerodendron splendens*, *Ficus repens*, *Passiflora pruinosa*. *Tristellatia austrulis*, *Thunbergia fragrans* and *T. alata* and *Vallaris hynei* are good for screening. For a very shady situation *Rhyncospermum jasminoides*, *Asparagus plumosus* and *Lygodium scandens* are suggested. *Caesalpinia sepiaria*, *C. scandens* and *Mimosa caesia*, *M. sappan* and *Capparis horrida* are impenetrable hedges, but not neat by any means, while *Bougainvillea* can also be formed into an ornamental and throny hedge.

Palms

Ptychosperma mcArthuri will grow 4-6 metres and not spread more than 1·5 to 2·0 m in width. *Rhapis flabelliformis*, on the other hand, while growing form 2-3 m in height, sends out runners which must be constantly removed. *Areca lutescens* grows as tall as the *Kentia* but bushes out more.

Distance apart to plant

This depends on the ultimate size of the plant, whether it is a tree, shrub or low-growing succulent. Trees should be planted 2-3 m apart, shrubs 15-50 cm apart and *Alternanthera*, etc., (edging) 2 cm apart if planted in a single row but when staggered double the distances. *Duranta*, *Lawsonia*, etc., can be thickened when the hedge has grown up, by having the pruned cuttings planted in between or on either side of the growing bushes. For hedge planting calculate 9 plants per metre row of planted singly 10 cm apart and 12 in a double row if planted 15 cm apart staggered.

CARE OF HEDGES

The first requirement for a hedge is impenetrability and the next neatness.

Any prickly plant, such as *Inga dulcis* or the thorny type of *Duranta*, will not ensure an absolute cattle or thief proof hedge in its earlier stages, so run a barbed wire through the bushes from the ground or plant a row of pineapple, *Agave*, prickly cactus or thorny *Euphorbia* at the base and the case is altered.

Always keep jungle away from the roots of a hedge. In the dry season fork up the soil and flood ; when Mendhi (*Lawsonia*) or *Duranta* are pruned, during the wet weather, plant the cuttings so as to fill gaps.

MANURING

Usually hedges receive little attention till they become thin. Then the plants are pruned heavily in the rains, add manure at the close of the Monsoon. Feed hedges, especially those that are clipped regularly by giving superphosphate of lime and bone meal 50 gms each, 12 gms sulphate of potash and 50 gms sulphate of ammonia per two metres row, every six months.

Once a year dig in cow manure as the rains break. This might seem superfluous but the results will amply repay the attention given.

PRUNING OF HEDGES

Some varieties have to be left to grow as in nature, i.e., *Pandanus*, *Euphorbia*, etc., but kept within bounds by the removal of side growth or the central head. In *Euphorbia* and *Opuntia*, the taller portions broken off can be replanted in the gaps to thicken the hedge.

For low hedges, 50 cm to 1·0 metre high, clip frequently during the rains but once a year cut back the old wood below the maximum height to restart a new top ; do this in May or June.

Plashing a hedge is cutting back side growth of overgrown and old hedges, partly cutting through the main stems and burying them in the line of the hedge by pegging down into position, a sort of layering that is only possible when the hedge is thin.

HOW TO PRUNE

Use a sharp pair of pruning shears for small twigs but a secateur will be necessary for larger stems. It is best to stick to a simple shape instead of attempting battlements, turrets, balls, columns, etc. Arches can be grown on an iron rod bent to shape, the shrub kept in position by being loosely tied with strong wire to the rod.

SHAPES OF HEDGES

A hedge is apt to become wedge-shaped, the top widening out, if not carefully clipped square. A rounded top is difficult to keep unless the type of hedge is slow, compact growing and small leaved. Hedges are also cut on a slope but here too the Mali often makes a mess of the shape. It is best to have wooden or iron stakes painted green, sunk in the hedge at intervals on which string can be tied and used as a guide. Stick to a square cut hedge.

TOPIARY

Topiary is practised only in few traditional gardens. The plants that have small foliage and are of slow growth are good for using in topiary. The results required takes years to attain and one careless clipping will spoil the entire design. Starting with a ready-grown plant, stems are bent and held in position with wire if they do not naturally grow at the required angle. A rough clipping to get the general outline follows and as new shoots develop these are either trained to fit in with the design or removed. Simple shapes, a ball, spiral, table, cube, etc., are not so difficult to obtain, it is when birds or beasts or even man is to be moulded that the topiarist tackles a tough proposition. Patience and plenty of it as well as perseverance are called into play.

Topiary work gives an old world appearance to a garden but these clipped bushes should not be scattered aimlessly all over the garden. A formal garden is best suited to topiary work. For simple shapes the following can be used *Hibiscus, Thuja* and *Cupressus, Putranjiva* and *Polyalthia* but for the more intricate *Murraya exotica, Duranta repens, Ehretia buxifolia* and *Tropis aspera* are used. *Myrtus communis* is too slow in growth.

When using wire to model the bush or tree to the rough outline care should be taken that this does not cut too deeply into the bark. Stoppage of sap will mean poor growth or death of a stem.

Although topiary is an important feature in a formal garden according to many this form of shaping trees, so called Art of Tree Sculpture is a parody of Art and Nature, and the distortions produced are not only a waste of labour but an unnatural method of Gardening.

EDGING PLANTS

While considering hedges one naturally turns to edgings. Duranta can be clipped to 15 cm and even lower if the shears are frequently employed but a neater edging is formed of *Alternathera* in many forms and *Aerva sanguinea* with dark red foliage and spanking forms given a pale copper.

Insects are rather fond of Aerva and will eat off all the leaves. Another low edging is *Eupatorium cannabinum* which is a trailer and has to be constantly pruned to keep it within bounds but makes a dark green edging. *Sarcolobus globosus,* called *Eupatorium foeniculaefolium,* is also a neat green edging requiring heavy clipping and one might add *Pilea muscosa.*

CARPET BEDDING

The many shades of red and yellow *Alternanthera* are the most suitable for this kind of works, the design is marked off on a sandy base and each variety set out as cutting. As soon as the roots are through, clipping commences•but must be stopped before the cold weather when the foliage assumes its best colours.

CHAPTER XIII

Propagation of Ornamental Plants

Plants usually reproduce in two ways : (1) by seeds and (2) by vegetative parts of plant. The latter method is very popular in the multiplication of fruit and ornamental plants.

SEXUAL PROPAGATION OR PROPAGATION BY SEEDS

This is the easiest method of propagation of plants. In this method the seeds are sown, covered with a layer of soil or leaf-mould and watered. After germination the seedlings are allowed to grow up to 4 leaf stage and then they are transplanted in the beds or pots. In some cases the seeds are directly sown in the ground.

These seeds originate by the union of male and female gamete. During pollination pollens of male reproductive organ come in contact with the receptive organ or the stigma of the female reproductive organ. When the ovules are fertilized by the pollens of the same flower the process is known as self-pollination. Cross pollination occurs when the pollens come from a different source and usually the pollinating agents are wind or insects. Self-pollinated seeds are likely true to type or variety, but - the cross pollinated ones may not resemble the parents for all the character. After pollination, male gametes fertilize ovules resulting in the production of seed.

All seeds do not germinate immediately after harvest and said to be resting. The rest period may be controlled by hormonal mechanism and chemical changes like acidity, enzyme activity. Increase in amino acid, etc., may also influence the rest period.

Dormancy is used when the seeds will not germinate either due to internal condition of the seed itself or existing environmental factors like temperature or humidity.

Inhibitor in the seed coats or the pulp of the fruit may also prevent germination of seeds. Glucosides, alkaloids may act as inhibitors for germination.

Rest period is caused by conditions within the embryo. Orchids, anemones often produce undeveloped or rudimentary embryo and the seeds fail to germinate. Seeds of apple, peaches, plums, etc., require certain enzymatic and chemical changes in the embryo before they can germinate.

Seed coat—In many seeds thick, tough or leathery seeds coat prevent intake of water and exchange of gas which result in delayed germination. Intake of water stimulates swelling of embryo and endosperm and greatly increase the enzymatic activities for germination. The rest period due to presence of hard seed coat can be overcome by mechanical or chemical scarification. These treatments weaken the seed coat and make it permeable to water.

After ripening and stratification—Seeds which require a period of after-ripening for breaking the rest period due to internal condition of the seeds, cold treatment and stratification are followed. The seeds are treated under conditions of abundant moisture, oxygen and cold temperature. The seeds are placed in moist sphagnum moss, or peat wrapped in polythene and exposed to temperature ranging from 1 to 5 °C for 1-7 months. In case of seeds with hard seed coat which also require treatment should be subjected to scarification followed by cold stratification.

Treatment of seeds—Trees and shrubs often form seeds with hard coats and are treated to increase the permeability. Seeds of vegetable and flowers have usually thin coats, and germinate without much difficulty.

Acid treatment—Concentrated sulphuric acid is taken in a acid resisting container like glass or earthenwire and the seeds placed on copper wire net are immersed in the acid for 5 to 60 minutes depending on the seeds.

Scarification—When the seed coats are scratched with abrasives, the process is called şcarification. It improves permeability of the seed coat. In foreign countries a number of machines are available, sand paper can also be effectively used for this purpose.

Water treatment—Soaking of seeds in water is a common practise of hastening germination of seeds. Seeds which are difficult to germinate may be soaked in warm water. Soaking facilitates germination by softening the seed coats. In some seeds it releases inhibitors.

Seed treatment for prevention and control of diseases. Various fungus and bacterial diseases are carried in the seeds of seed coat. Seed treatment can be classified into two groups : (i) seed disinfectants, (ii) seed protectants.

Formaldehyde, mercuric chloride and organic mercuric compounds are commonly used as seed disinfectants and zinc oxides, copper compounds as protectants.

A SEXUAL OR VEGETATIVE PROPAGATION

The following are the reasons for propagating plants vegetatively :

1. Many plants do not produce seeds under local condition or have lost the ability of production of viable seed. It is found in several cases that plants which readily root from cuttings do not produce seeds e.g., *Acalypha*, *Eranthenum*.

2. Plants which are cross pollinated and have different varieties in cultivation, produce seeds of heterogenous mixture. In such plants a particular type can be maintained only by vegetative method or by careful cross-breeding with the same variety.

3. Double dahlias when grown from seeds show a wide range of colour and also a mixture single, and semi-double. Apple, pear, peach, mango, etc., do not grow true to type from seeds.

4. Vegetative method of propagation results in earlier flowering and fruiting than those raised from seeds. Vegetative part of a fruiting plant is mature to bear, while a seedling take few years before the shoots ripen to produce flowers and fruits. Seedlings of *Amherstia nobilis* or *Brownea ariza* require 7-8 years to flower but a layer starts flowering in the second year.

5. Plants are also vegetatively propagated to increase their resistance or to develop immunity to a particular disease or pest.

6. A well-rooted vegetative part of a plant can adapt more readily to new environment and has greater possibility to flower and fruit than a seedling.

Many parts of plant are capable of giving rise to new plants under natural condition.

Bulbs—Bulbs are underground modified stem in which the central axis is much shortened and fleshy leaf scales are closely pressed. *Amaryllis*, *Crinum*, *Hymenocallis*, *Hemerocallis* and *Haemanthus*, are usually multiplied by bulbs which arise from the main bulb. *Cooperanthes*, *Zephyranthes* and tube rose are also mainly grown from bulbs.

Corms—Gladiolus produces new corms and cormels on old ones which are used for multiplication.

Rhizomes, *tubers* and *fleshy roots*. Rhizomes are defined as more or less cylindrical branches growing laterally or upward through the soil. Many ornamental plants such as *Calathea*, *Anthurium*, *Alocasia*, *Alpinia*, *Hedychium*, *Heliconia*, *Gloriosa*, *Canna* produce rhizomes or rhizomatous stem with buds on it which can be cut into pieces and each one will produce a new plant. Root tubers of dahlia are storage organs and shoots arise from stem attached to the tubers.

Runner—When a slender stem grows out of a crown and trails along the ground it is called a runner or stolon. *Chlorophytum*, *Episcia* send out stolons and produce young plants from the nodes. It is then detached and grown separately.

Offsets—Many ornamental plants are propagated by this method. *Sanseviera* and *Agave americana* send out branches terminating in rosette of leaves which ultimately grow as new plants. These can be separated from the mother plants. Chrysanthemums also produce offsets which are detached for multiplication of plants. Gerbera also sends out suckers on offsets.

Root sucker—There are some plants which produce suckers from roots and are detached from the mother plants for multiplication. *Millingtonia hortensis*, *Clerodendron splendens*, *Quisqualis indica* are few examples.

CUTTING

This is the simplest operation in the method of vegetative propagation. Cutting may be defined as a detached vegetative part of a plant which will develop into a complete plant when placed under condition favourable for regeneration. A large number of ornamental plants are propagated by this method.

Cuttings are classified into three main groups according to part of the plant used—leaf, stem and root.

Rex begonias are propagated by cutting leaf into pieces and the adventitous buds originate from the cut veins. In African violet buds and root develop from petiole. Many succulent like *Bryophyllum*, *Echeveria*, *Peperomia* are propagated from leaves.

FACTORT AFFECTING ROOT FORMATION

Temperature—Temperature of rooting medium and also air temperature greatly influence the root formation. For tropical plants range of temperature between 23 and 27 °C has been found to be optimum. Both high and very low temperature affect rooting.

Humidity—High relative humidity prevents the cutting to dry. This is more important with cuttings which are not easy rooting and takes a long time to root. In this country cuttings are usually taken in the monsoon, because of lack of facilities to create artificial humidity. Plants like *Plumeria*, ponisettia are propagated from cutting in early summer.

Rooting medium—It is not only a substratum for holding cuttings in position but provides condition necessary for growth and development of roots on which survival and subsequent growth of the plant depend. The media should be porous but it should remain moist and in close contact with the cuttings, Soft or succulent cuttings do not thrive in excess moisture and only sand should be used.

Sand is often used for rooting of soft wood or succulent cuttings. These type of cuttings may rot if planted in medium which retains too much moisture and favours bacterial and fungus growth. After formation of good root system the cuttings are taken out from the sand and planted in suitable compost.

Semi hardwood or hardwood cuttings which root very easily are often planted in sandy soil on raised bed.

A compost consisting of 1 part each of loamy soil, sand and screened leafmould is also a very good medium for rooting. Leafmould should be sterilised or completely dried in sun. Cutting can be planted in pots containing the rooting medium along the sides or in raised beds or propagation benches. The cuttings are kept in partial shed but not under any tree. Dripping of water during the rainy season will keep the rooting medium wet and the cuttings may rot.

Age of the plants—Cuttings taken from young plant root more easily than from an old plant.

Presence of leaves—Presence of leaves on cuttings promotes root formation. Amount of sugar in the cutting also influences the capacity of rooting. Cutting collected from plant having high carbohydrate-nitrogen ratio will produce more number of roots than those taken from plants with low ratio.

Stem cuttings are classified into three types :

(i) softwood, (ii) semi-hardwood and (iii) hardwood.

In general, herbaceous plants with softwood root better than the other two types and usually tip cuttings are used. In all types of cuttings the basal cut is given below the node.

Root-promoting chemicals—Growth substances have been found to encourage root formation in many plants which are naturally difficult to root from cuttings. In fairly easy rooting plants these substances markedly improve the number and quality of roots. Beneficial effects of the root-promoting chemicals can be summarised as follows :

(i) Larger number of cuttings produce root

(ii) Cuttings root in a shorter period

(iii) Produce better root system
(iv). Better survival of rooted cuttings.

Root formation in air and ground layers have also been greatly encouraged in many plants by using these chemicals. Indole butyric acid (IBA) and napthalene acetic acid (NAA) are the two most effective substances showing root-promoting effects. These are used as solution, powder or as paste. There are a number of commercial products which are used in cutting.

LAYERING

Gootie or Marcottage or Air layering—In this method a ring of bark about 3-5 cm in length is taken out from one-year old shoot. Care should be taken to remove the cambium without injuring the wood and presence of bud at the upper end of the ring encourages root initiation. A mud poultice is given on the cut surface covering about 2-3 cm above the ring. A layer of moist moss on the mud poultice helps to develop branched root system ; moist moss may also be used. It is then covered with a piece of alkathene and tied at both ends.

When large number of branched active roots are visible, the gootie is detached from the mother plant, planted in a pot and kept in shed for few days.

Soil used for mud poultice should be loamy, clay soil affects initiation and growth of roots. Addition of small quantity of well-rotted cake is recommended where the wood is hard.

GROUND LAYERING

Ground layering is done by fixing a portion of a branch in the ground and covering it with soil or by placing a portion of the branch in a pot containing soil. Many harbaceous plants of prostrate habit and some climbers which produce roots from the nodes can be propagated by covering one or a few nodes with soil. In comparatively difficult rooting plant, a tongue is made from a node of the branch, pressed in the soil and held in position by bamboo pegs.

TIP LAYERING

Tip of a branch is bent and a portion of it placed about 2 cm below the soil. When the roots come out from the node, the tip is detached below the roots and removed with soil.

SERPENTINE LAYERING

Flexible branches are alternately covered and exposed over the whole length. Roots are produced from the nodes which remain covered with soil and shoots develop from the exposed part. After root formation the plants with root and shoot are detached.

MOUND LAYERING

After pruning, shoots grow very close to the ground level and produce roots when the lower portion of the shoots are covered with soil in the form of a mound. After root formation the shoots are severed below the rooted zone.

GRAFTING

In this method, a part of a plant is inserted or placed on another in such a way that a union will be formed and growth will continue.

The success of graft depends on three conditions :

(i) Compatibility between the plants or its parts, (ii) stage of growth of bud of scion and (iii) contact of cambium. In this process, the operation of inserting the cambium layer of one plant in close contact with another is of maximum importance. The scion wood is selected from a desirable plant and the stock plant from a hardy species or variety.

Approach grafting is the method in which parts of the two plants are brought in contact for union when both the plants are on their own roots.

Thin slices of equal size are removed from both the plants and the exposed surfaces are firmly pressed so that margins of the cut surface with the exposed cambium layers remain in close contact. The cut portions are joined by means of string or polythene strip. After union the scion part is cut below the joint and the stock above the union.

SPLICE GRAFTING

This method of grafting is practised in plants which unites readily. The scion shoot is detached from the mother plants and inserted on the stock along a long diagonal cut.

WHIP-AND-TONGUE GRAFT

In this case, diagonal cuts on both scion and stock are made in a manner similar to that in splice graft. A tongue is made both on the scion and stock as shown in the figure and tongue fitted closely and the cambium layers come to close contact.

SADDLE GRAFT

Cut on the scion starts under the bark and brought diagonally towards the central pith in an upward direction. The process is repeated on the other side of the scion and central piece is removed. The stock is also diagonally cut on both side to form a saddle so that the scion fits in closely.

SIDE GRAFT

A long sloping cut extending downward through nearly one-fourth the diameter of the stock is given in the form of a tongue. Scions are selected from current year's shoot and cuts given on both sides to match the stock.

PATCH BUDDING

This method of budding is practised for grafting plants with thick bark. The stock and scion should be of similar age and diameter. A rectangular patch of bark is removed from the stock between the two nodes and similar operation on the scion shoot is done to remove the bud. The scion bud is then inserted in the space of the stock plant.

FLUTE BUDDING

A ring of bark is taken out from the internode of the stock plant. This is done in scion and the ring of bark with a bud is removed and fitted on the stock. During the operation desiccation should be avoided and operation completed as early as possible.

ROOT STOCK

The part of the plant which is used as stock for grafted or budded plant. Uses of root stock :

(i) For vegetative propagation of plants that cannot be propagated by other methods of asexual reproduction.

(ii) To change the form or shape of the plant. Quince root stock is used to dwarf varieties of pears.

(iii) To hasten production of a praticular type of plant.

(iv) To bring resistance to diseases and pests.

(v) To induce resistance to drought, cold and waterlogging.

INCOMPATIBILITY

Failure of union between scion and root stock is termed as incompatibility. Incompatibility may be of various types :

(i) Union may not take place between two varieties or species.

(ii) Number of unions are few.

(iii) Union forms but plant dies after detachment.

(iv) Deficiency symptoms may arise.

(v) Union may result in stunted growth.

(vi) Union may cause degeneration of tissue system and physiological disorder.

APOMIXIS

Some plants reproduce vegetatively without the process of fertilization though they form seeds. This form of reproduction is called apomixis. It develops from the tissue surrounding the embryo sac. Reproduction by apomixis has resulted similar to that in vegetative propagation. In citrus this type of embryos develop from the nucellus or the integument and are known as adventive embryos.

POLYEMBRONY

Formation of more than one embryo in a seed is known as polyembryony. A cleavage of zygote into two or more units is common in gymnosperms. Embryos may originate from cells of the embryo sac other than the egg. Synergids may give rise to embryo with or without fertilization. In *Citrus*, *Syzygium* and *Mangifera* embryos arise from cells outside the embryo sac.

PROPAGATION OF ORNAMENTAL PLANTS

TREES

Most of the species of trees, grown in tropical conditions are raised from seeds. The seedlings with tap root grow tall and large and give necessary support against storm. Some species, however, often fail or produce seeds irregularly.

SEED

Species of *Cassia* and *Poinciana regia*, *Thespesia populnea*, *Peltophorum ferrugineum*, *Couroupita guinensis*, *Acacia auriculiformis*, *Pithecolobium saman*, *Saraca indica*, *Spathodia campanulata*, *Lagerstroemia flos-regineae* and many other flowering trees produce seeds freely which germinate in seed compost consisting of garden soil and leafmould, one part each in bed or in seed pans. Seeds of mahogany have spongy seed coat and rot in excess moisture. Seeds of *Polyalthia* do not germinate if they become too dry. Seedlings of *Eucalyptus* and *Jacaranda* grow well in less humidity and temperature and should be sown in the spring.

Seeds of *Cassia fistula*, *Cassia nodosa*, *C. grandis* and *C. renigera* have hard seed coat and soaking in hot water or covering the seeds with garden soil helps in quick and uniform germination. It has been observed that seeds of *Cassia fistula* germinate for three successive years during monsoon from one sowing. Seeds of *Cassia siamea*, however, show quick and uniform germination. Seedling of most of the Cassias produce very long tap root and transplanting should be done at an early stage of growth as root injury causes death of seedlings.

Seeds of Chinese Cherry (*Muntingia calabura*) do not germinate in the usual way and it is propogated easily from gootie or airlayers. *Sterculia alata* var. Diversifolia a peculiar plant with dissimilar leaves, when grown from seeds produces seedlings mostly with uniform leaves. To perpetuate the curious character the plant is multiplied by gootie.

Cutting—Plumerias root easily from stem cuttings. Cuttings are made in spring as excessive moisture in soil causes rotting. These are planted in sandy soil and light watering is done after callus formation. Plumerias produce large fruits containing many seeds but the seedlings do not flower before four years. Cuttings from mature terminal shoot start flowering within few months. *Salix babylonica* and *Gliricidia* are also propagated from cuttings. *Millingtonia hortensis* (Indian Cork tree) produce many root suckers which are separated in the rainy season. In the case of *Spathodia campanulata* in addition to seed propagation, root suckers are also used.

Air layer and ground layer. Tabebuia rosea, T. spectabilis, Citherxylon subserratum, Erythrina cristagalli and Pachira rosea seldom form seeds at very high temperatures and can be vegetatively propagated by gootie. *Gustavia augusta, Brownea ariza* and *B. grandiceps* though produce few fruits every year but the seedlings are very slow growing and are also propagated by air or ground layering. *Magnolia pterocarpa, Peltophorum braziliensis, Eriolaena wallichii, Baikea insignis, Mimusops elengi* var. Variegata, *Caesalpinia cacalaco, Monodora grandiflora, Podocarpus macrophylla, Ficus canonii, Saraca thapingensis*, etc., are uncommon trees and seldom bear seeds. The above trees and also *Amherstia nobilis* are difficult-to-root from gooties and ground layers and application of root promoting substances like indole butyric acid (IBA) naphthalene acetic acid (NAA) and Seradix B-3, have been found to be effective in root formation. *Ficus elastica* and *Ficus krishnae* and *F. benjamina* are easily propagated from air layer.

Michelia champaca var. Alba is grafted on to common *Michelia champaca.*

Many species of trees have also been successfully propagated from cuttings under mist, viz. *Saraca indica, Milletia ovalifolia, Peltophorum ferrugimeum, Pterospermum acerifolia, Bauhinia triandra, B. purpurea, Thespesia populnea.* The plants raised from cuttings. are of dwarf habit are start flowering in the first or second year.

SHRUBS

Seeds—Few species of shrubs which produce seeds and the seedlings flower in one or two years without changing the character, are raised from seeds e.g., *Galphimia gracilis*, *Cassia glauca*, *Cassia didymobotrya*, *Solanum macranthum*, *Tecoma stans*, *Sophora tomentosa*, *Brya ebenus*, *Callindra speciosa*. *Bauhinia acuminata*, *B. tomentosa* and *Caesalpinia pulcherrima*. Plants like *Memecylon tinctorium*, *M. umbellatum*, *Catesbaea speciosa*, *Ochna wightiana*, *O. squarrosa*, *Carissa carundas*. *Jacquinia ruscifolia*, *Bauhinia galpinii*, *Portlandia grandiflora* and *Calliandra speciosa* do not root easily from cutting and layering and so seed multiplication is commonly practised. The above mentioned shrubs are slow growing and it has been found that root injury at the time of transplanting adversely affects the growth. It is suggested to sow one seed in a 10 cm pot and after the seedlings have grown about 10-15 cm plant them in ground or in bigger pots. *Barleria*, *Duranta*, and *Dodonaea viscosa* are grown both from seeds cutting ; *Coffea bengalensis*, *Murraya exotica* and *Wormia burbidgii* from seeds and air layers. To grow *Calliandra haematocephala* and *C. tweedii* from seed is a test of patience and as they root from air and ground layers, the latter methods are followed. Seedlings of *Calliandra brevipes*, however, has faster growth while *C. houstonii* does not produce seeds.

CUTTINGS

Though a large number of shrubs root from cuttings this method is followed on a commercial scale in plants which produce high percentage of root formation, much branched root system and rapid growth of shoots. Survival of cuttings depends on the quality of root system while its price is determined by the size of the plant, i.e., shoot growth.

All species and varieties of *Acalypha*, *Angelonia*, *Aralia*, *Asystasia*, *Buddleia*, *Cestrum*, *Daedalacanthus*, *Eranthemum*, *Graptophyllum*, *Justicia*, *Lagerstroemia indica*, *Malvaviscus*, *Pentas*, *Poinsettia*, *Russelia*, *Jasminum sambac*, *Brugmansia*, *Stachytarpheta* and *Thunbergia* are very easily propagated from cuttings. In *Aralia*, *Eranthemum*, *Pentas*, *Aphelandra* and *Daedalacanthus*, tip cuttings produce quicker and better roots. *Caryopteris mastacanthus*, *Clerodendron inerme*, *Hamiltonia suaveolens*, *Sanchezia nobilis*, *Strobilanthes* and varieties of *Ixora coccinea* are usually grown from cuttings. *Mussaenda frondosa* and *M. corymbosa*, *Hemelia patens*, *Brunsfelsia hopeana*, *Excoecaria bicolor*, *Gardenia* and *Tabernaemontana*, *Nerium* and many species and varieties of *Ixora* including *I. singaporensis* and *I. macrothyrsa*, though produce roots from cuttings, but shoot growth is very slow and are propagated by air or ground layering. Poinsettia and *Lagerstroemia indica* root better in spring, while in other shrubs cuttings are taken during the monsoon.

AIR LAYERING

Atalantia monophylla, *Brunsfelsia americana*, *B. grandiflora*, *Brunsfelsia hopeana*, *Cerbera fruitcosa*, *Dombeya*, *Excoecaria bicolor*, *Gardenia*, *Gmelina asiatica*, *Jatropha panduraefolia*, *Lemonia spectabilis*, *Magnolia mutabilis*, *M. pumila*, *Magnolia grandiflora*, *Hibiscus mutabilis*, *Pootea grandiflora*, *Cananga kirkii*, *Punica granatum*, *Quassia amara*, *Rondeletia*, *Stemmedenia bella*, *Tecoma gaudichaudi*, *Tabernaemontana*, *Vitex trifolia* and *V. agnus castus* are propagated by goolees. It is of interest to note that *Calliandra haematocephala* and *C. tweedii* root from air layer but *C. brevipes* and *C. houstonii* are layered in soil. *Atalantia monophylla* and *Stammedenia bella* are comparatively difficult rooting and root-promoting substances are used.

Most of the varieties of *Hibiscus rosasinensis* are propagated by air layering but varieties like 'Hawaii white', 'Daffodil' and 'Pride of Ceylon' root better by ground layering. Budding is also done in *Hibiscus*.

GROUND LAYERING

Shrubs which have thin bark and soft wood and do not root from cuttings are propagated by this method. Injury in wood at the time of taking out the bark as done in air layering causes drying of shoots. Ground layering is also practised in plants which require longer time to root. Plants propagated by this method form much branched root system and have more chance of survival than the air layers.

Dwarf bushy shrubs like *Turnera*, *Plumbago*, *Calliandra brevipes* and *Cuphea* can be easily layered in about 10 cm pots. *Magnolia fuscata*, *Olea fragrans*, *Calliandra houstonii*, *Mussaenda erythrophylla*, *M phillipica*, *Cassia calliantha*, *Randia macrantha*, *Malpighia coccigera*, all species and varieties of *Lantana*, *Gustavia insignis*, *Iochroma tubulosa*, *Wormia burbridgii*, *Clerodendron macrosiphon*, *Jasminum pubescens*, *J. grandiflorum* and *J. angustifolium* are propagated by ground layering.

Inarching—*Petrea arborea*, a large blue flowering shrub does not root easily from layers and percentage of survival is also very low. When grafted on *Petrea volubilis* they unite in about a month. *Allamanda violacea* does not grow well on its own root and inarching is usually done on *Allamanda nerifolia*.

CLIMBERS

SEEDS—Annual climbers like *Clitoria*, *Ipomoea lobata*, *I. purpurea*. *I. rubro-coerulea* and sweet pea are grown from seeds. *Aristolochia grandiflora* and *A. elegans*, *Derris scandens*. *Asparagus racemosus* and *Artabotrys odoratissima* are also multiplied from seed. Seeds of *Clematis fammula* are obtained in foreign countries and *Aristolochia* produces seeds in colder climate.

CUTTINGS—Few flowering climbers, *Thunbergia grandiflora*, *T. harrisii*, *Tecoma grandiflora*, *Ipomoea palmata*, *Vernonia eleganaefolia*, *Ficus repens* and a few species with handsome foliage like *Monstera deliciosa*, species of *Philodendron* and *Scindapsus* and *Cissus discolor* root from cutting. Several varieties of *Bougainvillea* root well from cutting.

Quisqualis indica produces many suckers which can be taken out with root and *Clerodendron splendens*, grows from root cuttings.

AIR LAYERING—*Congea azurea* and *Combretum* have been found to produce much branched root system in air-layers.

Ground layering—Almost all other climbers are propagated by ground layering. These include species and varieties, of *Antigonon*, *Aristolochia*, *Bougainvillea*, *Passiflora*, *Adenocalymna*, *Beaumontia*, *Banisteria laurifolia*, *Camoensia maxima*, *Clerodendron thomsonae*, *C. balfouri*, *Combretum densiflorum*, *Echites caryophyllata*, *Petrea volubilis*, *Stephanotis floribunda*, *Tristellatia australis* ; etc. Few varieties of *Bougainvillea* like Partha, H. C. Buck and Scarlet Queen are propagated from cuttings and the plants are ready for sale in the same year ; with other varieties ground layering is commonly practised.

GREEN HOUSE PLANTS

Green house plants thrive in shade and grow well in high humidity especially during the hot months. These are mostly grown for beautiful foliage though flowering plants like *Achimines* and *Pelargonium* need suitable protection during dry and hot season.

SEEDS—Plants can be raised from seeds of *Coleus* but to maintain a particular variety vegetative propagation has to be done.

STEM CUTTING—All the different species and varieties of *Aglaonema*, *Philodendron*, *Anthurium*, *Scindapsus*, *Monstera* and *Dieffenbachia*, have succulent stem which are cut into small pieces keeping one node in each and planted in ground or pot. The cuttings are planted horizontally about 1-2 cm below the soil with the bud pointing upward. Several species of *Dracaena* e.g., *Dracaena ugandense*, *D. victoria*, *D. deremensis* 'Bausii', *D. reflexa* 'Variegata' are grown from top cuttings. The erect stem can also be cut into pieces with few nodes in each cutting and planted in soil. Top cuttings produce well-shaped plants after root formation, while shoots from lower cuttings have slower growth.

Episcia, *Syngonium*, *Gynura*, *Fittonia*, *Pellionia*, *Coleus*, *Zebrina pendula*, *Setcrasea purpurea*, *Peperomia*, *Pillea* and *Strobilanthes dyerianus* are propagated from stem cuttings. It is safe to plant these soft cuttings in sand only. After root formation it can be transferred in pot or ground.

Foliage begonias and African violets can be propagated from leaf cuttings but division is a safe method under our climatic conditions.

DIVISION—Species and varieties of *Anthurium*, *Alocasia*, *Calathea*, *Maranta*, *Sansevieria*, *Begonia rex*, *Cyclanthus*, *Ctenanthe*, *Carludovica*, *Aspidista*, *Heliconia* and *Aglaonema pictum* are multiplied by division of rhizome. *Chlorophytum*, large number of species of *Anthericum* and species of ferns, e.g., *Nephrolepis*, *Pteris*, *Ptyrogramma*. *Polypodium* and *Davallia* are divided with crown and rhizome. *Pandanus*, *Bilbergia*, *Neoregellia*, *Cryptanthus* and *Rheo discolor* and palms like *Kentia belmoreana*, *Areca lutescens*. *Caryota mitis*, *C. urens* and *Raphis humilis* produce suckers which can be separated and grown as an individual plant. All palms produce seeds in suitable climate after attaining maturity. *Pritchardia*, *Caryota*, *Livistonia* and *Oreodoxa* often form seeds in Calcutta.

Dracaena terminalis and *Ficus elastica* var. Decora and varieties of crotons are propagated by air layering.

CHAPTER XIV

Pruning of Ornamental Plants

Pruning is one of the most important garden operations which many amateurs neglect. It is a specialised job because all plants do not react similarly to pruning and thus a general rule cannot be suggested. Each species of plant has its own particular method and season.

Removal of any part of a plant may be termed as pruning. This includes cutting of small and large branches, spent flower spikes and cutting of roots etc.

Pruning encourages growth of new healthy shoots which bear more flowers and fruits than on an old branch. It keeps the plants in shape and form. If left untouched for an indefinite period a shrub not only grows unusually tall and bushy due to constant production of weak interlaced shoots which do not bear flowers and also become a suitable home for insects and diseases. Sunlight cannot reach all the parts of the above ground portion and ultimately the plant becomes an undesirable.

Growth habit can be manipulated by careful pruning. It helps in utilisation of energy by elimination of unwanted shoots. It facilitates cultural operations like hoeing, weeding, etc. Hedges require constant pruning to keep it neat and in the desired form. After every few years quick-growing hedge plants can be cut low to remove woody branches and encourage new growth with sufficient foliage. Removal of flower spikes after blooming often causes appearance of another flush of flower. Pruning greatly helps rejuvenation of the old plants. On the whole, if you want to see your plants in best form for the maximum period of time, pruning is as essential as manuring.

TIME OF PRUNING

The purpose of pruning will not serve, if it is done at the wrong time. Sufficient time must be allowed for the new shoots to mature and flower. Season of flowering, age of the shoot bearing flowers and rate of shoot growth are the most important factors which will give an idea about pruning.

Diseased and dry wood must be cut from the base of the affected branch whenever detected. Branches which grow irregularly and affect the shape of a neat bushy plant should also be removed without waiting for the proper season. Deciduous shrubs should be pruned when the plants remain dormant i.e., about a month after leaves have fallen. In such plants, flowers appear on current year's shoot.

Spring and summer flowers are usually produced on one-year old shoot and such plants should, therefore, be pruned after flowering or fruiting to encourage new shoots to come to the stage of ripeness-to-flower in the following year.

General cleaning and trimming can be done during the monsoon because this is the season of growth for most of the plants.

Use secateurs or pruning knife for small branches and saw for larger branches. Tree pruner is very useful for taking down spiny shoots or branches beyond reach. Garden shear is a common tool for trimming hedges and topiary. Saw is used for removing large branches.

HOW TO PRUNE

First remove diseased and dead wood. Then start to take out thin-matted shoots. Old branches usually produce weak and slow growth, so it is necessary to prune such branches from the base than to remove a number of branches in a haphazard way. Always cut above a bud tending to grow in an outward direction. Cut surface must be clean and after removal of a large branch the surface should be painted with coal tar or fungicide. These exposed surfaces very often become the starting point of infection of disease or insect attack.

SHRUBS

Shrubs which produce very quick growth during a particular period of the year usually stand heavy pruning. Varieties of Poinsettia and *Lagerstroemia indica* are such plants which should be cut to about 30 to 40 cm and new growth will reach 1·5 to 2 m in four to five months. Poinsettia should be pruned in March just after the bracts have faded. They will grow about 1·5 m by July and another 50 to 70 cm before flowering. If a smaller plant is desired, they can be pruned a second time in July. Every four or five years, more severe pruning should be done and the plants be replaced after eight to ten years. *Lagerstroemia indica* varieties should be pruned in January after the leaves have fallen. All thin branches should be removed keeping only four to five of the strong mature shoots. *Lagerstroemia lancasteri* can also be pruned severely like the *L. indica.*

Caesalpinia pulcherrima can be safely cut back up to a height of about 50 cm from the ground in March-April. The plants will grow into a well-shaped plant and flower profusely on large raceme at the end of each shoot.

Crotons, *Hibiscus* and *Gardenia* do not stand pruning but old wood can be entirely removed from the base.

Acalypha can be pruned before the rains but pruning is done any time when grown as hedge. *Eranthemum* and *Polyscias* should also be pruned in June and during the rainy season plants will come to a shape with new bright foliage.

Varieties of *Ixora chinensis*, *I. coccinea* and *I. lutea* stand heavy pruning than broad leaved species and hybrids like *I. singaporensis*, *I. macrothyrsa.*, *I. westii*, where usually light pruning is done after flowering.

All species of *Pentas* except *P. kermesina* grow quickly and form untidy bush, if left untouched. Terete branches should be removed from the base and plants pruned up to a height of 25 cm or so in the Monsoon. In the later part of rainy season, it is often necessary to remove irregular branches. During winter the plants should be cleaned as the leaves dry very quickly.

Pruning of *Pentas kermesina* to a height of about 70 cm will produce bushy plant which continues to flower throughout the year.

Angelonia grandiflora often requires cleaning and branches are pinched in the rainy season. *Beloperone*, *Turnera* and *Crossandra* should be pruned severely during the Monsoon.

Hamiltonia suaveolens, a sweet scented winter flowering shrub looses its leaves in the spring when dry flowers stalks are removed and branches pruned to keep the plant in shape.

Dry branches at the centre of the bushes of *Plumbago capensis* should be removed during the rains, when it produces maximum growth. In *Plumbago rosea*, it is necessary to cut off the dry flowering spike in winter with portion of the shoot.

Some plants do not respond to regular or heavy pruning and affect the size, shape and flowering, and the plants loose its vitality. Plants like *Memecylon edule*, *Ochna wightiana* and *O. squarosa*, species of *Magnolia* and *Calliandra*, *Olea fragrans*, *Rondeletia speciosa*, *Petrea arborea* which usually grow slow or produce woody branches do not favourably respond to pruning. *Excoecaria bicolor*, *Jatropha panduraefolia*, *Lemonia spectabilis*, *Bauhinia acuminata*, *B. tomentosa* and *B. purpurea* though grow fairly fast, pruning does not induce formation of healthy shoots. In these plants diseased or undesirable branches are removed from the region of attachment to the main shoot.

Daedalacanthus nervosus, *Aphelandra cristata* and all the species and varieties of *Barleria* flower in the cold months, and should be cut back after flowering or in early rains.

In order to keep the growth of *Jasminum pubescens* under control pruning should be done after it finishes flowering in the summer. *J. pubescens* var. Rubescens, however, respond well to lighter treatment. *J. sambac* should be pruned during the late rains when the last blooms have faded.

Thunbergia erecta and *T. hybrida* grow rapidly and form bushy plants. These are cut back every year up to a height of 30 cm or so after the leaves have dropped off in the early spring.

Mussaenda corymbosa and *M. frondosa* flower in the summer and rainy season and pruning is done after the plants become almost deciduous in the winter. *M. erythrophylla*, however, is not touched except removal of old branches.

Cestrums are quick-growing scrambling shrubs, and heavy pruning is done every year. *Cestrum aurantiacum* and *C. nocturnum* are cut back at the end of the rainy season, while *C. diurnum* should be pruned after the fruiting in autumn.

Hibiscus mutabilis flowers after the rains and almost each shoot bears large blooms. After flowering the plants are cut to a height of one metre which encourages formation of long healthy shoots.

Caryopteris mastacanthus, *Buddleia madagascariensis*, *Callicarpa cana* should also be pruned in the early rains.

Oleanders do not like pruning and fail to flower in Lower Bengal till the new growth has reached a height of 1·5 m again. In drier parts, however, pruning keeps the plants dwarf and bushy. Prune *Cassia laevigata*. and *C. glauca* after two to three years to a height of one metre for obtaining bushy plants and profuse flowering. Do not use your secateurs on the Magnolias except when for removing few straggling branches of *M. mutabilis* and dry twigs of *M. pumila*, *M. fuscasta* and *M. grandiflora* should be left undisturbed.

CLIMBERS

Cleaning and pruning of climbers is a test of patience and skill for a gardener.

Antigonon is very quick-growing and can be severely pruned twice a year, once in October and again in March.

In most of the heavy climbers flowers are produced on new shoots. Thin stems of *Beaumontia* and *Congea* can be cut during rains. Clean and lightly prune *Echites* and *Derris* after flowering. *Bignonia venusta* should be cleaned after the flowers have finished. *Bignonia purpurea* may be left untouched.

Honey suckle, *Tristelletia*, *Stephanotis* do not like pruning, clean the plants if necessary. *Thunbergia grandiflora* is one of the most quick-growing climbers and can be cut back severely before the rains.

Quisqualis is another heavy climber which requires thorough cleaning and pruning of matted growth after flowering. New shoots arise quickly. *Clerodendron splendens* flowers during winter and should be pruned at least twice during the year. Thinning of *Passiflora* should be done in winter. *Clematis paniculata* can be cut to ground level when deciduous, prune *Jacquemontia* in July and replace the plant every three or four years. *Porana* can be cut back after flowering and will again be ready by next season to bear flowers.

Pruning of *Bougainvillea* is often neglected because of thorns. These are very quick-growing plants and should be pruned every year in May so that the new shoots attain maturity and bear flowers in the winter months. If pruned in the monsoon it sends out large number of succulent water shoots which are of no use and have to be removed again. Firstly, thin out interlaced matted shoots which will never bear flower and remove them with the help of a tree pruner keeping only the few healthy branches.

These branches will give rise to new shoots which will spread and cover and such shoots, in full sun, will flower profusely. The plants may be pruned severely to a height 50 to 75 cm once every three to four years, the operation will rejuvenate the plant. Pot plants should be cleaned, thinned, and the woody branches removed. Some varieties, showing vigorous growth even in pots like 'Mary Palmer', 'Thimma', 'Partha', etc., should be thoroughly pruned to keep the plant in shape and encourage flowering.

Combretum coccineum and *C. densiflorum* require removal of old branches and the best time to do it is early rains. *Derris scandens*, *Roupaliagrata*, *Rhynchordia wallichii* and *Hiptage madhabilata* are woody heavy climbers which should be thinned out every three years by taking out a number of large branches.

New shoots after maturity will produce more number of flowers. Cleaning and removal of branches growing out of place are frequently done. It is necessary to prune *Gmelina hystrix*, a shrubby climber twice, during and after the rains, new shoots arising after pruning will bear profusely in the next summer.

All the species of *Solanum* need only cleaning. Prune *Stigmaphyllon* lightly after flowering is finished, in early monsoon. Jasmines should be thinned out by removing interlaced growth which do not produce flower. *Petrea volubilis* does not respond well to severe pruning. In humid regions the shoots arising after pruning take two years, to bear flower. Except *Ipomoea horsfalliae* clean and prune *I. learii*, *I. palmata* and *I. bona nox* thoroughly.

TREES

Except few species, trees are not normally pruned. For avenue trees little pruning is very important to see that lateral branches are not allowed to grow at lower height and the mature trees have a clean trunk height of three to four metres. Trees like *Ceiba pentandra* and *Alstonia scholaris* are pruned to have the lateral branches only at the desired height. *Gliricidia maculata* is pollarded to the trunk up to a height of two or three metres. *Ficus infectoria* has been observed to maintain a lower height and good form by heavy annual pruning.

Height of *Polyalthia longifolia* var. Pendula can be effectively controlled by removing the upper portion of the stem depending on the height of the plant desired. For making topiaries pruning is done in *Polyalthia longifolia, Diospyros embryopteris* and *Diospyros montana*. *Mimusops elengi* is also sometimes pruned to give it a better form. All the species of *Cassia* except *C. fistula* readily produce new shoots when the branches break in storm. Odd branches of *C. nodosa* and *C. siamea* can be safely removed to regulate the shape of the plant. *Muntingia calabura*, a quick-growing tree with spreading habit, requires frequent pruning to keep the growth under control.

CHAPTER XV

Orchids

For the exquisite beauty of the flowers, variety of fragrance, brilliance in colour, unusual shapes, variation in form and attractive growth habits, orchids are considered as the most beautiful flowering plants. There are about 24,000 species and 32,000 hybrids of orchid, a large population grows in warm climate.

Development of new hybrids and commercial production of cut flowers in orchids are expanding rapidly in the USA, Europe, Thailand, Malaysia and Singapore. Thailand and Singapore are the two important countries exporting tropical orchids and the export value is approximately 6 million dollars per year. There is immense scope for improving orchids in India, because large number of species are native to this country and many of them have already proved to be important parent plants and contributed in the production of several outstanding hybrids in the world. Due to the diversity of environmental condition in India, it is possible to grow all types of orchids in suitable places without the control of environment.

Forest is the natural habitat of orchids. More or less similar environment can be created by growing the plants in greenhouse and protecting them from direct scorching sun, dry wind and by maintaining high humidity.

ORCHIDS FOR WARM CLIMATE. Orchids which suit warm climate condition and can be successfully grown in ordinary greenhouse include the numerous beautiful hybrids of *Cattleya*, *Dendrobium*, *Onicidium*, *Phalaenopsis*, *Rhynchostylis* and *Vanda*. Orchid species producing beautiful flowers, e.g., *Aerides longicornu*, *A. multiflorum*, *Arachnis crispum*, *A. maculosum*, *A. odoratum*, *Anoectochilus roxburghii*, *Arachnanthe catchcartii*, *Arundinia bambusaefolia*, *Calanthe densiflora*, *C. masuca*, *Coelogyne flaccida*, *C. ochracea*, *Dendrobium aggregatum*,

D. densiflorium, D. devonianum, D. fermerii, D. formosum, D. moschatum, D. nobile, D. parishii, D. pier ardii, D. transparens, Phaius macutatus, P. wllichii, Phalaenonsis manii, P. parishii, Pleione maculata, Renanthera imschootiana, Rhynchostylis retusa Saccolobium ampullaceum, S. dasypagon, S. trichromum, Thunia alba, Vanda coerulea, V. coerulescens, V. cristata, V. teres and many others grow and flower well in the above environment.

ORCHID HOUSE AND ITS MANAGEMENT—A free standing flat-roof orchid house shaded by spit bamboo or wooden batten is recommended for housing of orchids suitable for warm climate. The range of temperature which suits most of those orchids, is 65° to 85 °F. For satisfactory growth of orchids, atmospheric humidity should not be less than 30 percent at night and 70 to 80 percent during the day time. Monopodial orchids like *Vanda*, *Phalaenopsis* require high humidity, whereas sympodial type e.g., *Cattleya*, *Laelia* or those with leathery leaves need less humidity. The atmospheric humidity will increase if small tanks or lily pools are located inside the orchid house and the floor-space is covered with sand, soil, cinder, etc., instead of concrete. Free circulation of air is needed for the orchids to grow and flower and light intensity ranging between 1500 to 2000 feet candle in midday is good enough for most of the orchids.

SEED SOWING AND CARE OF SEEDLINGS—Seed pod of orchid grow after fertilization, and ripens in six months to one year. After ripening the seeds are collected and stored in a cool and dry place or in a desiccator. Millions of powdery seeds are released from each pod and they contain little or no food to nourish the embryo. Under natural condition, the seeds germinate when they find a right pocket of decaying vegetable matter on the trees.

Seeds of orchids are germinated and seedlings grown in culture media containing agar, inorganic nutrients and sugar. Disinfected seeds are sown in sterilized flasks containing agar-nutrient media and the seedlings grow for 8 to 12 months before they are transferred.

The seedlings are removed from the flask and planted in the community pots, 7 to 10 cm in diameter which hold about 20 to 25 small plants. The compost used for seedlings in the community pot is a mixture of equal parts of the finely chopped tree fern and dust-free crushed bark or moss. A shady but well-aerated location in the greenhouse will promote the growth of seedlings. In the community pot, the seedlings are watered daily and during the summer months they may be sprayed with water two to three times a day.

With the increase in size and vigour, each plant is transferred in a small pot, using the same compost recommended for larger plants, but at this stage they benefit by feeding with the weaker concentration of fertilizer solution.

VEGETATIVE PROPAGATION—Besides multiplication by seeds, commercial method of vegetative propagation of hybrids of *Cymbidium*, *Phalaenopsis* and *Cattleya* is done by meristem culture and large number of plantlets develop from a small piece of growing apex. Amateurs, however, propagate their plants by offsets, air layering, cuttings and division.

Offsets develop from *Dendrobium*, and some *Epidendrum* which can be detached and planted in small pots.

Air layering is practised on the monopodial types like *Vanda*. A slant cut is given halfway in the stem and wrapped with sphagnum moss. When roots are noticed in the moss, the upper portion of the plant with roots is detached and potted.

In *Arachnis*, *Renanthera* and to a lesser degree in *Vanda* propagation is done by cutting. As these large-sized plants produce adventitious roots, the stem is cut in sections 3 to 4 nodes, placed in a cool and dry place for healing of wound and allowed to root in moist sand or damp sphagnum moss.

Plants of many genera such as *Cattleya*, *Dendrobium*, etc., produce new growth from a lead and they can be propagated by division at the time of repotting.

POTTING AND COMPOST—A vigorous and healthy root system often indicates good vegetative growth of the plants which largely depends on the pot compost. Ideal rooting media will provide high degree of porosity and ensure adequate oxygen for root respiration. Water should drain out freely through the media and it should be resistant to rapid decomposition and decay.

Depending on the growth habit, i.e., terrestrial or epiphytic, orchids are potted in a wide variety of media and compost. Epiphytes like *Cattleya*, *Epidendrum*, *Phalaenopsis* *Vanda*, *Dendrobium*, *Rhynchostylis*, etc., are planted on a very light rooting media, consisting of various kinds of tree fern fibre or on larger pieces of hard charcoal. Terrestrial orchids like *Phaius*, *Calanthe*, *Thunia*, etc., thrive best in the mixture of leafmould, loamy soil, silver sand, dried cowdung manure, charcoal and chopped tree fern fibre. Epiphytic orchids are best grown in specially designed orchid pots with holes at the bottom and slits or perforations on the sides. Monopodial epiphytes like *Aerides*, *Phalaenopsis*, *Vanda*, etc., are particularly suited to basket culture because of the large aerial roots produced from these plants and straight growing habit. Many orchids are conveniently grown on the branches of the trees, charred wooden slabs or tree fern blocks.

Orchids, in general, grow better if undisturbed. *Phalaenopsis*, *Vanda*, *Laelia* and some species of *Dendrobium* should not be repotted unless it is absolutely necessary. *Cattleya* and many *Dendrobium* species and hybrid need repotting when roots become pot-bound.

WATERING DAMPING DOWN AND SPRAYING—As orchids are grown in a light and porous compost, watering is very important and if neglected, it will show miserable results. Epiphytes cannot tolerate under or over watering, but terrestrial orchids need more moisture.

Atmospheric humidity influences evaporation of moisture from the compost and orchids, in general, prefer high relative humidity. In a dry and well-ventilated atmosphere, damping down of the floor of the greenhouse, frequent overhead sprinkling of water will increase the humidity. But in high humid atmosphere watering should be less frequent.

Alkaline water is injurious to orchids and slight acidic water or at *p*H up to 7 should be used.

Newly potted plants should not be watered very frequently but the compost is kept moist by fine spraying. As new root emerges and growth starts, the plants need more frequent watering and it should be decreased again after flowering. Fine spraying of water is also very beneficial to plants during the period of growth or on warm dry days.

NUTRIENT SUPPLY—It has been observed that growth and flowering of orchids are improved markedly by the application of fertilizers in liquid form and a number prepared fertilizers are available in the orchid-growing countries. A balanced feed on nitrogen, phosphate and potash in the ratio of 10 : 12 : 10 and very small amount of magnesium, calcium, manganese, iron, boron and zinc has been found very effective on a large number of species and hybrids. For mature and flowering plants, 2 table spoonful of the above fertilizers mixed in 10 litres of water is sprayed once a week, while a more dilute solution is used on seedlings. Leaves and rooting media should be thoroughly sprayed with the fertilizer solution.

DISEASES AND PESTS—Orchids are less subjected to the attack of pests and disease. Scale insects, mealy bugs, green fly, thrips, red spider and snails may cause considerable damage, if they are not controlled in time. Application of Rogor or Malathion is very effective to keep the orchids free from pests.

Die-back is a serious disease in orchid which starts in rhizome and if left unattended, it spreads to other plants in the orchid house. Orthocide 50 and Cossan are recommended for controlling fungus diseases on orchids. Virus infection is also common in several species and varieties of orchids. Sometimes black spots appear on leaves and flowers turn yellow and drop off. This is not caused by fungus but due to faulty culture like over-watering, insufficient ventilation, too much of light or very dry atmosphere.

Cleanliness of the greenhouse and regular attention to the plants are very important to keep the plants free from diseases and pests.

CHAPTER XVI

Lawn

Lawn, similar to other essential and basic architectural features of the modern garden, has been subjected to a great evolution. They have suffered great alteration and changes governed by fashion and culture and these changes brought about a stabilisation in the development of turf and subsequent management of ideal lawn.

It has been observed that a well-planned lawn with its relationship to other furnishing of surrounding planting such as shrubberies, flower beds and specimen trees contribute greatly to the intrinsic value of the garden. It is a source of pride, everlasting pleasure, distinct charm, restful effect, and provides a great relaxation to the body and mind particularly after the hard labour of the day. There is an enlivened consciousness today among general public and others concerned with turf and interest is growing steadily in lawn making and upkeeping specially from scientific angle. Lawn also provides meeting place for social parties, marriage ceremonies, festival celebration and other gathering.

As a matter of fact, no garden is complete and beautiful without having a good lawn, because the beauty of a garden largely depends on the condition of the lawn.

In order to instil an invigorating and throbbing life in the realm of gardening, lawn is an inevitable 'must', because it serves as an important aid to beauty.

Lawns are always related to the design of the garden confirmating of mansion and houses in order to have perfect harmony with other garden features. For the excellent and brilliant growth of the turf, proper and thorough preparation of the soil is very essential. The subsoil should be retentive of moisture but must provide adequate drainage. The surface soil should be fertile loam at least 20 cm thick. Where the soil is very poor or gravelly the turf is liable to become patchy in dry weather, hence the top soil of good texture should be of at least 20 cm in thickness.

SELECTION OF SITE

The selected site for a lawn should get full sun and the best situation is the southern side of the house and the sites in south-east or south-west directions will serve the purpose. Grasses do not grow under the shade of a tree.

SOIL

Doob grass (*Cynodon dactylon*) can be grown on any type of soil. But for the establishment of a good lawn, fertile loamy soil rich in humus with good moisture holding capacity is most suitable.

So far soil acidity is concerned, a slightly acid soil having *p*H between 5·5 and 6·0 is suitable for good growth of grass. But high acidity is undesirable specially at the sowing time.

Where the *p*H of the soil is lower than 5·5, 300 gm of chalk or ground limestone per sq metre on sandy or a similar amount of slaked lime (calcium hydrate) on clay loam should be applied.

PREPARATION OF THE GROUND

It should be remembered that thorough preparation of the ground is very essential as the ground is the foundation on which lawn is established. The lawn is often hastily and imperfectly done, and a badly prepared lawn cannot be easily rectified afterwards.

In the hot weather, before the monsoon sets in, i.e., in April/May the ground should be dug up to a depth of 30 to 45 cm. The soil thus dug out and left in clods is subjected to the scorching rays of the sun for killing the weeds, insects, etc., and sterilising the soil. After few days when clods are partially dried, they are broken with the help of a bamboo or wooden rod. And thus the soil should be spaded 3 to 4 times at weekly intervals and each time the remaining clods are to be broken till the entire soil is brought to a fine tilth. The weeds including the roots and other foreign materials like rubbish, stones, etc., should thoroughly be picked up and removed.

MANURING AND CONSOLIDATION OF THE SURFACE

If the soil is originally fertile it is better not to apply bulky organic manure into the lawn, because cow dung and farmyard manure contain weed seeds and its becomes very difficult to make the lawn weed free. But where the soil is infertile, well-decomposed cow dung or farmyard manure should be applied to the ground at 100 kg per 100 sq metre and thoroughly mixed with the top soil up to a depth of 10-15 cm.

Once the soil has been disturbed it takes enough time to settle (consolidate) again. To ensure consolidation of soil the ground should be heavily watered 2 to 3 times at intervals. During this period weed seeds will germinate and nuts of Cyperus (motha) will sprout their sharp sword-like leaves. The weeds are removed before the next watering.

FINAL LEVELLING AND DRAINAGE OF THE GROUND

Proper levelling of the ground is essential for a good lawn. Doob grass will not grow in areas liable to becocome waterlogged. So it is advisable to raise the lawn a few cm above the paths or ensure effective drainage.

After settling of soil, the surface should be levelled by filling depression and by repeated rolling. A gradual slope from the centre to the edges is always preferred as it facilitates drainage of excess water during the heavy rains and irrigation. For perfect levelling spirit level can be used with advantage.

Like levelling, good drainage is also essential for maintaining a lawn in good condition. In small lawns where the soil is not so sticky, special arrangement of drainage may not be necessary.

But for the bigger lawns, it is always advisable to have surface drains at the ends or sides of the lawns with a proper outlet for the excess water.

SELECTION OF GRASS

In most part of India, doob grass (*Cynodon dactylon*) is successfully grown in lawn. The planting material, either seed or grass should be free from weeds.

PLANTING OF GRASS

Lawn can be made at any time of the year provided irrigation facilities exist. In the tropical parts of the country it is better to sow the seeds after one or two showers in the beginning of the monsoon or after the close of the rainy season. But the grass runner should be planted in the beginning of the monsoon to get quick growth.

Grasses are usually planted by dibbling, turfing or pasting of grass is also done.

(1) FROM SEEDS : To ensure even sowing it is better to divide the entire ground by string into equal plots of 200 to 300 sq. metre. Prior to sowing, the rolled surface is scarified with a rake to a depth of 2·5 cm. The seed lot is divided for each small plots, i.e. at 500 gm/200 sq. metre and mixed with double their bulk of fine sifted soil and broadcasted carefully by hand. Then the soil is raked over into two directions so as to mix the seeds with the soil. If the ground is dry, it should be thoroughly rolled with a light roller. Then water gently with a water can having a fine rose to keep the soil moist. The seeds will germine within 3 to 5 weeks.

After few weeks when the grass will be 4 cm high, the first cutting should be done with a pair of sharp garden shears and the surface is rolled so that when the mower is used, it will go over a more or less even and low growth. Thereafter, no hand cutting will be required as rolling and mowing at regular intervals will gradually improve the condition of the lawn.

In area where the seeds have not come up evenly, resowing should be done after little raking.

(2) DIBBLING : After thorough preparation of the ground small selected grass roots, free from weeds, obtained from either nursery or lawn scraping should be dibbled 7-9 cm apart preferably when the soil is slightly moist. Then the dibbled area should be lightly rolled and thoroughly watered so as to keep the soil moist till the grasses are established. After few week the grasses will be ready for cutting and in course of 4 to 5 months it will be a fairly compact lawn by frequent rolling, mowing and watering. Under West Bengal condition this method is commonly practised without any risk.

(3) TURFING : Turfing is the quickest method of forming a lawn. Turf or small pieces of grass should be cut uniformly thick from a place where the doob grass is free from weeds. They should be spread on the prepared ground side-by-side closely and slightly beaten down flat into position. Any cavity or interspaces should be filled with fine soil and entire turfed area then thoroughly rolled and watered liberally till the turf is established.

Another easy and successful method is to cut the off-shoots into small pieces and scatter them evenly over the prepared ground, followed by a top dressing of fine soil and sand about 1 cm thick Then light rolling is advisable if the ground is dry, followed by watering to keep the soil moist till the grass develops roots and new shoots come out. This method should be specially adopted in the rainy season and one is sure to have a brilliant and compact lawn during the next winter.

Once the lawn is properly established, it needs maintenance. To retain the verdure of the turf and its uniform colour, the lawn is raked, aerated, and topdressed with fertiliser and kept free from weeds.

ROLLING AND MOWING

The purpose of rolling is to bring the grass in contact with the soil and also to keep the ground level. After the first shower of rain, roll throughly with a medium roller both ways to make the level correct. Avoid rolling when the soil is too wet. Normally after every weeding or at weekly interval the lawn should be rolled to get an even surface.

Regular mowing of lawn is also as essential as watering. Never allow the grass to grow more than 6 cm high. During the winter season most of the lawns require mowing once a week and some time twice when the growth is rapid after the application of fertiliser.

WATERING

Watering must be through and as frequent as the weather condition requires. Frequent watering rather than heavy watering at long interval is beneficial for lawn as the doob grass is surface rooter and heavy watering may encourage the deep rooting weeds. Sprinkler irrigation is the best method for watering lawn as it distributes water evenly over a good area and also saves much of the Mali's time. Fresh water should be used and brackish or saline water burns the grass specially during the summer.

In winter, dew is a great help to growing grasses and it is always advisable to take the full benefit by brushing the dew into the lawn with a light bamboo stick or a piece of rubber hose every morning.

WEEDING

Both in old and new lawns weeds are found to grow along with the doob grass, and if left uncared, in no time weeds will cover the entire lawn supressing the growth of doob grass and spoil the beauty. So just after the establishment of lawn one should be very careful about the removal of weeds at regular intervals or when required. Take out all plants that are growing on the lawn except doob grass. More frequent weeding is necessary during the rainy season than in the winter months. The removal of shallow-rooted weeds is not so difficult as the deeprooted mothas. While weeding, care should be taken to remove the weeds including the roots, and never allow the weeds to produce seed.

SCRAPING AND RAKING

Due to constant rolling and mowing where a hard crust has formed on the surface and the lower part of the grass has become matted and woody, scraping and raking are always beneficial and hence considered essential for the maintenance of lawn. In such cases the entire lawn should be scraped with Khurpi followed by raking before the break of monsoon, i.e. in the month of May or early June. But in other cases where the condition of the lawn is good, only through raking in both ways will be sufficient to take out the old runners and loosen the soil. Then mow the grass throughly until the old stump of the doob is well-trimmed and the surface of the lawn cleaned and exposed to the sun. A top dressing of garden soil, coarse sand and leafmould in the proportion of 1 : 2 : 1 is beneficial. Hundred kgs of the mixture is sufficient to cover an area of 100 sq m to a depth of 2 cm. Bonemeal @ 1 kg per 10 sq m should also be applied.

TOP DRESSING AND MANURING

Again in the month of August/September before the beginning of the cold season, a top dressing of garden soil, coarse sand and screened leafmould with the addition of bonemeal in the proportion mentioned above should be applied in the lawn followed by rolling. After 2 to 3 weeks lawn fertilizer or turf mixture may be applied followed by watering.

Ammonium sulphate at 1 kg per 50 sq m should be applied once every month from October/November to February/March or a fertilizer mixture containing nitrogen and phosphorus may be used.

CHAPTER XVII

Dahlia and Chrysanthemum

DAHLIA

Dahlias are popular flowering plants, widely grown throughout the world for garden decoration. They are easy to grow both in ground and pot and small flowered varieties are used for floral decoration. With a remarkable diverstity of form and colour, dahlia caters for all tastes.

Mexico is known to be the original home of Dahlia. The species introduced into the old world were as *Dahlia imperialis* (tree dahlia), *D. coccinea*, *D. merckii* and *D. juarezii*. The latter is probably a hybrid of *D. variabilis* from which most of the garden types have developed. Continuous crossing between the species and varieties and by subsequent selection, it has become possible to produce varieties with most of the colours in the spectrum with the exception of blue.

In Mexico, dahlia grows wildly in the sandy uplands. Early reference reveals that the Dahlia was in cultivation in the gardens of that country as early as 1570. Seeds arrived in Europe only in 1789 being sent by Vincenzo Cervantes of the Botanic Gardens, Madrid. The plants were flowered by the Abbe either in that year or in the following autumn and were named Dahlia in honour of the famous Swedish botanical explorer, Andreas Gustav Dahl.

Cultivated dahlias may be classified as follows :

CLASS I (SINGLE-FLOWERED)

Flowers upto 10 cm diameter having one row of smooth ray florets surrounding a central disc, suitable for bedding purposes.

CLASS II (STAR-FLOWERED)

Small flowers having two or three rows of pointed petals which overlap very slightly, are somewhat recurved at the edges and form a shallow cup-shaped flower round a central disc. These are now seldom cultivated.

CLASS III (ANEMONE FLOWERED)

This class has an outer row of ray florets which surround a central group of comparatively long tubular florets, producing a pin cushion effect. They are also not very popular.

CLASS IV (COLLARETTE)

The blooms are usually about 12-15 cm across and resemble the single varieties in that they have a ring of flat ray florets surrounding the central disc, but in addition they have an inner ring of narrower florets (the collar) which are about half the length of the outer florets usually contrasting in colour.

CLASS V (PAEONY FLOWERED)

They possess two or three rows of florets which are generally flat with a central disc, the flower size goes up to 17 cm.

CLASS VI (DECORATIVE)

This is the most popular section producing fully double flowers. These cover a very wide range of colour and size, from globular blooms with florets slightly flatter than in the pompon type of blooms with curly florets approaching the cactus type. This section has again been subdivided into large, medium, small and miniature varieties of about 20, 15-20, 10-15 and upto 10 cm of diameter.

Large decoratives are the most popular type of Dahlia in Indian gardens. Small and miniature decoratives look like Pompon, but their petals are not completely tubular as in the case of a pompon. These are very popular in Europe as cut flowers and used for floral arrangement.

CLASS VII (POMPON)

These are fully double and are five to ten cm in diameter. They are practically globular in form having their central florets like the outer ones, only a bit smaller. The florets are incurved at their margins, short and blunt at the mouth.

CLASS VIII (CACTUS)

This class has fully double flowers which do not normally show the central disc. The flowers has straight or incurving petals which are partially revolute (inturned) along their length and tend to be narrower and pointed which give the flowers a star-like appearance. The tips of the petals of several varieties are lascinated or split, thus giving the flower an added lacy charm. Like the decoratives, the cactus dahlias have also been subdivided into large, medium, small and miniature.

PROPAGATION

There are three methods of propagation for dahlias—by seeds, by division of roots and by cuttings.

BY SEEDS

Only dwarf bedding singles are usually grown from seeds. Plants of large flowering types raised from seeds show a heterogeneous mixture. From a strain of double, there will be a large portion of single and semi-double flowers, also greatly varying in height and colour. It is interesting to grow and test out seedlings from good varieties with the hope that new and better variety may result.

Sow the seeds thinly in shallow boxes or seed-pans containing porous soil, cover it with a layer of screened leafmould and water through a fine rose. Under tropical condition, sowing should be done in September-October and the seedlings will be ready for transplanting in three to four weeks.

BY DIVISION OF ROOTS

When a grower has old roots that have survived the summer and rains, he could divide and plant them out. When dividing the roots, it is important to remember that each division must have an eye or bud on it. These eyes are situated on the crown of the roots where the tubers meet the old stem. The division should be made with a sharp knife so that the cut will be clean and a portion of the crown should be left attached to each tuber. Cut surface should be dusted with a mixture of lime sulphur to prevent rotting. This method of propagation of dahlias is not popular in tropical countries.

BY CUTTINGS

This is the most popular method of propagation of good varieties of dahlia. If the tubers of dahlia are stored properly, new shoots start to grow from the base and from the lower nodes of the stem. Shoots arising during rainy season usually become woody and the growths of mid-September to early November form good cutting material.

As soon as the young shoots have grown about 6-8 cm long, cuttings are made by trimming back to a point little below the node and removing the lowest pair of leaves. The young buds at the leaf-joint should be left uninjured, as they will facilitate formation and development of roots. In taking and preparing the cuttings, a sharp knife or a razor blade should be used so that the cuts may be clean. The rooting medium should be very porous and a mixture of leafmould and sand in equal proportion be used. Plant the cuttings in shallow boxes or pans about five cm apart each way. To encourage quicker and better rooting, the base of the cuttings may be treated with Seradix B—1. Cuttings kept under shade and protected from rains will root in 10 to 15 days. After rooting, the cuttings are hardened off by gradually exposing them to more sunlight.

CULTIVATION METHODS

In Ground. Dahlias grow well in any type of rich and porous soil. It is advisable to plant dahlias in the open space until chances of heavy showers are over i.e., not before the middle of October. Select a place in the garden which receives full sunlight throughout the day ; partial shade even for few hours will adversely affect its growth and flowering. The beds should be manured with well-rotted cow manure at the time of preparation of soil. Use about 150 gms of bonemeal to a sq. m. area and a small amount of potash.

Dahlias look very impressive in a single colour block in separate beds. Planting should be done at a distance depending upon the height of plants for a massive display of colour. Water thoroughly but no daily springkling is necessary. After about 30 to 35 days add 50 gms of 'Rallimeal', a mixed fertilizer with organic base to each plant and thoroughly mix it with soil without disturbing the roots. Feeding of plants at fortnight intervals till the flower buds show colour of the petals will improve the flowering. Application of oilcake in dilute solution also helps in getting fine exhibition blooms. When the plants attain a height of 20-25 cm, pinch the tip of the plants and allow four to five branches to grow and flower. Remove all the buds except the terminal one on each shoot. Too much of nitrogenous manure gives poor quality flowers, which wilts readily.

In Pots. Dahlias are also very favourite pot plants, because they grow well in pots and can be handled with more care and attention. Potted plants in flower can be used for the purpose of decoration. These are also very popular exhibits at flower shows.

Take 25-30 cm size pots and fill them up with rich compost consisting of two parts of well-rotted cow manure, one part of garden soil and one part of leafmould. Add one handful of bonemeal for every 25 cm pot. Some exhibition growers provide rotted cowdung and bonemeal at the bottom, just over the crocks. About a month after transplanting, stake the plants and dig a handful of Ralli meal in each pot at an interval of 15–20 days. Application of liquid manure from cowdung and oilcake will greatly help to produce healthy plants and exhibition blooms. If good cowdung or oilcake is not available, 30 gms of a mixture of fertilisers containing two parts of superphosphate, one part of sulphate of ammonia and ¼ part of sulphate of potash and iron dissolved in a gallon of water should be applied in five pots.

Regulate growth of shoots according to the number of flowers required per pot. Remove all the buds except the terminal one on each shoot.

STORING OF TUBERS

When most of the leaves dry up and colour of the stem turns yellow, the plants should be cut leaving 15 cm of stem and the roots should be taken out with a forked hoe. Remove soil from tubers and allow them to dry for three to four days in a cool shady position. While lifting the tubers, care must be taken not to injure the crowns. The top of the stem should then be dusted with lime sulphur. Then the roots should be correctly labelled. Pot the tubers in a well-drained sandy soil and keep the pots under shade during hot months. In the rainy season, the pots should be removed in open and kept slanting to avoid water-logging. Tips of shoots which will grow from the base of the stem in the rainy season or even earlier should be pinched off in September to encourage new shoots for making cutting.

There are not many pests and which damage the flower, but to keep Dahlia free from them, occasional spraying with Rogor and Endrine is recommended. Morestan can be used to prevent attack of aphids and red spider.

SOME VARIETIES OF DAHLIA

LARGE DECORATIVE

Name of the variety	*Description of flower*
AFRICAN QUEEN	Purple to crimson, very large.
AUTUMN TIPS	Deep cardinal red, some petals tipped with white. very large flowers.
AXFORD GOLD	Yellow with bronze shading, very big size and splendid depth.
ART LINK LETTER	Lemon yellow. very big size blooms.
BILLS WHITE	Pure white blooms of huge size, dwarf habit and fine formation.
CHALLENGER	Pale lilac striped with crimson, a distinct bicolour.
CROYDON APRICOT	Apricot to bronze, excellent of size and depth, very large.
CROYDON DELICATE	Pale mauve to pink with an attractive glistening sheem.
CROYDON LILAC	Very large, exhibition variety, one of the rarest colour.

CROYDON MASTERPIECE	Giant decorative, colour copper orange and tan, 35 cm blooms, very popular and exhibition variety.
CROYDON MONARCH	Choicest exhibition variety of exceptional quality.
GRACY HAY	Very big size over 30 cm, best red Dahlia.
MAJESTAT	Delicate flesh pink tinted salmon with darker reverses.
OUR FRIEND	A fine combination of phlox purple and mauve, huge bloom strong and vigorous growth.
THE DRAGON	Giant size flower, dark or blood red, petals wide, strong stems, very attractive.
UCHUU	A beautiful bright red and very large flower.

CACTUS

AMI PARDIEU	Terracotta red with bright golden centre.
ARAB QUEEN	Giant, exhibition bloom of salmon rose, blended with gold.
CAPISTRANO	Bright yellow, very large size bloom narrow petals.
NITA	Winner of 22 Medals in the USA, colour cyclamen purple with variegation of pink.
SILVER WEDDING	White suffused delicate pink very fine formation.

CHRYSANTHEMUM

HISTORY OF CHRYSANTHEMUM

The Chrysanthemum has a very long and glorious history. It was first cultivated in China and Confucious wrote on the

Chrysanthemum 'yellow glory' in 500 B.C. This was probably *Chrysanthemum indicum* a small yellow daisy ; *Chrysanthemum morifolium*, another species bearing rose pink to lilac flower was also used in Chrysanthemum development. In the early days, however, no systematic attempt was made to improve the flower in China and a law prevented the plants from leaving the country. Chrysanthemum became popular and fashionable as garden flower between 355 and 417 A.D. and thirty recognised forms were known between 960 and 1127 A.D. showing white, yellow, purple and pink.

Chrysanthemum first reached Japan in 386 A.D. via Korea and many colours—white, yellow, violet and even blue appeared in the first seedlings. The first period of glory for Chrysanthemum in Japan was from 800 to 1200 A.D. It not only became popular but the growers were interested to develop improved types. In 910 Emperor Uda proclaimed Chrysanthemum as the national flower and the Imperial Chrysanthemum Show was started. The second important period began in 1736 when the first known illustrated catalogue was published and it contained 100 varieties. During the World War II, cultivation of Chrysanthemum was confined only in the Botanic Gardens and about 150 cultivars were maintained at the Shinjuku Botanic Gardens.

Although Chrysanthemum was first bought to England in 1764, it was lost after a short time. In 1789 Mr. Louis Pierre Blanchad brought a large flowered variety from China to France and it was the first variety cultivated in the soil of Europe. This variety was sent to England in 1790 which developed great interest. A number of varieties were introduced in England from China and Japan between 1820 and 1826. Raising of seedlings in Chrysanthemum for developing new varieties first started in 1832.

In 1861, Robert Fortune during his visit to the East sent seven varieties of Chrysanthemum from which reflxed types were produced. In 1869 forty four-varieties of large flowering reflexed type were raised. From 1850, English raisers nave made tremendous improvement in form, size and colour of flowers ; and numerous varieties have been developed, many of which are widely cultivated by amateur and professional growers.

Few important English raisers who have contributed in the development of promising varieties and in the improvement of Chrysanthemum culture are H. Woolman of Shirley, H. Shoesmith of Woking, James Bryant in the Isle of Wight, H. J. Jones, William Wells, Keith Luxford, E. Riley and Ron Thistlethwaite.

Chrysanthemum 'Dark Purple' was first introduced in the United States by John Stevens in 1798 and a number of varieties were imported subsequently from China. Chrysanthemum varieties imported from Japan also contributed in the fine rays of colour and forms of the flowers developed in the USA. Many important hybrids were raised by Elmer D. Smith in 1889. A large number of American breeders are actively engaged in raising new hybrids and Chrysanthemum is now considered as the most popular flower in garden and vases in the USA. Freeman Lloyd Mulford, Alex Cuming, Ezra Jacob Kraus, F. L. Skinner, Glenn Viehmeyer and the Dunhams in Michigan are few leading raisers of many outstanding varieties of Chrysanthemum in the USA. The Yoder and Ball Firms have released many varieties of different types, particularly suitable for green house cultivation. They have markedly improved the technique of year-round blooming of Chrysanthemum and method of cultivation in pots.

In this chapter, the achievements of Thomas Pockett of Australia should also be mentioned. He developed many of the large flowering incurved varieties of outstanding quality in the 'Pockett' 'Turner' and 'Lloyds' groups, some of which are still popular. In India, Chrysanthemum varieties were mainly introduced from England. Several American varieties brought during 1960-64 proved very successful in different parts of the country and they are now popular exhibition varieties. Large and medium sized incurved and reflex varieties are more popular than other types. Though almost all the types of Chrysanthemums are found in this country, the number of varieties under each group are, however, very small.

Recently several mutant varieties have been obtained by radiation at the National Botanic Gardens and at the Fertilizer Corporation of India.

USES OF CHRYSANTHEMUM

GARDEN DECORATION

Chrysanthemum is grown in gardens in all parts of the world. In the northern parts of India, early cessation of rains and temperature in the autumn months provide a favourable condition for the cultivation of Chrysanthemum in beds. Several pompon varieties are grown in home garden in the southern parts of the country. In the drier parts of eastern India few hardy types, particularly anemones, pompons and singles are used for bedding. Chrysanthemum can also be grown for an effective display of colour in the shrubbery, rock gardens, mounds and borders and it will continue to flower during the late autumn and early winter when the winter annuals are yet to show their best display.

POT PLANTS

Chrysanthemums in pots are very useful in decorating steps, porches, garden paths and beautifying grounds for ceremonial purpose. The flowers stay well in sun and shade and the buds continue to open for a long period. All types of Chrysanthemum grow and flower well in pots.

CUT FLOWERS

Chrysanthemum is considered as one of the best cut flowers which often remains in good condition for 7 to 10 days. The flowers are displayed in attractive manner in bowls and vases and the flower decorators in all parts of the world find various types of Chrysanthemums very useful for floral arrangements in different styles. Small Chrysanthemums also make attractive corsages. In India, besides floral display, Chrysanthemum flowers are also used in garland and veni (clusters of small flowers used by women in the southern parts of India for hair decoration).

EXHIBITION

Exhibition of potted plants and cut flowers are also popular features in cities and towns and the competition to grow plants of outstanding quality and merit has caused marked improvement in cultural practices.

CLASSIFICATION OF CHRYSANTHEMUM VARIETIES

In Chrysanthemum, large number of varieties are found in a particular type. For all practical purposes, the different varieties of a type should be grouped under a common name so that like the varieties, the group also clearly indicates the type of flower it bears. With a varietal name in a type, a grower may form an idea about the colour, shape and size of the flower, whether single or double, reflexed or incurved. Classification is also necessary for the exhibitors to know the particular type of plants required for a particular section. There is no point in comparing a single flowered variety with large flowered incurved. It is also important for commercial purpose. A grower may obtain cuttings from a nursery a type of Chrysanthemum he wants to grow even if he does not know the name of variety in that particular type. For the sake of convenience, National Chrysanthemum Society of England and the USA have evolved the following classification systems.

The National Chrysanthemum Society of the United States classified in a simple way mainly based on the form, shape and arrangement of the corolla and size of the flower.

DIVISION A.

Ray florets ligulate or strap like.

SECTION I

Disc conspicuous with one or more rows of ray floret at right angles to the stem.

CLASS I SINGLE

Ray florets in not more than five rows. Short disc florets.

(*a*) Small, blooms not over 5 cm in diameter

(*b*) Intermediate, blooms 5-10 cm in diameter

(*c*) Large, blooms over 10 cm in diameter

CLASS II SEMIDOUBLE

Like single but bearing more than 5 rows of ray florets and not necessarily at angles to the stem.

CLASS III REGULAR ANEMONE

Broad ray florets arranged regularly, not more than five rows. Disc florets longer than in single, disc hemispherical in form, or free of ray florets.

CLASS IV IRREGULAR ANEMONE

As in Class III but with ray florets irregular in length. May be flat or quilled, twisted or tubular.

SECTION II

Disc may be present, concealed or absent.

CLASS V POMPON

Bloom globular in form, ray florets incurved and broad, disc concealed or absent.

(*a*) Small, blooms not more than 2·5 cm in diameter

(*b*) Intermediate, blooms 2·5 to 5 cm in diameter

(*c*) Large, blooms 5 to 10 cm in diameter

CLASS VI REGULAR INCURVE OR CHINESE

Blooms globular in form, incurve, full centred, nc conspicuous disc. Ray florets incurved regularly.

(*a*) Small, blooms 10 to 12 cm in diameter

(*b*) Large, blooms over 12 cm

SUB-CLASS : SKIRTED INCURVE

. Lower rows of rays not incurved but stand at right angles to the stem or stand vertically. Rest of the corolla-like regular incurve.

CLASS VII IRREGULAR INCURVE

Like a regular incurve, rays are both twisted and incurved irregular in their overlapping.

(*a*) Blooms, 12-17 cm across

(*b*) Blooms, over 17 cm across

GROUP B LIGULATE COROLLA REFLEXED

CLASS VIII REFLEXED OR DECORATIVE POMPON

Blooms like Pompon but rays broad, short and reflexed. Centre ray may incurve at an early stage.

SUB-CLASS : CARNATION FLOWERED

Ligulate corolla laciniated as in carnation.

CLASS IX DECORATIVE OR ASTER FLOWERED REFLEXED

Ray florets longer, narrower than in Pompons, pointed regularly or irregularly reflexed.

CLASS X REGULAR OR CHINESE REFLEX

Globular in form, like the regular incurve, no conspicuous disc but ligulate corollas reflexed.

CLASS XI IRREGULAR JAPANESE REFLEX

Like irregular incurves but ligulate corollas reflexed.

DIVISION B TUBULAR FLOWERED

CLASS XII SINGLE SPOON

Ray florets tubular opening at ends to form spoon or spatula like tips, florets not more than 5 rows. Disc conspicuous. Blooms small, intermediate and large according to the size.

CLASS XIIA SEMIDOUBLE OR DOUBLE SPOON

Floret spoon like but in more than 5 rows.

CLASS XIII QUILL

Ray florets long tubular, tip spoon like or closed, curved or hooked. Bloom double, disc not conspicuous.

CLASS XIV THREAD

Ray florets long, tubular, tip closed, straight or curved.

(a) Small, blooms not more than 15 cm in diameter

(b) Large, blooms more than 15 cm.

CLASS XV SPIDER

Ray florets long, tubular, tip may open spoon-like or closed but must be coiled or hooked.

In England and other European countries, Chrysanthemums are chiefly grown in glass house, hardy types are brought and planted in the open when the weather conditions become favourable. In Europe, USA, and Japan Chrysanthemums are commercially grown year round by controlling the temperatures and light period in glass house.

National Chrysanthemum Society of England has classified varieties mainly according to the time of flowering, shape and size of flowers.

OTHER GROUPS OF CHRYSANTHEMUM

CUSHIONS – Low growing plants, early bloomer and develops large number of small almost globular flower of various colour.

CASCADES The stem of the type is trained to arch or drop. The types which produce thin stems form best cascades.

KOREAN—Very attractive plant bearing single or double flowers in profusion and in various shades of colour. Cultivation is very easy, cuttings root easily, stopping or disbudding is not required.

CHARM—It is grown mainly from seeds only one stop is required at the early stage after which it will break and a good specimen may spread 60–90 cm across bearing many small single flowers of compact habit.

LILIPUT—The new group of dwarf Chrysanthemum developed by H. Woodman Ltd are very useful for bedding, dwarf pot culture and grouping. A plant bears large number of small flowers.

CARE OF STOCK PLANT AND PROPAGATION OF CHRYSANTHEMUM

A Chrysanthemum grower should secure clean, disease free stock. Culturing and indexing of stock for diseases in their various forms are normally carried out by plant pathologists in the USA, European countries and Japan. Visual selection should be done at the time of flowering, the plant should be true to type with all the best characters of the variety and colour, shape and size of the flowers should be as uniform as possible.

Although a disease free plant can be determined precisely by indexing, but several fungal and bacterial diseases causing necrosis, wilting, leaf spots etc., can be detected by visual observation. Virus diseases affect the flower and cause change in colour and malformation in flower and petals and the affected plants should be discarded.

TYPE OF STOCK :

Stool of the parent plant is commonly used for propagation. A stool consists of a portion of old flowering stem, its roots and then underground stem. Shoots arise from the main stem and from the rhizomes.

Another type of plant largely used in the USA is the stock plant. This is a young plant grown from a cutting or sucker and pinched several times to induce the growth of lateral shoots which are used as cutting for multiplication.

Cuttings from both types of stock will produce good quality flowers, if the environmental conditions are favourable and cultural practices are good. As the stools arise from a flowering plant, premature flower buds may appear on the cuttings. Another disadvantage with the shoots from stools that being in contact with soil and moisture, presence of eelworm cannot be avoided. Fungus diseases are common in the basal region. In India, Chrysanthemums are propagated from cutting or sucker and the former is made from stool or stock plant developed from sucker.

SELECTION OF SHOOT FOR CUTTING :

Thin shoots with long internodes developed from last year's stem do not make good cuttings. Suckers arising from the underground portion of the plant with lower part etiolated form good cutting and roots emerge better. Shoot selected for cuttings should not be too hard or very soft or those where growth is arrested or deformed. Hard or arrested shoots do not grow well, very soft cuttings often rot during rooting. Although cuttings from shortjointed thick shoots are hardy, those from vigorous shoots make better plants under favourable environment. Some varieties, however, do not produce basal growth and shoots are collected from upper portion of the stem for multiplication.

Five to seven centimeters long cuttings are made with a slant cut at the lower end and below a node and three to four leaves are retained on each cutting.

ROOTING MEDIA :

As the cuttings are rooted during rains in June-July, the media of rooting should be very porous. Fine sand, sandy soil or vermeculite are usually used. Mixture of sand and screened dry leaf mould in the proportion of 1 part each make good media, if watering can be regulated properly to avoid excess moisture in the media. When only sand or vermiculite is used as medium for rooting, the cuttings should be lifted soon after root formation, otherwise the rooted cuttings suffer from starvation and leaves turn yellowish. In sand watering should be more frequent so that it does not dry up completely during rooting. Cuttings are planted in bed, seed pans or shallow boxes and protected from excess moisture or rains. For the first few days before the root emergence they are kept in semi-shade and gradually exposed to more light during the development of roots. Root primordia appear within 7 to 10 days and the cuttings are well rooted within 14 to 18 days. Although in temperate countries where Chrysanthemum is grown in large-scale underglass, cuttings are rooted at a temperature between

60--70°F. In tropical region, the temperature during the season of propagation in July is higher than the effective temperature for rooting. Satisfactory rooting is, however, obtained upto 90°F, if other conditions remain favourable. Cuttings should not be planted very close to each other and crowding causes defoliation and rotting.

Watering of cuttings is an important practice. Frequency of watering will depend upon the weather condition. In sunny and dry day, the cuttings may need watering twice a day and after root formation they require more water than before. Watering should be done with a fine rose so that the cuttings are not disturbed and the media receive water uniformly and never in excess to make it soggy.

At the later stage of root formation, amount of water may be increased but the media should not remain very wet during night. Watering should be done in the morning and again in the afternoon, if necessary. After planting of cutting the leaves may droop down in the midday due to high temperature, even if the rooting medium is moist. It should not be considered due to water deficit and further watering will not improve the condition of the cutting. In such case the bed should be shaded or removed to a shady place, if the cuttings are in boxes or in pots.

In order to stimulate rooting the base of the cutting (1 cm) is treated with Seradix B-2. This root promoting chemical hastens rooting, produce roots in larger number of cuttings and develop larger number of roots which result in better and quicker survival of the rooted cuttings in pots. Chrysanthemum cuttings either rooted or unrooted may be stored at a constant temperature of 31°F in a air tight container from three to eight weeks depending on the variety.

The stock plant should be treated with insecticide and fungicide before the cuttings are taken and another may be necessary during rooting, if the sky is cloudy and the atmosphere is humid.

After root formation, cuttings are taken out gently with the help of a pointed stick without damaging the roots and potted as soon as possible. If immediate potting is not possible or rooted cuttings are to be taken to a place, the roots with a portion of the leafless stem are placed on a layer moist sphagnum moss, covered with a thin layer and gently rolled to make a loose bundle. The bundle is then covered with a piece of polythene or moist newspaper.

CHRYSANTHEMUM GROWING IN POTS

SHIFTING

For growing Chrysanthemum in pots, plants are shifted in pots of various sizes. The rooted cuttings are first planted in 8–10 cm pots. When the roots are almost pot bound and the growth of the plant is slowed after some time, the plant needs shifting. The condition of root growth can be verified by tossing out the plants from the pot. When much branched roots have made a network between the compost and the inner wall of the pot and the plant comes out of pot easily with the compost held by the closed network of root it should be repotted in bigger pot. If kept for a long time with roots in pot bound condition the growth will be severely affected and plants will develop closed jointed internodes and leaves become smaller in size. From a 8–10 cm pot, the plants are transferred in 15 and finally in a 20 cm pot. Large growing varieties often need 25 cm pot. The shifting is not optional but a necessity in chrysanthemum. Direct planting in a bigger pot will not produce quality bloom.

Rooted cuttings of chrysanthemum develop better root system when grown in small pots because soils in such pot do not remain wet for a long time and better aeration encourages root growth. Because of limited supply of intrients and restricted root system the vegetative growth is also not luxurient with soft and tender shoot. In Chrysanthemum rapid and luxurient vegetative growth are not desired. The plants should however, make steady and continuous growth throughout with semi-woody, erect and strong stem and much branched root system so that it can absorb sufficient amount of nutrients after appearance of flower bud for developing it into a large flower.

Pot : Burnt clay pot of uniform size and attractive appearance should be obtained for chrysanthemum, because the appearance of a pot is also important for a potted plant. The pot should have side and bottom holes for satisfactory drainage of excess water. Plastic pots have several advantages. It can be used for many years. As the moisture does not evaporate from the side of the pots, the soil remains moist for a longer period and frequent watering will not be needed. Too much watering in a plastic pot will, however, keep the compost soggy which is detrimental for newly planted rooted cuttings. Compost in a plastic pot maintains a higher temperature which is beneficial in cold climate. Used pot should be throughly washed and dried before using it again. From nursery, one can get cuttings with bare root or potted in a 5 cm pot. Though the difference in price between the two types of plants is not much, carrying of potted plant may be difficult. The rooted cuttings in small pot however, establish quickly and develop new growth within a few days after first potting.

FIRST POTTING : For first potting the soil should be of medium texture and not very rich. The compost should consist 3 parts of loamy soil, 1 part of dry screened leaf mould and small amount superphosphate, if bone meal has not been mixed in the compost at least a month before potting. Seive the mixture through fine meshes.

Put a crock on the bottom hole and some small pieces around it. A thin layer of coarse soil is placed over the crocks and 2/3rd of the pot is filled with compost and pressed with finger. The rooted cutting is then planted, the pot is filled with compost which after pressing will leave a gap of 1·5 cm at the top. Cuttings should not be planted deep into the compost and not more than 1·5 cm basal portion should remain in the compost.

Water the potted plants with a fine rose carefully and see that the compost is thoroughly soaked. The pots are kept in shady place protected from rains. At this stage, both excess water or drying of compost are harmful to the plants. After the cuttings have established and started new growth, the pots are brought in full sun and watered. In dry and warm day it may be necessary to water twice daily. Rapid drying of the small pots can be reduced by inserting about 2/3 of the pot in cinder or sandy soil. It also keeps the temperature of the compost lower and the plants grow better.

SECOND SHIFTING

In small pot, a plant usually remains for 30 to 40 days before it is repotted in a 15 cm pot. The compost should be richer and made of 3 parts loam, 1 part each of well-rotted cow or stable manure and leafmould. A small amount of wood ash and a tea spoon 'Sterameal' should be added in the compost for 15 cm pot. The compost should be mixed thoroughly but seiving is not necessary. Fill a clean dry pot up to 1/3rd depth and consolidate the compost by pressing. Take out plant from 10 cm pot, remove the crocks from the ball of compost and place it in bigger pot. Fill the sides and top with fresh compost, ram it and leave about 1·5 cm space empty for watering. After potting water the plant through a fine rose.

FINAL SHIFTING

About 40 to 60 days after second potting the plants become ready for final shift in a 20 cm pot. The time of repotting will depend upon the growth of the plants. If the roots in 15 cm pot is pot-bound the plants should be repotted in a richer compost and adequate nutrients promote growth and flowering. The compost for final potting should consist of four parts loamy soil, 2 parts well decomposed cow manure, 1 part leaf mould, and a table spoon 'Sterameal' and little wood ash for each 20 cm pot. Ramdown the compost upto 1/4th depth of the pot after placing adequate number of crocks at the bottom. Place the plants in position spreading the roots on the firm base of the soil in the pot. Then fill in the sides and the top with compost and ram it firmly and leave about 2·5 cm portion for watering.

WATERING OF CHRYSANTHEMUM

Watering of chrysanthemum is a very important task for its successful cultivation and will depend on several factors e.g, variety, stage of plant growth and atmospheric condition. Best way to check the moisture of the compost in the pot is to tap the side of the pot with a wooden tapper attached to a handle. If the pot has enough moisture it will produce a dull sound, whereas dry compost will make a sharp sound. Due to water deficit the leaves and the apical portion of the shoot droop down and they gradually regain their normal appearance after watering. High temperature and low humidity often cause drooping of leaves especially during midday even when the compost is wet. Temporary wilting is also observed when the plants get bright sun after a couple of cloudy or rainy days. It can be rectified by spraying the plants with water through a fine rose or sprayer and by watering the ground.

STOPPING AND TIMING

Stopping consists of removing the apical portion of the shoot of the growing plant. When a plant grows about 15–20 cm high, may produce a small flower bud at the tip, commonly known as break bud. After the appearance of bud, the apical growth is checked naturally and side shoots develop from the axils of leaves. This is 'natural break' of the main shoot caused by the formation of flower bud at the tip. The axillary branches will also develop flower bud which is known as the first crown bud. After the appearance of first crown bud or if the tip of axillary branch is removed, laterals will arise which again produce buds, known as second crown buds. Third crown buds appear in the same manner and they are often termed as terminal buds because appearance of third crown bud does not usually develop axillary branches.

The earlier the first crown bud appears, the larger the number of petals produced. Third crown forms smaller flowers of interior quality. Since the top growth rather than basal branching is preferred, pinching is suggested up to 2 cm tip to induce early lateral branches. At least two to four strong branches will shortly begin to grow upwards and uniformly. Branches arising from young shoots grow and flower better than those developed from older and woody stem. It has been observed that colour of flower is improved on second crown bud provided the number of petals and size of flowers do not reduce appreciably.

Timing means the fixing of the date or period in which flowering is to be made Timing is important when a grower desires to get bloom on a definite date of the season for a particular show. Under natural day length, if a grower wants to get bloom on a well-grown plant by the last week of December, the cutting should be first potted in the last of June, transferred in the middle of July and final shift made on first week of September. Stop the plant by pinching after about a week. The bud on the first crown will appear in the last week of October which will be in full bloom by the last week of December. Practice of timing mainly depends upon the growers experience with the different varieties and the local environmental condition particularly day length and temperature.

In Europe and the USA Chrysanthemum is grown round the year under controlled temperature and flowering is regulated by photoperiod. Varieties which are grown for cut flowers should develop large number of flowers of uniform quality. Exhibition varieties usually produce fewer flowers. Cut flowers varieties are mostly short break type and branches develope due to natural break and rapidly grows into a bushy plant. The long break varieties which usually grow tall before they break naturally need stopping to obtain a well-shaped plant.

MANURING :

Application of manures and fertilizer in the pot compost should ensure a balanced growth of the plants for a period of 4 to 5 weeks after final potting.

In England, the USA and Japan, complete and balanced fertilizer mixtures for chrysanthemum are available and fertilisation of chrysanthemum is a simple and effective treatment in these countries. In India, there is no standard fertilizer of chrysanthemum and method of feeding varies with grower and every one tries to maintain a secrecy for his success and beginner often gets an impression that chrysanthemum culture is very difficult. It is true with all types of plants that experience improves the cultural practices but by following certain basic principles and taking interest in the plant culture one can expect a fairly good success with chrysanthemum.

Acidity or alkalinity of the soil or compost should be tested and chrysanthemum prefers a *p*H between 6·0 to 6·5 ; a slight deviation on the alkaline side is safe but high acidity is injurious.

Though many growers in this country chiefly use organic manures for feeding chrysanthemum, e.g., mustard or castor cake solution or cowdung rotted and diluted in water. These liquid manures are no doubt safe and effective but in cities and towns, the arrangements are often felt cumbersome and the foul smell during rotting. will be a test of patience for the neighbour. The above method of feeding often discourages the beginners. Blood meal. wood ash. soot water are also used in chrysanthemum.

Chemical fertilizer, on the other hand, in balanced proportions if applied in a well-prepared compost during growth and flowering, at regular interval. beginning from 4 weeks after final potting till the buds show colour of the florets will produce good bloom. Nitrogen. phosphorous and potassium in the proportion 10–5–5 together with small amount of magnesium, sulphur, iron and calcium and minute quantities of boron and manganese make a good fertilizer mixture for chrysanthemum.

DISBUDDING :

It is a process of removal of unwanted buds for better growth of those which remain. Disbudding also includes removal of excess bud, axillary shoots between leaf and stem and also those arising from the base of the plant to prevent utilization of energy for any purpose other than development of desired number of flowers.

When the largest bud is slightly bigger than the size of a pea, disbudding should be started, smaller buds are not easy to handle. Large buds on the sides will squeeze and deform the specimen bloom.

Disbudding of the whole plant should not be done in one day but the buds removed gradually in 2 or 3 days. It should be started from top of the stem and continued downwards. The buds are removed with finger nails without damaging the desired bud or stem tip. Knife may be too big for this purpose.

After securing the crown bud, the axillary growths are removed leaving the leaves intact. If the crown bud is damaged or distorted, the next largest one is retained on the plant.

CARE AFTER DISBUDDING

The work of the grower does not end by securing the bud. The plant needs regular and thorough checking. Any bud left out during disbudding and new shoots which may arise from the ground should be removed. Constant attention and regular feeding and watering during the development of bud will improve the size and quality of flower.

DELAYING FLOWER BUD DEVELOPMENT

If crown bud is early by weeks, it may be removed and the second crown allowed to appear on a lateral below it. In case the desired bud is 7-10 days earlier to schedule, few laterals can be retained for some time which will reduce growth of the crown bud. The laterals are removed after a week or so.

PROTECTION OF BLOOMS

In India, chrysanthemums are grown in the open for decoration or exhibition. For exhibition, quality of each and every bloom on the plants is considered while judging. Delicate florets of chrysanthemum are easily damaged by sun, rain, wind, light, insects and fungi.

The flower may, to some extent, be protected by covering the bud before it shows the colour. Butter paper bag will be useful for this purpose as it will not collapse being wet in dew and remain inflated. The bag should be large enough to accomodate the bloom in full size and kept in position by means of support. The flower can be examined from time to time through a hole in one corner of the bag which can be clipped to close. Bud should be covered when dry and tied firmly. For covering large number of plants, a temporary frame may be erected, the top and part of the sides covered with white polythene. Covering of bloom also helps to form a globular shape of the incurved varieties without an open centre.

STAKING—Staking is almost a necessity for medium to tall varieties for keeping the plants erect with the sprays of flowers and large blooms on them. It is at the same time an art as bad staking often spoils display of the beautiful flowers. Normally a long stake is used for each shoot and if there are 4-6 shoots on each plant the stakes become more conspicuous than the flowers. In case of a plant bearing 1-3 branches, a stake placed centrally, tied firmly at the basal region and the branches tied loosely at several places on the central stake without bringing the shoots close to form a bundle of flowering branches. Bamboo canes normally used for staking should be trimmed round, painted green and the height should not exceed the stalk of flower. In case of varieties with large number of branches, one or more ring, made of bamboo or iron wire fitted with two stakes will keep the branch and flowers in position. Staking is often necessary after the final potting to keep the plant erect during wind and rains. Raffia or twine is used for tying.

CHAPTER–XVIII

Roses

HISTORY

Fossil remains of roses indicate that it is older than man. About three hundred species of roses have been listed by Dr. W. H. Lawrence of Cornell University but the number of true species according to Dr. A. Rehder is probably not more than 180. Few species of roses have been recognised as the ancestors of present roses. *Rosa gallica*, the French rose came originally from Caucasus and the middle East and is an ancestor of Moss Roses, the Centifolias (Cabbage Rose) and Damasks. The Tudor Rose, the Royal Rose of England which was first adopted as the badge of the Royal House of England in 1486 was a combination of *Rosa gallica* and *Rosa alba*. The Provence Rose, *R. centifolia* came to France in 1580 from the Mediterranean. It was widely cultivated in European countries and developed large number of varieties by mutations and natural crossing. The Damask Rose, *R. damascena* is a natural variation of the *R. gallica* and early record is noted 1000 B.C.

About the beginning of nineteenth century Bourbon Rose, developed as a result of natural cross between the Damask and hybrid China Rose, the latter developed by crossing China Rose (*R. chinensis*) and various members of *R. gallica* group.

Portland roses appeared in 1800 as a result of crosses between Damask and Gallica.

'Ena Harkness' can be traced back in direct pedigree to this variety. Soon after French Horticulturists, Laffay, Verdier and others crossed bourbons and hybrid chinas and crossed back with *R. gallica* variety and rigidly selected outstanding ones from thousand of seedling produced from pollination by bees or other insects. They produced the popular roses of the period, the Hybrid Perpetuals (HP). About the year 1820, the sulphur yellow rose was brought to Europe. It was called 'Tea rose' because its fragrance somewhat resembled that of tea chest brought from Bengal in the same ship. Tea rose was originally considered as varieties of *R. indica* var : Odoratissima (*R. odorata*) and in France as *R. Chinensis* var : Fragrans. The Tea Roses were actually dwaff segregates from noisette and *R. gigantea* crosses with free flowering exquisite flowers but not very hardy.

In 1867, M. Gullot introduced 'La France' by crossing tea rose and hybrid perpetuals. In 1882, Bunnett put out 'Lady Mary Fitzwilliam', a famous rose which became the parent of a number of modern varieties. M. Pernet Duchar (1898) first obtained new orange rose by crossing 'Persian yellow' rose. *R. foetida* var : Persiana on to 'Antonie Duchar', a hybrid perpetual and all the orange, yellow and flame colours now so conspicuous are derived from the poor orange yellow hybrid produced by Pernet Duchar. Thus all the important early hybrid roses came from France and only in the middle of the last century, first England and then Germany, Belgium, Luxemberg and Holland became important rose producing countries.

Simultaneously, another line of advance began by crossing different lines of *R. chinensis* with *R. multiflora* in Japan, and gave rise to Polyantha roses in 1873. These Polyantha roses were selected later on two directions for dwarf and climbing habits. The flowers are very small and borne in clusters for a long period. In 1912, M. Poulsen of Denmark introduced '[illegible]odhatte' by crossing Dwarf Polynatha and Hybrid Tea (H.T) roses. By 1924, with the release of varieties like 'Else Poulsen' they became very popular and began to be known as Floribundas. In recent years they have gained much importance. In America another group has been introduced as Grandiflora, which are actually cross between Floribunda and Hybrid Tea. They bear large flowers in small clusters which are very difficult to differentiate from H. T.

Many new varieties arose later from these groups as bud mutations. From one such mutant, Scott-Moncrieff in 1[illegible] introduced pelargonidin pigments in variety 'Paul Krampel' and developed brillant orange colour which was unknown in roses before. 'Paul Krampel' gave rise to orange scarlet floribunda roses like 'Independence', 'Heat Wave' and 'Golden Jewel'.

The race for search of new varieties of roses will continue till the civilisation exists and man does not forget or change his habit of enjoying the beauties of Nature.

TYPES OF ROSES

Roses which are very popularly used for the beautification and decoration of the gardens can mainly be grouped into six classes—Tea, Hybrid Perpetual, Hybrid Tea, Floribunda, Dwarf Polyantha and Climbing roses.

The Teas—This profuse blooming roses are known as 'Tea's for their fragrance which is very similar to the aroma of tea leaves. With the origin of Hybrid Tea the popularity of Tea roses faded away. Tea roses are not very hardy, grow as bushes of varied height with slender twiggy growth. These roses prefer light, loamy well-drained soil. Very little or no pruning should be done for the best performance of Tea roses. Some popularly grown varieties are 'Lady Hillingdon', 'Mme Falcot', 'Molly Sharman Crawford', etc.

Hybrid Perpetual—From crosses between European and Asian ancestors, this type of rose came into existence. Hybrid perpetuals (H. P.) are very hardy, with luxurious vegetative growth, moderately bearing large flowers sometimes with rich fragrance. They usually prefer well-drained good loamy soil, but can also be grown in clay or sandy loomy soil. Moderate to heavy pruning should be done to H. P. roses depending on the growth of the plant. H. P.s can be grown successfully in places of high rainfall and humidity where Hybrid Tea roses are found susceptible to adverse climate.

Hybrid Tea—H. T. roses are the most novel and exceedingly prized types of roses. This type owes its origin to crosses between Teas and Hybrid perpetuals and also crosses among themselves. Hybrid Teas are comparatively weaker than H. P. and Polyanthas, yet they surpassed all other types by their attractive colours, numerous varieties and fragrance. They also comprise many bicolour and multicoloured varieties.

For best blooming performance, H. T. roses prefer well-drained rich loamy soil with full sunshine and an environment free from dust and smoke. Dry and cold atmosphere encourage blooming. Medium to hard pruning should be done depending upon the variety and plant growth.

Some very popular and attractive varieties are 'Allegro', 'Anne Watkins', 'Bluemoon', 'Peace', 'Christian Dior', 'Colour Wonder', 'Confidence', 'Duet', 'Femina', 'Garden Party', 'Henry Ford', 'Intermezzo', 'Kalima', 'Montezuma', 'Superstar', 'Tyriana', etc.

Polyantha—This dwarf type with small flowers are usually preferred for their cluster of flowers, free flowering, and perpetual bearing habit. Polyanthas came into being from *Rosa multiflora*, formerly known as *R. polyantha*. Polyanthas are also largely used for the production of Floribundas. This hardy type needs very little pruning. Only cleaning of interlaced and diseased branches will serve the purpose of pruning. Widely used varieties are 'Cameo', 'Eblauissant', 'Gloria Mundi', 'Ideal', 'Paul Krampel', 'Yvonne Rabier' etc.

Floribunda—These roses have virtually replaced the old Polyanthas. They came into appearance by crossing Hybrid Tea with Polyantha. At the beginning, the flowers were larger than Polyanthas but smaller than those of Hybrid Tea. They bear flowers in large clusters, opening almost at the same time and producing a mass effect. By subsequent breeding with Hybrid Teas, the modern Floribundas have successfully combined the size and shape of Hybrid Tea with the habit of opening more flowers at the same time. Flowers of some recent floribundas have almost attained the form of Hybrid Teas and they are known as grandiflora in America. After removing old, weak shoots the plants need fairly light pruning. Some popular varieties are—'Ali Gold', 'Anna Wheatcroft', 'Arabian Nights',

'Border Coral', 'Circus', 'Chanella'. 'Concerto', 'Daily Sketch', 'Dearest', 'Delhi Prince', 'Evelyn Fiscon', 'Firecracker', 'Gold Marine'. 'Masquerade', 'Queen Elizabeth', 'Sea Pearl', 'Wotny Abbey'.

Miniatures—Recently the miniature roses with small leaves and exquisite little flowers are borne on small bushes. Most of them are useful for growing in pots and for edging rose-beds. Some popular varieties are 'Baby Masquerade', 'Coralin', 'Cinderella', 'Dwarf King'. 'Josephine Wheatcroft', 'Pixie', 'Sweet Fairy'.

Ramblers and Climbers—Ramblers owe their origin from *Rosa multiflora* and *R. wichuraiana*, while the climbers may be of Hybrid Teas, and Noisette roses. Both of them are free flowering and consist of many colours like white, yellow, pink, red, mauve, etc. Some popular varieties are 'Violette' 'Don Juan', 'Lady Waterlow', 'Goldi Locks', 'Marechal Niel', 'Golden Shower', 'Property', etc. Climbing roses grown in the lower part of West Bengal never give a good display of flowers.

CULTIVATION OF ROSES

Planting—In the plains of eastern India roses are normally planted from October-February. The beds are dug up to about 100-120 cm deep, a layer (about 15 cm) of stone chips or over-burnt bricks spread at the bottom to facilitate drainage. The beds should preferably be dug during the summer months so that the soil is thoroughly dried. For each plant, half a basket of rotted farmyard manure and a handful of bone meal or little super-phosphate are mixed with the top soil previously filled in. The bed should be raised about 20 cm above the ground level. If the soil is clay it is advisable to mix up 500 gms of hydrated lime per square metre before applying manure. The grafted or budded plants should be planted after the soil has properly settled down, so that the plants may not sink after heavy rains.

The rose plants collected for planting should be carefully handled. If the pits are not ready, the new plants may be kept in a cool place and water sprinkled lightly over the roots at regular intervals. The earth ball around the roots of the stock is cracked and planted in the pits keeping the point of union of the graft just below the soil. Addition of sand around the root in case of clay soil helps in initial development of root through the earth ball. Dry branches and flowers are removed before planting. After planting the soil around the root is pressed firmly and watered thoroughly. The distance of planting between plants and row is generally 75-100 cm for H. T., 70-80 cm for floribundas, 45-50 cm for polyanthas, and 250-300 cm for climbing roses.

Pruning—Pruning is the technique, which every rose-grower should understand and know properly. In the plains pruning and wintering of roses are usually done between the first week of October and first week of November. It is done mainly to encourage growth of strong new shoots which will ultimately bear flowers. All types of roses are not pruned in the same manner. It is done once a year except in the southern parts of India where pruning is done twice. General practice of pruning irrespective of any class of roses is removal of all dead and diseased shoot, thinning out of small, weak and interlaced branches in the middle of the bush and removal of all suckers which have grown from the stock. For pruning of shoots a sharp cut sloping inwards is made about 6-8 mm above a strong and healthy eye pointing outwards.

Method of pruning varies for the various types of roses. The severity with which a particular type is pruned again depends on growth of the plant, climate and whether blooms are required for exhibition or garden display. Hybrid perpetuals may be cut down to 40-50 cm from the ground. H. T. roses must be pruned moderately up to 30 cm leaving 4-8 eyes on each shoot. To obtain flowers of large size, the bush may be pruned to 22 cm and strong new shoots from the base are retained for replacement of the old framework. Floribundas and dwarf polyanthas like fairly light pruning. They produce many weak shoots which are removed and the plants cleaned. The younger shoots are shortened by about a half, to make a well-balanced bush with plenty of strong young growth to bear an abundance of flowers. Climbing and Rambler roses bear the best flowers on short branches that emerge from older canes. So they require only removal of tips. One or two main stem may be cut back severely after 3-4 years to encourage more lateral and sublateral branches.

In the first year, the bushes should be cleaned by only cutting flowering branches and removing thin and dead branches. Immediately after pruning the soil is removed to a depth of 15-20 cm and a diameter of 45 cm around the plants and kept exposed for about 7-10 days.

Manuring--As roses are strong growing plants and bear large number of flowers, they require a regular application of balanced manure. It is necessary to add organic manures under tropical conditions in order to supply of plant nutrients and to help to maintain a good soil structure. After pruning and wintering, adding about one-fourth basket of well-rotten cowdung manure, 30 gms of bone meal and 10 gms each of super-phosphate and sulphate of potash per plant to the soil removed from the roots and recovering the roots with the mixture. After manuring the plants should be watered thoroughly.

No further manuring and watering should be done until new growths are produced. A weekly dose of well-rotted oil-cake solution mixed with water followed by copious watering will hasten growth of new shoots. If it is inconvenient, a mixture of 10 gms of ammonium sulphate, 30 gms of super-phosphate 5 gms of sulphate of potash and 2 gms of ferrous sulphate is diluted in 5 litres of water ; a litre of the solution is applied per plant on moist soil every week.

Roses prefer soils having a *p*H range of 6·0-7·5 (slightly acid, neutral or slightly alkaline). While manuring, it is essential that the *p*H should be maintained between this range by carefully that adding lime or using ammonium sulphate as the source of nitrogen. The liming should be done during the monsoon.

Now-a-days ready mixed complete Rose-fertilizers like 'Rosemix' are available in the market. Two tablespoonful of the fertilizer should be added to the soil every fortnight. The rose grafts may show deficiency symptom of iron (chlorosis or areas between the veins are pale), magnesium (centres of leaves become pale), manganese (interveined chlorosis), or boron (terminal buds die) which are required in traces. Chelated compounds of iron, magnesium, manganese or boron are available in the market under names like 'Sequestreone Plus'. It may be added at a rate of one teaspoonful per plant after pruning. Foliar feeding or applying nutrients to the foliage through sprays is becoming popular. One gm of urea and 1 gm of potassium-dihydrogen-phosphate diluted in a litre of water with a little spreading agent may be sprayed in the early morning at an interval of 15 days.

PROPAGATION OF ROSES

Roses can be multiplied by various vegetative methods like cutting, layering, budding and grafting and also from seeds. Grafting was very popular few years back, but now budding is the most common method adopted for propagation of the majority of varieties. Seedlings and cutting are used as stock for budding or grafting. The seeds are used to test the crosses for developing new varieties.

Cuttings—Some varieties of vigorous types can be multiplied by cutting prepared from ripened branches during the monsoon or spring. This is a method specially suitable for the rambler, climber, polyantha and miniature roses. Each shoot should be cut clean just below the node and lower leaves are to be removed. The cuttings are generally planted in sand under shade. The rooted cuttings become ready for transplantin about 40-60 days.

Layering—It is a convenient method of propagating climblers and ramblers. By this method a plant can be multiplied without the risk of removing shoots from the mother plant before they have formed their own roots. Young shoots from current year's growth are most suitable. A cut is made with a sharp knife below a node without actually severing the stem and the portion is covered with soil in ground or in pot. The layer is held in position with a forked bamboo stick. Rooting usually takes place in 30-40 days and the layered shoot is detached 15-20 days after root formation.

Budding—It is a form of grafting by which a portion of a plant is transferred to a root system or 'stock' of a vigorous type. It has got another advantage of having more plant from the 'bud' stick with 3-4 buds instead of a single plant when propagated from cutting or layering. In eastern India, the common briar used as root-stock is a variety of *Rosa multiflora.* Edward is the popular root-stock for northern India. In Europe the root-stocks which are commly used is *R. cania, R. laxa* and *R. rugosa,* whereas in America varieties of *R. multiflora* are used as root-stock.

Now-a-days almost every rose-grower has resorted to budding as the most suitable form of grafting. Suitable buds or eyes (not to be confused with flower buds) can be selected from the half-ripened shoots of current year's growth of the desired variety. The thorn on an ideal bud-stick breaks off readily exposing the green tissues.

Stems that have just produced flowers, usually form small swelling. The stem with such eyes which have not started elongation are cut off and the thorns are removed. The leaves are removed but leaf-stalks are left. The bud or eye is a dormant growth situated in the axil of the leaf-stalk.

With a budding knife a shield-shaped piece of the bark with the eye is removed by cutting 1·5 cm below and then drawing upwards so as to come out again on the same side of the stem about 2 cm above the eye. The woody portion of shield-shaped bud is pulled away carefully from the bark. The prepared bud is inserted under the bark of the stock by making a 'T'-shaped incision. The incision should be just enough to accomodate the bud. The eye is bound in position with suitable fibre which should cover the incision from top to bottom keeping the bud exposed. Generally, budding should be done as low down as possible on the stock. One bud on a stem is considered to be sufficient. The best time for budding in eastern India is February to March. When the successfully united bud begins to grow, the top portion of the stock above the union is cut off and the fibre band is removed. It takes 3-4 weeks for the bud to unite. The side branches of the stock are removed which compete with the scion for supply of nutrient.

Grafting—This method is largely employed by Nurserymen in eastern India for the multiplication of Roses. In this method scion unites with the stock while it is still attached to the parent plant. The rooted stock plant with a ball of earth is placed near the scion. Current-year shoot with medium thickness, slightly woody at the point of incision should be selected from the scion plant. On both the stock and scion, about 3 cm. long cut is made through the cambium and slightly through the wood. The cut surfaces are brought together and the stock and scion tied firmly leaving the bud exposed. After the two have united the scion is severed below the union and stock above the point resulting in a new plant composed of a root stock and a grafted top. This method is known as approach grafting or inarching. The work is carried out from January to March and again during the monsoon.

CHAPTER XIX

Bamboos, Grasses and Reeds

The value of tall feathery grasses and light bamboos is not generally appreciated by amateurs. Perhaps the reason given that bamboos bring snakes may apply to old uncared bamboo stumps with holes and hollows, but in a small clean clump there is no room for a reptile.

The foliage of bamboos does not make good leafmould, and grass will not grow very well in the shade of bamboos, but the same is true of the environs of other trees as well. Actually there is no reason why these magnificent grasses should be entirely vanished from your garden.

How to grow: Any soil suits this class of plant, water logged localities are naturally abhorrent and extremes of temperature affect the growth but the most humus lacking soil will grow grasses and reeds. In pots make the compost light. When planting do not bury too deep and stake the new growth.

Every couple of years, tear the clumps apart and replant only a portion if you wish to keep the plants within bounds.

It is surprising how many of the bamboos, grasses and reeds which flourish at sea level do up to 1500 m, there is a certain moderation in growth which is quite natural but on the whole the plants do excellently.

Where to grow: Sun or semi-shade makes little difference too, any aspect or position will suit bamboo. Plant during the rains and be certain that the soil is deeply cultivated for all grasses are heavy rooting plants and it is as well to give full play to the root system. Leaves should be burnt and added to the soil around bamboo clumps.

What to grow: While there are a number of types that may find a place in a large garden, the amateur need not worry about more than the few noted below.

The best known is perhaps the dwarf bamboo grass, *Apluda aristata* (*Pogonantherum saccharoideum*) which finds a home in pots on so many verandahs. In the ground it grows 1 m high and can be clipped to hedge form or allowed to grow into a natural bush.

The variegated Danubian Reed, *Arundo donax* 'versicolor' and *A. mettallica* with a bronzy leaf are both handsome grasses. The former runs to green stems if given too much shade and grows 2·3 m high but the latter only reaches a height of 1·5 m and loves shade. Early in the rains thin out the inside stems and generally lighten the clump. New shoots will give strong growth and provide the best coloured foliage.

Among bamboos, *Bambusa aurea* 'variegata' the Golden Bamboo, *B. nigra*, the Whanghee or Black Bamboo and *B. siamensis*, a light feathery type are the best of the taller kinds. *B. nana* growing 3·4 m is used for hedges. Varieties like fortunei, aurea, striata and ruscifolia are 1 m high and excellent subject for the fern house or semi-shady borders. *B. pygmaea* which grows about 25 cm high is very ornamental.

Panicum (*Oplismenus*) *variegatum* should be used for hanging baskets or in the fernery ; it is a light growing grass with red and white variegated foliage. The Gardener's Garter, a miniature *Arundo variegata*, growing 30-35 cm high is *Phalaris arundinacea* var picta ; this spreads quickly in a fern house or shady nook and should be added to a collection of grasses.

Flowering grasses are represented by *Thyrsanolaena agrostis* which from February to May produces feathery sprays ; in foliage it is like a wide leaved bamboo and grows 3 m high.

The Pampas Grass, *Cortadeira* (*Gynerium*) *argentia* is a tall grass with lovely plumes of white flower, difficult to establish on the plains.

Ischaenum longifolium and *Saccharum arundinaceum* are tall coarse grass with white plumes. The flower sprays of *Eragrostis*, a dwarf grass, are used with cut flowers and *Pennisetum longistylum*, a taller kind bears pink bullrush like flower heads. If this latter variety is cut down at the end of the monsoon, the grass will flower again in the early cold weather though it is eassly reproduced by seed. *Andropogon helepensis* is a very strong spreading grass but if kept within bounds will provide lovely sprays nearly all the year round.

Grasses and reeds are easily propagated by division of clumps in the rains. Pennisetum and Eragrostis are propagated from seed.

Cyperus alternifolius is referred to in the Chapter on Water Garden, while *Papyrus antiquorum*, *Phragmites* and *Mariscus* will also be found in the same Chapter *Melocanna bambusoides*, the berry bearing bamboo, is a thin reed like plant that spreads rapidly, it is more a curiosity than ornamental.

The following are a few of the commoner and hardier grasses—*Andropogon assimilis*, *Pennisetum orientale*, *Neyraudia madagascariensis*, *Cyperus elegans* and *Rottboelia exaltata* that can be used in a small garden.

CHAPTER XX

Bonsai and Dwarfing by Chemicals

Bonsai comprises a tree or shrub planted in a small container for developing as a miniature plant showing the general appearance of that plant species found in nature. It differs from a pot plant where the foliage and flowers are important, whereas for Bonsai the appearance of the plant in a miniature form is to be maintained for many years.

Bonsai varies in shape and the following are common types :

1. A single tree with straight trunk
2. A tree with twisted trunk
3. A tree with slanted trunk
4. A tree with a large hanging branch
5. A tree with two trunks
6. A tree with several trunks
7. Several trees grown in a single pot
8. Tree grown on rocks

PLANTS SUITABLE FOR BONSAI

Although the suitability of plants for developing as Bonsai has been tested in Japan consisting mostly of sub-tropical and temperate plants, very little information is available on the response to the growth of tropical trees in miniature form, excepting the collection of dwarf plants of late Shri V.P. Agnigotri. He has developed a technique of dwarfing trees commonly found in this country and it has been a tremendous success.

The suitability of a tree to develop as a Bonsai depends on various factors :

1. The plant should be hardy so that it can be grown in a small container for many years with all the manifestations of a living plants.
2. The trunk should develop a natural appearance.

3. The branches should grow in natural but artistic forms.

4. The growth of the plant and its appearance should be harmonious with the shape of the container.

5. The miniature plant showing seasonal variations in growth and flowering is a very interesting feature of Bonsai.

6. Plants of low height and strong trunk, thick at the base are good as Bonsai.

Among the tropical trees that thrive well as miniature plants are : *Adansonia digitata*, *Anthocephalus cadamba*, *Bombax malabaricum*, *Adenanthera pavonina*, *Brassia actinophylla*, *Butea frondosa*, *Callistemeon lanceolatus*, *Ceiba pentandra*, *Chorisia speciosa*, *Caesalpinia coriaria*, *Erythrina cristagalli*, *E. parcelli*, *Ficus religiosa*, *F. bengalensis*, *F. infectoria*, *F. retusa*, *Jacaranda mimosaefolia*, *Kigellia pinnata*, *Melia azedarach*, *Melia azadirachta*, *Melaleuca leucadendron*, *Milletia ovalifolia*, *Putranjiva roxburghii*, *Tabebuia chrysantha*, *T. donaldsmithii* and *Thespesia populnea*.

Several tall shrubs like *Adenium obesum*, *Brya ebenus*, *Fortunella japonica*, *Hamelia patens*, *Hibiscus schizopetalous*, *Jatropha podagrica and Murraya exotica* form very attractive dwarf plants.

Woody climbers like *Combretum*, *Derris scandens*, *Hiptage madhablata*, *Roupellia grata* and *Jasminum auriculatum* can also be trained as Bonsai. Among the conifers grown in tropical conditions, *Juniperous prostrata* and *Pinus khasiana* will form good Bonsai.

HOW TO GROW BONSAI

Plants suitable for growing as Bonsai are planted in small containers. In tropical climate, the monsoon is the best season for planting or transplanting. For making Bonsai, plants growing wild or seedlings grown in the nursery for several years should be carefully uprooted, grown in ordinary pots for a year or two and then planted in a shallow container. Plants may also be obtained from layering of a large branch, grafting or by raising seedlings in a pot.

It is advisable to grow the plant in the ground for a year or two which helps in developing a strong root system and healthy branches. They are then transferred into a container after pruning the roots and branches. The plants grown in pots may also be planted directly in the container.

CONTAINERS

The containers should be unglazed shallow pots of various sizes and shapes. They may be round, rectangular or square, the size and depth depending on the plant to be grown.

SOIL

The soil for potting should be fresh, well-drained, and not very rich in fertilizer. It should not be highly acidic or alkaline. Clayloam or loam of different structures and clump sizes, obtained by sieving the soil is used in potting. It should not be very sticky or sandy. Well-rotted leaf mould is mixed with the soil.

PREPARATION OF SOIL

The soil is dried in the sun and sieved through meshes of at least three sizes. Large, medium and fine soil obtained by sieving are kept in separate containers. At the time of planting, the larger particles are placed at the bottom of the pot and a thin layer of medium-sized particles is spread over it. The tree is planted and the top soil consisting of small particles holds the plant in position and comes in close contact with the roots.

REMOVAL OF TREE

The soil of the plant to be transplanted should be kept on the dryside to facilitate removal of the plant from the pot. It may be necessary to remove thick roots and also the tips of some fibrous roots with a pair of sharp shears.

After pruning the roots, the shoots are also pruned depending on the growth habit and the desired appearance of the plant in miniature form, when the branches are crowded in any part of the plants. In the case of unbranched seedlings growing terminally, the main stem is cut to a height which may form a well-shaped Bonsai. If the branches are small and well arranged, pruning is not needed but the terminal growth is removed to minimise the height of the plant and to encourage the growth of auxillary branches. In case the branches have already grown to a size too tall for a Bonsai, they are pruned to 1/2 to 1/3 the length depending on the rate of growth of the plant and its response to pruning. Generally, broadleaved plants need harder pruning than small-leaved conifers.

PLANTING IN CONTAINER

The container is placed on a table or on a suitable platform where the planting operation can be carried out undisturbed. The holes of the container are first covered with crocks or plastic net. Then a layer of large soil particles is placed with a thin layer of medium-sized soil above it. The tree is then placed in the soil. Before it is finally planted, the side presenting the best view should have been determined. The medium-sized soil is placed around the root region and consolidated by means of a bamboo stick without pressing too hard. Then a layer of fine soil is spread on the top, levelled and pressed gently. While planting, care should be taken to keep the base of the trunk from where the main roots rise above the soil and to place the plant in the middle of the container. After planting, watering should be done with the help of a fine rose from the top of the plant.

CARE OF PLANT

The container is kept on a platform in a cool and shady place (not in a dark corner of a green house) for about two weeks to allow the roots to develop and the plant to establish. It is then gradually exposed to sunlight for longer durations beginning with the morning sun for two hours. The soil should never be allowed to dry up completely. In summer months with high temperature and low humidity, the plants may be placed in shade in the midday and afternoon. They also need protection from frost. It is, however, amazing to see 10–20 year old plants of Shri Agnihotri grown in shallow pans kept in the open during the summer months of Delhi. The miniature plants should be arranged in a planned fashion on a plantform or on stands of different sizes and heights so that the collection of plants looks like a garden. Proper spacing between the rows will façilitate watering the maintenance of the plants.

WATERING

Watering is very important for Bonsai as they are grown in shallow containers with small amount of soil. They should not be allowed to dry as temporary wilting of the plants adversely affects their growth. If the roots shrivel due to shortage of moisture in the soil, the plants are likely to die. Excessive watering often causes poor growth and waterlogging for a considerable period may cause rotting of the roots.

Bonsai is watered in two ways. The soil in the container is watered with an ordinary can or the whole plant is moistened through a fine rose.

DWARF PLANT ON A ROCK

Select a natural rock of medium size and attractive shape. For growing on rock, hardy plants like *F. religiosa* should be selected. The soil around the roots is removed thoroughly and placed on a lump of moist loam mixed with an adequate quantity of leaf-mould in a depression on the rock. The plant is tied to the rock by raffia. The roots are spread, covered with a thin layer of sphagnum moss and the plant together with the moss is again tied to the rock. The rock with the plant is then placed in a container, half of which is filled with soil and the block of stone tied to the container keeps it in position. The plant and the moss around the root are thoroughly watered. It should be treated as any other Bonsai grown in pots except that the plant on the rock needs more frequent watering.

PRUNING AND PINCHING

Removal of buds from Bonsai is an important practice. Pruning maintains the shape of the plant, stimulates branching and helps in the utilization of energy for the growth of other parts of the plant. The frequency and mode of pruning will depend on the growth habit rate of shoot growth, response to pinching and subsequent growth of auxillary shoots. Although pruning and pinching of tropical plants for Bonsai has not been standardised, the grower will be able to do it if he knows the growth habit of the plant. Pinching should not be done on a plant until it is established and starts new growth.

In order that the plant may maintain an attractive appearance, pinching is not done at the same length in all the directions. In the case of two axillary branches growing in two directions, one may be pinched at the apical bud, while the other one is pruned up to several nodes below the terminal bud. If the plant tends to grow fast in a particular season or continues to grow in length throughout the year it may be necessary to pinch more than once a year. But frequent pruning leads to the formation of thin and weak shoots which may wither in an unfavourable environment. Pinching or pruning should be done clean without damaging the shoot at the cut end. If the shoot is soft and succulent pinching can be done with fingernails ; woody or semi-woody branches will require shears and a large, thick and woody branch should be cut by a secateur. It should be ensured that the plants remain in a fixed position and the soil and root are not disturbed at the time of pruning.

ARRANGEMENT OF BRANCHES

Besides growing trees in a miniature form, the arrangement of trunk and branches is also an important technique to be followed to develop an attractive Bonsai. It is done to improve the shape and to help in the manifestation of natural appearance of the plants. In order to maintain the space between two branches the lower one is suspended by a strong twine or wire.

Before using wire, the portion of the branch is wrapped with raffia where the wire is to be tied. To improve the arrangement of the branches on the plant, wire is to be used very carefully and the technique needs experience, skill and proper tools. Wire cutter and pincers are normally used for the purpose. Copper wire is better than iron wire as it is softer and can be seen easily and does not rust.

Another very effective method of modifying the shape of the tree or arranging the branches is to tie wire around the trunk or branches so that they may grow in the desired direction and form.

TRANSPLANTING

Bonsai needs transplanting when the soil is completely exhausted or the container is filled with roots. In general, plants in the growing stage are transplanted once a year, and a full-grown tree once every two or three years. Containers should be used after thorough washing and drying. While transplanting, the old soil should be removed as far as possible, and dead roots and ends of fine roots pruned. Unnecessary branches are also removed to improve the appearance of the tree. Then the Bonsai is planted firmly in the container using the similar type of soil mentioned earlier.

APPLICATION OF MANURE AND FERTILIZER

Fertilizer is necessary for Bonsai as the plant thrives and grows in a small container. Apart from vegetative growth, attempts should be made to promote flowering and fruiting. Excessive use of manure is bad for the plant and causes root injury. In Japan, rape seed cake is commonly used in Bonsai but in our country a good substitute is mustard cake which may be used in liquid and powder forms.

One kilogram of mustard cake is diluted with six litres of water and allowed to decompose throughly. After about 3-4 weeks, the water above the decomposed manure is again diluted with 5-10 times the amount of water and the dilute solution is applied to the soil leaving the base of the trunk.

Thoroughly powdered cake is lightly mixed with the top soil slightly away from the trunk, in two or three areas using 1-2 tablespoonful of cake in each case.

The plants should be manured in the spring and again in the rainy season when they show vegetative growth. The frequency of fertilization is, however, determined by the growth of the plants. During the growing season the plants can be manured once a month followed by watering.

CONTROL OF DISEASES AND PESTS

Diseases and pests are common with Bonsai. Root rot is a common and serious disease caused by excess watering, drying of soil, poor drainage, direct contact with undecomposed organic matter, etc. The affected plant will show poor growth and decay of shoots. In the case of fungus infection either on shoots or on root, the diseased part should be removed at the earliest opportunity. Spraying of insecticides and fungicides should be a routine practice.

DWARFING BY CHEMICAL

Dwarfing of plants by using chemical is now a commercial practice for developing attractive pot plants of azalea, chrysanthemum, poinsettia and hydrangea. In recent years, a group of chemicals known as growth retarding chemicals or growth retardants which retard stem elongation without causing any malformation of plants has drawn considerable attention of horticulturists and commercial growers of ornamental plants.

Although a number of growth retardants have been synthesised, Phosfon—D (2, 4—dichlorobenzyltributyl phosphonium chloride) Cycocel or CCC (2—chloroethyl trimethylammonium-chloride) and B-Nine (N-dimethyl aminosuccinamicacid) are found effective on large number of plants. Compared to phosfon-D much wider plant spectrum is noted with Cycocel and B-Nine.

In addition to dwarf, bushy and compact appearance with dark green colour and thicker foliage, growth retardants also increase the number and size of flower in several species of annual and perennial ornamental plants. The treated plants also show increased resistance to drought and diseases and pests. Cycocel (liquid) is used as foliar spray or soil drench. Phosfon-D and Cycocel dust are applied in soil, while B-Nine is used as foliar spray. In case of perennial plants, chemicals are used when new shoots on pruned plants attain five to ten cm in length. Annuals are treated 20 to 3C days after transplanting.

Azalea : Cycocel, B-Nine and Phosfon-D effectively suppress the growth of treated plants. Maximum reduction of plant height is obtained by two applications of Cycocel at 0·25 per cent as foliar spray. The treatment causes early initiation of flower buds and increased number of flowers.

Chrysanthemum : In this plant also Cycocel, B-Nine and Phosfon cause marked dwarfing of the plants. Both Cycocel and B-Nine are used for commercial production of dwarf Chrysanthemum. The treated plants have thicker stem and dark green leaves.

Poinsettia : Two applications of 0·25 per cent Cycocel cause about 50 per cent reduction in the length of new shoots. The treated plants develop stronger and brighter colour of bracts of increased size and they are commercially better accepted than the untreated ones.

Bougainvillea : Two foliar applications of Cycocel and B-Nine with 0·4 per cent solution cause effective retardation of bougainvillea and the suppression of plant growth due to Cycocel is greater than with B-Nine. Treatment with the latter chemical, however, markedly increases the number and size of bracts, flowering also continues for a longer period.

Hibiscus rosasinensis : Single foliar application or soil drench with 0·4 per cent Cycocel solution retards the plant height by 40 to 70 per cent compared to the untreated plants and the effectiveness of the chemical remains for 300 to 400 days. Application of Cycocel dust in soil @ four to eight gm per pot also causes marked reduction of growth for a longer period and larger number of flowers develop on the treated plants.

Cycocel proves effective in inhibiting plant height of different species of Hibiscus and several other flowering belonging to family Malvaceae. Foliar spray with 0·2 to 0·4 per cent Cycocel solution causes dwarfing of *Hibiscus schizopetalus*, *H. mutabilis*, *Malvaviscus conzatii*, *Althea rosea* and *Malva sylvestris*.

Lantana camara : Treatment with B-Nine at 0·5 per cent results in dwarfing of the plant height to the extent of 53 per cent, the effective concentration also stimulates branching and flowering.

Barleria cristata : Cycocel and B-Nine at 0·4 and 0·5 per cent concentrations, respectively suppress the height of plants by about 45 per cent, compared to the untreated plants. These two concentrations also increase the number of flowers.

Hydrangea : Application of 0·5 per cent B-Nine solution not only suppresses plant height but also increases the number and size of flowers.

Rose : Two foliar applications of B-Nine with 0·4 per cent solution retard the shoot length by 30 to 40 per cent, depending on the variety. Treatment with the chemical increase the size and prolongs the life of flowers.

Dahlia : Height of Dahlia is reduced to almost half by treatment with B-Nine at 0·5 to 1·0 per cent, twice at an interval of 15 days after about 35 days of potting. The leaves become dark green in colour and almost all of them retain on the plants up to the last stage of flowering. Larger flowers also develop on short stalk.

In annual flowering plants e.g., salvia, aster, cleome, cosmos, petunia, zinnia, treatment with 0·2 to 0·5 per cent B-Nine develops dwarf and compact pot plants. Cycocel proves effective in retarding the growth of celosia, dianthus, marigold, antirrhinum and carnation.

CHAPTER XXI

Garden Sundries

Garden sundries constitute a number of diverse materials which are essential for gardening in an efficient way. So persons who are interested in gardening, should be well acquainted with different types of tools and implements and their uses. Quite a varieties of implements and other tools are required for carrying out the various gardening operations like spading, breaking of soil clods, removal of weeds, levelling of ground, planting of seedlings or saplings, manuring, watering and spraying or dusting of insecticides, etc.

The different types of tools and implements commonly used for garden works under Indian condition are briefly described hereunder.

FOR DIGGING

Kodali or *Phawrah* is the most widely used instrument for digging of soil. With the help of Kodali, the soil is dug up to a depth of 15 cm or so in one stroke. The metal (iron) blade and the wooden handle are the only two components of this simple implement. Very often the backside of the Kodali is used to break the large clod of soil during spading.

Kodali Fork—It is a combined form of Kodali and the weeding fork and is very useful while digging heavy soil. The four numbers of prongs of this handy implement goes deep into the soil and easily lift the clod of earth.

Garden Fork—Darjeeling type is also a very popular instrument for digging operations. When pressed with foot, the teeth of this fork go deep into the soil levering off clods of earth either towards or away from the user.

FOR WEEDING AND INTERCULTURE OPERATIONS

Weeding Fork—This is another very useful tool for loosening the surface soil and taking out the weeds. The weeding fork with a long handle can reach the centre of a bed and the danger of trampling down of small seedlings can be avoided.

Khurpi—Most of the interculture operations in India are done by this hand hoe, which consists of a sharp edged triangular blade fitted with a wooden handle.

Nirani—This commonly used handy tool has a slightly curved cutting edge with a small wooden handle. It is widely used for weeding and forking up of soil.

Hoes (Sabal or Khanta) is used for lifting large plants. The metal blade is like that of a Khurpi which is fitted with a long (60–90 cm) wooden or metal handle. This is also widely used for digging pits. There is another type with a curved blade which is commonly used for cutting edges.

FOR WATERING

Watering Can—Watering cans made of galvanised iron sheet are the best of its types. Two and two and a half gallon capacity cans are the best, larger size is difficult to handle. These watering cans are also fitted with a rose or spreader over the nozzle which is very useful to break the force of water and a wide distribution is obtained. A layer of paint outside and inside the can will protect from rusting.

Seedling Watering Can—To irrigate the seeds or newly sprouted seedlings, seedling watering can is a must. These cans have smaller capacity (1 gallon) and are fitted with fine rose at the end of long sprout. The working principle is same as that of the watering can but due to the fine rose, the water falls gently on the seeds or seedlings without disturbing or damaging them.

Buckets made of galvanised iron or polythene are also widely used for watering in a garden.

Syringe or *Pichkari* is usually 40–50 cm long, a brass made narrow cylinder fitted with a mouthpiece having many pores. It is often used for sprinkling water on the foliage of green house plants or indoor plants, with a little practice the spray can be made fine or coarse at will. A reversed nozzle may be used for syringing the under surface of the leaves.

Garden Hose—To use the water from the pipelines, garden hose will be required. Usually rubber or polythene hoses are used in gardens. Though the rubber hose is more expensive than that of polythene but the former type lasts longer. Rubber hoses have smooth or corrugated outer surface and one or two rows of threads are embedded in the rubber. Polythene pipes are light and can be handled with little effort. These will last for few years, if used carefully and continuous exposure to sun causes hardening and reduces the life of the pipe.

The fittings to the hose depend on the taps in the garden and the union can be done by screw or pressed with a rubber ring.

LAWN SPRINKLERS

'Garden Whix' is a sprinkler of simple design with convenient spike base and is ideal for small gardens or uneven lawns. It has one outlet which usually does not clog and covers an area up to 8 metres on each side.

'Jaladhara' is another sprinkler which is light in weight but quite sturdy and durable. The non-corroding alluminium alloy base and chromium plated spray arms rotate freely and spray even under low water pressure.

'Rainbow' is another dependable sprinkler with multiple adjustments and covers an area up to about 15 meters circle, if sufficient water pressure is available.

FOR PRUNING

A number of tools are in use for pruning of plants. For cutting large branches, *Bill Hook* or *Dhao* and also saw are usually used. The Bill Hook may be of single or double edge.

Secateur—A very useful handy tool for pruning of branches up to moderate thickness. It is usually sold in the market in different trade names viz. Singlecut, Doublecut, Supabuilt,

Klincut, Rolecut, etc. However, the Rolecut and Klincut are the most popular types of secateurs.

Tree Pruner—It is very effective for pruning tree branches having a diameter of about 6 cm or less. This pruning tool comprises one curved sharp edged blade fixed at the top of a long wooden handle and the other blade is blunt which gives support to the branches. The sharp blade is operated from below with the help of a long thick metal string. Tree pruner can also be used for pruning dead branches, withered flower spikes and also for collecting fruits from high branches.

Knives—A 'Budding' knife is rarely needed by the ordinary mali, the one he carries should be either a pruning knife with a single curved blade or a single bladed garden knife.

Garden Shears having blade size of 20, or 30 cm are commonly used for pruning of hedge and topiary work.

FOR CUTTING GRASS

To control the grass growth mechanically, lawn mower is widely used. Mowers may be operated manually or power driven. Though power mower is very useful for large lawns, play grounds, etc., no dependable power mower is manufactured in this country.

Size of a lawn mower depends on the length of the cutting cylinder and the different sizes are 24″ (60 cm), 20″ (50 cm), 16″ (40 cm) and 12″ (30 cm). The mowers may be with or without roller and the height of the cutting surface may be adjusted. The mower should be thoroughly cleaned after use and all dust and grasses removed. The nuts and bolts should be treated with lubricating oil.

Grass or *sheep shears* are very useful for cutting grass form the corners and edges of the lawn left after mowing. The size of the blades varies between 15 and 20 cm.

Skiffing knife with its long blade appears like a sword and is useful for cutting grass where lawn mower can not move. *Jhabow* is also commonly used to cut the grass and weeds to the ground level. *Hand scythe* or *Haswa* is another common implement for cutting grass. *Sickle* or *Kaste* with their serrated edge are also used for cutting grass and weeds which are large enough to hold with hand.

SPRAYERS AND DUSTERS

Plants have more enemies than friends. Numerous insects and diseases greatly damage the plants and may kill them if proper care is not taken to remove or destroy the enemies at the earliest opportunity. Effective insecticides and fungicides are now easily available in the market but application to all parts of plants becomes a problem without proper equipment. An amateur gardener often considers it an unnecessary expenditure to buy a duster or sprayer and somehow manage with domestic sprayer. Insecticide or fungicide are now mostly used as spray and a sprayer will save time and material. Container and nozzle should be thoroughly washed with clean water after use. Nowadays, a number of sprayers are available in the market. The following types, however, are most popular.

(a) *Hand Sprayer*—'Akela' and 'Ganesh' brands are the most popular. The former is a double action hand pump specially made for home garden, nurseries. The latter type is also an excellent pneumatic hand sprayer for pest control fitted with fine spray mist nozzle and can contain about 825 ml. of the insecticide solution. The 'Aspee poly sprayers' have a polythene body with a capacity of 600 ml. and are very hardy'. For small garden and kitchen garden the 'Aspee continuous atomiser' having a capacity of 200 ml. can be used.

(b) *Knapsack sprayer*—In this group 'Akela' and 'Shabnam' sprayes are found to be the most commonly used. 'Akela' has a high density polythene container of 5 litres capacity and the double action hand sprayer gives fine mist spray. 'Shabnam' sprayer is durable and dependable having a brass container of 9 litres capacity.

(c) *Bucket* or *Stirrup sprayers* are simple to use. The parts can be easily detached for quick and efficient cleaning.

With the help of the long delivery hose, spraying can be done very conveniently. 'Dipro' and the 'Aspee Leader' are the two popular brands.

(d) *Dusters*—Among the handrotary dusters, the 'Orient' brand is the most recommended one. This is a well balanced duster to rest comfortably on shoulder and is very easy to operate. The hopper capacity is 5 kg.

A FEW OTHER USEFUL TOOLS AND IMPLEMENTS

Garden rakes—One should procure a garden rake of 8 or 12 prongs. This is useful for collecting stones and brick bats in a beaten out bed, scarifying the grass surface, gathering leaves together, etc.

Wheel Barrow—Wheel barrow is useful for carrying materials like soil, manures, pots, etc., and collecting garden refuses. It is of two types—pan and box. Both the types are made from iron sheets and two iron handles are provided to operate the wheel barrow.

Baskets—Compared to the bamboo baskets, the cane baskets though heavier and more expensive, last longer. Baskets of medium size should be purchased and immediately strengthened by having the edges held down by coir rope. Woven in between the bamboo circles passing from the top to the bottom on four sides will double the life of a basket.

The *Pickaxe* or *Gaintha* may be omitted from the list of necessary instruments for a private garden because it is not of frequent use. It is required for repairing roads and paths.

Shovel or *Belcha*—It is often used to handle the manures, fertilizers, soil, sand and leaf moulds, etc.

Tool Box fitted with a lock in which the smaller implements can be stored should be provided to each garden. Otherwise, the implements will be dumped in any odd corner and will gradually disappear.

Sieve—It is necessary for screening soil and leafmould, etc. Screened soil and leafmould are necessary for the preparation of seed compost.

Labels—Among the different types of labels viz. paper, cardboard, wooden, celluloid, aluminium and plastic, the last two items are preferable. Paper or card board labels are for temporary use. Wooden labels painted with white paints will last longer but are gradually becoming outdated. Aluminium labels will retain writing clearly. Now-a-days plastic labels are becoming very popular and are widely used in different forms and shapes.

POTS AND PANS

Earthen Pots—Always purchase well baked earthenware pots ; sound them before use for often cracked specimens, or half baked ones, are camouflaged with red colour. Pots made with clay soil and well-baked with last longer than those made with sandy or loamy soil.

Sizes—Four inches (10" cm) pots are suitable for small annual seedlings, six inches (15 cm) for small palms, ferns, etc., eight inches (20 cm) pots are used for single specimen plants of annuals. Ten inches (20 cm) will contain three Salvia, Antirrhinum plants quite çomfortably and are also best for tall palms. Fourteen to eighteen inch pots should be placed in semi-permanent position as they should not be moved very frequently. Plastic pots are also available which are durable and easy to handle. As the water does not evaporate from the sides watering should be done carefully and very light compost be used in such pots.

For Orchids, shallow earthenware pots with slits cut in the sides are very useful. They are far more satisfactory than wooden blocks which rot within a few years.

Hanging pot and Baskets—These are made of earthenware, wood or wire, the last named material is most satisfactory for all purposes. They should be lined with coir fibre, hessian, gunny, or moss and will contain earth.

Seed Pans—The seedpans are shallow pots, used for raising seedlings and growing shallow rooted annuals and ferns. Boxes are often used for raising of seedlings. The size may vary from 25 to 40 cm in diameter.

Wooden Tubs a d other Containers—Oil casks sawn in half and charred inside to remove the oil, are more lasting than wooden tubs, unless these are prepared of seasoned teak wood. Pots made of cement are useful for growing perennial plants in permanent or semi-permanent positions.

TYING MATERIALS

These vary from Raffia and specially prepared Garden Twist to local twines of cotton, Jute or hemp. Coir, Jute and Nylon rope can be used to tie large plants. Galvanised wire should be carefully used as it is liable to cut into the stem of plants and cause damage. Whatever material is used should in any case be loosely tied to allow a little play between the stake and the stem.

SHADING MATERIALS

Shading Material differ in various parts of India ; hooglah or bullrush in one province, bamboo or grass stems in another. Whatever is used should be light and rainproof. In fixing the shelter no drip should fall on pans or the prepared bed. Hessian or tarpaulins are rather hot unless kept raised well above the sown seed. At present polythene sheets are widely used for protecting from rains and last longer.

Arches—Use strong angle iron or boiler tubes painted green whenever possible ; where wood is necessary paint thoroughly with tar or some antirot paint, especially the portion that go into the ground. *Pergola* is usually constructed by erecting pillars made of bricks at regular interval and climbers are supported on angle irons and wire netting placed on the pillars.

GLASS HOUSE

In tropical gardens, glass house becomes too warm to grow any plant inside particularly during the summer months. Glass top green house, however proves very useful for growing green house plants, orchids, etc. Frames with glass cover are useful for raising of seedling and propagating plants from cuttings.

PLANT SUPPORTS

This is where the average gardeners make a mess of his plants, he either does not stake at all or else uses sticks that are far too small or too large. Bamboos are the most serviceable material, if made of well seasoned bamboo these stakes will last for years. Prepare stakes of various lengths to use them on plants of different heights, dip the lower portion in tar or creosote oil and paint the rest green. Thin iron rods last long. Circular rings, supported by straight rods are used for carnation, petunia, etc.

Tree guards or gabions are seldom necessary in a small garden where few stakes will save the plant from being damaged, outside the compound, a strong iron or bamboo gabion must be provided. Bricks can also be used.

JAFEREY WORK AND WIRE SCREENS

Iron supports and wire netting provide a neat support for both light and heavy climbers. Use a strong type of angle iron, boiler tube or substantial wooden posts and bury the end at least 80–90 cm in the ground and place bricks around the base to prevent these uprights being drawn out by the weight of the creeper. The uprights should not be more than 2 metres apart. Run a thick strand of galvanised wire through holes in the supports at the top, bottom, and middle and on to this wire the galvanised netting. Use a largemeshed netting as this is cheaper and easier to clean of dead leaves.

Bamboo trellies should only be used as a last resort ; not only does it collapse when the creeper has covered the screen, insects and damp weaken it.

CHAPTER XXII

The Water Garden

One can become quite poetical over a restful lake, fringed with graceful reeds whispering in the wind, the surface covered with beautiful water lilies, the splash of leaping fish, the tinkle of falling water ; but alas, the serpent in this Garden of Eden is the mosquito larvae which make any water a risky business kept stocked with fish. No pond is sacrosanct but receives its film of kerosene and under such conditions no aquatics can thrive.

If a Water Garden can be provided without unnecessary risk, many plants can be grown in and around the pond.

HOW TO MAKE

Water lilies should be grown in a formal garden, geometrical in design or informal, with a depth ledge to suit the various kinds of water plants that may be added. The brick or reinforced concrete tank should be strongly buttressed or make with wire netting reinforcement. First cure the cement and test for leaks before you introduce the earth and plants. Arrange drainage if possible, though a siphon can easily empty the water. Allow the water to overflow occasionally if it gets discoloured or settle it with small quantities of lime or alum. Place a layer of stone chips or gravel on the soil to prevent it from washing away, replant every other year as the soil soon sours and ages the plant but do this operation in the rains.

If a cement tank is utilised build the corners carefully and round them off for this is where half the leakage takes place. A 25 cm retaining wall is enough but it must have buttresses into the surrounding soil.

A natural piece of water can be improved by irregular banks and graceful sloping sides. Allow 2 sq meter per water lily of the small kind and 6 meters for the larger type ; the very pigmy kinds require only 40 cm of water but 1 meter should be the average depth for the medium and 2 meters for the large kinds.

Leaks in a water pond are difficult to discover and repair, the water must be allowed to leak out and the dry surface watched for cracks or fissures, damp spots on an otherwise dry surface betray a leak. Chip off the cement on either side of a crack and when applying cement put a pound of ordinary washing soda into every gallon of water used in mixing the cement, this will make the mixture waterproof.

A method whereby repairs are done without emptying the pond and obtaining the services of a mason is by mixing the ash with the water and allowing this to leak out. It is on a par with the application of cow manure to repair a leaky root for the straw particles are washed into the cracks and seal the leak.

Running water has naturally a more ornamental effect than a silent pool and if a cascade or water-fall can be arranged and a rustic bridge added artificiality is reduced.

SOIL

For the compost, in which water plants are expected to grow use heavy virgin soil, cow manure and a small quantity of bone meal added at the spot where water lilies are planted.

For swamp planting, use pot plants in preference to those lifted from the ground for pot plants have their full complement of roots and can assimilate the nutriment immediately. Cut roots have to heal before they can actually enter upon their duties, while a plant may keep alive in water and it will not grow till new roots have formed.

Manure is seldom necessary for water plants, a tablespoonful of bone meal or such slow acting material can be dug in once a year and a basket or two of cow dung will provide the rotted matter that these plants receive in natural circumstances.

WHERE AND WHAT TO GROW

Certain varieties thrive in swampy land provided they have 30 cm or so of soil at the bottom. Others grow when their roots are continually submerged. With full sunshine a number of trees and shrubs stand swamp conditions where shade would prevent growth altogether.

BOG GARDEN, NEAR WATER

With proper drainage and raising the soil so as to prevent the roots of the plant being continually in water, nearly all hardy shrubs can be grown around a pond or within a meter of the water's edge.

Bog plants can be cultivated in pots if a large size container is arranged on the outside holding a layer of crocks and moss, etc., to keep the inside soil moist all the time.

IN THE WATER ITSELF—

Water lilies. A deep tank can grow *Nelumbium* (The Lotus) or *Nymphaea* (Water lilies) ; some of the *N. stellata* type in Bengal thrive in a meter of water, so will the Marliacea hybrids of which many beautiful varieties flower freely in India. *Nymphaea pubescens* type bloom in the cold months while *N. stellata* are more hot weather varieties. Nymphaeas are to be found all over Bengal and other moist provinces chiefly white, pink and a deep red but natural hybrids are met with giving many pleasing variations of shade. For instance the pink has dark bronzy red foliage but on occasion a natural hybrid will be met with pink flowers and a green leaf. The size of flowers varies, so too does doubleness.

N. stellata however, is deciduous and comes to life when the water rises in the paddy fields in the Monsoon, there is a small flowered type in pale blue and white but a larger variety is also met with in blue, blue fading to white, a pink shade and an intense blue manuve, possibly a cross with the *N. rubra pubescens.* The tubers of the *N. stellata* lie dormant in the dry fields for months without harm.

Victoria regia can only be cultivated in a large pond and is a magnificient water lily, the large cream coloured flowers with the base of the petals stained red are strongly scented, rather a fruity smell, and change to a carrunt red before they fade. The immense leaves measure 1·5 meters in diameter and have an upturned edge, the undersurface and stem being heavily armed with spines. This water lily is an annual and the hard canna-like seeds are germinated in a bottle of water, often the seed has to be slightly chipped or rubbed to assist germination. When the shoot appears, each seed should be tranplanted to a basket of rich compost and gradually lowered on to a mound of well-manured soil as the leaves develop. Victoria should never have less than 125 cm of water.

In transplanting water lilies, if tank earth cannot be obtained make a compost of equal parts stable manure and clay, soak for a few days and fill this into a basket. In the centre excavate a hole into which the tuber of the new water lily is to go and pack round with dry earth. To prevent the compost being washed away or parts rising to the surface when being submerged, lay gravel, coarses and or clinkers on the material before lowering the basket into the water. Sink the basket till a couple of cm of water lies over the tuber, as soon as the new leaves appear lower the basket to the full depth.

Eurale ferox, a little known aquatic, is like a mauve blue water lily with leaves heavily armed like the *Victoria regia* and sometimes 1·5 meters in diameter.

Water weeds. *Ceratophyllum verticillatum* (Jhanji) has foliage like *Asparagus* but unless periodically removed will fill the tank completely.

Limnantherum indicum, Water Snow flake (Pan shoole), is like a minature white water lily.

Several hardy ferns will grow in swampy soil, just above water level. *Pteris aquilina*, *Asplenium*, *Angiopteris*, *Acrostichum*, *Marsilea*, *Ceratopteris*.

Certain palms and allied plants stand moist conditions very well—*Carludovica, Cyclanthus, Acanthorhiza, Nipa, Areca lutescens, Rhapis flabelliformis.*

The following are miscellaneous collection of marsh loving types—*Acanthus, Funkia, Hemerocallis, Pancratium* (Spider lilies), *Commelina sellowiana, Typha angustifolia* (Indian Bullrush), *Crinum, Alpinia, Hedychium, Costus speciosus, Iris,* in variety, *Lasia heterophylla, Colocasia, Schizocasia, Xanthosma,* and *Polygonum.*

Exacum tetragonum, Dysophylla verticillata (Paneekala) *Oenanthe stolonifera* (Pan turaisi).

Tamarix both tree and bush forms, the several types of *Salix* (Weeping Willow), *Barringtonia acutangula, B. racemosa* and *Acacia farnesiana* are trees that will thrive in swamp land.

Aeschynomene aspera, the Sola pith plant, with floating stems.

Acorus (Sweet Flag), *Arundo, Calla* (*Richardia*).

Hygrophila spinosa (Talmakhna) a pink flowered under shrub.

Juncus effusus, the ordinary Rush.

Jussieua repens a creeping aquatic with white flowers.

Lemna, Duck Weed.

Nariscus, a sedge.

Monochoria hastoefolia, blue flowered, similar to the water hyacinth, but taller growing.

Neptunia plena with yellow mimosa like flowers the stems float on the surface, like the Sola.

Papyrus antiquorum and *Cyperus alternifolius,* both ornamental, help to make a piece of water interesting and can grow with their roots in water.

Phragmites, a type of bamboo.

Pistea stratiotes (Tekapana), Water Lettuce.

Pontadeira (*Eichhornia*) *crassipes,* Water Hyacinth, with blue flowers is well known.

Sagittaria sagitoefolia with white flowers.

Vallisneria spiralis (Jhanji), a water weed.

High elevation. A Bog Garden can quite easily be prepared and planted with a great variety of ferns, etc., that thrive near the water's edge. Many flowering succulents, *Primula*, etc., will add to the interest that an otherwise neglected area of the garden usually provides. Work as close to natural confusion. The selection naturally cannot be copied from the plains list but some are suggested overleaf to which many local bits of beauty can be added.

Aconitum, Alisma, Anemone, Artemisia, Arum, Astilbe, Butomus umbellatus, Caltha, Cardamine, Chrysanthemum maximum, Clethra alnifolia, Cornus canadensis, Eulalia, Eupatorium, Funkia, Gentiana asclepidea, Gunnera, Geum, Hemerocallis, Houttuynia cordata, Iris sibirca, I. aurea, I. ochroleuca, all beardless forms, and *Kirengeshoma palmata, Leucojum, Lobelia, Lychnis, Lysimachia, Lythrum alatum, Mimulus, Myosotis, Parochetus communis, Podophyllum, Primula pulverulenta, P. rosea, P. sikkimensis, P. denticulata, P. beesiana, Polygonum, Polygonatum, Pyrus melanocarpa, Ranunculus, Rheum, Rodgensia, Saxifraga peltata, Schizocodon soldanelloides, Spirea aruncus* and *S. giganteus, Solidago, Trillium, Troillus.*

Ferns—*Adiantum, Asplenium, Blechnum, Lastea, Onoclea, Osmunda, Polypodium.*

Pests and diseases. Water plants are particularly free from disease.

Caterpillars sometimes eat the foliage of water lilies and form a tent like structure while at work, grass and sedge and also destroyed by caterpillars. Snails eat the tender foliage of water lilies and a filmy under-water mossy algae chokes the new growth of plants.

CHAPTER XXIII

Vegetables

These short seasoned plants make a prominent position in the human and animal diet owing to their richness in vitamins and minerals. The role played by the vegetables as a protective food in the human nutrition need no advocacy. Due to their short life, intensive cultivation of vegetable is possible, which renders a high economic return per unit area. Besides these, every personnel of the family can take part in the cultivation of vegetables and thus it escalates the employment. So if land is available the cultivation of vegetables needs no more appreciation.

Now a question may arises that what should be the area of a vegetable garden for the average family ? If carefully cultivated with successional sowings and easily grown types half an acre should be quite sufficient. This works out to a plot 36×66 meters.

Soil condition : The plot of land which has been selected for cultivation of vegetables should receive full sun. Best soil for vegetable cultivation is loam or sandy loam rich in organic matter. The soil should be made very loose and friable by proper cultivation. This fineness in texture of the soil is specially required for the root vegetables.

We cannot always obtain an ideal soil for vegetables but it can be greatly improved by manuring and cultivation. If the soil is heavy and sticky put more organic matter in the form of farm or town compost to make the soil porous, lime and sand also improve the texture of the soil. First dig deeply removing all rubbish and stones, allow it to dry and thoroughly pulvarize the soil, mix well-rotted dry manure if you have not already applied it before. Prepare drainage, water channels, etc., before you think of planting seed for one must provide vegetables with plenty of water to obtain the best result especially during winter. Trenches should run north and south.

When to sow : On the plains the best time for sowing seed is from August-October. Cabbage, Cauliflower, and Tomato should be sown early as the seedlings are transplanted and take a longer time to mature. Acclimatised seeds give earlier crops than those raised from imported ones.

What to sow : Where winter conditions are short, choose the early varieties. In root crops e.g., Beet and Carrot, select the globe or short horn varieties in preference to long rooted varieties, in leafy vegetables which form heart quickly.

Obtain good seeds or seedlings of the best varieties from a reliable source as the quality of seeds is an important factor for successful cultivation of field crops and vegetables.

How to sow : To guard against unfavourable weather conditions sow small quantities of seed at intervals of a few days. Cover all vegetable seeds with their own thickness of soil except Beans, Peas and other large seeds which are planted direct in the open and buried a couple of cm deep. After watering, if the seeds become exposed, cover with fine soil. Root vegetables like Radish, Beet, Carrot, etc., should also be sown directly in the ground.

If sown directly in the ground, it is advisable to put 3–4 seeds in each hole or ridge and when the seedlings are few centimeters high to weed out all but the strongest. Soaked seeds germinate quicker than those direct from the packet. Grow everything in rows for they are easier to handle. Use space between long standing vegetable crops for those that are quicker maturing, such as Knolkohl, Lettuce, etc., and thus ensure a double crop from the same ground. Varieties that occupy ground longest are Brussels Sprouts and Cabbage and Tomato.

How to raise seedlings : Seedlings can be raised in shallow pans or raised beds. The seed compost should consist of 1 part each of leaf mould and loamy soil. The seeds are sown thinly and covered with leaf mould or fine soil. Excess watering should be avoided and seed beds protected from rains. When the seedlings come up, they are gradually exposed to more sunlight and before transplanting they should be sufficiently hardy to tolerate sun throughout day. The seedlings should be transplanted at the 4 leaf stage. At the time of removing the seedlings from the seed beds, care should be taken so that roots are not badly damaged.

Irrigation : It is better to flood and allow the moisture to dry out than to continually water with a can and rose. Fork up the soil, pull up weeds and allow the air to penetrate, then flood. The 'bolting' of vegetables is often due to erratic watering a poor strain of seeds, too early planting or to climatic conditions.

It is always detrimental to overwater any crop but more harm can be done by erring on the dry side. Celery, Leek, and Lettuce become tough, Peas and Beans stringy and Beet and Turnip fibrous if underwatered ; besides, if the plant is given a check, it takes a long time for free growth to recommence.

Transplanting : Cauliflower, Cabbage, Brinjal, Tomato should be transplanted and better result is obtained if it is done twice before planting at the site. Pumpkin, Cucumber and other crops of gourd family are usually germinated in a damp cloth and then planted. Carrot, Beet, Radish, Turnip, etc., are broadcasted thinly and the extra seedlings removed but if these are carefully lifted and transplanted, good results are also obtained. Leafy vegetables like spinach and other Indian spinaches are broadcasted and the thinned out plants can be consumed, while lettuce is commonly transplanted.

Manuring : One should always consider the reason for manuring before applying either liquid or dry manure. If for leaf production, do not commence until the vegetable is half grown say at least one month after germination of seed. If cultivated for fruit or seed, early manuring will strengthen the foliar development, therefore manure when the flower buds show. If grown for root or tuber attention is necessary just as the root commences to swell.

Dig over the land that can be spared early in the year and

sow Lucerne, Berseem or some other green manure crop, this freshens up soil wonderfully. When using natural manures make quite certain that they are well decayed and do not contain the grubs of cockchafers, etc. Natural manures are safest and oilcake is the best of these. One can not say what constituent is missing in the soil and unless an analysis is made the wrong chemical manure might easily be added. Weak doses of sulphate of ammonia and urea produce growth and can be used for most types of vegetable, use as liquid manure 4 kg. of oilcake, 4 of fresh cowdung, 30 gms. of superphosphate and ammonium sulphate in 5 litres of water; dilute ½ litre of this stock solution in 10 litres of water; and give once a week.

Salt is good for such crops as originated near the sea side, Asparagus, Beet, Cabbage, Carrot, Celery, etc. It prevents rankness of growth but should not be applied in larger quantities than 30 gm. per sq. meter, Peas and Beans require little nitrogen once they are started. Lime should be used for the vegetable garden, being dug in every three years as a general rule, especially where heavy manuring is carried out. Lime can be given safely to Cabbage, Cauliflower, Carrot, Capsicum, Onion, Eggplant, Lettuce and Spinach.

Phosphates when supplied to the following will give a better return. Beans, Carrot, Celery, Eggplant, Leek, Onion, Parsnip and Brussels Sprouts. Superphosphate seems to suit Potato, Spinach, Lettuce, Peas, Tomato, Chillies, Carrot and Beet. Potash with lime and phosphoric acid in the manure should be given to Beet, Lettuce, Knolkhol, Spinach, Swiss chard, Peas, Potato, Carrot, Parsnip and Radish. Sulphur, while being a deterrent to insects, is liked by Spinach, Celery and Beet. Root crops like soil which has been manured a year previously.

Over feeding of vegetables causes rot and splitting of Cabbage, Turnip, etc., while some root crops become coarse.

Rotation of crops: Rotation of crops in the vegetable garden is necessary to preserve the fertility of soil. Except for

Peas and Beans, do not plant the same variety in a plot for more than a couple of years.

Arrange a change of crop from one plot to another as suggested below. Dwarf Bean to Beet, Beet to Cauliflower, Cauliflower to Onion, Onion to Runner Bean, Runner Bean to Cabbage, Cabbage to Peas, Peas to Celery, Celery to Potato, Potato to Spinach, Spinach to Cauliflower, Cauliflower to Broad Bean, Board Bean to Turnip, Turnip to Carrot, Carrot to Dwarf Bean. Or a root crop followed by a legume and than a leaf crop. The Cabbage family is particularly severe on soil.

Storage : The storage of vegetables on the plains is limited to the keeping of dry types such as onion, garlic, etc., and may be potatoes for a short period. Where damp conditions prevail storage is governed by the time it takes certain vegetables to mildew. Lay everything out on a wooden shelf made of battens in a cool dry room, turn every couple of days and remove rotting leaves, etc., Tomatoes for instance, collected as they start showing colour, will keep for many days, To force these to colour the fruit should be wrapped in straw or grass, enclosed in a cardboard box and placed in the sun. Leaf types cannot be stored but herbs are dried and packed away in bottles.

Classification : A number of workers have classified the vagetables in a number of groups based on different factors of classification. Some of these classifications are based on botanical relationship, parts used as vegetables, seasonal growth, similar cultural requirements, hardiness, nature of origin (exotic or indigenous) and photoperiodic responses. Among these groups, the classification based on the similarity in the cultural methods of vegetables seems to be the best from the practical point of view, and it has been followed in this chapter while discussing the cultivation of vegetables. Accordingly vegetables are classified as cucurbitaceous crops, fruit vegetablcs, root crops, legume vegetables, leafy vegetables and bulb crops, etc.

Tuber crops : Now-a-days the tuber crops, specially the potato, covers an appreciable portion of the vegetables which are used in the human diet. These vegetables are rich in starch. By dint of proper storage arrangements tuber crops can be stored for a fairly long time.

POTATO (*Solanum tuberosum*) :

Potato is a modified stem. It prefers a loose, well drained, light loamy or sandy loam soil rich in organic matter. Excessive moisture in the soil causes rotting of tubers. A cool climate with bright sunshine is very essential for potato cultivation. The land should be manured with well-rotten farm yard manure 160 quintals/acre before the planting of tubers. The fertilizer mixture supplying 50 kgs N : 4o kgs. P : 50 kgs. K may be given as the top dressing in two or more doses at the time of earthing up operation, Potato is propagated by planting whole or pieces of tubers with two or three eyes. Plant in ridges with a row to row spacing of 45-60 cm and tuber to tuber 15-20 cm. Planting time varies with the altitude. In plains the tuber should be planted from September to October. The soil should be made loose and weed free by proper intercultural operations. Irrigation should be given at 7-10 days interval. The crop becomes ready in February-March. Tubers should be harvested when the plants have withered and the tubers do not peel off easily. Important varieties are Up to Date, Magnum Bonum, Gola, Great Scot, Darjeeling Red Round, Hybrid 9, O.N. 295, Phulwa, Satha, etc. Early and late blights and the virus diseases often cause severe damage to this crop. When the plants are about 20 cm high, Bordeux mixture should be sprayed at every fortnight to control blights. The virus-infected plants should be destroyed. Sprays of Malathion Metasystox, Endrine, etc., prevent the attack of insects and pests. Yield 100-150 quintals/acre.

Sweet Potato (*Ipomoea batatas*) :

It is a climbing plant producing tubers which are underground modified roots. A rich well drained sandy loam soil is very suitable to this plant. A warm climate with high temperature is essential for this crop. Propagated by cuttings of matured vines. Plant 30 cm long cuttings on broad ridges or shallow trenches. Row to row distance 30 cm and 22 cm between the cuttings. Plant cuttings from April-June. Irrigate when the soil becomes dry. The land should be hoed to remove weeds in the early stages of this crop. Harvesting should be done after 4-5 months when the tubers attained the marketable size. Prior to harvesting the vine, cuttings should be made and then collect the tubers with the help of spade. V-2 (F.A. 17-white), V. 6 (F.A. 17-red), C.L. 44. White Star, Pusa Sufed, Pusa Lal, etc., are some of the good varieties of sweet potato. Use insect free cuttings to obtain good healthy plants. Spraying of Bordeaux mixture helps to control the leaf spot disease. Yield 70-80 quintals/acre.

Elephant Yam or ol (*Amorphophallus campanulatus*) :

A well drained loamy soil is suitable for this crop. A heavily manured light soil also suits the plant. Plant the 'buds' from May-June with a spacing of 100-130 cm. Light irrigation at intervals should be done when the crop is matured. Dig up the corms when the leaves show signs of yellowing.

Yam (*Dioscorea alata, sativa etc.*) :

It is a quick growing climber producing large coarse looking tubers of varying sizes. Plant bulblets or cut portions form the top of tubers in a prepared pit 60-120 cm deep filled with light sandy soil and old cow manure in April-May. Spacing 1·5 meter. The crop becomes ready in 9 months.

Sankalu or Yam Bean (*Pachyrhizus tuberosus*) :

A strong creeper with a large edible tuberous root. The pods are also used when young and tender. Soil should be light and rich. Sow from March-June in position with a spacing of 1·5 meter. The plant must not be allowed to climb but grown on ridges like the potato and the vines allowed to ramble. The crop becomes ready in 4-6 months. Harvest the crop by digging up the tuberous roots when they are full grown tender and juicy.

Jerusalem Artichoke (*Cynara scolymus*) :

It grows up to an elevation of 1500 meters. Soil should be light and rich. Plant whole or cut like potatoes in February-March but place in soil immediately on receipt as they are apt to rot. Plant 85 cm apart with 1 meter distance between rows. Crop can be dug in 9-10 months.

Asparagus (*Asparagus officinalis*) :

A perennial. Sow from June to September. Sow fresh seed soaked in water for a couple of hours. When one year old, transplant carefully to trenches running north and south, give partial shade. Plant crown 15 cm below ground, 40 cm. apart, cover with 5 cm. soil. Draw soil gradually on either side till plant stand in a low ridge, irrigate in furrows, flood twice a month but weekly during cutting season, follow up with cultivating soil. Depth of trench 30 cm and about 60 cm at top, well drained.

Roots can be planted in March 5-8 cm below soil, cut down in October, or withhold water. Work a small quantity of salt and 22 gm of bone meal per meter sq. into the soil before planting roots and add rich manured soil in small quantities each year. Do not touch Asparagus in the first year and in the second season, only cut for a short period. During the cutting season allow no other shoots to grow. Then cut back and allow plant to winter. The plant reach maturity in the 6th year but can be cut from the 3rd and will last for 15 to 20 years. Blanch with light soil and sand and cut with a sharp knife. Weak doses of salt 500 gms per 10 sq. meter and soot dug in during the growing season is good as this increases the succulence of the shoots. When new shoots commence to get stringy, stop cutting and let the plant run to seed. Dig in old stable manure when plants are dormant, shoots can be cut from March to August. Manure with Guano, Fish Meal, etc. Best variety—Colossal.

Taro or Kanchu (Colocasia antiquorum) :

Its tubers, leaves and stalks are used as vegetables. The soil should contain plenty of moisture. Plant the small corms in March to May and earthen up in August-September. The leaves die down in December-January when the tubers can be lifted.

Cole Crops :

This group comprises of the three well-known vegetables which are Cauliflower, Cabbage and Knolkhol. Cole crops require a cold climate during their period of growth, otherwise in warm season it becomes pungent.

Cauliflower (Brassica oleracea Var. Botritis)

The soil should be fertile, well drained and have moisture retentive capacity. Medium to heavy soil is preferable. Sow the seeds from June-September. Transplant the seedlings 45 cm apart. Row to row spacing should not be below 60 cm. Before transplanting the land should be well manured, because cauliflower is a heavy feeder. Water should be given after every 10-15 days. The land should be free from weeds. When the flower first shows, the plants should be fed with plenty of liquid cow manure. Then as the flower grows, shade it with the leaves of the plant itself to keep the white colour of the flower. This crop requires a fair quantity of Boron, the deficiency of which results in the browing of the head. The crop become ready within 3-4 month. The crop should be harvested before the heads break open into segments. Early Market, Early Patna, Early Benaras, Snowball, Giant Snowball, China Pearl, etc., are some of the good varieties of cauliflower. Blindness of Cauliflower may be due to injury at the time of transplanting, drought, thick sowing, constitutional defects, insect attack or degenerated stock. Rogor and Malathion sprays will control the damages due to insects and pests. 30 gms seed will produce more than 2,000 plants and about 180 gms are required to sow an acre. Average yeild is about 10,000 kgs/acre.

Cabbage (*B. oleracea Var. Capitata*).

The climatic and soil requirement of cabbage is similar to that of cauliflower. Sow the seeds from July-November and transplant when the seedlings are 5 cm high to a seed bed 8 cm apart and then again to permanent waters. The spacing is silimar to that of cauliflower. Cabbage likes plenty of manure ; so add 130 quintals of well rotten F. Y. M. or cow manure as a basal dose at the time of land preparation. The land should be made weed free until the leaves cover the ground. Earth up plants when they are about 22 cm high. Liquid manure should be given once a fortnight when head forms. Irrigation should be done after every 10-15 days. The crop becomes ready for harvesting within 3-4 months when the heads attain the full size and are hard. Important varieties are Pride of India, Golden Acre, Early Drumhead, Copenhagen Market, Late Drumhead, Glory Enkuizen, etc. Mustard saw fly, cabbage borer, mustard aphids, etc., are some of the insects and pests which attack this crop. Spray Malathion or Rogor to control the insects. Damping off, club root, black rot, root, knot, etc., are some of the diseases which cause much damage to Cabbage. Yield—14000 kgs/acre.

Red-Cabbage :

This is another variety of heading cabbage with leaves finely netted and wrinkled. Red Cabbage requires less water than the ordinary kinds but should be treated identically. It is supposed to be much better in quality than the smooth leaved varieties. The cultivation is exactly the same as with the ordinary cabbage.

Knol Khol or Kohl Rabi (*B. oleracea Var. Caularapa*) :

It requires heavy rich soil. Sow the seeds from August-

November. Transplant when the seedlings are 7-10 cm high with a spacing of 25 cm between plants and row to row 30 cm. The seeds are also sown direct where they are to grow and better roots are obtained by this method. Thin out seedlings when they come up at the proper distance apart. Water profusely and give liquid cow manure once a week when the roots are half grown. The crop becomes ready within 2-3 months. Cut when about 7 cm in diameter. Harvesting should be done before the crop becomes tough and fibrous. Best varieties are Earliest White, White Vienna, Purple Vienna, etc.

Cucurbitaceous Vegetables :

This group includes a number of vegetables like gourds, cucumbers, melons, pumkins, squashes, etc. These vegetables are usually hot weather crops and most of them have trailing habit. The usual method of propagation is by seeds.

Pumpkin (*Cucurbita maxima* or *C. moschata*) :

It is a quick growing creeping or trailing plant bearing large globular fruit, green or brownish red in colour, eaten immature or ripe, boiled or in curries. The flowers and tips of vines are also eaten. The soil should be light but heavily manured, kept moist but not too wet. Sow from January-March in position for hot weather crop, June-July for rains crop. The summer type is grown on the ground. Spacing 1·5 meters. The crop becomes ready in 3-4 months. The mature fruit keeps for some time after being picked. Average yield per acre is about 11000 kgs.

Bottle Gourd (*Lagenaria siceraria*) :

An annual creeper, the tender tips and even the leaves being eaten while the immature gourd is used as a vegetable, boiled or curried.

A loamy soil rich in manures is best for this corp. Sow from June-July for rain crop and November-January for hot season in situ. Distance apart 2 meters. This crop does best on a scaffolding. During hot weather water once a week. The crop becomes ready within 3-4 months. Harvest the fruit when they are still tender. Fruits very considerably in shape and diameter. Pusa Summer Prolific Long and Pusa Summer Prolific Round are two very promising varieties of bottle gourd.

Ash Gourd, Wax Gourd or Petha (*Benincasa cerifera*) :

A large climbing gourd usually run on to a roof where it bears oblong fruit, used a vegetable or candied for sweetmeat. A light sandy soil will do for this crop. Sow the seeds from February-July depending on the earliness. It requires moderate manuring and little watering. Harvest the fruit for storage when it is fully ripe. The immature fruits are collected to be cooked as vegetable.

Summer sqush or Vegetable Marrow (*Cucurbita pepo*) :

A fairly fertile soil is required for this vegetable. Sow the seeds from November-March in places where winter is mild. Spacing between the plants should be 2-3 meters. Water twice or thrice in a fortnight. When the plant has made its fouth set of leaves pinch tips to make it break, pinch back again when the shoot have made four sets of leaves and the laterals now produced will bear. Remove sub-laterals. Failure of vegetabe marrow is often due to damp caused by execessive foliage, too rich soil, dull damp weather, or too much shade. Harvest before the seed ripens and fruit is soft with a light yellowish green colour. Patty Pan, Early Yellow, Prolific, Australian Green, etc., are some good varieties of this crop. Dust with ashes or use insecticide when it is attacked by fly, beetles and grab in fruit.

Palwal (*Tricosanthes dioica*) :

It is a trailing plant bearing small cucumber like fruit. A rich well drained sandy loam soil is most suitable for this crop. It is seldom grown from seeds, but roots planted in March to September. Plant in a shallow trench, 45 cm apart in well manured soil. Fill in the trench when shoots are 30 cm long and grow on the surface of the ground, do not water the ground till the stoots come through. The crop becomes ready in 4 months. The fruits should be collected at the young stage when they are still green.

Snake Gourd (*T. anguina*) :

It is a quick growing climber with long greenish fruit, striped with white or entirely green, 60-120 cm long and 4-8 cm in diameter. It thrives well on a rich loamy soil. Sow from March-June in position and give support. Distance 150-200 cm. The crop becomes ready in 3 months. The fruits should be harvested when they are full grown and still tender.

Ridged or Club Gourd (*Luffa acutangula*) :

A climbing plant which bears fruit 25 to 40 cm long, green with sharp ribs projecting from end to end used in curries when half formed. It prefers a rich well drained loamy soil. Sow in position from January-March for hot season, June-July for rainy season crop. Spacing about 1·5 meters. Pinch back the shoot to assist the fruit to set. Apply cow manure when fruits set. The crop becomes ready in 2-3 month. Harvest before the fruits become spongy. Pusy Nasdar is a very good variety.

Sponge Gourd (*L. cylindrica*) :

A very spreading climber usually grown up a tree, fruits are used in curries. Soil should be rich but light. Sow from January-March for summer and in June-July for rainy season crop in position. Distance apart 20 cm. The crop becomes ready in 3-4 months. Harvest the fruits when they are still tender. Pusa Chikni is a good variety of this crop.

Water Melon or Turbooza (*Citrullus vulgaris or C. lanatus*) :

A trailing gourd, fruit eaten as desert. Soil sandy with river silt, heavily manured with old cow manure, do not let collar of plant get too wet otherwise the stem will canker, usually cultivated in the dry bed of a river. Sow the seeds from January-March. Spacing between the plants—16 cm. Watering once a week should be done till the fruiting. The crop becomes ready within 4-5 months. Harvest only the fully ripe fruits. Asahi Yamato and New Hampshire Midget, Sugar Baby Charleston Grey, are the recommended varieties of this crop.

Round gourd or Tinda (*C. vulgaris Var. Fistulosus*) :

Rich sandy loam and silt loam soils are preferred by this crop. Sow from February-July depending upon the nature of the crop. Distance apart 16 cm. The crop becomes ready within 3 months. Discard the first flush of the fruits as soon as they born, because these fruits are very small sized. Gather the fruits of the second flush when they are still young tender and somewhat hairy. 'Whitsh green' types are better than the 'dark green' type.

Musk melon or Khurbuza (*Cucumis melo*) :

A trailing gourd bearing fruit which varies in size and shape according to variety. Melons do not like atmospheric moiusture which results in rotting. A dry hot period with a bright sunny weather at the time of fruit ripening imparts much flavour and sweetness to the fruit. Light loamy soils provided with good drainage condition is very suitable for this crop. Sow the seeds from October-February directly on the ground. Water after every fortnight or a few days more. The crop become ready for harvest in 3 months. The fruits usually are about 16–20 cm in diameter. Eaten when ripe as desert. The fruits should be harvested when they are fully ripe. The best known varieties are Pusa Sarbati, Haramadhu Amritsari, Faizabadi, etc.

Snap melon or Phooti (*C. melo Var. Momordica*) :

This is a trailing plant bearing fruits which are cylindrical in shape and lemon-yellow when ripe. The soil should be light, sandy and fairly rich. Sowing time is January-March and June-July with a spacing of 2 meters. Sow the seeds directly on the ground in holes or trenches. Water after every 7–10 days till the fruits ripe. The crop becomes ready within 4 months. The fruits burst when ripe so collect when they are fully grown and intact. It is used as a desert fruit with sugar, when unripe cooked as a vegetable.

Long melon or Kakri (C. melo Var. Utilissimus) :

This is a trailing vine with long narrow fruits which are pale green in colour when young. A heavily manured sandy loam soil is very suitable for this vegetable. Sow from November to May in holes or trenches with a spacing of 2 meters. In the summer grow the crop on the ground and stake the monsoon crop. Water once a week in case of summer crop. The crop becomes ready in 3 months. Harvest the fruits when they are still young.

Cucumber or Kheera (Cucumis sativus) :

A creeper bearing fruits 20–45 cm long and 6–13 cm in diameter, used raw in salads or when mature cooked in a variety of ways. Sandy to loamy soil is suitable for this crop. Manure the soil castor oil cake and old cow manure in equal parts with small quantities of bone meal. Sow from February to July and September to November, directly into the ground in circular hole of 45 cm diameter. Sow three seeds in a triangle 16 cm apart and use wood ashes to keep off beetles. Distance apart 2 meters. Water after every few days' interval depending on the soil moisture condition. Tip the vine when three or four fruits have formed. The crop becomes ready in 2-3 months. Good varieties are Japanese Long Green, Staright Eight and China.

Bitter gourd or Karela (Momordica charantia) :

Bitter Gourd are 20-25 cm long by 5-10 cm in diameter, green covered with warty protuberances, when ripe the fruit becomes orange in colour and splitting shows a number of scarlet seed within. It thrives best on rich sandy or silt loam soils. Sow seed from March-June. Sow in holes or trenches with a spacing of 2 meters water twice a week for the early crop. Harvest the fruits when they are fully grown but still green.

Balsam apple or Ucche (*M. muricata*) :

A small fruiting variety of the bitter gourd. Treat similarly like that of bitter gourd. Sow from September to November with a spacing of 2 meter between the plants. The crop becomes ready in 2-3 months. Harvest the fruits when they are green and young with immature seeds.

FRUIT VEGETABLE

This group comprises Brinjal, Tomato, Chilli and Lady's finger, etc. Here in this group fruits are used as vegetables. These vegetables are rich in vitamin A, B, and C and are seed propagated.

Tomato (*Lycopersicon esculentum*) :

This popular vegetable thrives best on well drained loamy soils. The soil should have a fine tilth. Sow the seeds from July to November. Tomato seed raised in the wet weather should be started in small pots and when thoroughly rooted, transferred to a ridge. Seedlings are ready for transplanting in 4 to 6 weeks. The seedlings should be planted with a spacing of 75-90 cm. Plant in rows and support on stakes, jaffrey or neeting. Start the seedlings in rather dry soil. If the plant forms too much leaf give a weak dose of sulphate of potash, if stunted use sulphate of ammonia. For early crop stake and remove all side shoots, tie lightly. Never let plants get too moist, this a fatal error. Fruit splitting is due to irregular watering. The land should be kept weed free. Manure is applied every ten days after the first fruits have reached the size of hazel nut, 10 gm per plant, super-phosphate 4½ parts, sulphate of potash 2 parts and Bone dust 1 part. Water heavily with liquid manure when in flower so that the fruit may set well. Go over plants every 10 days and nip off all shoots showing at the axils of the leaves, thin out fruit if the plant seems over laden. Pinch off leaders when 4 to 5 trusses of fruit set. Fruit with hard portions unripened and not colouring shows absence of potash ; use sulphate of potash in that case. Removal of too much foliage causes burn and green lumps in fruit. The sudden application of a garden fertiliser will often cause tomatoes to split. The crop becomes ready in 3 to 4 months. The fruits should be harvested when they are full grown and show distinct change in skin colour. Good varieties are Best of All, Oxheart, Ponderosa, Sioux, Pusa Ruby, Golden Queen, etc. Spray Malathion to control the insects and pests. Damping off, early blight, leaf curl, etc., are the few serious diseases of tomato. The yield varies greatly under different conditions.

Brinjal (*Solanum melongena*) :

It is a shrub 70-160 cm high, fruit purple or white or green differing in size and shape according to the variety, used in curries or fried in variety of ways. It grows on all types of soil but thrives best on rich loamy soil. Sow Amon, Muktakeshi, Aushee, Pusakranti, etc., in September-October and will be ready in February-May. Sow Kuli and Banaras in February-March the crops of which will ready in August to January. Distance apart 100-130 cm. Seedlings should be raised in a seed bed and transplant 2 or 3 times, at intervals of 15 days. Give shelter from northwinds. Earth up when 50 cm high. Manure heavily. A surface dressing of 250 gm cow dung and well rotted mustard oil cake in equal proportions per plant when fruits set give beneficial effect. Water twice a week in summer and once in a fortnight in winter. The crop becomes ready in 4 to 5 months. To increase size of individual fruit, pick off all but two or three when they are at the size of marbles. Harvest the crop when it is full grown but not ripe. The bright colour of the fruits should be preserved. Black Beauty, Pusa Purple (long and round) etc., are varieties of Brinjal extensively cultivated. Stem borer, fruit and shoot borer, Jassids, and Epilachna beetles are the chief insects which attack Brinjal. Most serious disease such as leaf curl, mosaic, etc., are caused by Virus. Spraying of Malathion, Endrine, are used for controlling insects.

Chilli (*Capsicum frutescens*) :

It is a small shrub bearing hot and pugent fruits. The fruits are 3-12 cm long with a narrow diameter. A large fruited type with sweet flesh of often used raw in salads or pickles. Chilli requires ordinary soil though a little old cow manure worked in will do good. Sow from July-November with a spacing of 70-100 cm. Irrigate once a week. The crop becomes ready in 2-3 months. Harvest the fruits when they are full grown and have a change in skin colour. Sanauri, Patna Red, Sirhindi, Balasore, Ceylon, California Wonder, Chinese Giant, etc., are some of the good varieties of chilli. Spraying of Bordeaux mixture controls anthracnose, wilt, blight and fruit rot.

Lady's Finger : (*Abelmoschus esculentus*) :

These plants grow from 100-200 cm high with horn like pods 12-20 cm long ; eaten either boiled or fried but objected to by many owing to the mucilage which appears when cooked. It thrives on all kinds of soil but prefers well manured light soil. Sow from January to March and April-July either. The seeds should be sown directly in the ground with a spacing of 50-70 cm. Irrigate once a week in summer. The crop becomes ready in 2 months. Harvest the fruits when they are still young and tender. Recommended varieties are Pusaswani, Pusa Makhmali, Lucknow Dwarf, Long Green Velvet, Smooth Green Velvet, etc. Jassids, spotted ball worms, etc., can be controlled by spraying BHC, Endrine or Parathion. Yellow vein mosaic caused by virus and powdery mildew are the two severe diseases of Lady's finger, use resistant variety and sulphur spray.

ROOT VEGETABLE

This group includes radish, parsnip, turnip, carrot and beet. The enlarged roots are the main edible portion of these vegetables and are rich in minerals, vitamins and carbohydrates.

Radish (*Raphanus sativus*) :

For the best performance radish requires rich sandy loam soil having good moisture retentive capacity. By thorough ploughing the soil should be made to a very fine tilth.

Radish should not be grown on too light soil because this makes it tasteless nor on too heavy as this makes it hard and woody, a rich loamy soil is best. Sow the seeds from July to February with a spacing of 10 cm, on ridges (about 50 cm high) in July. After sowing irrigation should be done and subsequent waterings should be done once a week. Keep the land weed free. Slight shade is advantageous. Never use too much manure or fresh material as this causes forking of the root. The crop becomes ready in 1-2 months. Harvesting should be done by pulling the full grown, tender and crisp roots. White Long, Japanese White, Scarlet Globe and Red White-tipped are some of the good varieties of radish.

Turnip (*Brassica rapa*) :

It is a root vegetable of easy culture. The European types are sweeter than the Indian types and can be taken raw. It grows best on sandy soils rich in organic matter. Sow the Indian types from July-September and the European types from October-December. Sow the seeds 20-30 cm apart. Water once a week. The crop becomes ready in 2-3 months. Harvest the crop when they are 10-13 cm diameter. Deshi varieties are white and red types and the European varieties are

Snowball, Goldenball, Purple top, Early Milan, Red Top, etc. For turnip fly syringe with a soap and water solution, 60 gm soap to 5 litres of water.

Carrot (*Dacus carota*) :

For the best performance carrot requires a deep, loose well drained loamy soil having a fine tilth. Sow the seeds from September-November with a spacing of 12-20 cm. Thin out plants when they have formed 4 leaves and again when the plants have grown thick, leaving them 20 cm apart. Irrigation should be done once in 10-15 days in winter. Roots are liable to split if kept too long in the ground or given too much nitrogenous manure.

The crop becomes ready in 3-4 months. Harvest the crop when the top of the roots have a diameter of 3-5 cm. Nantes, Scarlet Horn, Champion. etc., are some good and popular varieties. Average yield per acre is about 8000 kg.

Beet (*Beta vulgaris*) :

A root vegetable used for salad and also cooked as curry. Keep the soil loose by digging deep, rows running north and south. Soak the seeds in liquid manure and a better germination will result. Sow broadcast or in rows from September-October. Water once a week and give liquid cow manure once a fortnight. Thin out the seedlings to 20 cm apart. As roots form give 30 gm of sulphate of potash for every sq. meter. The crop becomes ready in 2-4 months. Harvest the crop when the roots have 8-10 cm diameter. Best variety Crimson Globe.

LEGUME VEGETABLES

This group includes the pod vegetables which are rich in protein, vitamins and minerals. The crops also have a beneficial effect on soil due to their nitrogen fixing ability.

Garden Pea (*Pisum sativum*) :

Peas can grow on a varied type of soils but rich loamy soils are best. Sow from September to January with a spacing of 100 cm. Plant in double rows, each row 30 cm apart and their own height between rows, running north and south. Sow seeds 5 cm. deep and when the plants are 15 cm high put in *dhaincha*, bamboo or jute sticks to support peas, a double line in each row and clamp in the plants 40 cm apart as they grow up the stocks, water heavily in dry weather otherwise pods will become stringy. If the plants fail to grow strongly or look pale coloured a weak dose of lime water is suggested. The dwarf varieties does not require much stacking but seldom gives a good crop. Water freely when in blossom, twice a week when pods form. To get full pods, pinch the tip of the plant when first pods form. If foliage becomes yellow it often means that the plant is short of nitrogen, use 15 gm of ammonium sulphate per meter row watered in. The crop becomes ready in 2-3 months. Harvest the crop by cutting the pods when they are well filled with tender peas changing in colour from dark to light green. Varieties—Early : Arkel, Early Giant, Early Badger. Medium : Bouneville,18-35 quintals of green pods/acre.

Cowpea (*Vigna sinensis*) :

A runner bean bearing long slender pods 15-30 cm. in length and the thickness of a lead pencil, used in curries or boiled as a vegetable. Soil light sandy loam. Sow from January to February for hot season and March-July for rains with a spacing of 170 cm in position. Give supports to the plants. The crop becomes ready in 2 months. Harvest the crop when the pods are full grown and tender. Best varieties are Pusa Phalguni, Pusa Barsati, No. 419 (Andhra), Gwalior K-3B, Gwalior K-11, Gwalior K-14 etc.

French Bean (*Phaseolus vulgaris*) :

It thrives best on a well drained, fairly rich, sandy loam soil. Sow from August to October and in February, 15-25 cm apart and 65-100 cm between rows. Give some shade to the plants. If planted early, grow on slope of parallel ridges 7-10 cm apart. When fruit has set pinch off tip. Harvest the crop by picking the pods which are not fully grown and the seeds are still small. Best varieties are Kentucky Wonder, Giant Stringless, Pencil Pod, Canadian Wonder, Earliest of all etc.

Country bean or sem (Dolichos lablab) :

There are many varieties of this twining bean, varying in size and shape of pod though most are flat and normally upto 15 cm. greenish white, green and purple in colour. Soil light with a little old manure worked in before planting. Sow in May-June in position giving support, 15-20 cm apart and 130-160 cm. between rows or up fencing, shrubs etc. Give shelter from north winds. Apply liquid manure when 100-130 cm high. The crop becomes ready in 4-6 months. Harvest the full grown pods which are still tender. Important varieties are Early Prolific, Indian Flat, Altapati Black and White, Ghiya, Makham, Baghnoke, Hatikhana etc.

Sword Bean or Bara Sem (Canavalia gladiata) :

A robust woody perennial climbing bean, bearing pods 25-40 cm long and 5 cm broad, eaten when young as a vegetable and seed when the pods manure. Does best up a tree. Soil ordinary with a small quantity of cow manure. A dwarf variety is a first class type for small gardens. Sow in position from March-June 10 cm deep with a spacing of 160 cm. The crop becomes ready in 4-6 months. Cut down to roots every year.

Velvet Bean or Leda Sem (Mucuna cochinchinensis) :

A climbing perennial bean, the large fleshy pods are eaten when tender as a vegetable or in curries, pod borne in clusters, each 10 cm long with dark green or black velvety skin. Soil ordinary. Sow from April-June direct in position with a spacing of 160 cm. The crop becomes ready in 4-6 months. Be careful of the variety with stinging hairs (alkusi).

Broad Bean or Balaka Sem (*Vicia fava*) :

Soil ordinary. Sow from September to December with a spacing of 20-30 cm between plants and 65 cm between rows. Broad beans do not fertilise their flowers if grown too strongly. Pinch out top and base shoots and do not water too much. The flowers often fail to pollinate because the keel is jammed and holds the stamens, release with the fingers by pressing down.

LEAFY VEGETABLES

This group includes a number of leafy vegetables which are rich in vitamins and minerals. They also due to their soft fibrous matter replete the stomach. These are usually seed propagated and can be grown throughout the year.

Palak (*Beta vulgaris*) :

Soil light but rich. Sow Indian variety all round the year and English variety from September to November. Broadcast or line sown. Thin out the plants with a spacing of 30-36 cm. Water freely. Give a lime dusting to the soil. Harvest after 2-3 months, Pusa Jyoti and Banerjee's Giant are some of the good varieties of spinach.

Ceylon spinach or Poye Sag (*Basella alba* ; *B. rubra etc.*) :

A perennial climber with fleshy green or purple stems and leaves, the tender shoots and leaves are used in curries, etc. Soil ordinary. The leaves and stems are mucilaginous. Sow from March to June directly on the ground giving support. The crop becomes ready in 3 months.

Indian Spinach (*Amaranthus species*) :

There are many types of these soft wooded annuals, differing in size and colour of foliage. The leaves and in some cases even the stems are used in curries as with spinach. There are a number of varieties more or less distinct and known under various vernacular names that are used as pot herbs. Each province has its own vernacular so that the Bengali names must not be considered out of this province. Known under the following names, Dengu Notiya, Lal Notiya, Kanta Notiya, Khara Notiya, Lal Sag, Puddo Notiya. *Amaranthus gangeticus* with a dozen or more races and forms, very variable in colour and shape of leaves. *Amaranthus polygamus* gives us Champa Notiya, Lal Champa Notiya. *A. spinosus*, a thorny variety Kanta Notiya, *A. frumentaceus*, Bhatua Sag. *A. bilitum* var. oleracea, Notiya Sag, Sada Notiya. Soil light and rich for the best results and occasional doses of liquid manure during the growing season. Sow from February-August ; broadcast or in drills 50 cm apart. To obtain in a succession crop plant every month, pluck when 30-35 cm high. The crop becomes ready in 1 month.

Sarson or Mustard (*Brassica species*) :

Sarson comprises a number of varieties such as Brown sarson (*Brassica campestris* var. *dichotoma*). Yellow sarson (*B. campestris* var. *sarson*). *Banga sarson* (*B. juncea*) etc. Sarson is not only an oil seed crop, it is also used as leafy vegetable. Sarson thrives best on well drained fertile soil. Sow from September to November with a spacing of 12-18 cm between plants and 35 cm between rows. Irrigate after every 10-15 days interval. The crop becomes ready in 1 month.

China Cabbage (*Brassica chinensis*) :

It is used like spinach and also lettuce but is actually a variety of mustard. Grow on well manured light soil giving it plenty of moisture at the growing season. Plant 50-65 cm. apart. Best variety Wong Bok.

Broccole or Kale (*B. oleracea* Var. *Acephala*) :

Kale and collards are types of non-hearting cabbages, the

leaves being used as greens on spinach. The former is cultivated in old climates and stands frost remarkably well. Collards is for hot situations. Treat as cabbage, plant them 35-50 cm apart. The crop becomes ready in February-March.

Brussels sprouts (*B. oleracea* Var. *Gemmifera*) :

Soil rich and heavy. A long growing season is necessary for this crop. Sow from August to November. Transplant after formation of second ieaf with a spacing of 65-80 cm. Earth up plants slightly when 30 cm high and keep soil firm. Water once a week when in full growth. Cut large leaves to compel the shoots to form, pinch out head if this of no avail. The crop becomes ready in 4-6 moths. Best varieties are exhibition, express, etc.

Celery (*Apium graveolens*) :

Soil light, heavily manured down below with well rotted stable or cow manure and a small quantity of bone meal. Sow from June-July. Seeds are very slow in germination. Soak seed in water for 24 hours. Sow in pots, transplant into trenches running north and south. Plant out when 10-20 cm high in trenches 50-65 cm deep but on a low ridge down the centre of the trench to avoid damage by wet or in holes 18 cm apart 35 cm deep. Water freely and when half grown give liquid manure once a week down the sides of trench. A number of amateurs procure seedlings from the Hills in September and save themselves all the troubles of raising plants. Remove outer stalks and earth up gradually every 10 days with dry soil after plants are 35 cm high, using thick brown paper or earthenware tiles round the stems before earthing to prevent soil getting into the heart of the plant. Six weeks later the celery will be ready to cut. Best varieties are White Gem, Golden Self Blanching, Celeriac, etc. Tobacco dusts can be used to prevent the attack of celery fly.

Leek (*Allium porrum*) :

This crop requires a rich sandy soil. Sow in September-

October with a spacing of 20-30 cm. Transplant when 12-20 cm high into narrow trenches 40 cm apart from 20 cm deep and earth up gradually 3 cm every 10 days when the plants are two months old. Trim tips of leaves 2-3 times to make stem swell. Give as liquid manure 3 weeks before pulling 45 cm. Sulphate of ammonia, 25 gm Muriate of potash and 25 gm. Superphosphate once a week. The crop becomes ready in 3-6 months. Best varieties are Musselburg, Prizetaker, etc.

Lettuce (*Lactuca sativa*):

A light soil rich in organic matter will do for this salad vegetable. Sow successively from July-January. Seeds take a long time to germinate. It can be transplanted from boxes. Early lettuce should be planted on the north of a ridge 25-30 cm high and will do in the rains. Frequent watering is necessary. The reason for lettuce bolting is not always due to a bad strain of seed, but also due to some climatic influence, lack of nutrition, or over manuring at too early an age. Slight shade is advantageous and the use of cheese cloth at a height of 20 cm will give good results. Force to obtain crisp leaves. Tie up 'cos' types when plants form 10-12 leaves and give liquid manure occasionally. The crop becomes ready in 2-3 months. Lettuce can be of three types—cos, cabbage or heading and loose leaf. Best varieties, Cos—Little Gem, Giant or Mammoth White ; Cabbage type—Unrivalled, Goldenball, Ideal, Supreme. All the year round ; Loose leaf type—Black-seeded Simpson.

BULB CROPS

Onion and garlic are the two bulbous crops which are cultivated in our Indian condition. A mild season, without any severence of heat and cold, is very suitable for the best performance of these two bulbous crops. The onion bulb is composed of fleshy scales, while an aggregate of a number of cloves or bulblets comprises the bulb of the garlic.

Onion (*Allium cepa*) :

A well drained loamy soil rich in organic matter is very suitable for this crop. The soil should have a fine tilth. Dig in a good quantity of wood ashes and old mortar. Sow from September to November. Acclimatised seed is very good. Seeds of onion take three weeks to germinate and so should be soaked in water. Transplanting can be done when the seedlings are 15 cm high with a spacing of 12-20 cm in rows and 27-35 cm apart. Manure well and water freely. When the onion is 3 cm in diameter remove the earth gently from one side of the bulb and then from the other but do not expose the roots, this will make the bulb swell. Thick neck and late maturing due to delay in forcing growth. Pickling onion are a smaller variety and should be sown thickly in unmanured soil and not thinned out too much. The crop becoms ready in 3-5 months depending on the variety. Harvesting is done by pulling out the bulbs when the tops are fallen over and the leaves are turning yellow. Best varieties are Red Globe, White Globe, Patna White and Red, Pickling White, White Portugal, Red Italian, Silver Skin, Sweet Spanish, etc. Thrips and blights cause much damage to this crop, use Rogor to control the thrips. Clean cultivation and spraying of Bordeaux mixture helps to control blights and mildew.

Garlic (*A. sativum*) :

The soil and climatic requirement of garlic is similar to that of onion. Plant the cloves or bulblets 15-20 cm apart and 20-25 cm between rows in October-November with a depth of 6 cm. Garlic can be planted in three ways—dibbling, furrow planting and broadcasting. Water after every 10-15 days interval, but sparingly when the bulbs start ripening. The land should be made free from weeds. The crop becomes ready in March when the tips show signs of drying up. Pests and diseases of Garlic are similar to that of onion.

CHAPTER XXIV

Fruits

Flowering and ornamental foliage plants please the eye and make one spellbound with their charm, beauty and gracefulness. But the fruit plants with their luscious juicy fruits lure the mind of people. Fruits are not only palatable but also rich in vitamins. These beneficial characters of fruits necessiate their presence in every garden. Of course due to the shortage of space in urban areas the scope of fruit plants with their huge vigour is very limited in comparison with that of the rural areas. A real fruit garden is only possible in the villages, where a few bighas can be spared and profitably devoted to a selection of well known varieties.

Before coming to discuss particularly about the cultivation of fruit trees, we should first consider the selection of site, soil condition, water supply and other factors related to cultivation of fruits. The factors which should be taken into account for selecting a site for commercial fruit growing are many such as the location or the distance of the nearest market, natural flora in vegetation with particular reference to the fruit trees to be planted in the orchard, soil condition, water supply, labour availability and transport facilities etc.

Soil condition is another factor which should be considered carefully, because soil is the medium for the growth of the trees and it also serves as anchorage. The soil condition, i.e. all the physical, chemical and biological properties of the soil should be ideal for the best performance of the fruit trees. Of course most of the fruit trees, however, are not very specific in soil requirement and can grow under a varied soil and climatic conditions. For example we can take the case of Mango. Though the best soil for Mango cultivation is deep alluvial having good moisture retentive capacity, yet Mangoes are found to grow in the gangetic alluvial soils, sandy soils, lateritic soils and in red soils or in other words from sea level to

1,500 meters above the seas in the Himalayas. However, in connection with the surface soil condition, another important factor for the depth and properties of the subsoil should be taken into account as the fruit trees have very deep root system. The soil should be fairly deep without any hard pan beneath.

Water is another factor which governs the plant life and fruit production. Lack of water causes poor fruit setting and water also affects the size, yield and quality of fruits. The fruit trees have their own water requirement and for the best performance this requirement should be repleted. But in our country fruit trees are hardly irrigated after they surpass their young stage. They are usually rain fed. But in countries developed in agriculture and horticulture, a number of irrigation methods such as Flooding, Ring and Basin method, Furrow method, Trench method and Overhead or Sprinkler method of irrigation, etc. are practised. In our country also instead of depending on the natural precipitation, we should follow regular irrigation practices to get the good yield from orchards.

Now, while discussing the cultivation of fruits a number of questions will at once appear before us—what to grow, when to plant, how to plant and what are the cultural practices, etc. Let us discuss them one by one.

WHAT TO GROW

Do not attempt the larger fruit trees unless you are prepared to wait for four to six years. Pomelo, Limes, etc. bear fruits in 3 to 4 years, Litchi and Mango take six to eight years before a bumper crop can be gathered. Of course the plants raised by vegetative propagation will come to flowering and fruiting much earlier than the one obtained from seed. They might bear at the very first year after planting, but precocious bearing should not be encouraged. It will hamper the vigour of the fruit tree. Where seedlings are planted, the fruiting period is protracted and one is never certain of obtaining a good type from a seedling unless careful selection has been practised. Plants propagated by vegetative means retain the good qualities of their mother without any deterioration. For instance, a seedling Kaghzi lime of a thin skinned mother, may have a thick rind and little juice while one propagated by gooties will perpetuate the thin skin character. Always buy from a reliable source as foliage differences cannot be depended on for judging the quality and type of the plant. Because to discover after eight years that a Langra Mango tree bears small acid fruits will be no recompense for having purchased the graft a few paisa cheaper from an unauthentic source.

If obtained from reliable source do not judge a tree by the fruit borne in the first two or three years : there is a marked improvement while the plant matures, especially in the Citrus group such as Pomelo and Orange.

WHEN TO PLANT

The rainy season is the safest period of the year for planting the fruit trees. Of course if irrigation facilities are available, the planting can be done at any time of the year.

HOW TO PLANT

As a general rule shrubs should be planted 3 to 4 metres apart, dwarf trees 4 to 6 metres and tall trees from 10 to 13 metres. There must be at maturity a clearance of a few metres between plants. Planting may be done in various ways such as Square, Rectangular, Quincunxial, Triangular, and Hexagonal method.

For planting trees, pits should be dug up to a depth of 1 to 1·5 metres and about 1 metre in diameter. The pit should be refilled with the excavated earth to which a basket of leafmould, same quantity of decayed cow manure and sufficient sand may be added to counteract any sticky clay tendencies that may exist and to make the compost porous. If possible irrigate the pit so that the soil settles down with proper compactness.

Before planting, selection of proper plants should be made. Choose plants where grafts and buddings are made low down on the stock. The graft union should be firm and care should be taken to see that the stock is stouter than the scion. A flexuose scion should be avoided. While planting grafts, see that point of union is half below ground. All other plants should have the ball of earth covering the roots buried a couple of cms. below the soil. Staking and fencing may be done, if required. No further manure is necessary till the plant has started fruiting. An annual dose of bone meal, oil cake, decayed cow or horse dung should be applied.

A catch crop like vegetables or papaya may be cultivated in the open space between the trees during the first few years till the fruit trees occupy the whole area. It should always be noted that the catch crop must not choke the permanent plants.

To guard against collar rot, white ants and also to prevent sunburn of the base of stem use half circles of earthen wire pipes placed three to four inches away from the stem and extending at least nine inches above the ground. When fruit trees are much exposed to the fierce sunshine and the stem burns, it should be white-washed with a thin coat of lime.

WATERING

Fruit trees should have an adequate and steady supply of water. The presence of too much or absence of sufficient water in the soil will result in injury to the plants. An excess of water suddenly following a prolonged dry period often results in the cracking of fruits which is often found in case of Citrus fruits. Shortage of water also on the other hand has many adverse effects. Never let a plant show signs of flagging leaves during the hot months. Stop watering altogether at the end of November, allow it to winter naturally, or artificially according to variety, and wait for the flowers to appear. As soon as the petals fall and the fruits have started to set, commence watering and also give liquid manure in small doses. This applies particularly to the bush and dwarf tree types. During watering do not allow the water to come nearer than 60-90 cms. of the collar of the plant.

PRUNING

Pruning means the removal of unwanted shoots and is usually done with an aim to maintain a balance between the vegetative and reproductive growth. Unlike the ornamental plants, pruning in fruit trees is not done for beautification. Fruit trees are usually pruned to secure good crop yields. Of course in our country for the evergreen fruit trees very little pruning is required. It is mainly restricted to the removal of dead old branches or branches infested with insects and pests. All unhealthy stems must be removed.

Root pruning or any injury to the root will result to temporary increase in fruit bud formation. Root pruning of fruit trees is better done half at a time carrying the operation to a second year. This permits the tree to partially recover from the shock. A regular practice of root pruning to induce fruit bud formation, however, has adverse effect on the plants and should not be practised every year.

While a tree is bearing well, do not prune ; simply clean out the dead branches.

Ringing, notching, etc., are some of the special orchard practices that usually results in increased fruit bud formation due to the carbohydrate accumulation around the operated region, provided the tree has attained the bearing age.

In case of root pruning of fruit trees, do not excavate the earth very close to the trunk. Digging of soil should be done at least 1 to 2 metres away from the main trunk. Only the thin weak roots should be pruned leaving intact the main anchor roots.

FRUIT RIPENING

Fruits are often forced to ripe by being wrapped in straw, damp grass, using ethylene, etc. Though the fruits become soft and show colouration yet they remain astringent or acid. The fruits which ripe naturally on the tree will have much better flavour and taste than the artificially ripened fruits. Certain pests, however, necessitate the removal of half ripened fruits if we wish to enjoy any return from the fruit garden.

Bananas should be cut as the deep green colouration of the fruit commences to change to a paler shade. Hang the bunch keeping stem downwards to obtain slow ripening. Other varieties of fruits should also be harvested with a portion of the stem, if possible. Never harvest the fruits until they show a definite alteration in tint.

The following is a selection of well-known fruit trees for cultivation on the plains of India. The major fruits like Banana, Citrus, Mango, etc., will be dealt first and the minor ones will be discussed later on.

MAJOR FRUITS

BANANA (*Musa paradisiaca*) :

Banana is a very delicious and nutritious fruit which grows over a vast area starting from southern end of India right up to an altitude of 2,000 metres at the foothills of Himalayas. Banana can withstand a wide diversity of soils and climatic conditions. It thrives between temperatures of 10° and 40°C. However, the most suitable climate is one with warm humid weather throughout the year devoid of strong winds. The Indo-Malay region is believed to be the place of origin of Bananas.

For vegetative propagation sucker is the most popular planting material. Among the suckers which arise from the rhizome, the sword suckers (having narrow sword-shaped leaves) are better than the water suckers (with broad leaves) and should be used. Banana suckers are usually planted in small pits or in deep furrows about 2-3 metres apart. A dose of 20 to 25 kgs farm-yard manure together with about 5 kgs wood ash per plant should be given at the time of planting.

Banana is a heavy feeder and so proper manuring is very much essential except in very rich soils. It responds well to potash. A heavy clay suits the Banana and the black earth from the bottom of tanks or ponds is an excellent soil compost for Banana plants. It requires much water and so irrigation at least three times a month should be done. The removal of suckers, dry leaves and old exhausted plants are the prime aftercare operations. Only one good sucker should be left per plant. Wind breaks should be installed in areas subject to strong winds. At the time of appearance of the flower spikes the plants should be staked properly. The flower buds should be cut off when most of the fruits have set. The clumps should be replanted after every 2 or 3 years in fresh soil.

The first fruit usually matures in 14-18 months and the second crop may be ready from 6-10 months thereafter. The fruits should be harvested when the first fingers show early signs of ripening with a change in fruit colour. A stem of at least 20-25 cms. length above the first row of fruits should be kept for easy handling of the whole bunch.

About 70 varieties are available in India. Our table varieties are all Bananas which we wrongly call Plantains. The real Plantain is the cooking type. Some of the important varieties of both Banana and Plantain are mentioned hereunder.

Banana—Amritsagar, Basrai, Chini Champa, Kabuli, Martaman, Robusta, Harichal and Poovan, etc.

Plantain—Monthan, Myndoli, Nendran, Gross Michel, etc.

Root stock borer weevil is the most serious pest of Banana. Application of Thimet 10G or Furadan 3G will give good result. Nematicides like Carbofuran has been found very effective against nematodes, which are at present adversely affecting the Banana production appreciably in India. A number of fungal and virus diseases also attack both the plant and the fruit. The Banana wilt commonly known as 'Panama disease' is a serious disease of Banana plants. The leaves gradually become brownish ; black streaks develop in underground stem and the plant dies ultimately. The affected plants should be eradicated and disease free suckers should be planted in a new spot. In India, of course, the Panama disease is not so devastating because a number of Indian varieties like Basrai, Harichal, Robusta, Monthan, Poovan, etc., are resistant to it. Anthracnose, Leaf spot disease, etc., are other important diseases which can be controlled by spraying Dithane M-45, Dithane Z-78 or Difolatan. The Bunchy top disease is another serious disease of Banana plants. The diseased plants have a crown of stunted leaves in bunches. The diseased plants should be destroyed immediately after the attack and new suckers from disease free area should be planted.

CASHEW (*Anacardium occidentale*) : Cashew is favoured both for its nut and apple. It is particularly a coastal fruit and can be cultivated up to an elevation of 700 metres. It thrives best in well drained soil with adequate soil moisture. The plants are propagated by seeds, air-layering, inarching and side grafting. Spacing varies from 6 to 12 metres depending on the type of soil. It requires very little aftercare except occasionally weeding and pruning. When the plants are three-four years old, manuring should be started. Annual manuring containing 250 gms of Nitrogen, 120 gms of Phosphorus and 120 gms of Potash in two split doses applied before and after the rains will improve the yield appreciably.

Plants bear at three years of age. But maximum production will be available from sixth year onwards up to seventy years of age of the plant. The fruits become ready for harvesting from March-May but in heavy rainfall tract, it continues up to November-December.

The tea mosquito and the Cashew stem borers are the two most serious pests of Cashew nuts. The tea mosquitos which cause the inflorescence blight can-be effectively controlled by spraying Endosulfan 0·05% at least thrice in October, December and January. The stem and root borers can be destroyed by using B.H.C. The Cashew nut plants are also affected with a few fungal diseases which of course are not so damaging.

CITRUS FRUITS

Among the major fruits in India, Citrus stands next to Mango and Banana. Citrus fruits comprise all types of oranges, limes and lemons. Citrus fruits are fondled for their refreshing and delicious juices which are rich in vitamins. Citrus are found to grow in almost all kinds of soil and climate though a dry climate with a rainfall between 60-120 cms. is preferable.

ORANGES

Oranges in India can be mainly divided into two groups— Sweet oranges (*Citrus sinensis*) and Mandarine oranges (*C. reticulata*). The typical examples of sweet oranges in our country are Malta, Mosambi, Sathgudi and Washington Navel, etc., and of Mandarine group are all types of loose skinned oranges commonly known as Nagpur Santra, Assam Santra, Coorg Santra and Sikkim orange etc. Unlike the Mandarine oranges, sweet oranges are tight skinned and heavy.

Sweet Oranges : Sweet oranges thrive under both subtropical and tropical conditions. Low rainfall tracts with pronounced summer and winter season are very suitable for the cultivation of sweet oranges. It can grow on a wide range of soils, from light sandy to heavy clays having good drainage system. Sweet oranges are usually propagated by budding. The trees should be planted 6-8 metres apart in July-September. The ground for oranges should be well ploughed. As this plant requires much nitrogen, use a green manure crop. For a plant of two years old 10 kgs. of F.Y.M., 1 kg. Bone meal and 250 gms. of Superphosphate should be used. From the fourth year this annual application should be doubled. All branches starting from a few inches of the bud union should be pruned, leaving about 60 cms. of clean straight stem with a few well selected branches. Before three years no crops should be taken. In case of bearing trees very little pruning is required. During harvesting a few cms. piece of stem should be taken along with the fruit, which will serve the purpose of pruning. Root exposure and withholding of water in proper time bring the plants into good bloom. After the first heavy application of water at the time of planting a second light irrigation should be given within a week. Thereafter the interval of irrigation will depend upon the climatic and soil condition. Grafted, budded or gootied plants should bear in 3 to 4 years but seedlings take 8 to 10 years and are seldom true to type.

Mandarine oranges—The soil and climatic requirements of Santra oranges are almost equal to that of Sweet oranges. Only the difference is that it stands more humidity than the Sweet oranges. Budding on rough lemon and seed propagation are better prevalent in Santra oranges. The spacing, planting time and method, pruning, manuring and irrigation methods are similar to that of Sweet oranges. In Santra oranges also the budded trees come to fruiting much earlier than the seedling trees and start to bear the crop from fourth year onwards while the seedling trees take at least seven years to bear the first crop.

LIME (*C. aurantifolia*): Limes are of two types—sweet and sour. Limes are small, round or slightly oval in shape and are only 3-4 cm. in diameter. Its skin is very thin and the juice is highly acidic. This dwarf tree thrives well in all parts of India where frosting is absent. Seed propagation and budding are usually practised in sour lime. Sweet lime is propagated both by stem cutting and seed. Planting method, pruning and manuring, etc., of Limes are same as that of Sweet orange. it bears twice a year, once in August and again in February.

LEMON (*C. limonia*): This struggling tree bears large heavy fruits with prominently long nipples. Unlike the Lime the Lemons have thick rind and the juice is less acidic. The Lemon can be cultivated up to an elevation of 900 metres but is susceptible to frost. Tahiti Lisbon, Eureka, Villafranca and Italian lemon are some of the notable varieties of Lemons.

GRAPE FRUIT (*C. paradisi*): It is very similar to the Pummelos. Its climatic and soil requirements are similar to those of Oranges. The multiplication of plants is usually done by budding or grafting and the tree bears in 4 years. Planting, irrigation, manuring and other intercultural practices are similar to that of Oranges, except lesser pruning is required. Harvesting season is November to January. The popular varieties are Duncan, Mc Carthy, Marsh seedless and Triumph, etc.

SHADDOCK (*C. decumana*): The Pummelo or Shaddock is a small tree which can be grown up to an elevation of 1,500 metres. The same soil as recommended for other citrus fruits suits the Pummelo. Plants should be grown from gooties or buddings. A basketfull of well decomposed cowmanure and a mixture containing equal proportions of Bone meal, Superphosphate and Muriate of potash at the rate of 250 gms. per plant should be applied in the 1st year. Increase 250 gms. of this mixture for every subsequent year with a maximum quantity of 2·0 kgs. per plant. Pummelo bears fruit in 3 years. Do not allow the plants to flower earlier, as this will weaken the plant. Reduce the number of fruits borne and thin out interlaced twigs. The fruit ripens from July to November. Stalkarts, Society's No. 1 and Society's No. 3 are some of the good varieties of Pummelo.

Pests and Diseases: Citrus plants together with their fruits are very much favourite of insects, pests and diseases. Different types of caterpillars, mealy bugs, scale insects, white flies, aphids and borers are some of the insects and pests which affect the Citrus plants and fruits to a great extent. To control these insects and pests Demicron 100, Zolon or Rogor should be applied at regular intervals. The bacterial disease-Citrus canker, is a great problem for Citrus plants and fruits. Bordeaux mixture can be used as a preventive measure against this disease. Gummosis, a fungal disease, is another problem in Citrus cultivation which can also be controlled by the application of Bordeaux mixture.

CUSTARD APPLE (*Anona squoamosa*): 'It is a dwarf tree suitable for arid climate on light soil. Cold and frost are detrimental to this plant. Both seed and grafting are the usual methods of propagation. Seedlings vary appreciably in their characters. Grafting by budding and inarching are usually done on Bullock's Heart (*Anona reticulata*) plants which is an allied species.

Seedling plants bear in 3-4 years while the grafted plants come to bearing in near about two years. A pit of 3′×3′×3′ should be made and be filled up with a compost containing soil, 10 kgs. well decomposed cow manure, 2-3 kgs. of wood ash and 500 gms. of bone meal. The trees should be planted in the early part of monsoon so that they get the full advantage of the rains. Planting should be done with a spacing of 6 metres or so. Application of oil cake before the monsoon and again at the beginning of winter will be beneficial for the trees. At the end of monsoon, 500 gms. of Superphosphate and 250 gms. of Muriate of Potash per plant should be applied to the soil. Flowering starts in April-May and the fruits become ready by September-November. Mammoth is a good variety. The plants are usually free from insects and disease attack. Mealy bugs and fruit fly sometimes attack the plants which may be controlled by spraying Sevin, Malathion, etc.

GRAPE (*Vitis vinifera*) : Grape is one of the oldest fruits which is in cultivation since at least 3000 B.C. Near about 1000 varieties are in cultivation all over the world covering an area of more than 27·5 million acres. In India, grapes occupy 25,000 acres of land. Though the grape vine grows luxuriantly on the plains it seldom produces sweet fruit. The grapes grow well up to an elevation of 1000 metres having dry hot summers and frost free winters. The grapes are usually propagated by stem cuttings. Seed propagation is used for breeding purposes. While pruning the grape vines, the pruned branches can effectively be utilised to make the stem cuttings for multiplication of plants. In northern India, pruning is done in the month of February and the stem cuttings are also made in the same time. But in Southern India, as the pruning is done in October, the stem cuttings are made in October. The cuttings are usually 10" long with at least three buds on them. The cuttings become ready for transplanting within 3–4 months. At the time of transplanting care should be taken that only one node with buds should be kept above the ground and all other nodes are kept under soil. Pits of at least 50 cm. × 50 cm. × 50 cm. should be made and filled up with equal proportions of soil and well rotten cow manure or compost. Aldrine or BHC dust of about 50 gms. should be applied to each pit before planting to prevent the termite attack, if present any. Pits should preferably be soaked with water for at least two days before the transplanting of the rooted cuttings. Transplanting of cuttings should be followed by a light irrigation. The spacing between plant to plant and row to row may be approximately 2·5 metres on each side. Bamboo sticks are usually used to help the vines grow vertically.

Pruning is a very important operation in grape cultivation. A number of methods like head system, cane system, cordon system and arbour or pergola system are in vogue. Vines are pruned only once in north India during spring and twice in peninsular region, first in April and again in October. While pruning, all side shoots are pruned keeping only the leaves at each internode.

In addition to the cow manure or compost, chemical fertilizers should be used at regular intervals. Application of Sterameal and blood meal at the rate of 500 gms. per plant after pruning will give good result. Potassium sulphate should be used to improve the fruite quality and colour. Watering should be stopped at least a week before harvesting. This will improve the keeping quality of the grapes and increase the sweetness.

The following varieties may be cultivated:

Northern India—Anab-e-Shahi, Gulabi, Kandhari and Thompson Seedless.

Southern India—Bangalore Blue, Kali-Sahebi, Cheema Sahebi, Anab-e-Shahi, Bhokri, Thompson Seedless, etc.

Grapes are attacked by a number of insects and diseases. The flea beetle, cock chaffer beetles, thrips and red spider mites are the most important pests which affect the grape cultivation. Application of Thimet 10G, Furadan 3G and Morestan, will keep the plants free from those pests. The most important diseases of grape vines are Downy mildew, Powdery mildew and Anthracnose. Regular spraying of Dithane M-45 and Dithane Z-78 will eliminate the disease attack.

GUAVA (*Psidium guajava*): It is a dwarf hardy tree which can stand hot spells and prolonged drought but is quite susceptible to frost. It is propagated by seed as well as by air-layering, ground layering and inarching. The planting distance should be about 5-7 metres.

Guava wants very little care and can grow on the most ordinary soil. Young trees should be pruned several times to avoid lanky growth. Heavy pruning induces fruit bearing new shoots. Flowers appearing within two years of planting should be removed so that the plant can take proper growth before their regular bearing stage.

Some of the guava fruits are pear shaped and others are round. Some are seedless and some are red fleshed typed. The important varieties are Lucknow-49, Allahabad-Safeda, Seedless, Harijha, etc.

Caterpillars, scale and mealy bugs are some of the insects and pests of guava. Regular spraying of insecticide like Demicron 100 or Rogor will give beneficial result to control the insects and pests. Besides these, wilt disease causes much harm to the guava cultivation. The affected plants should be uprooted and burned immediately after the outbreak of the disease.

JACK FRUIT (*Artocarpus integrifolia*) :

This huge tree with its enormous fruits are found to grow from sea level to 1,500 metres elevation. Severe cold and frosting is harmful to this plant. It is propagated by seed and inarching. The plants should be planted 12 metres apart. Seedling plants take about 6-8 years to come to bearing. Harvesting season is May-June but continues up to September in higher altitude. Important varieties are Singapore, Ceylon, Rudrakshi, etc.

LITCHI (*Litchi chinensis*) :

Litchi thrives well in loamy soils containing fair amount of lime. It is found to grow up to an elevation of 900 metres but frosting during the winter adversely affects the growth of plants.

Air-layering is the usual method of propagation. Ground layering, budding, grafting and inarching are also practised. Procedure of pit making, initial manuring and method of planting are same as that of mango. The plants should be planted 10 to 12 metres apart in the rainy season. The young trees should be protected from dry hot winds during the summer months and from frosting during winter. At the end of monsoon, 10-20 kgs. well decomposed cow manure, 2kgs. of Bone meal, 200-500gms. of Superphosphate and 200-500 gms. of Potash should be applied according to the age and growth of plants. The trees should be irrigated copiously as the fruits form. The practice of collecting the fruits with a stem of about 30 cms. long and some leaves serves the purpose of pruning required for Litchi.

Plants which are propagated by gooties bear fruits in 4-5 years. The harvesting time is May-July. Some of the recommended varieties are China, Purbi, Deshi, Bedana, Muzaffarpur, Gulabi, Kalkatia and Late Seedless, etc.

Litchi plants are in general less affected by pests and diseases. Mite is the most important pest which results in curling and thickening of leaves. They suck the sap from the undersurface of the leaves. The leaves ultimately dry up. Application of pesticides like Kelthane or Thiodan 35 E.C. will give good results.

MANGO (*Mangifera indica*)

Mango is the most popular fruit in India. Its reputation is world wide. The area under mango cultivation covers nearly half the total area under fruit cultivation in our country. Mango thrives under a varied range of soil and climatic conditions and can be found to grow from sea level to a height of 1,500 metres.

Mango is almost an evergreen tree and when the leaves fall entirely it is usually a sign that very few flower spikes will form that year. Grafted varieties are dwarf with more number of branches than that of seedlings which form a straight trunk with a tall stature.

Mango can be propagated by seed and by vegetative means such as budding, grafting, inarching, etc. Vegetatively propagated plants usually give good quality fruits. They also bear much earlier than the seed propagated plants. Prior to planting, the land should be properly ploughed and levelled. Irrigation channels should also be laid out. Planting distance varies from 8 to 12 metres according to the varieties of plants and the condition of the soil. The best planting time is the early monsoon. If irrigation facilities are available the trees can be planted at any time of the year.

Ploughing and harrowing should be done twice a year, one at the onset of monsoon and the other at the close of monsoon or in winter which have beneficial effects on growth of orchard plants. When young, the plants should be fed, annually in December with two to three baskets of well rotten cow dung along with 500 gms. of Bone meal. At the first bearing stage, i.e. when the plants are 4-5 years old, a few baskets of well rotten cow manure and 2 kgs. of Bone meal should be given. Superphosphate and Muriate of Potash should also be applied to each plant at the rate of 1 to 5 kgs.

according to the age and growth of the plant. Green manuring once a year should also be done. Vegetables or papaya may be cultivated as short season intercrop in the vacant spaces between the plants during the first four or five years. The plants should be irrigated at an interval of 7-10 days. Watering should be stopped during cold weather before flowering. Fog often interferes with the bursting of pollens and is a serious menace to the crop. The lighting of smudge-fire is recommended to disperse the fog in a Mango garden.

Pruning is occasionally resorted to and root pruning is done when a seedling tree refuses to bear after the 6th year. Slashing the trunk is a method employed by the Filipinos to produce fruit. This is done in the dry season but should not be done severely. While pruning, only dead branches should be cut down keeping the centre of the tree open.

Grafted plants bear in 3-5 years, seedlings in 8-10 years. Mango usually flowers in January-February but varieties like Dophallia, Baramashia, etc. have two or three crops in a year. The erratic or biennial bearing of Mango is a serious problem in Mango cultivation. The fruits are usually available in the market from May to July, the earliest being the Bombai type but with Dophallia, Bhadurea, Fazli (late) and some of the earlier types, fruits of one kind or another can be placed on the table right through the year. The matured ripe fruits should be carefully collected from the trees without allowing them to be bruised and may be packed into baskets or box with leaves of Debdaru (*Polyalthia longifolia*) or Ash Sheora (*Glycosmis pentaphylla*) etc.

While about 1000 named varieties with their different shapes, sizes, colour and tastes now exist in India, only near about two dozen varieties can be recommended for general cultivation. Some of the important commercial varieties growing in different regions are presented hereunder :

Early—Alphonso,Aman Dashehari Bombai, Gopalbhog, Himsagar, Mithua, Rataul, Zafran, Samurrad and Zardalu, etc.

Mid Season—Aman Abbasi, BharatbhogDasheharіFazrizafrani, Gulabkhas, Khasulkhas, Krishanbhog, Langra, Safeda Lucknow and Safeda Malihabad, etc.

Late—Bathua, Benishan, Chausa, Fazli, Karticka, Safeda No. 1, Sepia, Sindurai, Sukal and Taimuria, etc.

A fairly large number of insects are found to attack Mango. Among them Mango hoppers are the most serious pests. Besides the hoppers, the beetles, the borers, the fruit flies, etc. also sometimes cause much damage. Application of insecticides like Sevin, Malathion, etc. at fifteen days interval from the flowering to fruit maturing stage will give very good results for controlling these insects and pests. Among the diseases which cause considerable damage to Mangoes are Anthracnose, Powdery mildew, Fusarium, Fruit rot, etc. Out of these diseases, Powdery mildew is the most serious one and appears during February-March. A whitish powdery growth of the fungus may be seen on the young leaves, flowers and fruits which cause curling and distortion of leaves and result premature flower and fruit drop. Regular spraying of Dithane M-45 and Dithane Z-78 will control those diseases.

PAPAYA (*Carica papaya*): Papaya is an ideal fruit for small gardens. It prefers well drained, rich, loamy soil for the best performance. However, papaya is found to grow in different types of soil upto an elevation of 1,500 metres. Heavy rainfall and waterlogging are detrimental to this fruit plant. Low temperature has also adverse effect on it.

Papaya is propagated by seed which should be sown at the early monsoon. Seedlings of 30 to 45 days age and 20-30 cms. height should be transplanted in monsoon 2·5 to 4 metres apart. The pits should be 50 cm. × 50 cm. × 50 cm. in size. A mixture of 10 kgs. well decomposed cow manure and 1 kg. Bone meal should be mixed with the soil of the pit atleast 15 days before planting. Oil cake, Superphosphate and Potash in small quantities are good for the rapid growth of the plants. One male tree for every 15-20 female trees is sufficient. The plants should be irrigated once in a week in summer and every 10-15 days during winter. Liquid manuring at the time of fruiting will improve the flavour.

Harvesting of fruits can be done 8-10 months after planting. Papaya bears well up to 3 years of age. The fruits should be thinned out keeping only 20-30 per plant and should be protected with net against squirrels and birds. Papaya often bears two crops a year. Manure heavily after first crop, but keep only 15-20 fruits during second crop. The so called 'male' papaya bears small fruit on long stalks. Drastic pruning of male plants some-times changes the sex of the plants. The fruits should be harvested when they are still hard with a distinct change in skin colour. After three years the main stem should be cut to induce branching. It will send up 3-4 branches which will bear more fruits though somewhat smaller in size. Some of the commercial varieties of papaya are Washington, Ranchi, Honey dew, Singapore and Ceylon, etc.

Among the insects and pests, the red spiders are the worst. Regular spraying of Morestan, Morocide 20 E. C., etc. will keep the plants free from any attack of pests. Several diseases cause much harm to papaya plantation. Among them, stem rot, foot rot or collar rot, etc. are most common. Application of Dithane Z-78 and Dithane M-45 will give good result against the diseases. Virus diseases also cause much damage to papaya cultivation. The diseased plants should be uprooted and destroyed immediately after the attack.

PINEAPPLE (*Ananas comosus*) : This plant can be grown under full sun or semishade. Any well-drained soil is suitable for this plant. It grows well up to an elevation of 1,000 metres. It can not withstand extreme climate. Pineapple grows from suckers, stumps, side shoots or crowns, but is usually propagated from slips and suckers. In low rainfall areas with well drained soil, planting may be done on flat bed but in heavy rainfall areas planting should preferably be done on ridges. Planting distance should be 50-100 cms. on each side depending on the varieties. Early monsoon is the best season of planting.

Cow manure or Farm yard manure should be applied at the time of land preparation.

After the second year or earlier, if the plant growth is vigorous, keep the plants starved till the flower heads appear in February-March ; then irrigate well once a week. Thin out all extra suckers as they become large enough to handle and replant every fifth year. The same ground can be used, but should be deeply dug and well manured and the actual line of plants should also be altered.

Potash manures are beneficial for pineapple. Too rich manure on the other hand, though it may increase the size of the fruit, always reduces the sweetness and flavour. A very good manure, for the pineapple may be prepared as follows : 1 part of sulphate of potash, 2 parts of bone meal, 2 parts of superphosphate, 2 parts of oil cake and 1 part of sulphate of ammonia. This may be applied twice a year, once in March and again in September.

Pineapple suckers will give fruit a year ahead of plants raised from fruit crowns. Stake the fruit as it commences to swell and tie the leaves around it as it matures to avoid sunburn. When the fruits show signs of yellow colouration, it should be harvested with a portion of the stem and a few leaves.

The popular varieties of pineapple are as follows : Queen, Kew, Mauritius, Kew giant, etc.

Pest and disease attack are not a serious problem for pineapple cultivation.

MINOR FRUITS

ASPHUL (*Nephelium longanum*)

This species of plant can grow well up to an altitude of 650 metres. It is a round, grey, smooth skinned fruit similar to the Litchi, but much smaller in size and with a distinct flavour. The plants are usually propagated by seeds. The plants raised from seeds start fruiting in 8 years, but the grafted varieties bear fruits within 4-5 years. The fruits are harvested during summer months.

BAEL (*Aegle marmelos*)

This is a tree suitable for large gardens, grows up to an elevation of 900 metres. The plants are usually propagated by seed. Seedlings bear in 6-8 years but give best result after the 10th year. Fruits bear in March-June. The fruits are widely used to prepare drinks (sherbet), sliced preserved fruits, etc. The thin skinned large fruiting variety is the best.

BER (*Zizyphus jujuba*).

Jujube or Ber is a favourite fruit of Indians which grows on almost any soil and can withstand waterlogging and dry spell. But it is susceptible to frost. It is usually seed propagated but shield and ring budding are also common. Planting should be made 6 metres apart. Proper cultural practices induce better yield. Prune heavily after harvest. Asexually propagated plants will bear in 2 years. The round types are usually grown from seedlings which bear in 4-6 years. Fruits ripe in January-March. Fruit fly is the most serious pest. Spray Malathion, Sevin, etc., to control the fly. The fruit borer, a caterpillar can be controlled by spraying Rogor, Folithion, etc. The most serious disease is caused by Powdery mildew. Application of Dithane at regular intervals will keep the plants free from this disease.

BLACK PLUM (*Syzygium jambolana*)

It grows well up to an elevation of 650 metres. The trees are commonly propagated by seed but grafted plants are also available. This fruit has an astringent dark purple pulp. The fruits are harvested in May-June.

BULLOCK'S-HEART (*Annona reticulata*)

This tree will thrive up to 650 metres altitude. It prefers a heavier soil than custard apple. The usual method of propagation is by seed and inarching. The fruits are available from

January to May. A handful of bone meal with a basket of old cow manure and lime rubbish should be given in every winter.

CARAMBOLA (*Averrhoa carambola*)

It prefers a hot humid climate and can grow successfully on sandy to clay soils. The plants are propagated by seeds and air layering. The trees should be planted 8-10 metres apart. Pruning is not very essential. Flowering and fruiting almost throughout the year. Two types of plants having sweet and sour fruits are available.

CAROUNDA (*Carissa carundas*)

This thorny shrub grows up to an elevation of 650 metres and is usually propagated by seeds, cuttings and gooties. The plants are very hardy and require no special treatment. The plants raised through seeds will start bearing in 3 to 4 years while the air layered plants bear in 2 years. The fruits are harvested from May-August. The ornamental berries are used to prepare jelly, Pickle etc.

CHINESE CHERRY (*Muntingia calabura*)

It is a recent introduction from Hong Kong and a very quick growing tree of graceful habit. It grows on any soil and bears fruit up to an elevation of 600 metres. This plant bears from March-September. Red cherry like fruits are borne in clusters. The fruits are very sweet when ripe.

DATE PALM (*Phoenix dactylifera*)

It is a very hardy tree. It grows well on any type of soil varying from light to heavy and can also withstand a fair amount of salt. It can tolerate extremes of temperature, both hot and cold. It requires very little irrigation. It is usually propagated by suckers or off shoots. The spacing should be 5-6 metres. After harvesting, old and dead leaves should be pruned.

FIG (*Ficus carica*)

It grows well up to an elevation of 900 metres. The fig is insipid in lower Bengal but the full flavour can be obtained in a dry climate where the soil is calcareous and the climate is hot and dry. In autumn and winter, apply small quantities of bone meal, wood ash and lime by digging the soil encircling the root zone. The plants start fruiting when they are 2-3 years old. The fig ripens in March-May and should be sheltered from wind.

LOQUAT (*Eriobotrya japonica*)

It is a tree that bears well all over India up to an elevation of 900 metres. The plants are propagated by gooties which bear in 2-4 years. Seedlings take about 8 to 10 years to fruit. The soil should be well manured. Copious watering should be done when the fruit sets. The flowers are very sweetly scented and the fruit ripens in March-April.

MANGOSTEEN (*Garcinia mangostana*)

This tree grows well up to an elevation of 1,000 metres. Extreme climate with excessive heat during summer days or severe cold during winter is unfavourable for the normal growth of this plant. Plants are usually propagated by seeds. Irrigation at 7-10 days interval will give good result. The fruits are harvested in August-October.

PHALSA (*Grewia asiatica*)

This plant grows up to an elevation of 600 metres. It is a tree with small cherry like fruits which are taken when ripe. No particular care or attention is required to grow this tree. By pruning the plant is kept dwarf and the fruits which are borne on the new growth are larger in size. The fruits ripe from April-June.

POMEGRANATE (*Punica granatum*)

This tall shrub grows up to an elevation of 1,500 metres. Plants raised through cuttings or gooties bear in 3 years while seedlings take 6-8 years and are never to be depended on. The plants should be pruned to induce new shoots which will bear fruits. The only serious pest of the pomegranate is a caterpillar which affects the fruit. Spraying with Metasystox, Dimecron 100 or Rogor will keep the plants free from insects and pests.

ROSE APPLE (*Syzygium jambos*)

This is a medium sized tree, grows up to an elevation of 600 metres. The trees should be planted 8 to 10 metres apart. The fruits have a small quantity of nicely flavoured flesh around a large seed. Though layering is possible, it is usually propagated from seeds. The fruits ripe in February-March.

SAPOTA (*Achras sapota*)

It is a hardy evergreen tree. Well drained sandy loam soil is required for the best performance. Ground layering, air layering and inarching are the usual methods of propagation. Planting distance varies from 8-10 metres. Irrigation should be done once in every week except in monsoon. Vegetables may be taken as intercrops for the first few years. Pruning is not essential. Fruiting starts from 4-5 years and the plant bears crops twice a year. Baramashia is a round fruited type and the best to grow. Diseases and pests are not so much severe.

WAX APPLE (*Syzygium javanica*)

This tree do not thrive well at elevations of more than 650 metres. It is a fairly big tree bearing white, watery fruits which are quite sweet if riped before heavy rain starts. The fruits are harvested in March-May.

CHAPTER XXV

Layout and Management of Nursery

In horticulture, the word nursery represents an area for rearing of plants. It is the place where all sorts of plants (viz. trees, shrubs, climbers, fruit plants, etc.) are grown and kept for transporting, for using them as stock, for budding, grafting and other method of propagation or for sale.

Nowadays, a nursery is no longer an area where only plants are grown but an area where plants and flowers also seeds and other accessory materials like fertilizers, implements, etc. are offered for sale. It may be an area meant for an individual garden or for business purpose. Hence the area for a nursery can range from as small as is required for a private garden to a large area for commercial use. Yet, some principles behind the planning and management of a nursery remain the same and are outlined as follows :

SITE

The nursery should be established on a raised ground where the chances for water logging is minimum. Stagnation of water only for a few hours may cause casualty of the young seedlings or plants. A plot of land with some established plants will be preferred than an open ground, because semi-shady condition is also required for a nursery.

The nursery should be easily accessible to visitors and vehicles. Good transport facilities should be there for efficient movement of materials and plants.

PROTECTION

Nursery should be well protected by providing walls or barbed wire fences surrounded by thorny hedges against any pilferage or cattle damages. When the nursery is located as a part of a garden, the view should be cut off from the rest of the garden by a shrubbery or hedge line or by a screen.

Care should also be taken against the hot and cool winds and severe storms by planting tall trees around the nursery which will act as a wind break.

LIGHT

Light is an important factor for proper management of a nursery. There should be shady, semi-shady and open places for different types of plants having different light requirements. In general, semi-shady condition is necessary for most of the nursery plants especially during the summer months. Again one should be careful not to plant large number of evergreen broad-leaved trees which will result dense shade. So a combination of evergreen and deciduous plants should be planted inside the nursery area so that during the winter an appreciable amount of sunlight can be provided to the nursery plants. During the summer months, if required, temporary sheds with bamboo structure can be made. Cocoanut leaves, can be easily utilised as a shading material. Too much shade during the monsoon will also spoil the plants, and care must be taken that the plants should get the sunlight for at least few hours.

The seedling beds should be constructed in open space so that they can get full sun when required and the damages caused by drips from over-hanging branches can also be avoided.

WATER

While selecting the site for a nursery the foremost, considera-tion should be given to the availability of freshwater from a permanent source. The source of water should be within the nursery area or adjacent to it. The water should be free from high concentration of salts. As during the summer, daily watering will be necessary to keep the plants in fresh and turgid condition, provisions for supply of water in abundance shall have to be made before the establishment of a nursery. Hence a number of water taps or water reservoirs (cistern, well, pond, etc.) should be provided throughout the nursery area. For large commercial nurseries, provision of pumps with the regular supply line should be installed. Hose pipes will be very helpful for covering large area within a short time.

DRAINAGE

Proper drainage system is another essential item for successful management of a nursery. Raised seedling beds are safe from the possibilities of water logging. Construction of drainage channels at regular spacing will take out the excess rain water within a short time.

PATHS AND WALKS

Proper network of paths and walks made of cinder, muram or cement is desirable. The paths should connect all places and corners of the nursery. A minimum width of 1 meter is to be provided for the paths so that the wheel barrows can be used conveniently. From commercial point of view the total area allocated for making paths should not be very large.

CONSTRUCTION OF BEDS

Raised beds are generally constructed for raising of seedlings. It is always better to construct the bed with side walls made of brick. For annuals, vegetables and herbaceous plants, the bed may be of 6m x 1·5m x 30 cm in size. Seedlings of trees and shrubs may be raised on similar raised bed, or in beds of greater depth. A shallow groove can be made on the upper surface of the brick work for spreading insecticides to repal ants, etc. Before filling the bed with soil, a layer of sand (15 cm) should be placed as drainage layer. But in tree seedling beds, a layer (15 cm) of brick bats (2 cm dia) followed by a layer (15 cm) of coarse sand should be placed. Rest to be filled up with the compost consisting of 2 parts loamy soil, and one part each of sand and leafmould. For protecting tender seedlings from scorching sun or rain water, arrangements of shade should be made over the beds. Materials like hogla and polythene are usually used. For supporting the shutter three parallel iron bars lying on iron posts should be fixed along the length of the bed. The middle bar should be somewhat raised than the other two to have the necessary slope on both sides.

POTTING LINE

When plants are to be kept for more than one year in the nursery, it is necessary to prune the shoots and roots of the plants at least once during monsoon. The plants should be lifted out from the bed and after a day or two they may be replaced to the ground after pruning of shoots and roots. Rooted saplings having firm earth ball around the roots may be directly planted in rows in the potting line. Another practice is to bury the pots in the potting line. The pots are burried up to their rim. The potting line should be situated in semi-shady location, i.e., under the partial shades of trees. The length of the potting line may vary according to the available space. But the width in no case should exceed 1·5m and it will facilitate different cultural operations like weeding, watering, etc. Some space should be provided between two potting lines. The boundary of the potting line can be made of bricks.

POTTING SHED

A potting shed is essential for various purposes like storing of soil and composts, for potting of plants, etc. A shed open on three sides are generally constructed. On the open sides, a low wall about 1 metre high should be raised to get protection from rains. The floor of the potting shed should be above the level of the ground.

STORE HOUSE

For storing implements, fertilisers and other materials, a store house is a must in a nursery.

GREEN HOUSE

For rearing the indoor house plant in a proper way, a well

equipped green house is always necessary. Besides freshly transplanted plants can be kept in the green house for establishment. A green house can be constructed with iron angles and wire nets. The roof of the green house can be covered with light shading material to provide extra shade to the plants during the summer. A small lily pool inside the green house will add beauty to the green house and also helps to keep the internal atmosphere more moist than that of outside.

COMPOST PITS

Leafmould is an important component for seed and pot compost. The compost pit should be constructed near the potting shade and it will facilitate the collection of compost for storage purpose. It is better to make at least two pits, so that the rotted refuse may be used in alternate years.

SHOW ROOM AND SALES COUNTER

For exhibiting and selling all kinds of plant materials and various garden materials a show-cum-sales counter is a must for a large nursery. It may be suitably arranged near the nursery. If the nursery is at a distance from the city, the sales counter may be located in or near the city.

SUBJECT INDEX

SUBJECT INDEX